D0246226

Martin Lipton has enjoyed a 30-year career as a journalist. As well as being Chief Football Writer for the Press Association, *Daily Mail* and *Daily Mirror*, and covering England at six World Cups and four European Championships, he has also reported on Wimbledon, the Ryder Cup, Test and World Cup cricket, and two Olympic Games. A graduate of Oxford University, he has been an active Spurs supporter since attending his first game in 1972. He is now Chief Sports Reporter at *The Sun*.

WHITE HART LANE

THE SPURS GLORY YEARS

1899–2017

Martin Lipton

WEIDENFELD & NICOLSON

A W&N paperback
First published in Great Britain in 2018
by Weidenfeld & Nicolson

1 3 5 7 9 10 8 6 4 2

A CIP catalogue record for this book is
available from the British Library.

ISBN 978 1 4091 6927 7

Typeset by Input Data Services Ltd, Somerset

Printed and bound in Great Britain by Clays Ltd, Elcograf S.p.A.

MIX
Paper from
responsible sources
FSC® C104740

Weidenfeld & Nicolson

The Orion Publishing Group Ltd
Carmelite House
50 Victoria Embankment
London EC4Y 0DZ
An Hachette UK Company
www.orionbooks.co.uk

CONTENTS

LIST OF ILLUSTRATIONS

1. Erection of the Spurs Cockerel, 1909. (Tottenham Hotspur)
2. Arthur Rowe explaining his Push and Run philosophy. (Getty Images/Bob Thomas)
3. Bobby Smith and Jimmy Greaves denied by Benfica keeper Costa Pereira. (PA Images)
4. Jimmy Greaves wheels away in delight. (Getty Images/Popperfoto)
5. Alan Mullery celebrates with the Uefa Cup in 1972. (Getty Images/Central Press)
6. Bill Nicholson opening the gates at White Hart Lane. (PA Images)
7. Glenn Hoddle opening the scoring at the Paxton Road end. (Getty Images/Popperfoto/Keith Halley)
8. Graham Roberts holds the UEFA Cup aloft. (Getty Images. Bob Thomas)
9. Chris Eubank lands a right on Michael Watson. (Getty Images/Bob Thomas)
10. Osvaldo Ardiles with his coaching staff. (Getty Images)
11. Alan Pegg, White Hart Lane tunnel steward.
12. George Graham shows his frustration. (Getty Images/Phil Cole)
13. Ollie with his ticket on Bill Nicholson Way.
14. The view from the White Hart Lane press box.
15. Mauricio Pochettino hugs Harry Winks. (Getty Images/Dean Mouhtaropoulos)
16. Harry Kane scoring the last Tottenham goal at White Hart Lane. (Getty Images/Tottenham Hotspur)
17. Paul Jiggins hard at work in the White Hart Lane press box.
18. Rainbow over the East Stand. (Getty Images/Tom Jenkins)

FOREWORD

White Hart Lane will always be a special place for me. I've been lucky in my career. I've been at a lot of other clubs and had a good relationship with the fans and been lucky enough to score goals. But for me Tottenham is just special, different.

The Spurs fans knew what they were giving back to me and what they meant to me. Every time I put that shirt on I knew how important it was to them to see someone who cared as much as they did, who knew what it meant to play for Tottenham. I always told myself, as I was walking out: 'I'm playing for Tottenham Hotspur today.' Every game, every training session, I carried that and enjoyed that feeling.

And when I played at White Hart Lane, with that feeling of the fans behind me, with that relationship, I knew week-in, week-out, that I needed to score goals and be successful.

There were good and bad moments. You don't get on with every manager. But for me to leave as the fifth highest scorer for Tottenham Hotspur, the leading European scorer – when I look back I can only be proud and happy. I played with some unbelievable players there and if they hadn't been around me I wouldn't have been as successful as I was.

The day that stands out was Wigan at home, when I scored five. I remember feeling so emotional on the pitch. It would be hard to imagine a more special day.

As a young kid, all I wanted to do was score goals, but I never dreamed I would score as many as 143 for such a huge club. If I had scored just one for Spurs I'd have been over the moon, but to score five in one afternoon, at White Hart Lane, was incredible. I think only Alan Shearer and Andy Cole have scored five in a Premier League game, and I did it in one half! It was the best thing ever in football for me.

I still sometimes watch the game back because when I watch it that feeling comes back to me – the one I had that day. It was hard to find words but to have the whole stadium standing for me like that was just so special. That's why I cried when I left the club, because it has done so many things for me. People said I'd gone a bit soft, that I wasn't meant to cry, but it was such a special place for me and to leave that pitch as a Spurs player for the final time was a hard thing for me.

I had a box, just next to the tunnel, on the halfway line. Whenever I scored I'd look to see my family in there and run to them. It was something I loved doing.

I wasn't sure how I'd feel about the last few weeks at the stadium. It was tough. In one sense it was my home, somewhere I'd spent so many years, scoring goals, and I feel I should be satisfied about my part in the history of the place. But then there's the emotional response: 'That's it. White Hart Lane has gone.' And that was hard for me to get my head around.

But I will remember walking out of the dressing room and down the tunnel, the noise getting louder, people getting excited and shouting, that roar, the one that told me I had to be ready for those fans, for this club. I guess all any of us who loved the ground can do is embrace those memories, the ones we've got inside us, and just accept that we must keep them with us and be grateful about the time we spent there.

At the end of the day, I know the fans are grateful that I played at the club and I'm grateful I could play for such a big team.

Leaving Tottenham was so hard for me because of that. And I did it twice! The one thing that made it easier was that I wasn't signing for another Premier League side. I knew I was going to another country and that did mean it didn't hurt quite as much to leave.

It was really good for me, when I went back to the Lane after joining Sunderland, to see that I'd been replaced as far as the fans were concerned. They were brilliant with me, and it was great for me to get the chance to go back to the Lane one final time, although I don't know how I would have reacted if I had scored. But they had somebody else to chant for in Harry Kane. I thought that was great, because Harry knew what the club meant to the fans as well. It was a really nice thing to see.

I'm happy with everything I did as a Spurs player. I always worked hard in training. That's why I was still able to play at the top level in my mid 30s. When I was at Tottenham I never cut a corner. The fitness guys would tell you they missed working with me, and I loved working with the staff. I always knew that you get out of the pitch, in the matches, what you put in on the training ground, and I just wanted to do well for the club and give the fans something back for what they gave me. I always said that when I finished playing I would go back there to give something back to the club, helping the kids, anything. I know how important it was, every week, to put the effort in, to put that white shirt on and play for those supporters in that stadium. Every time I did it, I recognised how much it meant for all of them, too.

Jermain Defoe
June 2017

PROLOGUE

Seventh October 1972. The autumn sunshine streaming down. A shouting match, probably, before we walked out of the front door. Getting into the front passenger seat of the blue Ford Cortina, strewn in cigarette ash. No seatbelt, for the chain-smoking driver or his five-year-old passenger. Only a short journey, three miles or so around the North Circular Road, passing through Leyton before turning right, then Hackney Marshes and those countless games going on. Yet this was a Saturday about one game. A game that began everything, changed everything.

What do I remember? Possibly nothing. It's maybe all imagined. I might have merely told myself it was true, deluded myself with the passage of time. Falsely remembered that he really did sing those songs in the car. Although I'm absolutely sure I did, as my kids will tell you, inherit his utterly dreadful singing voice.

But I do recall it as the first time we went through what was to become the traditional pre-game ritual in the Lipton household. This was, of course, a different age. Recent, but utterly different. Before the Three-Day Week, when Margaret Thatcher was only known for her hostility to school milk. Before most homes even had colour televisions. When some families still did not have telephones, although the days of most people slipping out to nearby boxes to make their rare calls were dying out. When most people's idea of what a computer looked like came from Benny Hill's role in *The Italian Job*.

In the early 1970s not everyone had a car. You genuinely could still 'play out' in the streets, even in industrial north-east London. You could park on the side of most roads. And as he drove around the streets of N17, with the stadium suddenly looming in front of us, the first barrier. A policeman. On this afternoon, as he would do again and again in the next few years, the ritual. 'I'm sorry sir, you can't come through here. Not on a match day.'

'Is there a match on? Bloody hell, I wish I'd known. But come on mate, we're here to see his granny. She lives in that block over there. Number 41. She's not well, you know. He doesn't get to see her very much . . .' The truth was that Mabel Cohen was, at the time, in Johannesburg. Rosina Hatt was living in a 'Warner Flat' in Walthamstow. But the bluff worked. That time. Every time. The copper must have been in on it. Or incredibly stupid.

Then, after parking up, a smirk on his lean face, a glint in his eyes, the short walk. I didn't know what to expect, could not imagine what was going to be inside. Everything was so big, including him (even though, like his son was destined to become, he only stood 5ft 6in). Through the turnstile, for the first time. The fug of smoke. Along the concourse. Up the white concrete stairs. And there, suddenly, before me, the pitch. Not just grass. But a deep, magnetic green. From moment one exhibiting the pull which would bring me back, time and again, for four decades and counting.

Until very recently, I had not been able to find any video clips from that match. Even now I have, I cannot remember any of the seven goals, only that Spurs scored four of them – two from John Pratt, one from the glistening dome of Alan Gilzean, the winner by Ralph Coates. Apparently, David and his son, that tousle-haired dreamer, the boy whose eyes had just been opened like never before, were among 31,951 inside. But I do remember looking to my left from the spot on The Shelf, the elevated terracing that ran along the length of East Stand, that was to become a familiar place, home from home, that gave a sense of perspective, arguably the greatest vantage point in English football. And I know that I wanted to keep on going back.

This was the Spurs side, still under the wily hand of Bill Nicholson, that was to win the League Cup – against Norwich – at the end of that season. A team with Pat Jennings in goal, Mike England and Cyril Knowles at the back, Steve Perryman in midfield, Martin Peters and his late runs, Gilzean and 'Big Chiv', Martin Chivers, up front. A team that was running in the shadow of the one Nicholson had built a decade earlier, the one that is still cast over every subsequent Tottenham side.

The names and the cast-list change. Nicholson was to quit, his heart broken by the curse of hooliganism, replaced by Terry Neill and then Keith Burkinshaw, whose infamous parting shot towards the board when he walked out in 1984 was, at least legend will always recall it so, although perhaps that was not entirely accurate: 'There used to be a football club over there.'

Peters and co. gave way to Glenn Hoddle and Ossie Ardiles, who in turn were replaced by Chris Waddle, Paul Gascoigne, Gary Lineker, while Ardiles returned as manager, brought in the 'Famous Five' and promptly walked the plank.

Others, too. A revolving cast-list. Jürgen Klinsmann, twice. Teddy Sheringham twice too. Likewise, Robbie Keane and Jermain Defoe – also each twice. And for a whole generation of Tottenham fans, that spell at the start of the Premier League, the 'Dark Ages' where tenth spot was an aspiration, where the signings were Kevin Scott and Jason Dozzell, Ruel Fox and Grzegorz Rasiak. Players who made the much-criticised John Duncan, Chris Jones, John Lacy and Paul Price appear as giants in comparison. But also Luka Modrić and Gareth Bale, players who made it all worthwhile, who gave you reason to believe, even when everything else told you that you could not compete for a place in the top four elite when you paid, at most, only the sixth-highest wages in the division. A belief that is being fostered, stronger than ever, now, with a new young team, full of home-grown heroes, boys who can become men. Perhaps, after all these years, a team for whom 'Glory, Glory' can become an epithet, not an aspiration.

Those four decades have brought moments of hope, genuine belief, great games, the occasional Cup triumph. More frequently, though, they have brought disappointment, frustration, angst, misery. And the sale of the star asset, who could not stay when more money was on the table, when they needed to actually go and win something. The recognition that, as Alan Hansen once said: 'You can only really count on Spurs to let you down.'

Yet the constant was White Hart Lane itself. No matter what went on, no matter the pain, the ground, the stadium, was always there. The stage ready for the next performance, the next director, the next cast. But with so many of the same audience, 34,000 versions of Waldorf and Statler, heckling at the actors they wanted to be so much better but could not imagine ever forsaking.

Ninth of November 2014. The child is father of the man. And now that man is father of his own child. Hurtling towards my fifth decade, this was the day I passed on the baton, just as my own dad had 42 years earlier. And the same opponents, Stoke, on a similar, sunny, warm, autumn day.

No car journey or game of bluff with the Met's finest. It takes too long. There's nowhere to park and even if you do, it will then take an hour to get half a mile from the ground. And they're, understandably, a mirthless bunch, too. The last thing they need is aggravation and a smart-arse. Instead, a bus to Clapham Junction, train to Vauxhall, Tube to Seven Sisters and another bus down the Tottenham High Road. Talking, excitedly, all the way. This was the day I had promised Ollie, who has become another football-obsessed, Spurs-obsessed version of his dad, just better equipped with knowledge, Sky Sports and the iPhone Goals app. A five-year-old then, now seven, who can, and does, watch every game on television, every goal, who had made Harry Kane his hero, despite the young striker having made just a handful of starts. You see, I told you he was smarter, wiser, better-informed that his dad.

To the gatehouse, at the end of Bill Nicholson Way. Picking up the tickets for the Paxton Road stand. Directly behind the goal. Upper tier. Second row. Ollie, posing outside the main entrance, ticket in hand, a smile as wide as the Spurs defence were to be in the first half as Stoke gained revenge for that 1972 game (I'm sure that really was Mark Hughes' motivation).

It wasn't about the visit to the Spurs Shop and buying the blue-and-white scarf that he wore all that winter and beyond. Nor about the game, even if there was a second-half rally that was to prefigure the time, just a few months away, when Kane became a national hero, Chelsea were routed, Arsenal too. It meant far, far more to me and my family. This was a rite of passage. It meant Ollie was, officially, inducted.

And that is why I needed to write this book. For by the time he can *really* remember everything about White Hart Lane, about Spurs, the stadium will be long gone, knocked down and built on, part of a past that may have little apparent relevance, especially in an age in which technology is developing at a bewildering, terrifying pace. His Tottenham now play at the gleaming new structure being constructed not even a back pass away from the stand in which we sat that Sunday lunchtime. He has become part of the 62,000 who go there, an attendance that could, maybe this time will, help create the financial conditions to allow Spurs to be the genuine force I've spent most of my adult life wishing them to be. Hopefully, in 20 years or so, he will take his son or daughter, to transfer the baton on once again to the next generation.

But for him to be able to do that, as I did, he has to know his inheritance. Just like the thousands of other Tottenham fans need to know theirs. Yes, football is about the facts and figures. The dates, the results and the scorers. Those are incontestable. They genuinely, unquestionably, irrefutably happened. But in an era in which the concept of 'alternative facts' has become a meme, so too must we understand that, just as real, just as factual, just as much the 'truth' is the way we, as fans, lovers of the game, remember things. For every single supporter, no matter their club, their perceptions are as much a part of the fabric of their memories, arguably more so, than the small print of the official details. If they conflate games, get the years wrong, the opponents mixed up, it does not make those remembrances any less real. It is from those bricks that the whole house is constructed, with its faults and flaws, cracks and crumbling. A real house.

Because, at its heart, football is romance. Joy. Despair. If football was only about winning, there would be no supporters. Only one club can win. It is about more than that. It is about identification, history, about passion and devotion, about finding a way of living the moment through the deeds of others, yet making those moments part of what makes you who and what you are.

I wanted to speak to those for whom White Hart Lane was part of themselves. Not just the players and managers, but also the supporters and those who worked inside the ground. The people who will always have the Lane in their heads, even when it has been knocked down and transformed into homes and businesses.

Football is an emotional beast. It matters to people. It encapsulates the spirit of a body of human beings. And every club, every stadium, has a special meaning to those who care.

This is for Dave and Ollie, my father and my son. Emma, too. She might end up a bigger fan than any of us. For the thousands who shed a tear on that final afternoon in May 2017. But it is also for me. A piece of me disappeared that day. A huge part of what made me into the person I am. I needed to mark the passing of that part of my make-up. This is my homage, my tribute, my elegy. Come on you Spurs . . .

Martin Lipton
June 2017

1

THE BEGINNING: THE COCKEREL CROWS

It came down, for the last time, as the diggers were dismantling everything below. Or rather, one version of it did – the Tottenham cockerel, which had looked down upon that small patch of north London turf for more than 100 years, turning its beady eye to the men who were aiming to create history below. A constant presence, in one form or another, the symbol of a club whose foundation was in itself an unlikely tale. A gang of kids, knocking around the streets of a rapidly growing enclave to the north of London, seeking an idea. An idea that snowballed into a football side that galvanised a community. Then a professional outfit, proving southern teams could outplay the northerners. And eventually, one of the country's great clubs, playing at a raucous, passionate yet uniquely intimate stadium.

For 12 months from the middle of 2017, the Spurs stadium was to become a concept, a promissory note: We've moved, for now. But we will be back. Over there, in that huge edifice being created, rising up from ground level to overshadow everything else around it.

The name alone has more resonance than the traditional football suffixes. Not Tottenham Town or City. Not Tottenham Rovers or Albion. But Tottenham Hotspur. A romantic name, with Shakespearean overtones, recalling a heroic and warlike figure, who was driven by an overwhelming desire for honour and glory – even if the Bard's version of Sir Henry Percy, known as 'Harry Hotspur', in *Henry IV, Part One* was a literary version of the leader of the 1403 attempt to overthrow the Crown, based only very loosely on the true facts. Suitable and fitting, indeed, for an idea between a group of pals which was to grow into something far, far greater. A club that was to immerse its roots not just in the surrounding streets but in the hearts and minds of hundreds of thousands over the years to come. To create legendary sporting figures. To become a backdrop for feats that were to live on, first as memories and then as folk history passed down the generations.

On 14 May 2017, the longest part of that story came to a conclusion when the final match was played at the ground known for more than a century as White Hart Lane, but which was never formally so named: Tottenham Hotspur versus Manchester United. Two of English football's biggest beasts, locking antlers one last time. A day of nostalgia, tears and celebration. A day in which past, present and future were combined, as the 31,848 who had paid to be there, and the many, many more who watched on television from around London, the UK and the wider world, waved goodbye to a place that had become such a part of so many lives.

But when the famous copper cockerel, the symbol of the club that had been perched high above the ground since 1909, which had a link to one of Britain's greatest explorers and heroes, came down, it was *not* copper. It was plastic, fibreglass. It was not even the original bird. Yet many fans had believed that this was still the first cockerel, which was widely known to have been cast in copper.

The Lane was so often a place of hope and fervent wishes, each new season fostering the belief that success was round the next corner. A feeling that was always at the back of so many minds, irrespective of the realities of the club's condition, and one which finally did come to pass in those last two seasons, as a team worthy of the club's grand traditions emerged under the hand of Mauricio Pochettino. Now, though, that ground, that setting, is only a memory, still fresh in so many minds, while its replacement is soaring into the skies.

But without that group of kids from the Grammar in Somerset Road and St John's Middle Class School, described at the time as 'a Scotch Presbyterian Academy', who gathered around their regular meeting point at the second lamp-post on the High Road to the south of what was to become White Hart Lane, all aged between 12 and 16, none of the following 135 years could have happened. At least, not as they did. Without those boys getting together to play football, all those years ago, there would not have been a Tottenham Hotspur or a White Hart Lane. We would not, perhaps, know some, maybe many, of those who were to wear that famous white shirt. We would not have seen the next stage of the club's dream being made concrete and real.

Edward A.C. Beaven, Stuart Leaman, Robert Buckle, Hamilton and Lindsay Casey, John and Thomas Anderson, Edward R. Wall, Frederick W. Dexter and John and Philip Thompson. The 11 original founders. Now just names, ghosts, but then a group of middle-class kids, which meant something very different in late-Victorian England – their fathers' occupations included a printer, a boot manufacturer and a signwriter. They were members of Hotspur Cricket Club, who decided they would play 'by Association' (rather than rugby) regulations. While the first name proposed was 'Northumberland Rovers' they eventually decided on Hotspur Football Club, a nod to the Percy family, whose ancestral lands in the vicinity bore the name Northumberland Park, and to Henry 'Harry Hotspur' Percy, the defeated leader of the insurrection against Henry IV who was killed during the Battle of Shrewsbury in 1403. It has been suggested that the Casey brothers, known as 'Sam' and 'Ham', were the driving force and that their father John built a set of goalposts.

Each of the boys paid sixpence to join the fledgling club, whose first game was against the Radicals on 30 August 1882, with Robert 'Bobby' Buckle believed to have been the first in a long run of captains which leads through the years to Hugo Lloris. The first home 'ground' was Tottenham Marshes, public parkland close to Northumberland Park railway station, between the tracks and the River Lea. They shared the pitches with University College Hospital's rugby side and Park FC, among their first opponents, alongside Stars and Latymer from nearby Edmonton, as well as Homerton College. Ham Casey subsequently recorded that 'our first meetings used to be held in some unfinished houses in course of erection in Willoughby Lane, and our light used to be tallow candles' but while 'impromptu' committee meetings were still held at the lamp-post, the team then began holding their informal club meetings at the Tottenham YMCA.

The club grew swiftly, new members having to pay double the initial fee to join the original gang of boys. By August 1883, the official strip had been agreed, too: 'Dark blue jerseys, white breeches, dark blue stockings and cap.' On the left side of the shirt, there was a scarlet shield with the letter 'H' emblazoned. And, even from those initial stages, they attracted supporters, their numbers growing to 4,000 or more within a decade.

More than a century on, some modern fans have a long-standing family connection to those early days of the club. Alan Swain and his wife Eunice went to the final game, 65 years after Alan had attended the stadium for the first time to watch the white shirts in action. But Alan can trace his line back to the formation of the club. His father, Sonny, would talk to him in reverential tones about the journey across London to Stamford Bridge in 1921, when Spurs lifted the FA Cup for the second time, 'drooling over players such as Jimmy Dimmock, Tommy Clay, Jimmy Seed and Arthur Grimsdell'. And his grandfather, William, 15 when the club was formed, was not only a supporter of the club as it grew from those initial days on the Marshes but also a steward at the Lane, opened in 1899.

Even in those days, gangs of boys fought for territory. Pupils at St John's (known as 'Saints') were frequently attacked by the

'Barker's Bulldogs' of Lancasterian School and the 'Simmonds Greyhounds' who attended Park Lane School. Twice the boys were evicted from their headquarters for being, well, boys. Their stay at the YMCA, their first home, ended in 1883 after one of them kicked a ball and broke a light fitting, plunging the room into darkness. The ball was then booted up a chimney, leaving it covered in soot, although it was the swing of a foot which accidentally sent it slamming into the face of a YMCA councillor that got them all into trouble. Yet the suddenly homeless club had a saviour. John Ripsher, a clerk in an iron factory, a bible-class teacher and the Warden of the Tottenham YMCA branch, who had been involved with the cricket club, agreed to become first president and treasurer of the club. He set them up at a property in Dorset Villas in Northumberland Park, before two of the boys were caught playing cards when they should have been attending prayers, and they were evicted again. Ripsher then established a new home at 808 Tottenham High Road. For many years afterwards it was simply known as the Red House, just a matter of steps across the road from the original lamp-post meeting point. Ripsher was to remain a leading figure in the development of the club over the next few years as it evolved from a boys' club into a professional outfit. Yet this man of God and benefactor left London for Dover in 1894 to live with his sister, ending up blind and penniless, and he sadly died in the town's Union Workhouse in 1907, buried in a pauper's grave. It was not until 2007 that his grave even had a headstone, when Spurs were able to honour his contribution to the club's formation.

Under Ripsher, the club had grown, taking in players from other local clubs that had disbanded, and was able to field a second team which played 30-odd fixtures each season. In 1884 they appended the club's location to their name to differentiate themselves from a team operating out of Syon Park, near Brentford. Mail meant for both sides had allegedly gone missing. They were now Tottenham Hotspur Football & Athletic Club, and they also switched from their original kit of navy tops to mimic the light-blue and white quarters of Blackburn Rovers. Changing rooms were found, first at Somerford Grove and then The Milford pub in Park Lane.

Success on the pitch – while most matches were friendlies, the two teams were winning a high percentage of games and entered the London Association Cup for the first time in 1885, beating St Albans 5–2 in front of 400 supporters, many of whom 'carried Billy Mason and Billy Hartson shoulder-high to the dressing room' after the final whistle – brought issues off it. The crowds were both large and extremely boisterous as they congregated, standing at the side of the pitch, with visiting teams complaining that they were intimidated by the baying hordes, even claiming they had been pelted with rotten vegetables, turnips, mud and other missiles. So, in 1888, the club moved to private land at Asplins Farm off Northumberland Park, occupied at the time by Foxes FC and a local tennis club. It meant they had to pay rates – £17 per year – but could charge entrance fees and bank the gate receipts. The first game, a reserve match against Stratford St John's or Orion Gymnasium (even the club's original official history, published in 1921, named both of those sides as the initial opponents) saw around 80 supporters paying 3d each for a grand total of 17 shillings. Given the support the club was now getting, one suspects a first-team match would have seen a somewhat larger gathering.

Four years later, Spurs, now fully established as a thriving club, joined the newly formed Southern Alliance. Modern-day fans will be shocked to hear that for five years from 1890 the kit was a vivid red shirt with navy breeches and socks, before they went three seasons wearing brown and gold stripes. It was only in 1898 that the club's now traditional strip was established, as a tribute to another Lancashire club, Preston North End. There were proper, albeit primitive, standing areas and an enclosure on the east side of the ground – the posh stand, as it were. And behind one goal was the 'Dunn Stand', a black shed renamed in honour of the Old

Etonian star striker Arthur Dunn, who had peppered the Spurs goal with a series of shots, some of which thwacked against the wooden construction, in an 8–3 drubbing in 1888. But football was still very much an amateur game, as Spurs were to find out in October 1893 when Ernest George 'Ernie' Payne, a winger who found himself unable to break into the Fulham team, was asked to play for Tottenham against Old St Marks in a London Senior Cup tie. Payne arrived at Northumberland Park with no playing equipment – his locker at Fulham had been emptied – and 'in a sorry predicament'. Spurs gave him strip and shin-pads. But none of the other players' spare boots fitted him so he was handed the princely sum of ten shillings to go and buy a pair from a local shop. Fulham complained, alleging Spurs had not only poached Payne but were operating as a professional side by offering him an inducement to play. The FA found Tottenham guilty of misconduct, suspended the club for two weeks and closed down Northumberland Park for the same period, while Payne – who repaid the money he had been advanced so he could remain an amateur and formally joined the club a year later – was banned for seven days.

This grievance fostered a growing determination to prove Spurs had been wrongly treated. And things were changing off the pitch as well. Now the dressing rooms were at the Northumberland Arms, while club meetings had moved to The Eagle on Chestnut Road. When Ripsher left for Kent, he was replaced by a very different character in John Oliver, a furniture manufacturer. He had a factory in Old Street, which allowed him to offer legitimate inducements to players to join and work for him. He had also been the president of the Southern Alliance. Oliver lent the club money for a wooden stand, seating 100, which was subsequently blown down and then rebuilt, incurring a club debt to Oliver of £60. One neighbour also took advantage of the growing interest in the club by undercutting Spurs, building an improvised platform on the adjoining land he owned and charging fans just 2d to stand and watch. The committee decided to block that scheme by erecting some boarding to hide the pitch from view.

But injuries were a problem and soon the big question of professionalism had to be answered. As a *Tottenham Herald* journalist wrote, ahead of a meeting at The Eagle on 20 December 1895: 'Every other matter, locally, so far as football is concerned, pales before the adoption of professionalism by the Spurs. For some weeks past the necessity of adopting this course has become more and more apparent.' Unsurprisingly, it was Oliver who most fiercely advocated the decision, supported by founder member Bobby Buckle. Only one member opposed the resolution.

Professionalism meant payments – one player was given a 25 per cent rise to a whopping 25 shillings per week, while another was sent packing by the club for 'misconducting himself in such a way that he had become an undesirable companion for the other players'. One can only hazard a guess at what John Oliver would have made of modern-day players like Mario Balotelli, whose off-the-field antics have driven a series of managers and various clubs to distraction. The following season, Spurs joined the Southern League, a professional competition that had been formed in 1894. The club was going places, and by 1898, when Tottenham issued 8,000 shares priced at £1 each to become a limited company, it had appointed its first full-time manager, Frank Brettell. Barely 1,500 of those shares were actually sold, to just 296 people. And with debts rising Oliver resigned, to be replaced by the man who was to dominate the off-field side of the club for almost half a century, Charles Roberts.

On Good Friday of that year, 8 April, a record crowd of 15,000 thronged to Northumberland Park to see a goalless draw with Woolwich Arsenal. Part way through the game, reported the *Tottenham Herald*, 'about 80 men and youths scaled the zinc roof of the refreshment bar, taking no heed of the warning by the police and officials. Suddenly a crashing sound was heard, which announced the improvised stand had broken under the weight'.

There were five minor injuries, but the incident caused concern at the club about the suitability of the ground. The club needed to find a new home and Roberts looked for a suitable site.

'One of my apprentices [a copper caster in his company] told me that a new football club was going to start on the vacant space at the rear of the White Hart,' he said. 'Being puzzled as to what enterprising club it was, I went and saw mine host, who informed me it was solely his idea. He would like to have a football club playing there.'

The site, just off the High Road, was a former nursery, now vacant land, owned by the Charrington brewery. According to Roberts's account, he agreed a deal within 24 hours of that initial chat with the landlord of the White Hart. Spurs had to guarantee crowds of 1,000 for first-team games and half that for reserve matches, ensuring plenty of passing trade for the pub – and groundsman John Over, who was also in charge of preparing the wicket at The Oval, got to work. Finances were eased when Roberts agreed to sell off the remaining five-year lease for Northumberland Park back to the landlords, who wanted to use it for housing.

It was at this time, and before Spurs could complete the move to their new home, that the club's enduring love affair with the FA Cup was first kindled. Brettell had been replaced by one of the players he had signed, Everton's Scottish midfielder John Cameron, who was named player-manager. His first game was a tie against the mighty Sunderland, seventh in the First Division, and Cameron scored the winner as Spurs came from behind to progress 2–1.

Every ground must have a name. Except White Hart Lane did not. It was initially, and colloquially, 'The High Road Ground'. Other options discussed were Percy Park, Champion Park and the early front-runner, Gilpin Park. Writing in 1921, in *The History of the Tottenham Hotspur*, subtitled 'A Romance of Football', Roberts explained: 'The ground was not christened, however, and for convenience sake it became known as White Hart Lane.' This despite the fact that the actual White Hart Lane is to the north of the stadium (much closer to the northern tip of the new ground) and on the opposite side of the High Road, as is the railway station carrying the same name.

A 'military tournament', featuring bareback wrestling and a 'balaclava melee', drew an audience of 5,000 for the first event at the new ground, and on 4 September a similar-sized crowd watched Spurs beat First Division Notts County 4–1 in the debut match at the Lane, generating receipts of £115. Those in the stands, which were dismantled on Northumberland Park and rebuilt, saw Tom Pratt cancel out an early own goal for the visitors before David Copeland scored a hat-trick. However, there were still issues that needed to be overcome. Roberts said: 'As time went on we found our new venue did not rid us of the continual nightmare of how to provide proper accommodation for the increased gate. Tons of concrete had to be blown up in making the ground. Adjoining land at both ends had to be acquired from the owners. For economy, wooden stands were erected. The upkeep, however, was alarming.'

On the pitch, though, things continued to blossom for a team that was to become known as 'The Flower of the South'. Spurs won the Southern League in 1900, breaking the grip of south-coast sides Southampton and Portsmouth, and bagging gate receipts of £5,592 for the season. The next year then saw history made. League football was a cartel of the Midlands and the north. Aston Villa were the most southerly of the 18 clubs in the First Division, Woolwich Arsenal the only side from south of Birmingham in the Second. Southern clubs, therefore, saw the FA Cup as their chance to show they deserved better treatment. Preston (after a replay), Bury, Reading (another replay) and West Brom were all vanquished by Cameron's side on the way to setting up the club's first appearance in an FA Cup final, against Sheffield United, whose goalkeeper was the legendary (and huge) William

'Fatty' Foulke. The crowd at Crystal Palace was a record 114,815. Tottenham's team included eight from the side that had won that first game at the new ground against Notts County, Pratt being one of the three casualties: George Clawley, Harry Erentz, Sandy Tait, Tom Morris, Ted Hughes, Jack Jones, Tom Smith, John Cameron, Sandy Brown, David Copeland, Jack Kirwan.

The list of goods delivered by caterers for that first game included: 55,120 portions of cake, 10,000 Bath buns, 20,000 French pastries, 24,000 scones, 1,728 gallons of milk, 200 rumps of beef, 300 quarters of whitebait, 22,400lb of potatoes and 2,000 cabbages and cauliflowers. And the flickering footage that has survived of the match shows a very different pitch to the one we are now accustomed to. There were no penalty boxes, but instead a goalkeeper's area that consisted of two ten-yard semi-circles along the goal-line that met in the middle of the goal, with another two lines further out, spanning the width of the pitch. Two goals by Brown put Spurs ahead but a controversial equaliser was awarded for the Yorkshire side by referee Arthur Kingscott when he ruled the ball had crossed the line, whereas the Tottenham players were adamant that goalkeeper George Clawley had fumbled the cross wide of the goal. But with no nets to give better evidence, the 'goal' stood. A week later, at Bolton's Burnden Park, in front of 20,470, Spurs came back from a goal down at half-time to win 3–1, courtesy of strikes from Cameron, Smith and Brown, who headed in the killer third. It was Brown's 15th of the competition and he had scored in every round. Those Spurs fans who had travelled north invaded the pitch while another FA Cup tradition was launched as the wife of director Morton Cadman tied white and blue ribbons to the trophy. On the train home, one Tottenham bricklayer persuaded Roberts to let him hold the Cup. He promptly filled it with beer and even FA Chairman Lord Kinnaird, on the same train back to London, took a sip. A crowd of 40,000 waited back in the capital for the victorious players to arrive home at 1 a.m., and they 'dragged them in two broughams [carriages normally drawn by horse] from South Tottenham Station' before fans flocked to the ground on the Monday evening to watch a 'kinematograph show including pictures of the cup tie'. A celebration dinner was also held, at the King's Hall in Holborn.

Over the next few seasons, the Lane was upgraded. By 1903, a wooden roof covered most of the East Stand, while crash barriers were put up on the open stand at the Park Lane terrace. Now the fans were able to watch Vivian Woodward, Spurs player and England's star striker, who scored 23 in as many games for the Three Lions. The pitch was returfed and in 1905 the club acquired the freehold of the site for £8,900, with a further £2,600 used to acquire land to the north. Stadium capacity was increased to 40,000, with the establishment of a tram network serving the outer boroughs expected to bring even more supporters to N17. And in 1908, exasperated by their dismissive treatment by the Southern League – 'This is the last straw,' exclaimed Roberts at a board meeting – the club applied to join the 'English League', as the Football League was then known. To the disbelief of Roberts and the board their application was unsuccessful, for they were beaten in a ballot to replace Lincoln City by Bradford City. Spurs faced a season with no competition but in June Roberts was informed by Stoke City they were resigning from the league on financial grounds. Lincoln, Rotherham Town and Southport were competitors, with Spurs and Lincoln tying in the first ballot. But the league's Management Committee gave the nod to Tottenham, aware of the potential for football to take a bigger step forward in the capital.

These days we have become used to players jetting around the planet on promotional tours but Spurs' decision to travel to Argentina ahead of their first league campaign would have been a real eye-opener to Edwardian fans. Five wins, a draw and a solitary defeat made it a success on the pitch but off it the travelling party were caught up in a mini-riot that left five dead and were also held at knifepoint by boatmen demanding an 'extortionate fee' for getting them to their ship before it departed. They also witnessed a horseback charge by sword-wielding members of the Argentinian cavalry when some fans stormed the turnstiles to scramble into a match for nothing.

Back at the Lane, it was set to be momentous too, with the first significant architectural step, although the official club history only mentions the 1909 construction of 'the present grand stand' in passing. For whole generations of Tottenham fans, the beginning of Archibald Leitch's masterpiece, starting with the West Stand, symbolised the birth of the modern Spurs. The link between Hotspur and the spurs worn by fighting cocks had long been made but it was only now that the connection between the bird and the club was made tangible. Former player William James 'W.J.' Scott, whose career spanned 13 years up to 1895, worked for F. Brady, a coppersmith based in Euston Road. Scott was determined to mark the new stand with a fitting monument and cast a cockerel, perched on top of a ball, that stood 9' 6" tall. Scott's son Roland was to lay the roof on top of the Old Bailey. He was also the cousin of Robert Falcon Scott, better known as Scott of the Antarctic, who was to embark on his doomed mission to the South Pole within months. Maybe that is why the cockerel, placed on the West Stand gable, originally pointed south not north. And why supporters believed it was unlucky when the north-facing version, a later addition, was turned round in the 1980s.

In any event, the original cockerel stayed on the West Stand until 1958, when it was transferred to the East Stand, facing the other way, where it stayed until 1988. Which is where Paul Gascoigne comes into the story. Club historian John Fennelly, who first started to watch Spurs in the mid 1960s, told me: 'I was working at the *Herald*, and Irving Scholar asked me to come along with a photographer because the cockerel had to come down. The East Stand was being rebuilt and so the cockerel had to come down. We got it down, eventually. The rumour was that the ball was full of gold sovereigns. We needed to open it up, but the only way to do that was to get a hammer and crack it open. And it was full, that much was true. But not with sovereigns. Inside was just a load of old papers. A Spurs handbook that had been there since 1934. Of course, the suggestion was that somebody might have been up there before, shinned up the pipes, opened it up and had it away with the sovereigns. But it was still intact, just in a mess. Nobody had opened it before we did. It was still sealed. All that was in it was an old club handbook and some newspapers in a plastic bag.'

And seemingly it was in a genuine state. Fennelly said: 'It was falling apart. It was all dented and pretty much knackered. The story was that the dents had been caused when it was hit by bomb fragments during the Blitz. But the truth was that the damage was done by Gazza – with an air rifle. I don't know why he had one with him at the ground, but we were training one day, and he was accurate enough to hit the ball from the other side of the ground, over by the tunnel. It was quite ridiculous, the sort of thing only Paul would do. He was bonkers like that. Of course he tried to deny it, but he'd been spotted, although it was only later we realised he'd actually managed to hit it.

'So when we got it down we realised it had to be replaced and instead we commissioned a couple of new versions, exactly the same size but made of plastic, fibreglass. They were much more solid and wouldn't fall apart. That original one, or what's left of it, is now in storage. It was in the cabinet in the VIP area, by the Arthur Rowe Suite.'

Leitch was to continue his work on the ground over the subsequent quarter of a century. By 1913 there were 5,300 seats and a standing paddock, 'the Enclosure', which could house a further 6,000 fans in the West Stand. The East Stand was covered in 1909 and enlarged two years later, taking the capacity to 50,000. Fortunes on the pitch had taken a dip, though, with only the outbreak of the First World War preventing the side being relegated from the First Division after six years in the league. That was despite the efforts of Billy Minter, top scorer for five straight seasons from 1908 to 1909 and who spent 32 years at the club, the first 18 as player and subsequently as both manager, for three seasons, and administrator.

During the conflict, with the Lane required for the national effort, Spurs split their home games between Clapton Orient's Millfield Road ground in Homerton and Highbury, which had recently welcomed interlopers from south of the river. Spurs had first met 'Royal Arsenal' in November 1887, a game abandoned with 15 minutes to go because of darkness when Tottenham were leading 2–1. But it was either side of the Great War that the rivalry and animosity between the sides, much of which remains to the present day, first surfaced. Spurs, along with Orient, Chelsea and much of the London media, had protested at Gunners owner Sir Henry Norris's proposal in 1913 to up sticks from their Plumstead home to Islington, in a bid to breathe life into a club that appeared to be dying a death. Despite their protests, the FA sanctioned the move and Arsenal became a north London club from September of that year.

The 1914–15 season was a shocker and, having finished bottom of the table, Spurs were due to be relegated before the war intervened. But when football emerged after the global conflict, ahead of the 1919–20 season, the Football League decided to expand the First Division by two clubs, up to 22. Both Spurs and Chelsea, who had finished 19th of the 20 clubs, believed they would be re-elected at the March meeting, following precedent. Chelsea were, with other clubs, deciding they had been the 'victims of a certain match, alleged to have been pre-arranged'. That was a reference to the 'Good Friday Betting Scandal', which subsequently saw three players from Manchester United and four from Liverpool banned for life for match-fixing – the two points 'won' by the Old Trafford club meant they finished out of the drop zone, although it was determined the fix was a plot by the players who bet on the outcome and was not designed to ensure United's top-flight survival.

But not Tottenham. Instead, they were manoeuvred into the Second Division by Norris. While Arsenal had only finished fifth in the Second Division, Norris enlisted old pal and league president John McKenna of Liverpool to lobby for his cause. The vote was: Arsenal 18, Tottenham 8, Barnsley 5, Wolverhampton Wanderers 4, Nottingham Forest 3, Birmingham City 2, Hull City 1. McKenna justified the outcome by stating: 'Arsenal had been a member of the league for longer than Tottenham.' Arsenal have remained a top-flight side from then on, the only club, other than recent top-flight arrivals Bournemouth, to have attained that status never since to have been relegated.

Roberts and co. must have been seething, and in *The History of the Tottenham Hotspur*, when the affair was still very raw, Roberts green-lighted the official line: 'Surprise throughout the whole country and consternation in Spurs circles was created by the league's decision. But Spurs would obtain by the verdict of the ball what they had been denied by the vote.' It was a feat they accomplished at the first time of asking. Peter McWilliam had been a fleet-footed left-half and three-time champion with Newcastle, known as 'Peter the Great' in his native Scotland. Appointed to Spurs, his first managerial job, in 1912, he was fired up by the sense of indignation that the league's decision had caused. His team responded and 'practically an unbroken series of brilliant successes' saw them romp to the Second Division title, with McWilliam's 'astute generalship' being hailed in the official club publication. Spurs accrued a record 70 points, which would have amounted to 102 under the modern system of three points for a win. Not until Reading won 106 points to get promoted in 2005–06 was that revised tally surpassed. And two months after it was printed, it was not just Spurs fans who were sending bouquets McWilliam's way.

A *Topical Budget* newsreel of the 1921 FA Cup final against Wolves at Stamford Bridge, running for seven minutes, proclaimed: 'The greatest event in football history' and 'A great Cup final'. It was perhaps the wettest, too, a torrential downpour all day turning the surface into a mud-heap – an unfortunate introduction to England for Australia's cricket captain Warwick Armstrong and his side, who were to retain the Ashes that summer with a 3–0 win over the home team, captained by Johnny Douglas. The newsreel's description says it all: 'A terrific storm marred the first period of play. It was practically impossible for the players to keep their feet.'

Despite the shocking conditions, skipper Arthur Grimsdell, who was nine years into a 17-season stay at the club, and Bert Smith took control of the match. And five minutes into the second half winger Jimmy Dimmock burst into the box – there was no 'D' at this time – from Bert Bliss's pass, slipped in behind the Wolves' right-back and shot left-footed across the keeper low into the bottom corner. Wolves pressed as Tottenham tired but the defence held. Exactly 20 years after becoming the first London club – and still the only non-league side – to win the FA Cup, they won the trophy a second time to remain the only team from the capital since the formation of the Football League in 1888 to have victory in the competition to their name. They would retain that distinction for another nine seasons. Grimsdell did not raise the Cup into the air when, finding shelter under the one covered stand, he was presented with the trophy by King George. He merely walked down the rickety wooden staircase that had been erected.

The Cup run added to the club's finances, while the following season Spurs finished second, this time with the cockerel badge on their shirts for the first time. The profits were used to cover the terraces at both the Paxton Road and Park Lane ends of the ground, replacing the small roof which had kept the rain off half of the fans at the northern end. Now the capacity had reached 58,000, more than two thirds of them under cover, and in 1934, the same year the electric clock with a cockerel motif was erected on the High Road, Leitch unveiled his crowning glory.

White Hart Lane's East Stand, built at a cost of £60,000, was something out of the ordinary, a triple-tiered construction with a ground-level paddock and seats in the upper area. And between them, running the entire length of the ground, was The Shelf, a raised standing area that had a life of its own and was to become part of the very soul of the ground. In total, the East Stand offered room for almost 24,000 supporters, with 5,100 seats and space for 18,700 to stand, taking the total capacity to just shy of 80,000. In a bridge to the present, and the club's ambitions to ensure their next home provides all the comforts of executive quality, the club programme proudly trumpeted that 'the catering arrangements here are the finest on any sport ground in Great Britain. When you enter either of the restaurants you will find yourself in such surroundings that you will imagine yourself in a West End establishment.' One suspects that of more interest to most fans was the notice that the club had obtained an agreement with Charrington's to serve alcohol at the ground, although only between 1 p.m. and 4 p.m. on first-team match days.

Although the crowds flocked in, it didn't do any good for the side on the pitch. There was a stunning, record-breaking crowd of 75,038 to see Spurs lose to Sunderland in a 1938 FA Cup tie. But it was far from a golden era. McWilliam quit in February 1927 with his team headed for relegation. The prolific scoring feats of £5,500 record signing Ted Harper, who scored 36 in 1930–31, were insufficient to lead them back into the top flight until Percy Smith's team secured promotion two years later. But despite coming third in their first season back, the new East Stand witnessed a relegation fight, which had a deep impact on the captain of the team, a man who brooded about the crushing disappointment until he himself had the chance to put it right. A man named Arthur Rowe.

2

PUSH AND RUN

You did not have to look hard to find monuments to Bill Nicholson at Tottenham. Even the entrance road to White Hart Lane carried his name. His bust took pride of place inside the main entrance to the stadium. And rightly so. But evidence of the man who influenced Nicholson more than any other, the architect of the first Spurs team to win the title – they are the only two members of the elite club of title-winning Tottenham managers – was much more difficult to discover. And without Arthur Rowe, without his footballing philosophy, insight and intelligence, it is quite easy to believe that Nicholson would perhaps never have been in a position to create the greatest side in the club's history.

Nicholson, famously, lived around the corner from White Hart Lane. His commitment to the club was total. Yet while Nicholson came to embrace and extend the club's philosophy, he was drawing on the groundwork laid by a man actually born in N17, who was also to serve the club as player and manager before being fatally undermined by his own boardroom.

For proof, just read this explanation by Rowe of what he brought into his side: 'My philosophy was that the easier you made the game, the easier it was to play it. So I used to tell the players to push the ball to a team-mate and then run into space to take the instant return pass. It was made of the "one-two". When not in possession, get into position. Make it simple, make it quick. It was easier said than done, of course, but I got together a squad of players with the football intelligence to make it work.'

If you listen to Nicholson's players discuss his approach later on, there is no doubt that Spurs' greatest manager did more than just learn from the man he played for in that 1950–51 title-winning side.

But Rowe had also learned from the men before him, especially Peter McWilliam, who used the club's arrangement with nursery club Northfleet United to try to instil the 'Tottenham Way' – close, quick passing as the means of transferring the ball up the pitch, rather than a big hoof – into the mindset of the coming generations of players. Rowe, raised and educated in Tottenham from his birth in 1906, and who recalled sneaking under the White Hart Lane turnstiles to get in for nothing, never lost the soft Cockney accent of his youth, which was clearly discernible when he recalled his memories of the victory over Wolves in 1921: 'I was at the FA Cup final at Stamford Bridge with my father. I was rolled over the heads of the other people, horizontal, down to the fence round the ground, as were a lot of other boys. It wasn't unique, even then. It was what happened when you had large crowds and the boys couldn't see very well.'

As a McWilliam protégé, Rowe was part of a school of thinking that can be traced all the way through to Rinus Michels's 'Total Football' with Ajax and Holland, and even Pep Guardiola's Barcelona: killing opposing teams simply by destroying their spirit with your own excellence. Initially an outside right, his professional career was as a centre-half, although it took five years for him to graduate from signing amateur terms and turning out for Cheshunt and then Northfleet to playing for his parent club. And it was another two seasons before he made the first of his 182 first-team appearances in a 1–1 draw with Burnley in October 1931. The crowd: less than 29,000.

Within two seasons he was club captain and, for one afternoon, in a 4–1 win over France at the Lane, an England international.

Just like Nicholson some two decades later, Rowe gained a single England cap, although, unlike his future wing-half, he did not score with his first touch as an international player.

Back in the club ranks, Rowe skippered Percy Smith's side as they returned to the top flight for two years before a sustained stay in the second tier – admittedly interrupted by the Second World War – only ended when he took up the reins, although the indignity burned deep inside him for the following decade and a half.

Forced to quit by injury at the age of 33, Rowe became one of the army of English football's global travellers, men whose internationalism makes the myopia and inward-looking approach of so many of their successors of the past half-century appear truly shocking. While others went to South America, Germany or Scandinavia, Rowe opted for Hungary. A lecture tour – he had been recommended by future Fifa president Stanley Rous – made such an impression that he was appointed in 1939 as the government's official coaching instructor. It was planned that he would be the 'football professor of the first Hungarian course for football trainers' and he was also charged with preparing the national side for the looming 1940 Olympic Games, scheduled for Helsinki. Events elsewhere in Europe, overseen by an Austrian-born former painter and soldier who took his first political steps in Munich, were to put a stop to all that, yet among those who were profoundly affected by Rowe's brief spell in the country were Ferenc Puskas and the man who was to oversee the Mighty Magyars' double humiliation of England in 1953 (3–6 at Wembley) and the following year (7–1 in Budapest), Gusztáv Sebes.

Rowe spent the Second World War back home, eventually coaching the Army side, before being appointed manager of Chelmsford City in 1945 and leading them to the Southern League title, making his name as an innovative, effective and winning coach. By then Spurs had been idling for three years post-war under Joe Hulme, so it was no real surprise when Rowe was approached to return to White Hart Lane in May 1949, with the side still seemingly stuck in the Second Division. Not for long.

In many ways Rowe was the prototype for the modern British style of management. He did not just content himself with looking after the players under his command but he also oversaw recruitment and the organisation of the entire club, effectively rendering the influence of the board redundant. It was a stance that was eventually to have fatal consequences for his reign. As a Tottenham boy he recognised the value of the local connection and Spurs' first-team squad included the likes of Eddie Baily, Charlie Withers, Les Bennett, Les Medley, Tony Marchi, George Robb and Sonny Walters, all also brought up kicking tatty balls on the narrow streets of north London, within a few miles of the stadium. They were players who were ripe to take on board Rowe's philosophy.

But the critical change was the application of genuine tactical nuance, something utterly out of keeping with the concepts of the 'English game'. That meant hours discussing set-piece organisation and the tactical tricks they could pull off, not just free-kicks and corners but also from throw-in positions and the kick-off. One tactic which had great success was from free-kicks on halfway, with the far-side winger sprinting off his flank from deep and wide as the ball was played forward, capitalising on the wide acres between the defensive line and the keeper. Obvious today but trailblazing in the late 1940s.

Interviewed on camera in 1982, 11 years before his death at the age of 87, Rowe remembered how he was able to transform the mindset of a club seemingly beset by paralysis and indecision. He said: 'They had a group of very good players but they were all willing to be advised by the manager. When I first mentioned push and run, a few people didn't understand what I was talking about. But it was easy for me.

'We trained in a car park when it was dry, and I used to give them a ball and tell them to kick it off the wall, run forward, pick it up and turn and do it again. Then I said: "That was easy, wasn't it? So what we'll do is stick a player there and when he passes the ball you'll find out it's just as easy. And it's just as easy on the field if you believe in it and if you do what you're doing now."'

According to the *Evening Standard*'s football correspondent Bernard Joy, in his 1963 book *Soccer Tactics: A New Appraisal*, Rowe was even more direct. Joy wrote: 'The first time Arthur Rowe met his players after becoming manager of Tottenham Hotspur, he took them on the pitch for a demonstration. He asked Welsh international half-back Ron Burgess to take a throw-in and he stationed himself ten yards from the touchline. When the ball came, Rowe hit it first time to Les Medley, who was a few yards up the wing. "How long did it take?" Rowe asked the trainer, who was timing the movement. "Two seconds," came the reply. Burgess repeated the throw and this time Rowe trapped the ball before pushing it as quickly as possible to Medley. "Four seconds," called the trainer. For the third throw, Rowe performed the normal reaction of a player, even in a fast-moving match. He trapped the ball with his "good" foot, the right, tapped it forward with the left and used the right again to send it speeding to Medley. The operation took eight seconds. Back in the dressing room, with the players sitting around on the benches, Rowe asked one of them to walk briskly while being timed. In two seconds he reached five yards, in four he doubled the distance and the dressing room was not big enough to measure the space he covered in eight seconds. "Now put that in terms of running in a match," Rowe told the team. "If you hold the ball instead of moving it straightaway you give defenders all the time they need to mark your colleagues who have moved into the open spaces. Worse still, a team-mate will have time to run into position and then out again before the pass is made."'

Rowe later explained his ideas to journalist Norman Giller: 'We used to operate in triangles, with Eddie Baily, Ronnie Burgess and Les Medley particularly brilliant at the concept out on the left. It was amazing to watch as they took defenders out of the game with simple, straightforward passes and then getting into position to receive the return. Over on the right Alf Ramsey, Billy Nicholson and Sonny Walters were equally adept at keeping possession while making progress with simple passes. Of course, you cannot play this type of game with confidence unless you have the foundation of a good defence, and from Ted Ditchburn through the entire rearguard we were rock solid.'

So they were, and entertaining too, with an average crowd of more than 54,000 for the Second Division championship season in 1949–50. However, not everyone believed the style of football that had propelled Rowe's side to that success would prosper against the big boys, with Arsenal and Newcastle the best exponents of the 'WM' formation, which was a response to the 1925 change to the offside law, meaning only two defensive players needed to be between the forward player and the goal for him now to be deemed onside, rather than three as previously. That view was crystallised when the newly promoted side's first game in the top flight brought a 4–1 home defeat at the hands of Blackpool, inspired, as so often, by the wing mastery of Stanley Matthews.

It would have been easy to buckle, to revert to the norm, especially when a long ball up the middle would have pandered to the initial instincts of the supporters and his two arch-critics in the boardroom, Eddie Dewhurst Hornsby and William Heryet. But Rowe was not for turning. He had told the board, before the start of the season, that he would stick with his principles. He believed that the key to success was ball possession, not casually frittering it away. No matter what the situation, the short pass was preferable, the determination to play out from the back. More than six decades later, as Mauricio Pochettino's side searched in vain for a late winner against West Brom at the end of the 2015–16 season, the Argentinian pinpointed Hugo Lloris's decision to start kicking long from the back, rather than feeding short to split centre-backs Toby Alderweireld or Jan Vertonghen, as the moment when his side lost the discipline that had enabled them to challenge Leicester until the last fortnight of the season. Whether knowingly or not, Pochettino was proving himself the natural inheritor of that golden thread, the one Rowe had put in place so long before.

Within the sanctuary of the dressing room, however, there was faith. Just as Nicholson was to make Danny Blanchflower the on-field manifestation of his vision, so Rowe leant on the wisdom of Burgess. Speaking two decades later, in his soft, lilting Welsh accent, the former skipper said: 'There was no individual more important than the rest. We had that vital all-for-one-and-one-for-all spirit, which I suppose was a spill-over from the war. We'd all been in the forces during the war and knew the importance of teamwork. If you have to single out one man, then it has to be Arthur Rowe. It was his philosophy that we followed. Keep it simple, keep it quick, keep the ball on the ground.'

Keeper Ted Ditchburn agreed that Burgess was the heartbeat of the side: 'Ron was poetry in motion. He was fantastic. And if you bear in mind he'd been invalided out of the RAF with a bad stomach, it made it even more impressive. I never saw him have a bad game.'

Ditchburn's memories were matched by playmaker Tommy Harmer: 'Ron had everything. He was fit, strong, good in the air. He was a good teacher and an honest, calm player. A very good player.'

It helped, too, that Rowe had a receptive audience. Baily, who was to go on to play 'bad cop' to Nicholson's 'good cop' but who himself earned nine England caps as a testament to his talent, said: 'There was a group of players here who already had the basic principles but Arthur told us he wanted to pass the ball. What we'd get from him was a lot of little sensible quips. He told us "Pass and Move", "Pass and Move". And it's the same today, if you do it properly. Ted would say he never had a strong kick and that he could throw it further than he could kick it. But he used the ball intelligently. Arthur would drum into us: "He who holds the ball is lost" and "Make it simple, make it quick". The basic, simple principles of football. I played for the love of the game. That was the most important thing. We kept ourselves to ourselves, as a team. We were a team that did everything together. That was it.'

Harmer said: 'Arthur wanted them to play the ball up to Len Duquemin, who was a big lad. He played it back and then it was Bump! Bump! Bump! Within fifteen seconds they were having a shot at goal. They didn't run as much but they were quicker than anybody else because the ball was doing the work.'

And Ditchburn reiterated the mantra: 'I liked to take control of the box. I'd shout a lot and my favourite saying was "Up!" As soon as we had the ball we would clear it. Normally I'd throw it out, because my kicking wasn't very good. Len would come back deep and I'd throw up the middle to him. Len would stop the ball, play it back to Eddie or Les Bennett and then it was off, push and run, all the time.'

Channel Islander Duquemin had hid in plain sight among the monks, working the fields of a monastery on his native Guernsey throughout the German occupation. There was no hiding place for 'The Duke' on the pitch, however, when he scored 134 goals in 308 appearances as a one-club player. 'The movement would make the openings,' Duquemin said, before going on to make one of the long-standing critiques of those at the helm of the club. 'There was always somebody to take over in possession. If I moved out to make an opening somebody would come through to take it over. I signed for £8 in the winter, £6 in the summer. I had to play twenty-one games before it went up to £12. We'd get a £2 bonus if we won, £1 if we drew. But it was a lot of money compared to what other people, the fans, were earning.'

On the pitch, with huge crowds flooding to the Lane, including attendances of more than 60,000 in two of their first three games and a club-record average of 55,509 across the whole campaign, Rowe's team were adjusting quickly. They lost narrowly at Liverpool and to Wolves but picked up a few points here and there before embarking on an eight-match winning run from the end of September, culminating in a 7–0 thrashing of a Newcastle side who had travelled south in second place but were destroyed in front of slightly over 70,000 fans. Burgess, out through injury that day, subsequently said: 'That was the finest exhibition of football I have ever seen. It was only by becoming a spectator that I realised just how special this side was. We paralysed Newcastle with our push and run tactics that a lot of so-called experts had said would not work in the First Division.' Joy's report in the *Standard* noted: 'This was superb football. I thought Spurs had reached their peak against Portsmouth (a 5–1 win in their previous home match) but this exhibition was even better.'

Spurs suffered just four more defeats all season – two of those to the Huddersfield side that also knocked them out of the FA Cup. Indeed, that home loss to the Terriers on 14 April opened the door, slightly, to the chasing pack, led by Manchester United. It was only the second home defeat of the season, the first since the opening day, while Rowe's team had won 15 of the other 17 matches, a formidable run as the increasingly raucous Lane became synonymous with a new brand of football. On 28 April 1951 they faced Sheffield Wednesday at home, knowing a win would land the title for the first time in the club's history. Not that you would necessarily have known that from the close-typed front page of the *Official Programme and Record of the Club*, which began by welcoming Wednesday 'to our enclosure today' before adding, with understated simplicity: 'After our drawn game at Middlesbrough last weekend, two points more would assure us of the championship, if considerations of goal average are not taken into account' before ending with a death notice which resonated with me when I read it at the end of the club's final season at the Lane. It marked, with regret, the passing of 'ground superintendent' Will Over, who had first joined the club in 1930 to work under his father John, Spurs' original groundsman when the club moved to the Lane in 1899. Further evidence that, even then, the lifeblood of the club was passed down through the generations.

The crowd was 'only' – by contrast with some of the previous huge attendances – a little more than 46,000, all of whom watched Duquemin, supplied by Baily, find the net shortly before the interval to score the winning goal. Strangely, by another quirk of the fixture list, ten years later when Nicholson's team clinched their title, the Owls were the opponents at the Lane in the decisive game. Maybe it was a bit of a shame for Mauricio Pochettino and his players that the South Yorkshire side were eliminated in the championship play-offs in 2017.

For Rowe and his side, a last-day win over Liverpool completed a stunning upset of a campaign. Tottenham's tally of 60 points was the highest since Arsenal had racked up 66 some 20 years before and saw them finish four clear of United. Few begrudged Spurs their triumph. Perhaps, though, it was the two inside the club, Hornsby and Heryet, who were most upset. They had written programme columns demanding more long-ball football even as Rowe's side were en route to the crown and continued to complain even after the success. In the *Tottenham Weekly Herald*, correspondent 'Concord' wrote: 'Spurs have proved beyond all doubt the vast superiority of their new-style soccer. Successful application of this style will, I predict, create a revolution in British soccer. Just as clubs found it necessary to discover an answer to the third-back game [WM system], so they will have to remould their ideas to counter the Spurs system.'

Unfortunately for Rowe and his team, they did. When teams played Spurs the next season, they no longer marked tight, leaving themselves vulnerable to the instant lay-off and ball into space. Instead, they dropped deeper in midfield and defence, frustrating and foiling in equal degree, while the opposition wingers stuck tight to the full-backs, negating Ditchburn's instinctive out-ball as a weapon that could be used to get the passing game going. When Rowe's champions suffered a revenge humiliation at St James's Park for the previous campaign's humbling, defeated 7–2, the beaten manager told his players: 'You lads ought to be flattered to have seen a better demonstration of your own game than you've given all season.'

Not that Spurs disintegrated. Far from it. A 6–1 thrashing of Stoke was proof of the team's qualities when everything clicked. But it clicked too infrequently. They were no longer quite so captivating or imperious, losing four at the Lane and 11 in total as they finished runners-up to United, this time four points behind rather than as many in front, to pass over the crown. Nicholson, looking back some three decades later, said: 'We found, when the team started going over the top, that there was more to this push and run than it appeared on the surface. You had to have good vision, good movement off the ball, excellent anticipation and to be able to pass the ball first time, with accuracy. Even though we had good players afterwards, we could never maintain that push and run of the 1950–51 side.'

Maybe, had Rowe been allowed to rebuild and prosper, the title season would not have proved a flickering moment of success. After all, Spurs were FA Cup semi-finalists in 1953 and again in 1956, this time under Jimmy Anderson, narrowly losing both times at Villa Park, to Blackpool and Manchester City respectively. Had they won those games, we would not remember the 'Matthews final' or Bert Trautmann's bravery.

But the internal sniping took its toll, and a heavy one, with Hornsby and Heryet relentless and implacable opponents of Rowe's footballing philosophy. Time, too, won its battle with the legs of Rowe's side and a 16th-place finish in 1953–54 ramped up the criticism, resulting in the manager suffering a nervous breakdown during the following campaign and temporarily – in fact, effectively for good – handing over the reins to Anderson before resigning. Rowe was to resurface as a coach at West Bromwich Albion, Orient (as they were named at that point) and Millwall, and had a two-year spell – and a second subsequent stint as caretaker manager – in charge at Crystal Palace, including their promotion campaign in 1960–61. As it was the season when their team lifted the Double, most Spurs fans will recall that campaign for different reasons.

Rowe's health never fully recovered. His legacy, though, did live on. Not only through Nicholson and the philosophy about bravery on the ball, but also thanks to his last Spurs signing, a Northern Ireland international from Barnsley named Danny Blanchflower. As for his recollections and achievements, modesty remained his watchword. 'All you need to remember,' he said, 'is that fifty per cent of the people in the game are bluffers. So a decent manager's halfway there when he starts out.' Not just a decent manager, a decent bloke too. In that final TV interview, Rowe was asked what Spurs meant to him. The tears began to well up in his eyes: 'I like them. They're a great club. To be associated with the club just feels nice.' The move away from the old stadium marked the perfect time for the Tottenham board to make a clearer, and more public, signal of Rowe's place in the club's history.

3

THE GREATEST

On the sand-brown wooden walls of Tottenham's spectacular new training complex at Hotspur Way in Enfield, just on the left, going north out of London, near where the A10 meets the M25, runs a series of inscriptions, quotes that sum up the ethos of the club. 'It's no use just winning, we've got to win well'; 'There's no use being satisfied when things are done wrongly. I want perfection'; and, finally, 'It is better to fail aiming high than to succeed aiming low. And we of Spurs have set our sights very high, so high in fact that even failure will have in it an echo of glory.'

When the club released their kit design for 2014–15, the first campaign under Mauricio Pochettino, the latter words were sewn into the design. Many suspect they were actually originally said by Danny Blanchflower, rather than Bill Nicholson, even if they were used by Tottenham's greatest manager in his foreword to Ralph L. Finn's instant history of the 1960–61 season, *Spurs Supreme*, published just months after the Double triumph. But in truth, that does not matter. As in so many memories, what people believe to be true *becomes* true. And what is incontestable is that every Tottenham manager has walked, and probably always must walk, in the shadow of William Edward Nicholson.

Player, and member of the first Tottenham team to win the League Championship. Manager of the other. Symbol of the club. The man who made the final decisions for 16 years, who presided over the golden days when the cockerel crowed loud and proud.

Who was cast into the abyss by the ungrateful men who employed him, only to be brought back, resurrected as the ultimate judge of which players were good enough for the club he built and cherished, and, finally, returned to his place atop the Tottenham pantheon. As Steve Perryman, signed by Nicholson and whose entire career at the club took place with Nicholson as the guiding spirit, eloquently described it: 'Bill was part of the fifties success, the sixties success and the seventies success. In the eighties, when we started to do well, some really good things, it was a team that still had Bill's thumbprint on it. He represented everything that was good about Tottenham.'

He certainly did. All that was good about Tottenham, and more. The bust of Nicholson, which long stood in the main foyer in the West Stand, bears a simple, homespun inscription, fitting for a man who did not have time for airs and graces, who lived most of his adult life in the same small house in Creighton Road, a seven-minute walk from the ground where that piece of ironwork has resided since it was cast:

BILL NICHOLSON

MANAGER

OCT 1958

AUG 1974

Seven words, two fewer than the number of major trophies he won. But the architect of the Glory years has, rightly, become more of a legend as those days have fallen further into the halcyon distance. And if there is doubt over whether Nicholson said everything attributed to him, there can be none, whatsoever, that those who played for him listened, strained to hear, whenever he chose to speak to them.

Nicholson was born on 26 January 1919, the second of nine children, to Joe, a groom in the winter who drove a horse-drawn cab along the sea front in the summer, and Edith, at 15 Vine Street in the North Yorkshire town of Scarborough, a house long since demolished. At the age of 17 he had come to the attention of Ben Ives, Tottenham's chief scout – recommended by, of all people, the local dentist who ran the Young Liberals team for which he had started playing – and had accepted the offer, three years before the outbreak of the Second World War, to leave Yorkshire behind for the capital and a place on the club's ground staff. The 3 March edition of the *Tottenham Weekly Herald*, under the headline 'On Trial', stated: 'Spurs are giving a month's trial to an amateur, Wm E. Nicholson, an inside-right of Scarborough Working Man's club. He recently celebrated his 17th birthday. His height is 5ft 8ins and weight 10st 12lbs.'

Wiry and ginger-haired, Nicholson passed the first test, signing for the ground staff at £2 a week on the same day as Ron Burgess, who was to captain and play alongside him in the first great Spurs side 15 years later. Their main role was working with the groundsman, with football training only on two evenings a week, and matches every Saturday for the club's feeder side, Northfleet United, in the Kent Senior League. But on 22 October 1938, 'Billy' Nicholson made his first-team debut in a 3–1 defeat at Blackburn in the Second Division, one of eight appearances he was to clock up before events in Europe and beyond brought a seven-year hiatus to league football.

Unlike the First World War, which saw thousands of footballers on the front line and several hundred killed, the Second World War was not so brutal. Even so, by April 1940 some 629 professional footballers had joined the services, 514 of them in the Army, including Nicholson, who served as a PE instructor with the rank of sergeant in the Durham Light Infantry. It is believed 80 of those died in the conflict, including 15 top-flight players. Demobbed at the end of the war, Nicholson returned to north London, initially as a centre-half but after two seasons in the right-half role which was to prove his forte. When Arthur Rowe arrived in 1949, he saw that Nicholson was the ideal man to play in front of Alf Ramsey, a key part of the side that followed promotion in 1950 with capturing the crown 12 months later.

And while he was to earn just a solitary England cap – scoring against Portugal at Goodison with his first touch, just 19 seconds in – his contemporaries recorded their admiration. Joe Mercer, another from that rich seam of managerial gold, remarked: 'You had to play with or against him to appreciate what a great defender he was and when the opposing manager was looking for a weakness in the Tottenham defence, the name Nicholson never came up.'

Retiring at 36 in 1955, Nicholson was swiftly appointed to the Spurs coaching staff under Jimmy Anderson, who had been effectively managing in place of the stricken Rowe for much of that season. He put to use the FA coaching badges he had earned upon his discharge, spending one day a week, as a strict disciplinarian, putting the Cambridge University squad through their paces. Not that Nicholson was overwhelmed by the quality of the Varsity players: 'Intelligence doesn't make you a good footballer. Oxford and Cambridge would have the best sides if that were true. It's a football brain that matters and that doesn't usually go with an academic brain. In fact, I prefer it when it doesn't. I prefer players not to be too good or clever at other things. It means they can concentrate on football.'

In hindsight, many felt that Anderson had only been appointed to keep the seat warm for the emerging Nicholson. That appears somewhat harsh, given that Tottenham finished runners-up to the 'Busby Babes' of Manchester United in 1956–57 – twice drawing with the champions – and, an admittedly distant, third behind Wolves and Preston the following season. But his work had been noticed and he was appointed assistant to England manager Walter Winterbottom for the 1958 World Cup in Sweden, where this most attack-minded of coaches was deemed responsible for the approach – based on the theory of isolating any weaknesses and eliminating them – which enabled England to hold eventual winners Brazil to a goalless draw. Anderson, stricken by ill-health and assailed by bad results – Spurs picked up just nine points from their opening nine games – fell out with wing-half Danny Blanchflower at the start of the next campaign. The manager resigned and Nicholson stepped up to the plate on 11 October. He never denied the story that he had not even told his wife Grace, always known as Darkie, who eventually discovered his elevation at second hand, presumably after his reign began the same afternoon.

Nicholson recalled Tommy 'the Charmer' Harmer, with a team that included full-back Peter Baker, Danny Blanchflower and Bobby Smith, the only members of it who would be in the side that were to make history within three years, although Terry Medwin did make 15 appearances in the Double-winning campaign. Tottenham 10 Everton 4, still Spurs' highest league score, with the home side 6–1 up at half-time, Alf Stokes and Smith scoring two, George Robb and Medwin one each. Further efforts from Harmer, two more from Smith and centre-half Johnny Ryden completed the rout. It was, though, a false, if glorious dawn, as Spurs flirted with relegation all season. Nicholson recognised the club was not what he had hoped.

The changes came thick and fast. Terry Dyson had joined Spurs after being demobbed from the Army in 1955, the same year Maurice Norman was signed from Norwich. Full-backs Ron Henry and Baker had been reared in-house but while Cliff Jones had joined from Swansea for £35,000 at the start of the year, he had only made a handful of appearances. But it was the quartet of signings the following year that transformed the side: the Scottish trio of goalkeeper Bill Brown, who cost £16,500 from Dundee, the brilliant playmaker John White, a £22,000 arrival from Falkirk and Dave Mackay for £32,000 from Hearts, and finally Les Allen, plucked from Chelsea's reserve ranks and installed as inside forward and Smith's raiding partner.

Nicholson had no doubts about the value of the new men. He

said: 'I was able to change things quickly because of the players I had. I brought in White, Mackay, Bill Brown and Jimmy Greaves. They were the men that allowed me to change everything. Mackay was so much for Tottenham. When he first came here he transformed everything. It was remarkable. I can't explain it really. But he came into the training sessions and from the first day everybody went "Wow! What have we got here?" Everything was so important, everything was dynamic. There were squabbles galore over goals, whether they were or weren't, even in five-a-side matches.'

Mackay did not attempt to deny his appetite and approach, or his willingness to join Spurs. He said: 'If Hearts wanted to sell me I just thought there had to be something wrong, so I'll go to Tottenham. I signed for £35,000, a record for a midfielder, and £20 per week. I remember going to London and it seemed like Benny Hill because everybody was not exactly running but almost running. They all seemed to be in such a hurry, completely different to what I was used to. But I've got to be a winner. I go crazy to win.'

His impact was instant, too. Jones said: 'Dave was an inspired signing. We had a lot of very good players but Dave gave us that spark, that bit of dynamite. From that time on we started to become a great team.' Dyson said: 'No matter how bad a game he was having, he would always want the ball.' And Smith, that burly bruiser of a centre forward, said before his death: 'Dave Mackay could do everything. He was wonderful.'

Nicholson looked his squad up and down and realised he had something special: 'I felt like the luckiest and proudest manager in the game. There was a common denominator about our game. We had a certain silkiness. The man without the ball makes them play – when you're not in possession, get in position, play the way you're facing. Time equals yards. You have got to have good vision and good movement off the ball, excellent anticipation and to be able to pass the ball first time, with accuracy.

'You don't particularly have to have eleven stars to make a football team. But you do have to have eleven players who understand each other's game and can play with each other and fit in a system. You've got to have a system to play.

'I used to say that for any craftsman, you need an ordinary tradesman as well. You need a labourer to carry the bags or do the rough stuff. In a football sense, that was the people who did the hard work, the running. Terry Dyson did it for Dave Mackay. They were both left footers but Dyson didn't have the quality Mackay had. He would run about for ever for Dave, and there were one or two others who really worked hard. Peter Baker did the job for Danny. People looked at Peter and said "He never marks his man", but that was because Blanchflower was such a good player going forward that Baker, instead of going to get close to his man out wide, and leaving space inside, which is the danger area, put himself in the position rather than be miles away from the goal.

'People didn't realise he was doing it for Danny. But that was part of our team work. That was important. Other players were involved like that too. It's team work. And with good team work, with players who were in the main pretty good players, that's how it all worked out. They all played for each other. They had a great friendship, their camaraderie was excellent.'

Dyson and others shared that view. The little winger, in his autobiography *Spurs' Unsung Hero*, said: 'The camaraderie among the players developed at a tremendous rate. It was brilliant in the dressing room. We used to sit in the bath together, chatting about the game and having a laugh. There was no "us and them" in the squad. The so-called big stars like Dave, Danny and John mixed in. We were one unit.'

If Mackay represented the 'heart' of the team, Blanchflower was the 'brain', although it needed him to be dropped early in Nicholson's reign, with the manager preferring the defensive attributes of Bill Dodge alongside Jim Iley, for the bond to be formed.

Dodge's professional career was to amount to ten games, nine of them that season. What might have been. But as Blanchflower wrote in the programme notes he penned for the manager's testimonial in 1984: 'Nick did it properly. He told me first and said he needed a better defensive balance in the half-back line. I shrugged my shoulders and hung around without animosity for a month or so. There were other places I could go. But there, I might have had to start all over again. Then I asked him for a transfer but he refused my request. That meant he didn't want me to go. So I hung around some more, biding my time. In the March, we played at Wolves. He didn't travel up with us. We were on the brink of relegation and they were League Champion favourites. He arrived late and hustled us into a private room in the hotel for a team talk. He said he was making me the permanent club captain and told the players to respect my authority. There was no more relegation talk after that. We were on the move again. Nick had decided to build around me.'

That game was drawn 1–1 and in the next match, at home to Leicester, the new skipper scored the opener in a 6–0 victory, his only goal of the season. Symbolic indeed. Eloquent and thoughtful, the Ulsterman was Tottenham's philosopher king, his essence illustrated by the words that were still plastered over the walls of the photographer's room, in use as a press overspill area when I sat down to compose my second edition 'rewrite' reports during the Champions League run under Harry Redknapp: 'The great fallacy is that the game is first and last about winning. But it's nothing of the kind. The game is about glory. It's about doing things in style, with a flourish, about going out and beating the other lot, not waiting for them to die of boredom.'

Nothing encapsulated better the vision the two men shared. Blanchflower's view of the game was equally romantic, although he was actually talking about his spell at Barnsley when he said: 'A football club is like a family, in the town or city. It represents the city because of that. I used to have a trainer who told me every elephant is an animal, but every animal isn't an elephant. What he meant was that there is a variety of people and the great key to football is to get unity out of a variety of characters. There is nothing more magical than that.'

In the summer of 1960, though, it was Blanchflower who first suggested the 'impossible' was, in fact, possible, telling chairman Fred Bearman: 'We'll win the Double for you.' Blanchflower related: 'I felt that it couldn't be done with a weak heart and that the team which might do it would have to really believe they could. I said it to the players and they agreed, as if they didn't disbelieve me. I mentioned it to Bill. He looked at me cautiously, he might have been thinking the same. "I think it can be done, too," he said.'

The pair kept that belief to themselves, although Mackay shared it. He suggested: 'There were only eight games left when I signed. My debut was against Manchester City, I played at left half and we beat them 3–1. We were second bottom of the table and in trouble but while I only played four of the last eight games we didn't lose any of them. That was just the start. It took off. Cliff Jones had suffered a broken leg but the following year everybody was ready.' Actually, not quite ready. Spurs began the 1959–60 campaign with a 12-game unbeaten run before losing – in a prefiguration of the future – to Sheffield Wednesday. In the end, they fell just short, finishing second, two points behind Burnley, but 21 wins and just ten defeats were a signpost to the immediate future, of a team that was finding itself and building momentum for what was to come. Mackay recognised he was in the right place at the right time: 'It was a marvellous team to play in, the best team I ever played in through my career. In that dressing room everybody expected to win. Really expected to win. We all thought we were that good. But we also believed we had to entertain, because entertaining came with it.'

And after Spurs began with a record 11 straight wins, everybody was talking about it. Everton, Blackpool, Blackburn, Blackpool again, Manchester United, Bolton, Arsenal, Bolton for the second time in a week, Leicester, Aston Villa and Wolves. Played 11, Won 11. Goals for: 36. Goals against: 11. The football was dashing, mesmerising, seemingly inevitable. Even a 1–1 draw at home to Manchester City in game 12 failed to stop the momentum, with further goal-laden triumphs over Nottingham Forest, Newcastle, Cardiff and Fulham before the first slip, at Sheffield Wednesday on 12 November. Smith was not worried: 'We won our first eleven games and other teams looked at us and thought: "Oh dear." We'd effectively won the league by Christmas. We had no pressure in the league.'

The blend of players was perfect. So was the leader on the pitch. Mackay said: 'Danny was a skilful player, quite tough as well. But the most important thing was that he was so influential. He knew about things, about life – he was too clever for the rest of us. He was the perfect captain. Everybody respected him. I was an adventurous player and liked to get forward but I could do that because I knew Danny would always be there, looking after the defensive side for me.' Jones, haring up and down the flank, could look back down the field with certainty. 'Danny was the organiser, the general,' said the Welshman. 'He was a great captain. Not just on the field but off it too. He bridged the gap between the boardroom and the dressing room. He was tremendous. Danny was a little bit older than most of us and he was a father-figure, a great captain. You could go to him for a chat about things. He would always have the answer and that helped us a lot.'

There was a natural, philosophical link between the manager and his captain, Blanchflower said: 'Bill and I became partners. Now we had lots in common with the best interests of the club at heart. We had total respect for one another when we learned that our different experiences and angles could blend into better teamwork. When he had doubts I could give him a second opinion. When I was too flippant he would bring me down to earth. It was not all buttering up. We often disagreed. But we agreed to disagree. After that, almost all our dreams came true. It was a hell of a time we had together. And every time we meet now that feeling is still there between us. You could call it a satisfaction that would be very hard to beat.'

Like that team, although Nicholson could be a harsh taskmaster. 'It's a cornerstone of my life as a player, coach and manager that the basics of the game are important,' he later insisted. 'Any player coming to Spurs, whether he's a big signing or just a ground-staff boy, must be dedicated to the game and to the club. He must be prepared to work at his game. He must never be satisfied with his last performance. And he must hate losing.'

Those who played under him for the next decade and a half attested to that view. Jones, Nicholson's lightning winger and still a match day host at the Lane, acknowledged: 'Bill was a great authority on the game. He knew his football and his tactics but he made training good too. When you have to train for nine months it can be a very boring part of football but he made it as entertaining as possible and his training was always geared to our performance. He said "The way you train is the way you will play" and if you train with effort that will be rewarded in the matches. Bill made us think. He was the most important member of Tottenham Hotspur. My respect and admiration for him just grew the more I saw of him. He knew more about the game than anyone I ever met and knew how to convey it. He was the complete manager.'

Jimmy Greaves, the cutting edge of Nicholson's 1960s side, agreed: 'Bill knew a lot about his players although he never actually said a lot. The Spurs fans would love to see a decent side. To give Bill credit, he used to say: "There's sixty thousand people out there who paid money to come and see you; now go out there and don't let them down." That was one of his edicts. He used to say that. It was a responsibility on us. You have a responsibility to play for your crowd. That's it.'

Mackay, lauded by Nicholson himself as his most important signing, in turn saw the Yorkshireman as gifted: 'Once he said something, then he meant it. That was how we had to do it. There were some great managers. Bill Shankly, Matt Busby, Alf Ramsey. Bill Nicholson was as good as any of them.'

For three glorious seasons, arguably better. To get a better gauge of the Double-winning side, they won the title by eight points, despite losing two of their final three games. But, admittedly in a 42-match season, if you convert to the modern three points for a win system, they would have earned 97 points, 15 clear of Wolves, who would have finished second rather than Sheffield Wednesday. They won 15 of their 21 home games, with three defeats suffered at the hands of Leicester (in February), Newcastle (a month later) and, in the final game of the season, with minds already turning to Wembley, West Brom. And they scored 115 goals, with a goal difference of plus-60. The supporters came too. An average of 53,124 at each home game, with 13 crowds in excess of 50,000 and six of those cramming in more than 60,000 – the London derbies were huge draws, with a season-best 65,930 for the visit of West Ham – all amid growing bedlam. Nicholson's Spurs had, as the season played out, become a phenomenon, extending their appeal way beyond industrial north London.

As for the football they played, it was a fusion of the best of the continental, patient, passing approach, mixed with trademark British physicality. A refined version of 'push and run', utilising the quality Nicholson had gathered, and which was designed to drag opposing teams out of shape, creating the opportunity to strike with devastating thrust and clinical finishing. Reading Ralph Finn's account in his 1963 book *Spurs Go Marching On*, it is hard not to draw parallels with Pep Guardiola's Barcelona side and their determination to destroy their rivals' spirits before demolishing their hopes: 'The ball goes from full-back to half-back to inside forward, back to the full-back, out to the winger, back again to the full-back, inside to the half, forward to the inside forward. It shuttles back and forth until the opening is made. The ball is worked from one position to another. Players move around, take up places where it is safe to receive a pass. Patterns of incredible complication are drawn on the field of play by moving the ball and the darting players.'

The title was won against the first team to have beaten them. Almost exactly ten years earlier – minus just 11 days – Nicholson had been a member of the Spurs side that beat Sheffield Wednesday 1–0 to lift the crown. Once again, the Owls were guests at a coronation, with 61,205 paying guests, Smith smashing home left-footed to cancel out Don Megson's scrappy opener, before Allen crashed home on the volley for the goal that was to seal the triumph, although nerves were stretched in the final minutes as Wednesday sought in vain for the equaliser. Dyson recalled in his autobiography: 'There was an incredible roar that must have been heard for miles.' Nicholson later said: 'Obviously they wanted to celebrate winning the league, so I said to them: "Okay – celebrate, enjoy . . . but don't forget we've got the other one to win as well. So if you could forget about the league and start to think about the Cup."'

By now the backdrop to the performances was the White Hart Lane version of the 'Battle Hymn of the Republic'. And any doubts that this team was capable of Glory, Glory were banished three weeks later, at Wembley. Spurs had brushed aside Charlton, Crewe – just the five this time, not the club record 13–2 of the previous season – Villa, Sunderland (5–0 in a White Hart Lane replay) and Burnley, and were heavy favourites against Leicester, even more so when the Foxes' Les Chalmers was reduced to a hobbling passenger after being caught by Allen in the first half.

Instead, on one of the few occasions during that campaign, Nicholson's side missed their lines. Eventually, Smith found space in the box to put Spurs ahead in the second half before Dyson's header gave Gordon Banks, in the Leicester net, no chance. The Double was won. History had been made. The first team to lift both trophies in the same season since Aston Villa in 1897, when Queen Victoria was on the throne. A feat that had been deemed beyond credibility in modern football. Smith recounted: 'It was a dream for me to score in the final. I was really pleased, really happy. We felt the pressure because nobody had done it. We were on edge, instead of relaxing. We didn't let things flow. But we managed to get through it.'

The manager, though, was not satisfied. 'Bill was unhappy after the final,' said Mackay. 'He was happy that we'd won, of course, and that we'd won the Double. But he wasn't happy with the way we played. Bill was really upset because we hadn't won by six or seven. He wanted us to win but to entertain as well.' Nicholson, even with the passage of time, did not demur. 'It was a great success to win it at Wembley but we should've done better, although it meant we'd won the Double.'

As Blanchflower lifted the FA Cup into the Wembley air on 6 May 1961, Nicholson recognised he had achieved what many had deemed inconceivable. Then again, to those who knew him, it would have come as little surprise. He was not a man who could ever have rested on his laurels. That would have been a betrayal of everything he held dear. Nicholson wanted more. And he knew exactly who could provide it.

It is said the three great falsehoods are lies, damned lies and statistics. But sometimes the statistics can reveal a greater truth. And while Bill Nicholson could not have foretold that James Peter 'Jimmy' Greaves would score 266 goals in just 380 games for Tottenham, he might have been willing to estimate that he would be somewhere in that vicinity. The numbers alone, though, only tell a fraction of the story. For a whole generation of Spurs supporters, Greaves was, and is, simply the greatest. An effortless, instinctive predator, capable of scoring goals of such sublime, infeasible genius there was the expectation, every week, that he would take the fans' breath away with his audacious impudence and deadly finishing.

Nicholson, too, knew what he was getting: 'Jimmy was an excellent player, an excellent goalscorer and he had more skill than people gave him credit for. He had good passing ability but most important was his ability to get the ball in the net. I tried several times, even talking to people like Ardiles, to say: "You get in these positions and yet you don't score." When Jimmy Greaves got in those positions, he didn't try to blast the back of the net out. He simply placed the ball just inside the post as if he was passing to the stanchion at the back of the net.'

The signing from AC Milan was one of those mischievous deals that were Nicholson's hallmark. And the best part of 12 months in the making. 'I'd bumped into Jimmy at the Café Royal, in the toilets there, when there was talk about him leaving Chelsea,' Nicholson later recalled. 'I said "What's this nonsense about you going to Italy? Why the hell do you want to go there?" When I heard things weren't going so well for him I found out he'd like to come back and said if that was the case I'd be very pleased to negotiate.'

Greaves did not need a second invitation. His relationship with hardline Milan coach Nereo Rocco had disintegrated, even though, on the pitch, the striker was delivering, with nine goals in ten appearances. He said: 'I went to Milan but the coach was anti-British. He was certainly anti-me! He kept telling me the wrong things. He told me to be at training at ten a.m. and then I'd turn up for then and be fined for being late. Mind you, discipline was never my strongest suit.

'I was playing well and scoring goals. So for the Italians, when I said I wasn't happy, that didn't make sense. They kept offering me more money but I just told them I wanted to go home. I was scoring goals out of misery and eventually they realised I was prepared to do anything to go home. And suddenly I could earn £100 per week back home.'

The abolition of the maximum wage earlier in 1961 – until then no player could be paid more than £20 per week – had altered the equation. And Greaves felt he needed the money, although the move was not entirely smooth. 'Bill Nicholson came out, with

John Battersby of Chelsea. They decided that they were both going to bid the same – £100,000,' said Greaves. 'But Bill actually decided he'd bid £99,999 for some reason best known to himself. I just wanted to go to Tottenham. They'd just won the Double but I also felt that after going to Milan I had to have a reason to come back home. Tottenham gave me that reason.

'I came back totally skint. Milan never paid me any of the money we'd agreed in the contract. Why should they? They held all the money back. We'd sold our home before I went there so when we came back we lived in a two-bedroom council house with Irene's family, her brother and sister, for four months before Tottenham found us somewhere. And I came back for £60 per week . . . Chelsea had offered £120 but I was so happy to play for Tottenham.'

Not that, initially, the players in the Spurs dressing room were entirely convinced. 'It was a bit difficult for me at the start,' Greaves explained. 'That dressing room was intimidating. I'd developed a reputation, unfairly I thought, of being a spoiled brat, although I might have been! I remember going into the dressing room for the first time and they were all getting ready to go out for training. One of the reserve players said: "Here she is!" And I thought: "Here we go!" I knew I had work to do but I was lucky because it was the greatest team you will ever see. I came back into a very great side but after what had happened in Italy I had to prove myself all over again to a great team and a great bunch of players. It would be wrong to say I wasn't accepted but it was difficult to come into that dressing room. I had to get down to doing what I did, to become part of the team on and off the field.'

Greaves being Greaves, though, he did it in his own inimitable style. On 16 December 1961, in front of 42,734, he put Blackpool to the sword. The *Sunday Express* match report gushed: 'In the 39th minute that white-shirted Spurs storm-trooper, left-half Dave Mackay, took a quick throw-in on the left. Straight as a bullet the ball flew to right-winger Terry Medwin. A superb back-header by the Welsh international arched to Jimmy Greaves standing hemmed in by Blackpool's defenders in front of goal. Like a flash of black-and-white lightning, Greaves struck. With an acrobatic continental leap he volleyed the ball into the roof of the net.'

There were two more to come, a header from Mackay's cross and another, also with his head, from Allen's corner. Debut. Hat-trick. Point made. 'Tottenham fans aren't the easiest to win over,' Greaves said. 'A lot of players have suffered because of that. They were looking for something a little bit special from me and I managed to give it to them on that day, with three goals. After that I was part of it, of them. From that day on I struck up, immediately, a great relationship with them. The most important part of football is the supporters. They are the lifeblood of the game, of the club. And they were the most important people in my life.'

A bond was swiftly struck up with his team-mates, too: 'Bill said he was lucky with the quality of the players but you can't guarantee a hundred per cent as the manager of a team that they are going to gel. You might buy great players but it's not always going to work. So in that respect Bill got lucky. But everybody brought something individual. Peter Baker had been around for a long time. I remember going to Spurs as a schoolboy and he was playing full-back then, when I was at school. Ron Henry and Bill Brown were solid, big Maurice Norman was what he was, Danny was an incredible guy, one of the most intelligent men I ever met in my life. He guided the club as a player, along with Bill. Dave Mackay was the greatest player to play for Tottenham. Cliff Jones, well, he was Welsh! John White was a great player and Bobby and myself, along with Terry Dyson, who used to go through a tremendous amount of work and was underrated. Smithy had more skill than people thought. Yes, he was a big, bruising player but he had a deft touch. I was a goalscorer. My job was to get the ball into the net, however I had to do it. You don't have to blast it. You pick your spot. But if I'd scored every goal I missed, and missed every goal I scored, I wouldn't half be in the record books!'

He is still, of course, but for all the talent in that team, they did not dominate as they should have done. Maybe Europe was a distraction, but the only other domestic trophy won by Nicholson's first side was when they retained the FA Cup in 1962, Greaves, Smith and a Blanchflower penalty seeing off Burnley. Promoted Ipswich, under the guiding hand of Ramsey, shocked football by snatching the title off Tottenham. Mackay believed that, for a rare occasion, Nicholson was out-thought by his old Spurs team-mate. He said: 'We went down there to Portman Road and we didn't know who to pick up. They had three through the middle and no wingers. Peter Baker was saying: "Hell, there's nobody on the wing, what do I do?" They beat us home and away but only because of the system. When we then played them in the Charity Shield at Ipswich we beat them 5–1 because we had sorted out our formation to counteract theirs.' Too late. Spurs had actually finished third behind their Wembley victims, and they were second, six points adrift of Everton, in 1962–63. Time, now, was taking its toll, alongside injuries. And, in a horror moment of inconceivable tragedy, another of Nicholson's greats.

Greaves said: 'We should've won the league back to back but we let it slip and Ipswich won the title. We were under-achievers. Then the team broke up. Danny got injured, John White was killed, one or two others started to crack.'

White's death, on 21 July 1964, was a hammer-blow, in many senses. Sheltering under a tree on the ninth hole at Crews Hill Golf Course, barely a mile and a half from the site of what is now the club's shiny new training headquarters, the 27-year-old was cut off in his prime by a lightning bolt. 'We called him The Ghost,' said Dyson, aware of the irony. 'Nobody could mark him. He was a superb athlete. He'd been a cross-country runner and had so much ability. He used to float. Nobody could get near him.'

Smith shuddered in a television interview as he said: 'The day before he died he asked me and Cliff Jones to play with him at Crews Hill. We told him he was mad because of the weather so he went on his own. That was the last time I saw him. I couldn't believe it.' Mackay added: 'Killed by lightning playing golf. How unlucky is that? It's a billion to one chance. It was heartbreaking for all of us. We all played at Crews Hill. I just couldn't believe it. It took me a long time to get over it. He had everything – right foot, left foot, bravery, a very good player, with pace too. John was brilliant. He had stamina like nobody else. I remember one game against Forest when the defender who was marking him was absolutely knackered by half-time. He was so strong. He could knock the ball from one end to the other with both feet.'

The 'Brain' of the team had retired, the invention snatched away by an act of God. It was never the same again. Nicholson was to rebuild, building good sides. But not another great one. As Greaves conceded: 'Bill got a new side around him but we were under-achievers through the sixties. A side that was good enough to win the league but didn't. We should have won more.'

4

CALL ME BILL

That Nicholson was, in modern parlance, a workaholic, is clear. First in to the ground, from 7 a.m. Frequently the last out. And no day of rest. 'In all those sixteen years I never had a long holiday, not even during the close season,' he conceded in his retirement. 'I popped into the ground every Sunday to work. We could have moved to a bigger house in Hertfordshire but that would have meant more time travelling. Being in such a state through overwork was entirely my own fault. No one asked me to work every day. But I ran the club and wouldn't trust the smallest job to anyone else.'

The impact was felt by his family. Not just Darkie but their daughters, Linda and Jean, who revealed in 2014: 'Dad always expected the players to aspire to perform at their best – and for many, many years we watched as they rose to the challenge. They played for him and they played for the glory of Tottenham Hotspur. He was an inspiration to others and it was nice to know that he was well respected by people inside and outside of the game. Dad also loved to watch and support youth football as they were the players of the future.

'He also loved the fans as much as they loved him. Dad used to say: "Without the fans there wouldn't be a game." It was a wonderful atmosphere, whether sitting or standing, at the Lane. It was such an exciting place to be on a match day singing "Glory, Glory, Tottenham Hotspur and the Spurs go marching on". But at the end of the day, when dad came home to his "other family", all he ever wanted was a quiet family life. He often found time to kick a football around in the garden with his three grandsons, and even give them a few hints.'

What hints they would have been. 'I was in awe of him,' admitted Steve Perryman, his voice now growing slightly hoarse. 'Maybe too much so. He'd won the Double and Cups, signed some big players. But I felt you had to look up to him and that was very big for me as a young player. He was the big man. I couldn't point to one single day where I came home from a session that I knew was going to last me for my football life. I wouldn't say I ever reached that single moment. But there was the constant messaging, the rules, which didn't have to be drummed into you for you to recognise they were the right things. You didn't need to be fined to not break them. I never heard of Bill Nicholson fining anyone, or anybody calling him anything other than "Bill" – from the young apprentices to the senior pros. He said the same to every single one of us: "Call me Bill." I would never dream of calling him anything else, "boss" or "gaffer". He was just "Bill". A proper, proper man, running a proper club. And that meant we had proper supporters, too, because they recognised his place in their history. He was straightforward. He told you what he expected. There was no nonsense, no spin, none of that from Bill.'

Perryman's memories are not rosy-hued. They merely come from a deep affection and a recognition that he was just one among many who were made by this son of Scarborough, the single most important figure that Tottenham Hotspur has ever known.

And Alan Mullery, who replaced Mackay as captain, also had no doubts: 'Bill was the best coach I've ever seen. And he was a coach, a real coach. He wasn't one of those who would stand on the sidelines and put out the cones while the trainer did the hard work with the players. Bill worked with us, every day. Him and Eddie Baily had both been good players. Eddie scored five in nine games for England and they were in the title-winning side in 1951. The thing with Bill was he was very strong about what he wanted us to do and the football he expected us to play and if we didn't live up to those standards, he'd let us know.

'I'd been at the club for a few months, ten or twelve games, and we beat Birmingham 4–1. I was at home the next morning, the Sunday, reading the papers to find out how people thought I'd played – because we always used to do that, with marks out of ten. That day I'd played quite well and was getting nines. The phone rang and my wife answered it, asking who it was. "Bill," said the voice at the other end. "Bill who?" she asked. "Bill Nicholson." So she told me who it was and handed the phone over. "Hello," he said. "I thought I'd tell you that was probably the best game you've had since you been here."

'So I was thinking: "Great; he really fancies me, that's good." Then he went on: "But in the eighty-second minute you gave the ball away for their goal. I don't want to see that again." And put the phone down. My wife looked at me, because she could see something was up and asked if I was all right. "No!" I said. "I've just got a bollocking for giving the ball away when we've won 4–1!"

'But that's what Bill was like. He wanted perfection from us, in every game. He wanted us to please the crowd, to send those supporters away happy every week. Winning wasn't enough for Bill. It had to be winning with style. That was the reputation he had and it was his philosophy throughout his career. All of us now miss him because of what he did for us. He wasn't a laugh or jovial. He was a dour Yorkshireman. But he just wanted everything to be perfect.

'He was ahead of his time, don't doubt it. He was doing things, fifty or sixty years ago, that are talked about as modern and far-sighted now. There's been this belief that coaches are a modern invention. People point to Mourinho, Klopp, Wenger, as if they're something new. But that's rubbish. Bill, Jock Stein, Bill Shankly and Matt Busby were wonderful coaches. Bill was a working man's manager and I wanted to manage like he did. He had that wonderful knack of going round to every player before a match and telling them exactly what they'd be facing and had to do. So that's what I did when I went into management – exactly the same, working with the players. He would do that, every day. But he was extremely helpful in showing me what he expected me to do and how to do it. And if you didn't perform well enough, he'd let you know, there and then.'

Mullery's view of Nicholson is echoed by others among his charges. Martin Chivers had a love–hate relationship with the manager which eventually mellowed into reverential respect.

And Scottish striker Alan Gilzean, whose balding pate and dynamic leap made him a fantastic partner for first Greaves and then Chivers joked: 'I was only in Bill's office twice in ten years. He moaned a lot. After a game it was: "Christ, Gilly, you shouldn't have been doing this or that." But he was a very honest man. He laid down what he expected from you. He expected me to go round like Bobby Smith, knocking people for six, but that wasn't my style. He kept saying: "Bobby Smith would've had the keeper in the net." So I'd reply: "Sorry, you'd better go and get Bobby Smith back again." He was good and bad to me. But I was only in his office twice so he must've liked me!'

As did the man plucked from Watford to replace Bill Brown, the safe pair of hands in Nicholson's greatest side, Northern Ireland's Pat Jennings. He said: 'Bill expected you to do the ordinary things well. If I dropped a ball he'd go on about the one I dropped rather than the ten I'd caught or the saves I made. The only compliment he ever gave me was after a game at Grasshoppers when he said: "You lot should give your bonus money to the keeper tonight."

'When Bill entered the dressing room to change before training there was a general hush . . . nobody clowned around when Bill was about, not even a joker like Jimmy Greaves. Before a game he'd go round the dressing room and every player. He'd tell me who to look out for, the dangers, what they would do, what their strengths were, who would come through from midfield. There was no video in those days but he was so thorough. I've never heard anything now or from any of the managers I've worked with since that I didn't hear from Bill Nicholson fifty years ago.'

That Nicholson demanded hugely, of himself and others, is unquestioned. It was perhaps fitting, then, that his first opponents were Everton. While Tottenham's motto, 'Audere est Facere' ('To Dare Is to Do'), has been plastered around White Hart Lane for the past decade, the Goodison side's 'Nil Satis Nisi Optimum', translated as 'Only the Best Is Good Enough', would perhaps be a more appropriate epitaph.

For those in doubt, here are some of the things Nicholson definitely did say:

'If you don't win anything, you've had a bad season.'

'It's better to fail aiming high than succeed aiming low. It's no use just winning, we've got to win well.'

'There's no use being satisfied when things are done wrongly. I want perfection.'

'Spurs have got to be the best in the land, not the second best.'

'If you don't have to drag yourself off the field exhausted after ninety minutes, you can't claim to have done your best.'

Perryman, who was to have his own spell sitting in the White Hart Lane dug-out, allied himself to Nicholson's enduring philosophy. He said: 'Bill had such a massive influence on me. I listened and learned from him every word he said. With Bill it was about common sense. He had standards he expected, for football and for life.

'We discussed things with Bill and Eddie Baily, how the game was changing, but what they did with us was amazing. The directors didn't understand it at all. I was playing for Bill Nicholson more than Tottenham. I was playing for the fans, and he would tell us that all the time: "It ain't you. It ain't me. It's the supporters. They stick with this club through thick and thin. They pay their money every week and they allow us to buy better players. They're the most important people at this club."'

One of Perryman's fellow trainees, who joined him in the elevator to the first team, was Ray Evans. For 30 years, the right-back had been a coach in the United States, living in Washington State, first near Seattle but then on the other side of the Cascade Mountains. But while he left the club in 1975, a part of him remained in N17: 'We knew that Bill was looking to bring though local talent,' he said, his Edmonton inflection still strong in his voice despite three decades away from London. 'Maybe because there had been so many local boys in the Spurs team he played in, even if the Double team was put together from all over the country. But there was a bunch of us, local kids who'd got apprenticeships, and he wanted to try to bring us through, rather than paying £100,000 for somebody else – when that was a lot of money, remember. It was incredible for me to be part of that.

'Bill did everything he could to try to instil the history and importance of serving this club. What the stadium meant. He had that sense of compassion for the fans. It's a different world now and he wasn't a natural communicator with us. That wasn't his strong point in terms of players, and he could be stern and strict with us. But it was about making us feel his pride in being part of the club, the privilege we had to be the next chapter in that history. He didn't have to say too much because it came from everything he did. And when he did lighten up, occasionally, everybody saw it and laughed along.'

Of course, even those who harboured affection as well as respect for Nicholson conceded he was, to borrow the most common adjective used by most of them, 'dour'. So, too, did those who had to deal with him in a different professional sense. BBC commentator John Motson said: 'I was quite in awe of Bill Nicholson. I started on *Match of the Day* in 1971 and Bill was still in his prime. I remember going to see him in his office in the Red House and he was absolutely charming, extremely kind. I interviewed him on camera a few times and he always made me feel welcome. I could see why the players held him in such reverence. He was scrupulously honest, a man who believed in the values that he wanted all his players to live up to. He worked at the ground every hour that God sent.'

Former *Daily Express* football writer Steve Curry said: 'I was scared of Bill, absolutely petrified. I used to have to steel myself to ring him up. He was very dour but he was a kind man in many ways. I wouldn't say he was at ease with the press but he was so loyal to his players.'

And Brian Scovell, who co-wrote Nicholson's autobiography and also penned *Bill Nicholson: Football's Perfectionist*, said: 'He was a very decent, totally honest man. He wouldn't have dreamed of fiddling a penny on any move. When I was writing his autobiography and started going round to his house, sitting down and talking to him for hours I found it amazing he was living in the same house, around the corner from the ground, where he'd always lived since he joined the club as a player. His wife, Darkie, was a revelation. She'd ride her bike round, shopping by bike. One day she brought it into White Hart Lane and said to Bill: "Something's wrong. Can you repair it?" And he looked at her and said: "I'm too busy."

'He was a decent man but very dour in interviews. Somebody told him not to say too much to the press and he took it literally. He was like Alf Ramsey in terms of offering information. He didn't say very much. He'd make you wait for an hour after a match before coming to speak. There wasn't a press room for interviews then. You had to do it outside, in the rain. Once he started talking tactics he would go on for half an hour or more. But if you asked about transfers or controversy, he didn't want to know.'

There was, though, another side to this austere man who

wanted glory and perfection, who would devote every moment of his working life to the club and who sadly conceded, at his daughter's wedding in 1970: 'I never saw her growing up.' The Nicholson who tended his prized allotment behind his house – named Peasholm, a nod to the Scarborough park near which he grew up – on his knees wearing a pair of Spurs shorts as he dug up the weeds, who took pride in his blackberry bush and apple trees, chasing away the local kids who nipped over the rickety fence to help themselves to the fruits of his labours, who meticulously cleaned his car inside and out.

Nicholson was held in esteem, not just by his players but also his managerial rivals, Jennings recalled: 'I joined Watford and played in the Irish youth team. I'd never been further than Belfast before that but then in 1964 I got a call from Bill McGarry to say he needed me back to do some extra training. He picked me up at Heathrow and he said: "Do you know why you are here, son? The great man, Bill Nicholson, is waiting for you at Vicarage Road."

'I didn't sign that day. There was a money problem! I went back to Ireland but then got a call from Bill asking if I'd thought about it because he had to go and sign someone. Getting money from Bill was like getting blood out of a stone but I signed for two years. The first contract was £23 per week plus £25 if I made the first team. I said I wasn't joining the great Tottenham for that and Bill said: "£35 per week." I said I took that home at Watford but Bill didn't want to back down. In the end I signed for £40 per week plus £10 if I played for the first team. Two or three years later I thought to myself I must be worth another contract. I plucked up the courage to go and see Bill and he asked what I was on. So I told him £40 plus £10 and he offered me £45 plus £5 per appearance!'

Nicholson had created a club that players wanted to become part of. Gilzean, who also joined in 1964, even spent a quarter of a year out of work; so keen was he to play for the manager. 'Dundee wanted me to join Sunderland but as a kid all I wanted to do was play at Wembley in the FA Cup final,' he said. 'I looked at Sunderland's record of getting to Wembley and they didn't go very often. Tottenham had a record of getting there and I wanted to go to Tottenham. But I had to spend three months on the dole because they wouldn't let me go.

'Finally Bill Nicholson agreed a fee with Dundee and within a couple of days I decided Tottenham was my club. I knew John White. He was my room-mate with Scotland and talked me into signing but sadly I never got the chance to play with him at Tottenham. I saw Greaves play when England beat us 9–3 at Wembley and could see he was some player. He ran amok and then I played against him for Scotland under-23s at Aberdeen. So I thought: "If you can't beat 'em, join 'em." He was down to earth but so quick, quicksilver, and showed such calmness under pressure. When I watch Lionel Messi now, that was exactly like watching Greavesie all those years ago. He was that good.'

The pair formed a formidable strike-force even if the only tangible reward for the mid 1960s team was the FA Cup final win over Greaves' first club Chelsea in 1967. 'It was my dream to play in a Cup final,' Gilzean said. The game, the first 'Cockney Cup final', was far from a classic but goals from Jimmy Robertson, who had arrived as a teenager from St Mirren and was to go on to become the first man to score for both teams in north London derbies, and Frank Saul proved enough for Spurs to lift the trophy for the fifth time despite a late effort from Bobby Tambling. Spurs' right-back that day was Joe Kinnear, who was deputising for broken-arm victim Phil Beal. Gilzean recalled that before the game 'Dave Mackay said to Joe: "Don't worry, son. If we lose, I'll give you one of my medals." Dave looked at Chelsea in the tunnel and said: "You don't fancy it, do you?" That was the sort of character he had as a captain. He had that big, barrel chest and just wanted us to attack, attack, attack. He was the heart of the club.'

Yet the heart was losing its beat. The previous year, in what was an iconic moment, captured on camera, Mackay turned on his Scotland team-mate – and subsequent successor as national captain – Billy Bremner when the flame-haired midfielder had deliberately booted his left leg, which he had twice previously broken, in retaliation for a minor touchline scuffle. Mackay felt for years the picture of him grabbing Bremner by the middle of his shirt, with the referee rushing over to try to prevent an explosion, portrayed him as a 'bully', although he did concede that 'I could've killed him.'

But Mackay's response to the tackle and the damage it might have inflicted on him signalled his realisation that injuries had already taken a toll. He pinned the blame for his waning powers on the horrendous tackle by Manchester United's Noel Cantwell at Old Trafford in 1963, an injury compounded when he broke his leg again in a reserve game at Shrewsbury as he made his comeback. Even 40 years after the event, and a decade before his death, his anger towards his assailant had barely abated: 'It wasn't a tackle!' Mackay added: 'After I broke my leg, I always had problems with my weight and I'd never had problems before that. In 1968 we played City and they were far better than us. They beat us easily at White Hart Lane (a 3–1 win, en route to clinching the title later that month). I knocked on Bill's door and said: "I want to pack up now. I don't want to finish up playing badly at Tottenham Hotspur after all these years." I had no intention of asking for a transfer but that game finished me off. I didn't want a team coming to White Hart Lane and playing us off the park.'

Others, though, were not allowed to leave on their terms, no matter how long-standing their service. When he felt the need, for the good of the club he was so determined to improve, Nicholson retained a brutal, cold edge. Even at the expense of those who idolised him, like Greaves and Mullery. Shortly before the debilitating stroke he suffered in 2015, Greaves returned to the savage end of his goal-laden Spurs career. 'I wish Bill was around to give his version,' he said. 'The day it happened I moved house. I got a phone call from Bill Nick. It was a strange call because he said: "Is that you Jim? I've got Martin Peters in my office."

I wondered what he was talking to me about Martin Peters for. Then he said: "I'd like to buy him but Ron Greenwood wants you in part-exchange. It needs to be done in the next hour because of the transfer deadline."

'I said: "That's a bit sudden, Bill." He replied: "We need to think longer-term. I'm serious. You're not required and that's it. That's the truth." I thought that if that was what the club wanted, I'd better do it. But after nine years at the club, for it to end like that left me disillusioned. I've got no more admiration for any man on earth than Bill but for him to do that left a bad taste. It was very hard because I didn't want to go. I never asked for a transfer or even intimated to Bill I wanted to leave the club. I just wanted to find my form, do the rally and come back the following season. I felt I still had a lot to offer Tottenham. Even when I went, my heart was still at White Hart Lane. I had nothing to offer West Ham.

'The following day I went in to White Hart Lane to pick up my boots, to say goodbye to all the lads. But there wasn't a soul there. He'd taken them all down to Cheshunt to train. The only person there was Johnny Wallis, the reserve team manager, who had my boots. He gave them to me. I thought that was a little bit nasty. So I walked out of White Hart Lane, there wasn't a soul there, and that was the end of my stay. Believe me, I didn't want to leave Tottenham Hotspur. It never even occurred to me. That was it. It was a very sad day. I was heartbroken. If I could put the clock back to that day I'd have said: "Bill, let's think this through another day." I'd probably have stayed at Tottenham and things might have returned to normal. But it never happened. That's the sadness of it all. I don't know what was on Bill's mind. The team was decimated and he was very tough in getting rid of people. He was ruthless. I don't know if it was personal or not. I didn't bear a grudge.'

But he did carry the scars, which probably contributed to his descent into alcoholism and surely played a factor in his distancing from the game, especially after the final partnership of his career, the on-screen one with ex-Liverpool midfielder Ian St John, had the plug pulled on it. As Gilzean noted: 'It broke my heart the day Jimmy left. He was rushed into leaving. But he lost faith in his own ability and that was so very sad. He was one hell of a player.'

Two years later, equally out of the blue, it was Mullery's turn. 'I'd been the captain in 1972, we'd won the Uefa Cup and I came back for pre-season,' the former midfielder told me. 'I was at the training ground at Cheshunt after one morning training, he called me over and said: "Come and have lunch." So I sat down and he said: "Alan, I'm thinking of bringing in another midfielder. I've got one or two lined up."

'"That's fine Bill," I said. "It doesn't bother me because I will keep my place."

'"Well, I'm thinking of letting you go . . ."

'"What?" I said.

'"I've had six phone calls in my office from clubs who know you're available. I'd look at those if I was you."

'And that was that. I'd been bombed. I went into the office and there was a list of clubs that wanted to buy me. I couldn't believe it. I had no option but to talk to them and that was it. One minute I was captain of the team, the next I was on my way and everything had changed completely. But he did the same with Dave Mackay and Jimmy. To be treated the same way as them was a bit of a privilege. He had just decided he didn't fancy us any more. That he had to move us on and get someone else in and that was that. I can't even remember who it was he brought in. I know he had Phil Holder coming through and I'm not sure who he ended up bringing in. But he didn't fancy me any more, so I was out of the door. I was thirty-two, he was looking to the future and didn't see me in it.'

Two years further on and Nicholson himself was leaving, although he had also picked up two League Cups along the way, Martin Chivers scoring twice against Third Division Aston Villa in 1971, before substitute Ralph Coates, on for the injured John Pratt, shot low and across Norwich keeper Kevin Keelan in 1973. For a man who placed such great faith in the importance of European football, it was sadly ironic that the turning point, the day when Nicholson lost faith in the game and all the sacrifices he had made for the good of the club, came at what should have been one of the high points, the 1974 Uefa Cup final second leg at Feyenoord's atmospheric De Kuip. As the curse of hooliganism began to spread into virulent contagion, Tottenham supporters did not have the same reputation as those of Manchester United, Leeds or Millwall. Nevertheless, during the first half of that game, with the Dutch side edging ahead on aggregate, Spurs fans dragged the club into the dirt.

Chairman Sidney Wale had recorded a message urging good behaviour before the game. As the ripped-up seats rained down from the upper tiers, he tried again. 'You are disgracing yourselves as Tottenham supporters,' Wale told them. 'You are disgracing the British public and the club will undoubtedly face a heavy fine.' It was to no avail. And so, instead of rallying his troops for the second half, Nicholson was urged to see if he could have any impact. He later recalled: 'They asked me if I'd speak to the supporters at half-time, which meant I couldn't do the team talk. I said I'd do that. I went to speak to them over the loudspeakers but it didn't seem to make any difference at all. And that really gutted me.'

Mike Collett, then just 21, vividly remembers the rioting in Rotterdam when he came face to face with his own mortality for the first time. He said: 'Our fans were going crazy, ripping up seats and attacking the Dutch fans in the neighbouring pen when the riot squad arrived, smashing heads with their truncheons. This was on the highest tier of the stand, and as the police poured forwards we were all being pushed down towards the front of the tier, and there was just a small metal railing running along the length of the edge of the stand that was starting to buckle. I was being pushed nearer and nearer the railing and realised it could give at any minute and if it did we would all tumble over the edge, fall fifty, eighty, a hundred feet and probably die. I didn't fancy that ... so I somehow darted back towards the riot police, got smashed on the back with a truncheon, but survived. I got behind the police lines and ended up fifty metres away in another section and watched the rest of the game but it was a miracle no one was killed up there.'

Nicholson's view was one of barely hidden disgust: 'It was very bad to think that Tottenham Hotspur couldn't control their supporters, although might I say I fail to see how any club can control their supporters who want to behave in the way they behaved. There were a lot of reasons for it. A lot of people thought they weren't completely and entirely to blame. A lot of people thought the police were to blame. But the poor old police always catch it. It was a saddening thing.'

That word 'saddening' appears crucial. Nicholson had been shaped by his background and war service. He believed in decency, in proper standards of behaviour and that football was, while a huge part of people's lives, still a sport, a diversion from the humdrum of the working week. Not an excuse for violence and weekly outrages that offended his moral code. Mullery said: 'He didn't recognise what was happening in football and society. There was a big surge of people fighting each other at grounds, really horrible people who spoiled the game and that wasn't Bill, wasn't what he thought football was about.' Brian Scovell agreed: 'What happened in Rotterdam, when he tried to talk to the fans and they didn't take any notice of him, severely damaged his love for the game.'

The light had been diminished. Nicholson knew it and the start to the 1974–75 season confirmed his view. Four straight defeats to start the new campaign saw him offer his resignation, which was accepted on the condition he stay on until his successor was appointed. Events a few months earlier at Liverpool, where Bill Shankly had bowed out with his assistant and close ally Bob

Paisley hand-picked by the outgoing man to fill the void, were the template Nicholson wanted to follow. He too let the board know what he felt was the right path.

Morris Keston, who grew close to Nicholson during his spell as Spurs' most well-known fan, was among those in on the plan: 'Bill's life was the club, no question. He actually wanted them to replace him with Johnny Giles and Danny Blanchflower as joint managers but the board told him "No".' Nicholson confirmed: 'I thought Danny would have made an exceptional manager. He had similar ideas to mine and was the outstanding candidate. I interviewed him for the job and he decided he'd like it. He would have had Johnny as his player-coach. I felt contented I'd done my best to ensure the running of Tottenham Hotspur would be in good hands.'

Wale and his colleagues, though, ignored Nicholson's advice. Instead, they failed to invite him to a board meeting called to appoint the new manager, Terry Neill, who had spent 11 years at Arsenal as a player but had then made an early managerial impact with Hull City to put himself in the shop window. The chairman, quizzed in the car park, appeared unaware of Neill's Arsenal past – and, seemingly fearful of having a backseat driver on the premises, cast Nicholson out entirely, rather than offering him the chance to stay on-board in an advisory role, although not before the final indignity of a 4–0 home League Cup defeat by Middlesbrough.

Unwanted, slighted, hurt, Nicholson sought comfort, spending time at London Colney, where Bertie Mee, just a month his senior, remained in charge at Arsenal. He then went to work at West Ham's Chadwell Heath training ground, where he was asked to help by another old friend and rival Ron Greenwood. The Hammers' chief did not seem to bear a grudge over Nicholson's intensive efforts to entice Bobby Moore to cross the capital in the months before English football's greatest day in 1966.

It was a job. But not *the* job. Mullery said: 'Tottenham was his first love, for the whole of his life. After he stepped down and went to West Ham, that broke him. Tottenham was his club. He lived in that same house, just around the corner from the ground, six or seven minutes away. He was always the first in and the last out. Once that stopped and he wasn't able to have that input into the club every day he was an entirely different man. I used to see him at other games and would always sit next to him. He'd point at a player and just dismiss him: "He's a five-a-side player; you can't have him – he only runs twenty yards." Even when we'd stopped playing he was still Bill.'

Nicholson, though, was to have a second coming. Not as a manager, but as an *éminence grise*, chief scout, talent-spotter, sounding board and confessor to the man who replaced Neill in 1976, Keith Burkinshaw. The younger man, like Nicholson born in the White Rose County, although he came from Higham, near Barnsley, showed his strength of character in doing what many would have counselled against.

Burkinshaw said: 'A lot of people said I was making a big mistake when I brought him back into the club. They told me he'd been such a big manager here and asked: "Can you handle that?" I said: "I think I can" and we got on like a house on fire, no problems at all. He'd gone off to West Ham, but I spoke to him and said: "Come on Bill, come back with me as chief scout." He was delighted. Tottenham Hotspur was his life. He didn't normally get it wrong on the player. We would always meet, maybe once, maybe two or three times a week, sit down at White Hart Lane and talk football. That was fantastic for me. Who could you talk to with more experience than Bill Nicholson?'

Who indeed. And while Burkinshaw was working on the training ground, Nicholson was out on the road once again, finding the raw materials. David Pleat, who was to spend a quarter of a century of his life connected to the club, has his own memories of Nicholson. Pleat said: 'I remember when I was at Luton that I persuaded Bill to come with me to Wrexham to watch Paul Price play for Wales against the Soviet Union in 1981. They had Aleksandre Chivadze at the back, a great player. We drove up together. Bill was my hero. I had Milija Aleksic and Paul and I tried to persuade him to buy Price. He rang me a few days later and said: "We've decided we will take both Aleksic and Price." I drove them both to Tottenham. My assistant at the time said: "I can't believe it; take them in a wheelbarrow, and sooner rather than later." He didn't fancy Price at all. But I drove them up to White Hart Lane to see the club secretary, Geoffrey Jones. The offices then were in the house on the right-hand side as you go into the main entrance, on what used to be Bill Nicholson Way. I remember just driving up and looking at the stadium. It took my breath away, even though this was 1981, when the West Stand was being rebuilt. Bill took me round the new stand. The boxes hadn't gone in at that stage but Bill gave me a tour of the ground and I just thought it was wonderful.'

His pride had been rejuvenated. His eye for a player remained and when Burkinshaw built a team in the early 1980s Nicholson played key roles in the recruitment of bargain signings Tony Galvin, Graham Roberts and Gary Mabbutt, as well as the schoolboys Paul Miller and Mark Falco, while he never hid his sheer love of the glittering skills of Ossie Ardiles, offering advice to his successor over how to get the best out of the Argentinian.

Miller said: 'I first came to the ground as a twelve or thirteen year old. Mark Falco was already here. I've known him since I was eleven. We were all East End kids. There were two ways out of that background – sport or crime! I went to a few other clubs, including Chelsea, and I played for Senrab (the East London Sunday League club which has spawned players including Ledley King, Sol Campbell, Jermain Defoe, John Terry and Ray Wilkins, to name just a few). But then I got a call to see Bill Nicholson. Me and my dad took the bus together. The 253 and then the 149 and we walked through the gates to meet Bill. He said: "I think we can make you a player." I said: "I am a player" and he put me in my place: "No son, you've not done anything yet."'

For Roberts, it was a slightly different sell: 'I was going to sign for West Brom on the Tuesday after I'd played for Weymouth against Nuneaton. I played well, we won 6–0, and I went up to West Brom. I was going to sign when I got a call from Weymouth to tell me Tottenham had made an offer. I was in Ron Atkinson's office but said I wanted to go down to Tottenham and talk to them before I signed. So I went down, met Keith and Peter Shreeves and trained with the first team. I'm not sure I touched the ball although I kicked a few people. My ex-wife wanted me to go to West Brom but I made the decision. I came out of Keith's office and spoke to Bill Nicholson and he explained how it had come about. He'd gone to Swansea but the game was called off so he'd decided to just pop over to Weymouth, a train from Swansea via Bournemouth, when he'd seen me and liked what he saw. He just said: "Don't do anything different to what you did that day." And I knew I had to become a Tottenham player.'

Mabbutt, too, could not say no to Nicholson. He revealed: 'I'd broken into the first team at Bristol Rovers. Bill was the chief scout and he wanted me to join Tottenham and put my name forward to Keith. I drove up to meet Bill and even pulling up to those gates for the first time felt very special. There was me, someone playing in the Third Division with Rovers, meeting Bill, a living legend, and he wanted to show me around the stadium before driving me to Cheshunt to meet Keith.'

Nicholson outlasted Burkinshaw by seven years, remaining as a consultant until 1991, giving his successors sage advice, even when that meant hard decisions still. Pleat said: 'I know Roberts and Miller didn't like it when I sold them because they'd been regulars under Keith Burkinshaw and Peter Shreeves. Miller was very disappointed because he really loved the club although I believed Roberts wanted to go because he knew Rangers wanted to take him. But they didn't know why I sold them. That was after

Bill Nicholson said to me one day: "What do you think of our centre-halves? Don't you think the free-kicks they concede put us under pressure?" That was how he dropped things in. He didn't need statistics, he just saw things. And when I looked into it, he was right. They did put us under pressure from free-kicks.'

Always on duty, always trying to improve the club he served, after being appointed club president, until his death on 23 October 2014. His ashes were buried under the centre-circle of the stadium he helped transform into a footballing citadel and he left behind a love affair that was mutual, as far as the fans were concerned. For many thousands, there could be no words that spoke to them as loudly as his: 'We must always consider our supporters, for without them there would be no professional football. It would be better to have more fans watching football the way they like it played rather than have a few fans watching football the way we would like it played. The public can't be kidded. They know what they want to see, what is good and what is bad and what is just average. I always said it was an honour to serve Tottenham Hotspur and I feel the same every time I walk back into the stadium.'

5

GLORY GLORY NIGHTS

'When you've been in Europe you know what it's like. It's magnificent to be in Europe at this club and clubs like Tottenham. If we're not in Europe, we're nothing. We're nothing.'

Bill Nicholson

While White Hart Lane was dismantled in 2017, when Britain was preparing to negotiate the nation's way out of Europe, it was sometimes hard to reconcile the fact that for many years our football teams were desperate to sit alongside the continental elite. But on 12 September 1961, as Nicholson and his team flew out to the coalfields of Silesia in southern Poland, they did not know what was waiting for them, or that the adventure they were beginning was to bring three trophies, moments of sheer elation and also lasting anguish.

England's pretensions to being the best team in international football had been obliterated, not just by the humiliation of the 1950 World Cup defeat by the USA in Brazil but also by their double destruction at the hands of Hungary's Magnificent Magyars – 6–3 at Wembley in 1953 and then 7–1 in Budapest the following year – on the eve of a World Cup in Switzerland in which Walter Winterbottom's team had been eliminated by Uruguay at the quarter-final stage. At club level, there were few such conceits, although many still wondered if the Busby Babes of Manchester United might have gone all the way and ended

Real Madrid's reign had it not been for the horrific events as they took off from Munich in February 1958. The Football League's haughty arrogance in banning Chelsea from the inaugural European Cup in 1955–56 was washed away by the tidal wave of national mourning that followed that night of desperate tragedy. But while United had reached successive semi-finals, Wolves and Burnley were put firmly in their place over the following two seasons, and Madrid reigned supreme, winning the first five tournaments and seemingly impregnable, with a team featuring Alfredo Di Stefano, Ferenc Puskas and Francisco Gento, before being displaced at the top of the tree by Benfica.

Nicholson, unlike some, had a sense of destiny, a recognition that European football represented both an ideal and a mighty challenge. At the outset of the 1961–62 season, with Spurs having beaten an FA XI – effectively an England side, including Jimmy Armfield, Bobby Robson, Johnny Haynes and Bobby Charlton and managed by Winterbottom – to win the Charity Shield on home turf, the manager set out his aims: 'Now that we have the Charity Shield to place between the FA Cup and the Football League Challenge Cup, the boardroom looks nice and tidy. We are not being big-headed when we say we have done the Cup and League Double, but we must have a new target – to win the European Cup. It has not been done before by any team from this country. Neither has any team from Britain yet reached the final – a state of affairs we mean to change.'

Bullish words but after 45 minutes of being put to the sword by Górnik Zabrze, they appeared hollow ones. Nicholson selected the team which had seen off Leicester at Wembley a few months earlier but in Chorzów they were a mess, picked off far too easily as they threw bodies and men forward with almost reckless abandon. Dyson recalls seeing prisoners digging up the roads under the watchful eye of armed guards but it was Mackay's determination to seemingly take no prisoners that infuriated the home supporters, although they had plenty to shout about as well, as

Spurs veered on the brink of embarrassment. Norman put one through his own net inside eight minutes and by the break further goals from 18-year-old striker Jerzy Musialek and Erwin Wilczek left Nicholson's men spluttering like miners down one of the local pits that dominate the skyline behind the ground. It got worse, too, with home skipper Ernest Pohl making it four three minutes after the restart and it was not until the last 20 minutes that Jones and Dyson gave them some semblance of respect – and a toe-hold into the tie with a goal apiece. Nicholson was forced to admit: 'We did not know how to play in Europe. We did not know how to play games over two legs. We had tried hard to play our normal attacking football. We threw caution to the wind and paid the price. Maybe we learned more in that ninety minutes than we had learned in ninety years before. Europe was certainly a different place. We had to learn quickly though.'

But first, there was a tie to win. And on what would be the first of 95 European nights at the Lane, spread over 56 years, Tottenham ran out wearing an all-white strip which was the manager's tribute to Madrid, in front of just under 57,000 spectators, who were in for the night of their lives.

The Polish media, working on behalf of the club, had complained that Spurs 'were no angels' in the first game. So, half an hour before the kick-off, three Spurs fans, Peter Kirby, Dave Casey and Mike Curly, ran on to the perimeter track – dressed as angels. They each wore sandals, false beards and white sheets, with placards reading 'Rejoice! This is the night of vengeance' and 'Glory be to shining White Hart Lane'. Spurs were electric and remorseless, a force of nature, leading 5–1 by the break, with Jones scoring a hat-trick, and 8–1 by the final whistle, Górnik bedraggled, battered and desperate for the journey home.

That decision by Nicholson was to have ramifications. Alan Mullery, who inherited Blanchflower's No. 4 shirt, admitted: 'The thing that really stood out, for me as a player, was seeing the kit laid out in the dressing room, with white shorts. As a kid, when

European football started, it was dominated by Real Madrid, all in white and for me us wearing white from top to bottom sent out a statement that we believed we were as good as that Real Madrid side, the one with Puskas and Gento. It was such a brilliant idea for us to play all in white, especially under the floodlights which picked the strip out so strongly. It felt like a different, unique experience, something we all wanted to savour and it did inspire us as a team. I've got to be honest, as I was putting it on, ready to play, I went back to being a kid and thinking of playing for Real Madrid. It felt like that. And you felt that every night was going to be something else. I know it was just a kit but it did feel different.'

Graham Roberts, who was to become the third Tottenham skipper to lift a European trophy, agreed: 'Every game I put on that shirt was a famous game. But European nights, with the white shorts, were special. That was the tradition going back to Bill Nicholson's team. It was different and told us, and the fans, that this did mean something different. You'd put on white shorts, at home, run down the tunnel and it felt different, more intense, from the second the fans saw us.'

That first campaign saw Spurs swiftly find their feet. Next up were Feyenoord of Holland and despite Nicholson being without Mackay, Allen and Smith, with Tony Marchi, Eddie Clayton and Saul coming in, they won 3–1 in De Kuip, Saul scoring twice, before stumbling through a tame 1–1 draw at home, memorable only for Mackay's determination to come back on after 23 minutes of treatment for a hairline skull fracture and the match starting half an hour late because the officials got lost on their way to the ground. So far, so good, despite that mini-stumble, but it was to get tougher when Tottenham drew Dukla Prague the following February.

Nicholson, wary of a repeat of events in Poland, left out Dyson to bring in Terry Medwin and played Marchi as an extra defensive body. Even so, Brown was the star with a series of outstanding saves, somehow keeping the deficit down to a single goal, which

Spurs easily overcame, on a snow-covered, ice-bound Lane 12 days later, Smith and Mackay both scoring twice. Blanchflower said: 'It was a night for the bold and the brave. The Czechs are nice people, but they play soft football. They couldn't adjust themselves to the conditions and didn't seem aware of defence at times.'

Enter the big one. Holders Benfica and their emerging super-star Eusebio. The semi-finals. The biggest test yet and one that left a sour taste decades afterwards. Greaves, who made his European debut in Lisbon, ruefully cast his mind back: 'That still rankles. We were robbed, no question about it. In both games. We were refereed out of it. He can sue me if he wants, the referee. We didn't deserve to win but we'd had two perfectly good goals disallowed, one from me and the other by Smithy. I got the ball, beat two men, inside and out, then pushed it past the keeper and was given offside. They wouldn't get away with it now. Something fishy went on, definitely. I'm convinced it was. We were done out of it.'

Still, the 3–1 deficit was not insurmountable and Benfica coach Béla Guttmann, moaning about the White Hart Lane pitch being over-watered, appeared to be preparing his men for the worst. The angels were out again, this time carrying a placard predicting 'Lisbon Greaves tonight' and the expectation of a Spurs triumph filled the air. Guttmann's concerns saw him even keep his players inside the dressing room until the very last few seconds before kick-off, so that they would not be overawed by the sheer burning intensity of the crowd, so much closer to the action than at the Stadium of Light. Greaves added: 'We felt that if we got a bit of luck we would do it, but we didn't get that luck at all. There were shots cleared off the line, everything. We needed to score early but they got a clever goal at the far post and it was always going to be an uphill struggle from there.' That goal from José Águas did not prevent the Lane from believing. Nor Nicholson's team. Greaves, again: 'We felt hard done by but were determined to right those wrongs.

'We thought we were back in the game but I was given offside when I came from the back of the defender and hammered it in, the second goal that had been disallowed for offside in the tie. We felt the odds were against us. Bobby Smith got us level on the night but it didn't go for us. Eusebio hit the bar for them. We gave everything and played really well. John White won a penalty which Dave Mackay scored and we only needed one more goal. We were so near. They were hanging on through every bit of courage they had, because they were a good side. In the last minute Dave hit the bar with a header. If that had gone in there would have been a replay, and we'd have won that. But it wasn't to be. If we'd beaten them we would've won the European Cup.'

It was defeat, but glorious defeat. A night those Spurs fans who were there still talk about in epic terms. 'I said to the lads: "The one thing we've got to do is give everything we've got," Nicholson later reflected. "If we lose while playing a controlled sort of game so many people are going to say 'they can do better than that, they're bloody fitter than that and they can get involved more'. So if we're going to go down, let's go down fighting." It was desperately disappointing because we'd have had a crack at Real Madrid in the final and I felt we could've beaten that Real Madrid side.' Meanwhile, new chairman Fred Wale, who had replaced Fred Bearman after the Double season, predicted: 'I think you know that we are a club who don't boast much, but we are going to be alright next season, and then we're going to win the European Cup. It's the only thing that really matters to us, and now we've been so far we've got to win it one day.' It was to be another four decades before they were to even get the chance to win it.

In the days of the Champions League, when we are used to seeing four English teams in the groups stage – if rather fewer than that in the later knock-out rounds – the initial set-up of European football seems brutal and almost primitive. But while Ipswich had stolen Tottenham's crown in 1961–62, the FA Cup win over Burnley saw entry to the fledgling Cup Winners' Cup for the 1962–63 campaign. And this time there was to be no mistake.

Rangers, with 'Slim' Jim Baxter the fulcrum, came down for the first leg of the opening tie in ebullient mood but could not cope with Greaves' right-wing corners, which brought two first half headers from White. Despite goals from Willie Henderson and Jimmy Miller, Spurs led 4–2 at the break after Allen's looping header was followed when his shot was turned into the visiting net by Gers skipper Bob Shearer and any doubts among the 59,000 crowd about the result were ended when Norman crashed in on the half-volley from another Greaves corner. Smith came back from injury for a similarly pulsating return at Ibrox, delayed by a week after fog postponed the initial tie. Greaves scored an early opener before Smith, who had replaced Allen, netted twice to complete an 8–5 aggregate win.

Things started tougher in the quarter-final as Tottenham travelled east again, this time to take on Slovan Bratislava. On a bottomless mud-heap in which the ball constantly stuck, Spurs, missing the injured Blanchflower – who had been crocked during the Rangers win – were lucky that the woodwork and Brown conspired together to limit the damage to 2–0 but back at the Lane, on another pitch that had little grass, it was a different story. Mackay broke Slovan's resistance from a distance, Greaves and Smith, too strong for the keeper, put them in front on aggregate by the break and there were another three in the second half, courtesy of Greaves, Jones and White. A feast for the 61,504 to savour.

Next up was OFK Belgrade. Spurs won 2–1 in the Yugoslav capital, thanks to White's volley and the instincts of Dyson, still smarting at being spat at earlier in the game, when he intercepted a sloppy back pass, although it came at a cost. Greaves claimed: 'I got sent off because of Bobby. Him and the centre-half were having a right go at each other and Smith gave him one. The centre-half went down. The ref came over and sorted it out but the guy marking me then had a little kick. I had a go back and the referee looked at the size of Smithy and the size of me and came over and sent me off. I marched down the tunnel and Cecil Poynton, the trainer, came over and said: "You're the first Spurs players sent off since 1928." I said: "How do you know that?" And he looked at me: "Because it was me! I was the one sent off in 1928."'

There was no Greaves on a surface turned into a treacherous sea of mud by the winter conditions for the second leg, but Spurs' quality shone through the grey clouds and the drizzle while Mackay, Jones and a diving header from Smith ensured Spurs would have their chance to become the first English team to lift a European trophy in Rotterdam. Their opponents? Not Real Madrid, but the Bernabeu side's nearest neighbours, Atletico.

At least Greaves was available for the final, but as the striker recalled: 'Bill's bottle had really gone. Dave Mackay wasn't fit so he had no choice but to play Tony Marchi and he was going to drop Danny Blanchflower. He felt we needed to be more defensive because they were so good. Danny wasn't really fit but Bill gave a team talk which really built them up into something they obviously weren't. At the end of that we all felt a bit down, we were looking at our boots. But Danny stood up and said: "Hang on. We've not got a bad team here ourselves. We've got 500 caps and there aren't any better players in Europe. Cliff Jones is the fastest thing on two legs, John White can do things nobody else can, they'll be scared of Smithy and Greavesie can knock one in." We looked at each other and saw he had a point – we weren't as bad a side as all that and suddenly we went out with a completely different attitude than we would've done if not for Danny.'

Blanchflower was right. Greaves put Spurs in front with a glorious half-volley, White found the roof of the net from near the penalty spot although Atletico were rightly awarded a penalty of their own when full-back Henry punched one out of the top corner with goalkeeper Brown stranded and reduced the arrears. But there was to be no stopping Spurs. Dyson scored from miles out on the left when his cross was misjudged by Atletico keeper Edgardo Madinabeytia, Greaves volleyed in a fourth before Dyson's 25-yarder screamed home – 5–1. Sensational.

'Little Terry was a great player, the sort you always want to have in your team,' said Greaves. 'He made up for what he lacked in ability with effort. And that was his night. It's different now. After a final the players are jumping up and down but we'd go in, light up a fag and sit there with a bottle of beer. We came into the dressing room and Terry was giving it the big one. And Bobby Smith said to him: "If I was you Dyson I'd pack it up now – because you're not going to have another night like that."'

Smith's words were prescient. But after that first incarnation of Nicholson's vision we were never again to have a night like that as injuries, age and the tragic and freak death of White conspired to take their toll. They surrendered their hold on the trophy with a first-round defeat by Manchester United in the first all-English European tie the following season, despite winning 2–0 at the Lane in the first leg, and had just one more European season, back in the Cup Winners' Cup in 1967–68, before the end of the decade, with the manager furious his side conspired to lose on away goals to Lyon despite scoring four at home in only the second round.

So it was that in September 1971 a very different Spurs side set off to Iceland to play Keflavík in the first round of the Uefa Cup, a team including, on what was to prove his only Tottenham appearance, off the bench, a very young Scottish midfielder named Graeme Souness. The one who got away. The aggregate score of 15–1 was evidence of a total mismatch but at least Spurs were off and running.

After a stalemate in Nantes, Martin Peters scored the only goal in the return leg although the waning of interest in football throughout the country was demonstrated as the crowd was only 32,630 – barely half the number which had watched Nicholson's side in those first two seasons of European football. That was followed by two Romanian excursions. Rapid Bucharest were put away 5–0 on aggregate, Jimmy Pearce making an unlikely seven-minute cameo appearance off the bench in the away leg in which he scored and was then sent off for fighting. Nicholson described the home team as 'the dirtiest side Spurs had ever played', adding: 'After the game there were bodies lying everywhere in the treatment room. I have never seen a dirtier team or a more vicious attack on a team of players than that. It was so bad Bucharest have refused to hand the film of the game over to the BBC.' Fortunately the quarter-final against UTA Arad was less unsavoury, Spurs effectively winning it with first half goals from Mike England and Roger Morgan in the away leg, although nerves were on edge before Alan Gilzean popped up ten minutes from time to secure a 1–1 draw and preserve Spurs' unbeaten European home record. In those first 14 European games at the Lane, spread over more than a decade, Tottenham had won 12 and drawn the other two. And it was merely the start.

Nicholson knew the next challenge in the semi-finals was intimidating: AC Milan, including Fabio Cudicini, whose son Carlo, also a keeper, was to play for Chelsea and Spurs, Romeo Benetti, Gianni Rivera and Germany's Karl Schnellinger. It was a task that appeared to have become even tougher when Benetti fired the Italians in front. Enter, wearing blue shorts – Milan had refused to change out of their white ones – a 20-year-old Perryman: 'If I had to name a personal night, it was that one. I never try to think personally. I was part of a team but if you ask the question, then yes, it was that night. I wasn't having a particularly good season and the doctor told me Bill was thinking about leaving me out. It's a good job he didn't.

'I scored two goals from outside the box to turn it round after we'd gone a goal down. It was the only way we were going to score against that Milan team. They had good players all over the pitch, proper players. And they had a defensive style, were happy to defend the eighteen-yard box. Maybe the goals had to come from outside the box. For me to score two like that, in a game of such importance, made me proud. I wasn't known for my goal scoring, but I was that night.'

Mullery was the rascal of the night, provoking Riccardo Sogliano into picking up two bookings in a matter of seconds. And it was his corner which was cleared only as far as Perryman's right boot for the second goal. 'I'd had a pelvic injury and had gone back to Fulham on loan,' said the skipper. 'But Bill had some injuries and I was brought back for AC Milan. I scored over there and we got a 1–1 to reach the final.'

Perryman added: 'We still had a tough job on in the San Siro but Mullers scored from the edge of the box with a drive after I laid the ball off to him, a typical goal from him, into the far corner from just on the edge of the box and that settled things down. It was the first goal and despite the hostile atmosphere we were able to draw 1–1 to go through.'

Where they would meet, of all sides, Wolves, with the first leg at Molineux and where the key man was the striker with whom Nicholson developed a love–hate relationship, Martin Chivers. Mullery, though, still wants his share of the credit: 'We went to Wolves and won 2–1 with a couple from Martin, a header for the first and then a stunner when he came off the left and thrashed it home from miles out.

'But people don't remember what I did for that goal, mind. When Martin picked up the ball I made a dummy run past him as he came in off the left. I did an overlap outside him and was screaming for him to give me the ball. I'd run forty yards, shouting, but then he smashed it in and all I could say was: "Great goal." If he'd passed to me that wouldn't have happened but he smacked it home. Afterwards Martin told me it was the best dummy run he'd ever seen. It meant we were in a really great position going into the second leg, with those away goals in the bank. We knew at White Hart Lane we only really needed to keep our nerve and play as we could to win the trophy. It probably made it something of an anticlimax and we certainly put in a better performance at Molineux than we did in the home game.'

Two weeks later, 54,000 flooded into the Lane, the majority of them expecting to see something special. Only a few thousand Tottenham fans had been in Rotterdam in 1962. Now ten times that number could experience the joy of seeing their team win a European trophy, and a new one as well – the old Inter-City Fairs Cup had been replaced by the Uefa Cup that season – on home soil. The game they got, though, was forgettable. It was the result that mattered. 'I will never forget that night,' Mullery said, laughing, 'because it was the last game I ever played for Tottenham. I thought I was going to stay but Bill had a different idea! I guess it's not a bad way to go out – to score the winning goal in a European final in your final game, but it might have felt a bit different had I known I wouldn't be playing there in a Spurs shirt again.

'Of course, my goal was a header – and they were very few and far between – and from six yards out as well, when I didn't really get that close to goal too often. It was a role reversal goal as well. Normally it would have been me trying to take the free-kick and Martin Peters looking to get on the end of it. It was his job, as a rule, to make those near-post runs. But he'd been brought down by Jim McCalliog and stood over it. When I saw he was out there and lining up to take it from the left I just thought I'd make Martin's type of run and into that position, across the keeper. When I got there I knew I just had to get something on the ball because the keeper wasn't going to be able to keep it out. I just got the touch, in front of Phil Parkes, and it flew home. I got knocked out but I recovered enough. And I think both sides knew that was going to be enough for us to win the Cup, even though they pulled one back.

'I can remember the fans lifting me on their shoulders with the trophy after the final whistle. It wasn't one of our better performances, far from it, but it was enough. But Bill wasn't happy. He came in after, while we were celebrating, and told us: "The best team lost." That killed the evening a bit. When you win a trophy you normally want to celebrate but he was adamant: "The best team lost." It was a bit of a killer to come into a dressing room and get a rollicking after winning a Cup.'

It could have been the start of another glory era. Spurs had won the League Cup the previous year, thanks to Chivers' double against Aston Villa, and won it again in 1973, a season in which they were dethroned as Uefa Cup holders by Liverpool on the away goals rule in the semi-finals, missing out on another final against Borussia Moenchengladbach. And then, in Rotterdam, the scene of his greatest European night back in 1963, Nicholson suffered the heartbreak of seeing Tottenham's supporters drag the club's name into the gutter as they lost the Uefa Cup Final to Feyenoord. But Spurs were in decline and Nicholson was ready to pack it in.

So it fell to another Yorkshireman, Keith Burkinshaw, to take the club back into Europe, following their FA Cup win in 1981. And straight away they felt at home. It was as if the eight years on the outside had not happened, starting with a 3–0 mauling of Ajax. Ossie Ardiles, the tempo-setter in midfield, said: 'European nights were always special. It was absolutely brilliant. Playing on a Saturday was one thing and we loved that, but a European game at White Hart Lane, under the lights, was special, different. Part of it was playing different teams, who had different ways of playing. With the English teams, we more or less knew what to expect but we didn't have a lot of information about teams, even sides like Real Madrid and Bayern. It all felt new and that novelty made it great. The atmosphere inside the ground was just fantastic. White Hart Lane was a place to play. I remember the happiness I had there, especially those European nights and that incredible atmosphere.'

That first run, to the Cup Winners' Cup semi-finals, saw Spurs destroy Ajax, scoring three in each leg, although they then scratched out an edgy, nervy and unconvincing aggregate win over Dundalk, a tie in which complacency seemed the biggest enemy.

By the third round, it was more of a fight. A 2–0 first leg advantage over Eintracht Frankfurt was wiped out within 15 minutes of the start of the return game before Glenn Hoddle stroked home left-footed from Chris Hughton's lay-off ten minutes from time, to score the away goal that deflated the German side.

It meant a first meeting with Barcelona, the initial game in north London. And while one side tried to play football, they were not wearing red and blue. Roberts still shakes his head at Barca's approach: 'They kicked us off the park. People talk about Barcelona now as the perfect football team but I promise you that version weren't. I know football was different in those days but I swear I have never seen a team go out just to kick the opposition in the way they did to us, not in my entire life. Clem made a rick to let a speculative long-ranger through his hands, the sort of shot he'd save without trying normally.' It was a howler. Antonio Olmo's effort from 30 yards appeared to be heading down Ray Clemence's throat but he misjudged completely, helping the ball into the back of the Park Lane end net, sinking to his haunches in disbelief and throwing away a clod of mud. Roberts nipped in at the back post to convert Hoddle's late free-kick but Denmark's pocket dynamo Allan Simonsen scored in the opening minute of the second half in the Nou Camp and Spurs could not respond.

The following campaign, back in the Cup Winners' Cup after a Wembley victory over QPR in a replay saw Burkinshaw's men retain the FA Cup, was short-lived. Northern Ireland's Coleraine were swatted aside, 7–0 on aggregate, but Bayern Munich were far too strong in the second round. Yet revenge, glorious revenge, was only a season away, as Burkinshaw built up to the perfect end of his eight years at the helm, although there was no obvious sense of the fireworks to come even when Spurs put 14 past Ireland's Drogheda over two legs in the opening round of the Uefa Cup in September 1983, to set up yet another European meeting with Feyenoord.

The Rotterdam side featured two Dutch greats, Johan Cruyff

and Ruud Gullit, at either end of their careers. But one man stole the show entirely. From a personal standpoint, I have never seen a more dominant first 45 minutes from a Spurs team in my 45 years of watching the side, although the performance against West Brom in January 2017 did come close. And it was orchestrated by a midfield genius, Glenn Hoddle.

Burkinshaw expected a searching encounter. Instead, Steve Archibald and Tony Galvin both scored twice before the break. Burkinshaw said: 'I looked at them and thought: "They're a good side, this lot; it's going to be tough to go through against them." They had Cruyff as captain, Gullit as well. Before the first game Cruyff said he felt we were struggling, that Glenn was a fancy Dan player. That helped me because Glenn read those things. He went out and I've never seen him more determined and he was absolutely marvellous. We played possibly as well in that first half as we ever played under me, absolutely fantastic.' Midfielder Micky Hazard agreed: 'It was almost as if Glenn had said: "Right. I'm playing against Cruyff, one of the greatest players who has ever lived – and I'm going to show him how good I am." And he did. He was poetry in motion.' And Roberts had no doubts either: 'They just couldn't get close to Glenn at all in the first half. He was just brilliant and we were 4–0 up at half-time. They pulled two back in the second half and a lot of people thought we'd thrown it away. Instead, we went over to Holland and won 2–0 in the away game. But that first 45 minutes at home, with the crowd going mad for us, was incredible. It was the sort of night you can never forget.'

There were more to come. Burkinshaw's side were more than slightly unfortunate to lose to Michael Rummenigge's late goal in the Olympic Stadium but turned the tables on a tumultuous night back in north London, despite a rapidly mounting injury list. Roberts rose to nod down a Hoddle free-kick, which Steve Archibald scrambled home and then with time running out more Hoddle vision, turning and clipping back into a pocket of space, saw Mark Falco's left foot finding the bottom corner off the inside of the post. Roberts said: 'We wanted that. We'd been knocked out by them pretty badly the previous season and I remember Mark Falco scoring the winner, across the keeper into the far corner.'

By contrast, the win over Austria Vienna was clear-cut. There were, however, 84 anxious minutes after Hazard's free-kick put Spurs ahead of Hajduk Split on the away goals rule in the next round – Falco had netted in a 2–1 defeat in the Balkans – before a spot in the final was clinched. We now know, of course, that the opponents should have been Nottingham Forest. Anderlecht had bribed the referee of their semi-final second leg and Brian Clough's side truly were robbed. But that was not recognised at the time and the 1–1 draw in Brussels in the first leg, courtesy of Paul Miller's header, gave Tottenham the initiative.

That win came at a heavy price, with Perryman picking up the booking that ruled him out of the home leg, and the injury crisis that had dogged Burkinshaw all season showed no signs of improving. On top of that was the knowledge that the manager's bitter fall-out with chairman Irving Scholar meant the Anderlecht game would be his last in charge of the team. 'For the second leg, if you look at our team, it was unbelievable,' he said. 'Glenn wasn't available, Steve Perryman was suspended, Ossie was sat on the bench, the goalkeeper didn't play, so we had Tony Parks in goal and a load of young kids. We battled away.'

Ardiles said: 'The final was a very special night because of everything that happened. Glenn was injured and Steve was suspended for the second leg. A couple of days before the second leg Keith had to decide to play with me or Gary Mabbutt in midfield. But I was only forty per cent fit, no more than that and there was no chance I could last ninety minutes, so we agreed it made sense for Gary to start, and that I could come on later. There were big question marks about me and Keith felt I couldn't play. I agreed but as it went on and we were a goal down, with time running out, we had to make a change.'

Mabbutt confirmed what a gamble it was: 'It was a big problem for Keith. There were so many injuries. Ossie had a knee problem and I actually needed a hernia operation, which we'd scheduled to take place as soon as the season was over, so he had to choose between the two of us to try and keep Enzo Scifo quiet. It was felt I'd be better able to nullify Scifo and I lasted seventy-five minutes and Ossie came on.'

And Roberts said: 'People remember Tony Parks saving the crucial penalty but not that he was only playing because Ray Clemence was injured. But with Steve suspended, I was captain, Glenn was out, Garth Crooks too, while Gary was only fifty per cent and Ossie was only fit enough to be on the bench. We had a lot of players who had come through from the youth team. Chris Hughton, Paul Miller, Micky Hazard, Tony Galvin and Mark Falco had all been at the club from being kids, while the injuries left us so stretched that we had Mark Bowen and Ally Dick on the bench.'

Despite which, Spurs were favourites, although that altered with just half an hour to go when Alex Czerniatynski streaked through the inside left channel to flick right-footed past Parks and into the net. Maybe not panic stations, but time for one of the night's two heroes to step forward. 'Winning the Uefa Cup, at home, scoring a goal and a penalty, was the best night of my life,' Roberts told me. 'No question. We wanted to win it so much, not just for ourselves but also for Keith, because we all knew it was his last game at the club. But it was a Cup final, in front of our own fans. You don't get the chance to do that very often in a career, if at all. It meant so much. But I wanted to win it so much. I was the skipper, the captain, and felt it was down to me to lead by example, to make sure we took any chance we had. For a long time it seemed as if it wasn't meant to be. We couldn't find a way through. In the build-up to my goal Ossie, who had just come on, had smacked it against the bar from a couple of yards. They scrambled it away but Micky hoisted it back into the box. Bilko [Falco] pushed the bloke in front of me and that gave me the space to chest it down. It will always live with me. The goal was *the* moment. I could see it coming towards me and I felt it was the chance we had to take. I remember I brought the ball down and bulldozed my way through a couple of defenders. The next thing I knew I was in front of the keeper and knew I had to keep my nerve, that I couldn't afford to miss because we might not get another chance with only five or six minutes left. I slid it past the keeper and the place exploded. In my mind I just stood there but when I look back at the tapes now I wheeled away to the corner and waited for everybody to join me. You never want to lose that feeling, the emotion of that moment, for the rest of your life. It was something special for me.'

Ardiles can now joke about it: 'I wanted to make Graham Roberts famous, so I missed when I couldn't miss from a yard. I hit the bar from a yard – but only because I knew Micky Hazard would put it back in so Robbo could score . . .'

But Roberts' goal only tied it up. Extra time failed to produce a goal. It came down to a test of nerve from 12 yards, at the Paxton Road end of the ground. 'People remember the goal, how I just kept going through the Anderlecht defence to score and that it was very late in the game and took us into extra time,' Roberts said. 'But I also took the first penalty, to put them under pressure. Before the game I had a chat with Keith and we'd agreed that if it went to penalties I'd take the first one because he was confident I'd score.'

Roberts did and Parks saved from Morten Olsen, putting Spurs in command. With Falco, Gary Stevens and Archibald all scoring, Tottenham were one Danny Thomas kick away from the trophy. He shot to the keeper's right but Jacky Munaron guessed correctly. Thomas was crushed, heartbroken, fearing he had blown it. The defender trudged, mournful and crestfallen, towards the halfway line, holding his head, his team-mates desperate to console him. Up in the stands, Perryman could barely look. But his ears were working. He said: 'I've always said that Spurs fans are at their most loyal when things aren't going well and for me that was summed up during the penalty shoot-out, when it looked as if we were going to lose. Danny missed his penalty and you could see on his face that he thought he'd blown it for us. But they chanted his name all the way back to the halfway line. We all felt that, saw what it meant, how much they were with us. And I wasn't even playing because I'd been suspended!'

It was time for Parks to write his name in folklore. Arnor Gudjohnsen, whose son Eidur was, briefly, to play for Spurs under Harry Redknapp, shot to his right but the young keeper parried and set off, arms aloft. Mabbutt said: 'I wasn't exactly known for my speed but if you look at the video I killed all of them for pace and was the first to get to Tony . . . I always felt the European nights were something else. The atmosphere created on those nights was like nothing else I've known. And that 1984 final, beating Anderlecht, had some amazing scenes, not just on the pitch when we won like that but also after the game when we celebrated with the fans in the big building next to the ground on the High Road. There were thousands of supporters there and we were on the balcony, showing off the Uefa Cup in front of them.'

Hazard recalls: 'It was an amazing evening. But it was also a sad one because we knew that it was Keith's last game, and he'd signed me as a youngster. I think back to that day as the one when the club started to go downhill and not be the massive club it was. But that day had everything, winning it on penalties when Tony Parks made the key save, then the celebrations afterwards. I'd been picked for the England squad but I remember still sitting in the Bill Nicholson Suite at 4 a.m. when I had to be up at 7 a.m. to travel to Hampden.'

Roberts, wearing the armband, got the opportunity to be at the heart of the iconic image, the man to hoist the trophy into the north London night. 'For me, with all that emotion, excitement, tension, passion, it was just a wonderful night. I got the chance to lift the trophy. And that's something I still recall and think about all the time.'

The holders, now under the hand of Burkinshaw's deputy Peter Shreeves, were back in the competition the next season, 1984–85. They were to make more club history, this time unwanted again, although not before reaching the last eight by way of ties against Braga, Club Bruges and Bohemians Prague. The reward was Real Madrid, the team who had inspired that all-white kit a quarter of a century before, although the Spanish side's change strip of magenta looked far from natural. And it was the Real giants who had the incisive, decisive moment, with Perryman's efforts to beat Jorge Valdano to Emilio Butragueño's right-wing cross only succeeding in diverting the ball past Clemence and into his own net for the only goal. It was, after 35 wins and seven draws, the first time Spurs had tasted a European defeat at White Hart Lane. And a goalless draw in the Spanish capital sent them back to the European wilderness for seven years. Nicholson, unsurprisingly, was proved right. As he said all those years before: 'When you've been in Europe you know what it's like. It's magnificent to be in Europe in this club and clubs like Tottenham. If we're not in Europe, we're nothing. We're nothing.'

6

UNEASY LIES THE HEAD

The bronze plaque on the wooden door carried a simple message: 'The Manager'. And, unsurprisingly, the 18 men who have occupied the role over the 43 years since Bill Nicholson stepped away have all been judged in comparison to the man who made Tottenham. A few, very few, have tasted success. Most have been branded by failure. Some managed to combine both – winning rare silverware but whose passing was celebrated rather than mourned.

Terry Neill probably recognised, even as he walked through the White Hart Lane gates in September 1974, that he was always on a hiding to nothing when he accepted the challenge. The vacuums left by Sir Matt Busby and, more recently, Sir Alex Ferguson at Manchester United, Don Revie at Leeds and Brian Clough at Nottingham Forest offer object lessons in how not to replace a successful manager, with Liverpool, who managed the succession from Bill Shankly to Bob Paisley so masterfully, remaining the exception. You can see, even now, why the board at the other end of the Seven Sisters to N17 remained so reluctant to part with Arsène Wenger as readily as many supporters demanded in the latter part of his Arsenal reign.

Nevertheless, Neill, aware that he was not Nicholson's choice, felt he had to accept the chance to return to north London and leave Hull, despite his affiliation with Tottenham's fiercest rivals: 'I'm an Arsenal man and will be to the day I die. That's me, cast until death.' Indeed, the club programme for the home game with Middlesbrough, Neill's third in charge of the team, hinted at an awareness of some of the disquiet: 'Mr Neill, who took over shortly before our victory over West Ham in our last home match, has a soccer pedigree and background well known to most of our supporters. He is tackling his task with enthusiasm and determination. He is well aware, from his past knowledge of London football, that only the best, in performance and achievement, will be good enough for Spurs. He cannot be expected to achieve instant success. He is as impatient for success as the most fervent Spurs supporter but needs time to put his plans into practice.'

'I had done well at Hull,' Neill said. 'I was only thirty-two and Spurs came to me out of the blue. You've got to be a bit mad but I was young and foolish and thought I could walk on water. It was the challenge. You've got to test yourself. I've always said there is no shame in failing but there is shame in failing to have a go.

'But it didn't take long for me to become disillusioned with the board. On the day I was unveiled, Bill stayed behind after the press conference. We sat in his office – it took a while to decide who would sit where, because it had been his place – for a couple of hours talking about personnel. I asked if he'd been treated properly and he insisted everything was fine and that he just needed a break. I asked if he wanted to come to the games and he said he wanted to stay out of my way. But a few months later I found out he'd been given a mere £5,000 – and that wasn't a lot for sixteen years of service, even then – as a thank-you present. That was the beginning of the end for me. A few months after I joined one of the directors came to me and said he'd been playing golf with one of his pals and been told that I'd played for Arsenal. He couldn't believe that, he said, so wanted to know if it could possibly be true. I'd only played there for eleven years.'

The players Neill found knew, though. All too well. Every manager alters things but some players in the dressing room feared the consequences from day one. 'When Bill left it was the beginning of the end for me,' said right-back Ray Evans, who had come through the apprentice ranks to make himself a fixture under Nicholson but was sold to Millwall before the season was out. 'As far as I'm concerned, letting Terry Neill through those gates was the worst thing that ever happened to White Hart Lane. In terms of management, he was a fraud, he was fraudulent.

'I was the first to go but between January of 1975, when I left, and the end of that season there were plenty of us he let go. I felt he was trying to destroy what he had inherited. And it wasn't just him. His assistant, Wilf Dixon, was an absolute joke. I could never respect either of them. But I felt the real blame should have gone to Sidney Wale. He'd looked at Neill getting Hull promoted from the Third Division and got completely taken in by that. So rather than having it out with Neill, I let Wale know what I felt when I left. I rang him up and told him what a terrible mistake he had made, that he'd hurt the club. I had to tell him, to make him realise.'

On the pitch, the side Neill had inherited survived the drop by the skin of their teeth, winning 4–2 against Leeds – who had an infamous European Cup final against Bayern Munich on the horizon – two days after the scheduled end of the season. A few weeks after Wale had publicly suggested it would need a 'miracle' for Spurs to survive, Neill was crowing: 'I've been pilloried for saying I was not going to react suicidal to the crisis, but saying that I wanted the players to enjoy themselves. The trouble is that people surmise that if you are not winning then your method must be wrong. If you are winning then your method is perfect. But the game is just not like that.'

The next year was markedly better, losing to Newcastle in the semi-finals of the League Cup and finishing ninth in the table. Another future Spurs boss, Gerry Francis, was skippering the QPR side that finished runners-up to Liverpool by a single point. And had one audacious coup come off – its failure and the rift that developed as a result signposted the end – things might have been different. 'We thought we were on our way,' Neill added. 'We had young Glenn Hoddle, Neil McNab, Pat Jennings, Stevie Perryman, John Duncan knocking in goals. We were starting to move. And I tried quietly to sign Johan Cruyff. I sounded him out through a very good friend, Dennis Roach. I didn't let the board know. We were making progress. We had some quiet conversations and a meeting and I was trying to get one or two sponsorship deals in the City so there was not so much of a discrepancy in the wages between him and the other players. But the story came out. Steve Curry had it in the *Express*. Suddenly the directors called an emergency board meeting. One of them slapped a copy of the paper down in front of me and said: "Mr Manager, who do you think you are?" I said I didn't want to go through another season of dicing with relegation and wanted to move ahead and be the best. I thought to myself that I was working twenty-four hours a day, seven days a week, driving three thousand miles every week and neglecting my young family, and for that lot . . . I walked away because I couldn't get on with the board.'

It was his decision to walk out on Spurs for a return to Highbury that caused outrage. Perryman, although all too aware of the passion of the supporters, does not condemn Neill. Indeed, as he explained to me: 'Terry did well for me. I speak to some groups of Spurs fans and they don't want to hear that, because they see him as an Arsenal man, like George Graham. Terry did always have that Arsenal tag attached to him and I felt people didn't give him an even break but he certainly didn't do me any harm. In fact, he did me a lot of good. A lot of people would disagree with that but I'd point out that we didn't get relegated with him in charge. We got relegated under Keith Burkinshaw. That's not to say Terry was brilliant. Keith was a better manager and initially was just in the wrong place at the wrong time. It was bad timing to take over when he did.

'Under Bill I used to play behind the ball, as a safety net. But Terry suggested I would improve as a player if I could go in front of the ball two or three times each half. So when Pat Jennings would clear it I'd run past the centre forward two or three times. At one point I scored six in twelve games, so Terry brought a different aspect to my game, a new dimension to the way I played. Of course, I ended up as more of a defensive player but for my development as a player, a coach and a manager, it was good to see what simple instructions could bring you.'

Neill's departure was to herald the advent of Tottenham's second most successful manager. Not that Burkinshaw expected to get the chance. Indeed, he was ready to be sent packing. 'When I joined Spurs it was my first time in London,' he remembered. 'Terry and his assistant Wilf Dixon came from the North-East and I was the first team coach at Newcastle. They looked at the way we played the game and thought they'd get me down because they wanted to play that way. After the season ended, before Terry left, we did a round the world trip. We went to Canada and the USA, Australia and New Zealand. Terry was a little bit fed up with the way things were going. He and the chairman didn't always agree on how things should be done. I went on holiday and halfway through the holiday I picked up a paper and saw Terry had left and gone to Arsenal.

'I thought to myself: "Christ, I've travelled from Newcastle, got a house and probably haven't got a job!" So I told the wife I had to go for it. I didn't think I'd get it but felt I had to have a go. Unbeknown to me, the players had gone to the directors and told them they wanted me to get the job. I was fortunate there. I liked it that Tottenham has the tradition and that I had to build a really good footballing side to compete with those traditions.'

Not that Burkinshaw's reign began smoothly. In truth, Tottenham were a shambles. The lowest point was an 8–2 crushing at Mackay's Derby, one of 16 away defeats. And despite nine home wins, just two years after playing in that second Uefa Cup final, Spurs finished 22nd, joining Stoke and Sunderland in the down elevator. Burkinshaw feared the worst. He said: 'All the senior players who had a good idea of what was needed to stay up, they all left. We didn't have the strongest side in the league and we struggled all season. There were times I felt: "I'm not going to be here next season."

'We finished bottom of the league but the chairman came up and said: "Keith, we took you on because we thought you were a good manager. I still think you are a good manager. But you've got to get us promoted next season." I said: "Okay, thanks a lot." We just managed to get back up, in third.'

They did, just, after ten tortuous months. And not before the pre-season campaign embroiled Burkinshaw in another period of drama which could have proved fatal. Pat Jennings had made himself into a symbol of the club, even if, initially, it had not been easy for the Irishman to win over the supporters. As 50-year supporter and Fleet Street photographer Lawrence Lustig said: 'When Pat first came the fans didn't take to him. It wasn't because he was replacing Bill Brown, although they loved Bill because he was an immaculate keeper. But more because he was a bit susceptible to making mistakes. He made a few clangers and was unorthodox. He'd come out of Gaelic football and was very different with his handling. He was a young kid, but he won the fans over eventually.'

By the mid 1970s, though, Jennings' status among the fans was unquestioned. As was evident on the day White Hart Lane staged its final game – he was, and always will be, a Tottenham legend, one of the Spurs greats. He had missed much of the previous season through injury, a factor in the debacle of relegation in last place, although Burkinshaw did not blame his understudy, Barry Daines. And, heretically, in the eyes of many, was to let Big Pat go. Burkinshaw explained: 'He wanted a substantial pay rise because his contract was up and the directors said no. I thought it would be a shame for him to go down to the Second Division. I knew Arsenal and Ipswich had tapped him up. I was half happy for him to go to a big club because he was a great player and a great chap.'

Maybe so, but that was not how Jennings saw it, and Irving

Scholar, who was to play the key role in Burkinshaw's subsequent departure, said: 'Pat actually told me, and I guessed this, that he didn't want to go. Pat had been injured a lot the season before and he wasn't playing as well as he had done in the past. Keith suggested he thought it was time to give Barry Daines a chance, because whenever Barry had played he'd done very well. Keith decided to let Pat go but deep down there was a lot of disapproval from the fans about that decision, not just letting Jennings go to Arsenal but him then doing so well there. And he did bloody well.'

His good performances were fuelled, clearly, by a sense of injustice and anger. 'It was unbelievable,' said Jennings, his soft Newry tones becoming edgier as he thought back to the circumstances of his departure and his belief that the club did not treat him with the respect he deserved after more than a decade of service. 'I was Footballer of the Year in 1976 but the next season I missed twenty-one games because of an Achilles injury and I couldn't get back in the team. I think that if I'd played just ten or twelve games at the end I might've kept them up. I was fit again for the last month of the season but by then we were more or less gone. Then I read in the papers that I was available for transfer. I wanted to know what was happening. Keith said that Bobby Robson at Ipswich had wanted me but that he couldn't let me go. Even so, I knew the writing was on the wall.

'The next summer we were about to head off to Sweden for a pre-season tour when at eleven a.m. Keith came up to me and asked if he could have a word. I thought it might be a tactical thing but he said I could go if I wanted and that he didn't want to take me to Sweden because it would be embarrassing to Barry. I thought: "You want me to apologise for being a good player?" Then Keith asked what I thought I was worth. I knew what I was worth but didn't think the club should be getting that for me. After all, I'd been there for thirteen years, after being bought for £25,000, and they were giving free transfers to players who'd cost £200,000 five years earlier. And they wanted to sell me. I thought they should have let me go on a free. I said: "It's going to be like that, is it?"

'Keith said that Bobby Robson would be ringing me at six p.m. and that at six-thirty p.m. he wanted to know what I was doing before they went to Sweden. I told him I wasn't going to make a decision in half an hour and he then said that Terry Neill wanted me at Arsenal but that he didn't think I should go there. When Terry rang the first thing I said was: "There's no way I can go to Arsenal. It can't happen and won't happen." I agreed a deal with Bobby, to stay at home and travel there two days a week. I had United and Villa interested and then Bobby rang and said he had an injury so he had to spend the money we'd agreed for me on an outfield player. I'd gone to the ground to say goodbye to the players because I knew I'd be gone by the time they got back from Sweden. We hugged and shook each other's hands. Everybody was on the coach with me standing there and suddenly the directors came out of the office. Every single one of them totally blanked me. I didn't even get a phone call from one of them. So I went home and said: "Give me Terry Neill's phone number quickly." I wanted to create the biggest embarrassment I could for those directors. Peter Day, who was the assistant secretary, tried to stop me. He asked if I really wanted to be transferred, saying he'd make a call to the chairman and Keith but it didn't make any difference to them.'

Jennings' subsequent successes over seven seasons at Highbury were a constant punch in the guts for Tottenham supporters and had Burkinshaw not managed promotion, courtesy of a goalless draw at already-promoted Southampton – in their final game – denying a Brighton side managed by Mullery, it seems infeasible he would have been allowed to stay on, let alone orchestrate the transfer coup that transformed everything.

England's failure to qualify for the 1978 World Cup was a national body blow. Scotland, aka 'Ally's Army', blew up against Peru and Iran in the group phase and attention in the UK swiftly switched to the teams at the business end of the competition. Before each Argentina match – they played in Buenos Aires and Rosario – ticker tape rained down from the stands, almost obliterating the grass from view and it served to accentuate the interest in strikers Mario Kempes and Leopoldo Luque, skipper Daniel Passarella and the diminutive playmaker and ball-carrier wearing the No. 2 shirt – Argentina gave out their squad numbers in alphabetical order – Osvaldo Ardiles.

The Argentinian said: 'The day after we won the World Cup I'd got back to Cordoba when I received a phone call from the president of the club. He said to me: "Ossie, there's an Englishman," – and he said it like that, an Englishman – "who wants to talk to you; he wants you to go and play in England." So on the Saturday I was there with the translator and they told me about Tottenham. Of course, I'd never heard of them before that day.'

But Spurs had heard of Ardiles. Burkinshaw's memory of the signing is strong: 'Bill Nick was at the club and a phone call came through. Harry Haslam, who was at Sheffield United, asked: "Do you think Keith would like to sign Osvaldo Ardiles from Argentina?" Bill said: "I'll go and ask him." I'd seen this little fellow playing on the television and he was marvellous. He'd been player of the tournament so when Bill spoke to me I said: "You're taking the piss here, you!" But Bill said he was serious. Harry had a fellow in Argentina and he seemed to know everything over there. Harry got on the phone and said he was going to Argentina on Friday, did I want to come? He said I'd get this fellow Ardiles if I did. I asked how much and Harry said it wouldn't be massive money. He said: "I must tell you Terry Neill is interested in Ricardo Villa, who came on as a sub in the World Cup." But then Harry said in the next day or so that Terry wasn't coming because the Arsenal directors didn't want any foreign players.

'We jumped on a plane on the Friday and got to Argentina the next morning. When we got off the plane, we were met by Antonio Rattin, who'd been the Argentina skipper who was sent off in the 1966 World Cup game against England. He was the nicest guy you could ever meet and he looked after me. On the Sunday Ossie came with his wife and immediately there seemed to be something happening between us, that we liked one another. His wife really wanted to come, and that helped me. We did the deal and Ossie cost me £340k or something like that. I said to him: "Thanks for that." He said: "Would you like to sign Ricardo Villa?" I said: "Yeah, I might be interested . . ." First I had to see if we had the money in the coffers. I rang the chairman and asked if I could bring in Villa for the same money as Ardiles. "Let me have a look," he said. Half an hour later he was back on the phone: "Yeah, we're okay for the money." I saw Villa the next day and straight away he signed. When we went out I didn't realise how big a thing it was going to be. It was seen as unbelievable that we were taking them to Tottenham.'

It certainly was. In a few strokes of a pen, Spurs were at the centre of a maelstrom. Ardiles said: 'The way they welcomed us was incredible. That doesn't mean everybody was happy. There were some MPs who were unhappy but we were the first South Americans playing in England. It was a kind of adventure to go to a new country. It's a lot easier now, but in 1978 it was a big decision to make. I never regretted it at all. From the very beginning I felt in the hearts of the Tottenham people and it was great. I thought I was coming for three years and then I'd go back home and buy a ranch. Instead I was here ten years as a player and then as a manager.'

Promoted Spurs were the talk of the country, especially when Villa scored the equaliser in a 1–1 draw at champions Nottingham Forest on the opening day of the season. Four days later, just under 48,000 crowded inside the Lane for the pair's home debut. The pre-game routine of El Monumental was recreated in N17 as the ticker tape streamed down, followed by thousands streaming *out* well before the end, as Spurs crashed to a 4–1 defeat.

Worse was to come, with Spurs humiliated 7–0 at Anfield,

although it wasn't all doom and gloom. Burkinshaw said: 'The game after Liverpool was at Leeds and we beat them and that lifted us again. We finished midway in the league and it was gradually coming together. I could see how good a squad it was but we were lacking people up front and I could see we needed to get players in that position if we were going to do well.'

First, though, he started to look at the youth ranks, and used Nicholson's ability to sort potential diamonds from the less valuable minerals in the lower divisions and non-league scene. Among those launched into the team that term was Paul Miller, who had joined as a schoolboy and was to end up winning domestic and European medals – and marrying the daughter of superfan Morris Keston. Miller remembered: 'I got my chance after we lost 7–0 at Liverpool. We lost 5–0 at home to Arsenal on Boxing Day and Keith started to think about the very good reserve team he had – we'd won the Football Combination three times – and that we deserved to be blooded. We didn't have the funds so Keith played a number of us. When I wasn't in the team I was knocking on Keith's door every Friday, driving him mad. Eventually I got my chance and when we won the Cup in 1981 that vindicated everything he'd worked on, as seven of the twelve of us were home-grown.

'At thirteen or fourteen you think you've made it but there we were in the ball court behind the West Stand where we used to train indoors, me, Chris Hughton, Glenn Hoddle – I couldn't get the ball off him, even then – Mark Falco, Gary Brooke, who went on to be the nucleus of the team that Robbo and Tony Galvin joined under Keith. It was a remarkable journey. I left school a year early – nobody knew I was here – and signed as an apprentice for £30 a week in 1976, asking Peter Shreeves for my expenses.

'I remember getting carried away and drinking five pints after my first youth-team game. I still feel like I'm that kid. We were lucky, coming through together here, learning to drive, learning to drink, learning to play together. And we started playing here, too, a proper stadium, with a big crowd, against proper players who wanted to kill us, every week. So for us, winning trophies was great, but doing it here, doing it with your mates, your friends, then going round the world, enjoying ourselves and getting paid for it, then, now, when we've retired, still playing golf together, coming back to watch games, taking the piss out of each other, meant so much. That's forty years with the same people, a lifetime of memories. And it's still my club, our club, something special.'

Galvin, born in Huddersfield to an Irish family (he earned representative honours wearing green), a graduate in Russian from Hull University and spotted playing for Goole Town, was to be Hoddle's out-ball, a willing, tireless forager on the left flank. But the cutting edge arrived in 1980, as Burkinshaw, aided and abetted by wisecracking assistant Peter Shreeves, decided the days when the line was led by the likes of Gerry Armstrong, John Duncan, Ian Moores, Colin Lee and Chris Jones were over. Instead, he paid a combined £1.45 million to land Steve Archibald from Aberdeen and Stoke's Garth Crooks. It was to prove a masterstroke. 'They got forty-seven between them that season, which was great,' said Burkinshaw. 'We were going places from then on.'

Places including Wembley, although Burkinshaw admits they were lucky: 'We were very fortunate. We were drawn at home just about every game. We beat Leeds when they were pretty strong and had a couple of lower division teams. Then Wolves in the semi-final. I always felt we were a better side than them but it was a draw because the referee, Clive Thomas, gave them a penalty that was *never* a penalty. I told the press afterwards: "Only that man would have given that decision on that occasion." The FA said he was the ref for the replay at Arsenal on the Wednesday. So I said: "Well, we'll not be playing if he's bloody refereeing." And they listened to me, gave it to someone else. And we won the game.'

Villa scored twice, including a belter from distance, setting up a clash with John Bond's Manchester City. Burkinshaw said: 'I always felt we were a better footballing side than the opposition, so I said: "Let them worry about us rather than us worrying about them." In the first game they kicked us off the pitch. There were some terrible tackles going in. We didn't handle it as we might have done and we were very fortunate to get the draw, when Glenn's free-kick ricocheted off Tommy Hutchison into the net.' That was no surprise to Burkinshaw's No 2. Shreeves said: 'They had Gerry Gow in midfield. And he was an animal. His job was just to stop Glenn from playing. I pulled Glenn and warned him that he was going to make life difficult. Glenn said: "Don't worry, I'll sort that out. It's a big pitch at Wembley." I told Glenn the actual measurements of the pitch were the same as White Hart Lane: "He will nail you, so be on your job." Glenn didn't have the best of games. After it he said: "All right Peter; spot on. But you watch me on Thursday." And he was the best player on the pitch by a distance in the replay.'

Although Hoddle was the star performer, the attention and the glory was claimed by the man who had arrived as the less-heralded part of the Argentine double-swoop. The television cameras picked out Villa, head bowed, dragging himself around the greyhound track towards the dressing rooms as it seemed Spurs were slipping to defeat before Hutchison's inadvertent late intervention. 'Ricky had a terrible game on the Saturday and went off in a huff,' Burkinshaw said. 'I walked into the dressing room and Steve Perryman came up and said: "You can't play him again on Thursday, Keith." I don't know why but something in me said "he's got to play". I said: "Steve, he *will* be playing." And as soon as Ricky knew he was playing, it was like a flower opening up.' Shreeves added: 'In the first game you're supposed to go out, hear them singing to the Queen and wave to your family. But you couldn't warm up, which was ridiculous. But in the replay it was different. You could warm up so I got some balls and went out with Ricky. He went one side of the band, I went on the other, and it was "chip it, try and knock one of their caps off, see if you can hit one of them on the head" and I could see Ricky looked happier.'

Setting the scene for one of Tottenham's, and Wembley's, greatest moments was a thrilling match won by one of the most memorable and remarkable goals to ever settle a Cup final and one that remains iconic for its sinuous beauty. Villa scored with virtually his first touch in the replay after a rebound fell at his feet but a stunner from Steve MacKenzie and Kevin Reeves' penalty, conceded by Miller, put City in front before Crooks prodded home the leveller. Enter Villa: 'There was no middle ground for me – I either played good, or bad! On the Saturday, when I was off the pitch, thinking my chance to win the FA Cup was gone, I wanted to cry. But Keith picked me again for the replay. When I got the ball, I thought: "I can win this game." I believed I could win it. I just told myself I was going to score. I went past everybody and rolled it into the net. It was perfect. It was an Argentine goal, scored at Wembley. It happened at the perfect time in the perfect place.' Burkinshaw added: 'Like everyone else I was expecting him to pass it because there were other players in a better position. Nearer to goal, every step, then he stumbled a bit and the ball was in the net. A wonderful goal – and he's lived a great life on that goal!'

The Cup victory was a stepping stone. Burkinshaw was able to improve his squad from a position of strength, recruiting Ray Clemence from Liverpool and Gary Mabbutt from Bristol Rovers. In 1982 they retained the FA Cup with a win over a QPR side led by Terry Venables and including future Spurs players Terry Fenwick and Clive Allen, but were beaten by Liverpool in the League Cup final despite leading with three minutes to go, tasting Wembley defeat for the first time and finishing fourth. 'I thought we had the best side in 1981–82,' added the Yorkshireman. 'But the problem was that we were in everything – the semi-final of the Cup Winners' Cup, we had a chance in the league, the final of the League Cup and we won the FA Cup. Before the FA Cup final we'd played eight games in sixteen days, which is absolutely ridiculous.'

Behind the scenes, though, things were changing. Scholar had taken over as chairman, ousting the old guard and his relationship with Burkinshaw was beginning to grow increasingly uneasy. According to the manager, the beginning of the end came on 21 March 1984. His choice of words indicates a rift that has never been repaired, even after 30 years: 'We had a new fellow come in as owner of the club and we didn't really get on, the pair of us. We played in the quarter-finals against Austria Vienna, away from home. About four p.m. in the afternoon he came to my bedroom with the assistant chairman and they said: "You're not going to be allowed to run the club as you've been doing. We are going to bring in the players. We're going to decide how much they will get as wages." And it went on and on. I said: "Don't you think this is the wrong time to be coming in here, at four p.m. when we've got a quarter-final at quarter to eight?" That started it all off. In the end I knew he'd been looking for another manager. I knew it. And he'd made a proposal to one of them.'

He had, indeed, made that approach, to a manager who was already in demand after first upsetting the established order in Scotland, as Aberdeen usurped both Celtic and Rangers and then won a European trophy. Scholar believed that the other manager was ready to come. A man who was to become British football's most successful boss. But at Manchester United, not Spurs.

'The truth was that I had been talking to and negotiating with Alex Ferguson about a deal,' Scholar said, 'and he and I had had very long and detailed discussions. I told him that I was a very old-fashioned type of chap and that the most important thing was that once you agree something, once you shake someone's hand, it's in concrete. Once you do that, then you do not – under any circumstances whatsoever – you do not go back on it. It's over. I told him that, when I first met him. So we had this big thing about the handshake. And he went on and on and on, discussions, negotiations, down to the minutiae of the contract.

'Everything was agreed. So I said: "Can we meet?" He agreed and I said I'd like him to meet someone else on the board, Paul Bobroff. He said that was fine and we arranged to meet in Paris on a Sunday morning, just by the airport. The idea was this was the moment, the seminal moment, of the handshake. We'd built up to this for weeks. So we met. I said: "Are you ready?" He replied: "I'm ready." I said: "Are you sure you're ready?" He said: "I'm sure." So we had this seminal moment of the handshake. As you know, unfortunately, he didn't keep to it. He never told me why. I had my own theories but that's water under the bridge now. It doesn't matter any more. But it was a disappointment. Thinking back, he stayed at Aberdeen for another two years, so it was unfortunate.'

Ferguson's recall of the discussions and their breakdown is somewhat different. Ferguson insisted his reticence to join was as a result of the length of contract Spurs were prepared to offer – originally two years when he would have wanted five. Spurs later improved their offer to three years, but Ferguson was not convinced that was long enough to do the job.

By this stage, Burkinshaw had departed, although with a withering parting shot that reverberated for years. 'I felt there was no way I could stay the next season. So I said: "Okay, I'll leave." And that was it. I know for a fact that if I'd stayed we'd have won more stuff because we had players who could do it. But he didn't allow it. I was really sick about it. And the way the club was run was being changed. Clubs were becoming Public Limited Companies. So they were being run as businesses rather than football clubs. So I said to one of the reporters: "This used to be a football club here."'

Or did he? Not if you listen to Scholar: 'I asked him about that because it was a very cutting statement that I felt was completely untrue. He actually said to me that he didn't say it but that he was very close to Peter Blackman, who worked on the *Evening*

Standard, and, you're right, certain things stick with you and that was one statement that stuck. I'm sure it damaged me. Yes, I'd say it probably did. What hurts most of all was that it couldn't have been further from the truth. If there was one thing that would have been blasphemous for me, it would have been to have behaved like that. That would be the worst thing and it was completely without foundation. I've seen Keith a few times since. I like him a lot and he's a nice man. I admired and respected him. He did a great job while he was at Tottenham. And when Alex Ferguson changed his mind, Peter [Shreeves] took over and did really well. We opened the season winning 4–1 at Everton. We won at Arsenal, from a goal down, on New Year's Eve and went top of the league. But we had some key injuries at key moments. Gary Stevens got a very bad injury and he was playing out of his skin in midfield.'

Shreeves – or Shreeve as he confirmed in the 2008 book, *The Boys From White Hart Lane* by Martin Cloake and Adam Powley: 'My real name is Shreeve, but over the years I've had so many people getting it wrong that in the end I thought: "Why not – it's Shreeves." I've looked in the club handbooks and I see that one year my name is spelt with an "s" at the end, the next it is without' – finished third in his first season but only tenth in 1985–86. It brought his demise, although he was to return for a third season under Venables five years later: 'It was a strong team but the response of the players wasn't the same as I'd had with the other group. When you're the coach, you're Uncle Peter. When you're the manager, you're that idiot Shreevesie who isn't picking them. It was a difficult time. They didn't have the same passion for the club as the other group.'

He was replaced by a manager whose direct connection with the club was to stretch to more than three decades and counting. Listening to David Pleat today, still as busy, determined and full of insight and opinion as ever, as we chatted while he was heading to St George's Park for a meeting of the League Managers'

Association board, it was obvious it was a relationship that was always meant to be consummated. 'Tottenham captured my imagination in 1960 – 15 October 1960,' he recalled. 'They came to Nottingham seeking a record eleventh successive win at the start of the season and they were wonderful. An absolutely wonderful performance. They won 4–0, John White got the fourth, and they captured my imagination. I had a great feeling inside.'

As it happens, Pleat is, slightly, wrong. The Forest game was Spurs' 13th of that season. They had drawn at home to Manchester City five days earlier – the only point dropped from their opening 16 matches: 'I then made my debut for Forest reserves, when I was seventeen years and thirty-three days old, at White Hart Lane', Pleat said. 'Everybody can name the Spurs Double side, and they were a great side. But I can name the *reserve* side. Mel Hopkins was at left-back. He was the understudy to Ron Henry but a Wales international. There was Tony Marchi, Eddie Clayton, Johnny Hollowbread. I remember looking around, thinking: "What a wonderful stadium; what a wonderful place; what a thing Tottenham Hotspur is." So when I hear the words Tottenham Hotspur they mean something to me. It was a club that, for me, was all about character and imagination, playing the right way, so when the club came in for me in 1986 it was a no-brainer.

'In my mind I always thought I would get a chance to do the Spurs job. The name means certain things but excitement is at the top of that list. Things like Bill Nicholson winning his first game 10–4. And my attacking philosophy fitted with that. I had five offers to go while I was at Luton, from bigger clubs, spoke with them but turned them all down. But I always felt that if Tottenham came in for me I would go. The year before I eventually came, Scholar, in his wisdom, kept Peter Shreeves for an extra year and I followed him the next season.

'When I arrived at Spurs and was asked to compare the clubs, I said: "It's like going from Woolworths to Harrods; or changing fish and chips for smoked salmon." That upset the people at Luton but it was true. I felt the animosity from Luton was unbelievable given what I'd done at that club. It was a great season, no question, with the system, the five midfielders supporting Clive. I thought our football was mesmeric. People say I didn't worry too much about defending. I wouldn't agree totally but I would admit my first thoughts as a coach were always about imagination and forward play. For me it was about scoring goals. Tottenham believed in scoring goals and the club wants a romantic manager, somebody who will play expansive, expressive football and encourage imagination from the players. After we beat West Ham 5–0 in the League Cup, John Lyall rang me – he was a magnificent man but we'd beaten them 5–0 – just to say that I must be proud to be in charge of such a group of players. It was almost unheard of for a manager who had just been beaten, crucified, whitewashed, to pick up the phone the following week to give me praise like that. It felt marvellous and there were some wonderful games. We should have won something. We got to the FA Cup final without any replays and then lost. That was tragic but in extra time, after I'd already used my substitute, both Gary Mabbutt and Richard Gough were limping badly. That should have been the triumph we deserved for the football we played but Gary put through his own net, of course, and Coventry won.'

Yet within five months Pleat was out of a job, following disclosures about alleged incidents during his spell at Luton, stories fanned, Pleat is still insistent, by the vengeful Hatters chairman, David Evans, who was by this stage also the Tory MP for Welwyn Hatfield. 'I felt Irving Scholar could have supported me much better than he did,' said Pleat. 'There were strains after we lost the Cup final. And I don't know, but I suspected he had already spoken to Terry Venables . . .'

Out of the role and out of employment. But not, in Pleat's own head, out of the club: 'For me, once it's established, the link with Tottenham can never be broken. Tottenham, the club, what it stands for, is the love of my life. I always feel comfortable there.

For the people there, it's the same thing. Tottenham was always about glory. Not necessarily about the result. But always about glory. For people with the club in their hearts, their blood, that is it. Still, whenever I go to White Hart Lane, everybody who sees me says: "I'll never forget your team David. I'll never forget the link play of Ardiles, the class of Waddle out wide, the brilliance of Glenn Hoddle with both feet, the goalscoring of Allen." Nobody forgets that season. So I'm a proud cockerel. I always will be and always want to be.'

Ready and waiting for the call which was to come again, but not before a series of appointments: Venables, whose fall-out with Alan Sugar, Spurs chairman from 1991 to 2001, was to go as far as the High Court, sparking a highly public, embarrassing and damaging inquiry into the darkest financial secrets of the game and costing Venables a fortune; Shreeves again, for one season; an unlikely pairing of Ray Clemence and Doug Livermore; Ardiles; then Gerry Francis; before, more than slightly implausibly, the chairman plucked out a balding Swiss, who spoke in clipped, halting and frequently mystifying English, Christian Gross.

There are still many who remember Gross at his unveiling. Few, though, know how ridiculous the whole thing was. When I got my chance to ask a question, I asked what Gross knew about the club, its traditions and history. I expected something bland and nebulous. Instead, his hand went straight to his inside jacket pocket, from which he produced a small piece of card. It was a Tube pass. Probably the one and only occasion on which he used the Underground. 'Here is the ticket,' he said. 'I hope it is the ticket of my dreams. I came on public transport because I wanted to experience how the fans feel. I wanted to show I am one of them.'

If only Gross's team had been as entertaining. Instead, he drilled his mantra into them. A simple one, repeated time and time again: 'Hard work; we must work harder.' The players, though, did not want to listen. Darren Anderton said: 'Alan Sugar started paying players good money and wanted them to earn it and wanted a manager who would train us two or three times a day. It was as simple as that. With his business head he wanted value for money. He thought: "I'm paying big money and that's what I want." Football isn't about that. It's not about how long you work for on the training ground but what you do. It's about quality of time, not quantity. And it was tough. Really tough. Christian was a nice guy. But it just didn't work. He brought in lots of new things. I'm sure lots of clubs do now but it wasn't for us. We didn't have a grasp of it. When you bring in different ideas and the team is winning, players are happy and will go for it. But if you're not playing well, not playing a brand of football that the fans want to see and the players want to play, it becomes really difficult. He lasted eight months.'

And in even such a short time he fell out with Mabbutt and the man brought back to the club just before 25 December, Jürgen Klinsmann. Upon his return, sitting in the tiny room used for press conferences at the Chigwell complex, Klinsmann said: 'I'm not Father Christmas.' Nor did he, or Mabbutt, feel much good-will towards the Swiss. 'I wouldn't say we didn't get on,' Mabbutt said. 'But . . . it was my last year at the club. My contract was up at the end of the season but I spent most of that season on the bench because Christian Gross was playing his love child, Ramon Vega. To be fair, Ramon had all the attributes to be a top player. He was very fit, good in the air. But sometimes he thought he was Franz Beckenbauer.

'We were dropping towards the bottom of the table. Jürgen had come back. We were room-mates and couldn't understand how it was going. Christian had some very good ideas but his man-management was poor to say the least and that was a big problem in the dressing room. When a manager arrives at a club he has to get his feet under the table and see how things work and then see what he wants to do. The first week Christian was there he wanted me to go back to the hotel with him to talk about the club. We spoke for about six hours, talking about the club, how things were done and how they had been done in previous years. I left that meeting and I don't believe he listened to a word of what I said.

'He wanted us to stay in a hotel, European style. So we'd finish training at noon on a Friday and he'd have us together for the next thirty-six hours. He asked me if I thought the players would want that and I said I wasn't sure, that we should ask them. I phoned the entire squad to ask them. We had twenty-six players – nineteen wanted to stay at home and seven wanted to go to the hotel. I went back and told him the vote was 19–7 and he said: "That's not a big enough margin; so we'll go to the hotel."'

Indeed, such was the scale of the divide between Gross and his players and the looming fear of relegation that Sugar, terrified of the potential outcome, considered ditching Gross before the end of the season and asking Mabbutt and Klinsmann to fill the void. Anderton added: 'I wasn't overly aware of the plan. That was what people would have liked to have seen because it had got so bad. Jürgen came back to help and Christian didn't want his help. So they clashed. And because of what Jürgen had done before, people saw he was doing us a favour and Christian Gross was dismissing it really. There was a huge clash and we were in a relegation battle. Jürgen was a top lad, great guy, bright and intelligent. But he had an edge. He was a winner. When he was playing for a team that was struggling and he could see why, he wasn't going to just sit there.'

Mabbutt, pressed about the near-miss, laughed. 'I think that's your answer!' he said. 'Ahead of Wimbledon there was a feeling that things could be about to change but then Jürgen came up with that fantastic performance and that saved us from the threat of relegation.'

It was time for Pleat again, with Sugar having brought him back to the club as director of football after ignoring his advice when he appointed Gross in the first place. 'I didn't want to go in 1987 but when I came back under Alan Sugar I felt that was destiny. He had a vision about going forward with me as director of football. That was destiny. With Gross, Alan Sugar was the one who decided: "He's got to go." And he was the one who brought him in. When he was thinking about the appointment he asked me if I knew anything about Gross. I said I didn't so he asked me to ring Alex Ferguson, because he was sure he would know. I rang Alex and he didn't know anything about Christian either, but Sugar told me: "I've appointed him."

'His agent was a bloke called Andy Gross [no relation to Christian Gross], who was also Jürgen Klinsmann's agent, which was quite ironic as the pair of them didn't get on at all. For me, the players let him down. They wouldn't accept him. It was about communication. Christian believed you had to train the players hard. That meant more sessions, warm-down sessions on Sunday afternoons, and they hadn't been treated like that before. The previous regime had been a lot more soft. Things didn't go well and in the second season Sugar said to me: "I'm going to have to get rid of him." I suggested he give him a bit longer but Sugar wasn't having any of that. He'd made his mind up. On the Saturday before he was sacked we'd just won at Everton but he was sacked anyway. Christian was in tears. He was a good man.'

Gross's fate was settled when he felt himself at least temporarily safe, a few weeks into the following season and during an international break. England were playing the opening Euro 2000 qualifier in Stockholm and two days before, with the press conference delayed, some of Fleet Street's finest enjoyed a long lunch awaiting the arrival of Sol Campbell. It meant they were prepared to press harder than they might have done and Campbell, having indicated he was not entirely keen to discuss club affairs, said: 'Whoever is manager you want them to be able to teach you things. I want to progress as a player, I want all the team to progress and improve, improve me as a player and improve the team.' 'Does Gross do that?' he was asked. 'I'll pass on that . . .'

Even as England were stumbling to defeat, Sugar was loading

his gun, with Gross sent packing. On the Monday, I arrived at the training ground in Luxborough Lane around lunchtime, under grey skies. Various players eventually came out, although I recall only Ian Walker stopping, briefly winding down his window and offering understandably bland comments about looking ahead. An hour or so later, as it was beginning to get darker, Pleat also emerged through the gates. Seeing me standing there, he was more abrupt than conciliatory. 'Lipton,' he bellowed. 'You're supposed to be a Spurs fan!'

I was just doing my job, which also meant covering the reaction to Sugar's next appointment. While Wale and his fellow directors seemed oblivious to Neill's Arsenal past in 1974, nobody could not be aware that George Graham, a member of the Gunners' Double team in 1971 and, to that point, their most successful manager since Herbert Chapman, bled red and white. He even had a mosaic of the Arsenal crest in the bathroom of his home in Hampstead. He had kept that despite being forced out of the club he loved at the height of his powers over a £425,000 payment he received – and eventually handed over – from Norwegian agent Rune Hauge. After Arsenal, he had gone to Leeds, building the foundations of a side that was to reach the Champions League semi-finals in 2001.

The surprise for many was that Graham took the job, and not just because of his association with Arsenal. Venables was a close pal, the man who had given the Scot his first chance to learn the coaching ropes at Crystal Palace when, long before he was El Tel, the former Chelsea and Spurs midfielder was building what was dubbed 'The Team of the 80s'. Many assumed, given the brutal fall-out between Venables and Sugar, just a few years earlier, that Graham would not have gone within a million miles of the place. Instead, as he explained: 'I always make my own decisions. My view was that when I made any decision I had to have nobody to blame but myself. Terry didn't know I was going to Tottenham. We're still great friends. We met as players at Chelsea. He was instrumental in me having a great career but I had to make my own call on the job, not his background with Alan Sugar.'

Pleat, who held the reins for the first of his three caretaker spells, said: 'George did all right but he was the wrong man for the club. Sugar asked if it would be a problem. I knew George and felt he could do a good job. But the problem was what the crowd knew about him. George wanted to come back to London and his agent, Steve Kutner, persuaded Sugar he should take him. I got a call from Sugar to say he wanted me at his house. I arrived and George was there. Sugar asked me what the worst possible scenario was. I said the big problem was the termination payment, and the issue was whether he could carry that. He said he could, so that was that. George was different. He said: "I'm taking over a C-grade club. So how do we become an A-grade club from being a C-grade one? You've got to sign C-grade players before you can sign A-class ones." He made a good point. Unfortunately, he signed too many C-grade players. He brought lots in from Wimbledon, Øyvind Leonhardsen, Ben Thatcher, Neil Sullivan, Chris Perry. But you don't sign Wimbledon players for Tottenham. I was the director of football but he was the manager so I had to give him his head.'

Graham, unsurprisingly, takes a different view: 'I knew what I was letting myself in for. I'd done a good job at Leeds, left them fifth and qualified for Europe. But I couldn't see us improving at Leeds. The guys who owned the club wanted to move on and sell it again. I didn't think the funding was going to be there to make them any better than fifth. I saw that there were going to be very limited funds and I then discovered Tottenham were interested. I wanted to move back to London for my private life in any event. My girlfriend at the time, who was to become my wife, was in London with her family.

'On a professional level it was a good move. Alan Sugar had taken over at Tottenham and he had great things for the club in his head. He was talking about taking the club into the top two or three, so it was a move I felt I had to make. I knew I was going to have to put up with some hostility. I was an ex-Arsenal manager. For some people that was always going to be difficult, and of course I knew there was going to be criticism. Even now people ask me, flat out: "Why did you do it?" It's simple: it was a job. I am a football manager. They wanted to employ me. And that's it. I didn't look at it from the fans' point of view but I was ready for a lot of stick. It was water off a duck's back as far as I was concerned. But I believe a lot of the problem was that most people, certainly most fans, don't understand how managers and players think. For us, it's a job. It isn't about love for the people who are employing you because there aren't too many who have grown up at the club as a kid, come through the youth team into the first team through the reserves. If that is the case, then it might be different. But most managers move around, go from club to club. So despite what was said at the time, it really was no big deal for me even though it was also a job in north London. It was just my job. I wanted to come back to London. It wasn't the love affair some of the fans want and maybe it had to be for some of them to accept me.'

In truth, some of them were never going to accept him, although within the squad it was different. Anderton said: 'People thought when George came in it was going to be boring, all 1–0 and 0–0. But we were really good that year, especially at home. We scored loads of goals. We were entertaining but more solid. I enjoyed playing for George. He was a winner. And he came after Christian Gross, so that helped. George was a winner. He came in and won a trophy. Fair play.'

Yet even that trophy, the League Cup in 1999, with Allan Nielsen's late goal sinking Leicester despite Spurs having Justin Edinburgh sent off for a retaliatory slap at wind-up merchant Robbie Savage, was not enough to improve the fans' view of Graham. Even their songs in support of the side omitted the manager's name. Graham, still 'Gorgeous George' in his mind, with a sharp sense of humour and not even a hint of doubt, dismisses it all now, as he did then: 'When I got the stick, all that "Man in the Raincoat" stuff, I just laughed it off. I expected it. I was well aware that it might come and I was prepared for it. The bigger issue for me was the squad I found when I arrived. It was pretty clear, right from the start, that the squad wasn't as good as I thought it was. I had a lot of work to do to turn things around. But I love coaching. I don't think it will be a shock for people to hear me say I always think the best route to get a club moving in the right direction is to sort them out at the back, to get the defence right. That was paramount for me, to get that right, and I think we did that. When we won the League Cup in 1999, beating Leicester in the final, I felt that was a good start.'

A start but not enough for Sugar, who was still under pressure from the supporters who were unhappy at the state of the team. Some, equally, had lost some faith in his stewardship of the club as a whole. Yet under the Amstrad owner, the post-Taylor Report rebuilding of the Lane had been completed, including the upgrading of Paxton Road with a new upper tier of seats and a second giant Sony 'Jumbotron' screen for fans to watch highlights and match action during games. He also increased the capacity up to 36,240. As much as anybody, Sugar had left his imprint on the fabric of the stadium.

Not that any of that was to save Graham, although it was Sugar's successor, Daniel Levy, and the new ENIC consortium, owned by Bahamas-based billionaire Joe Lewis, who ended the Scot's spell in charge. Graham saw the writing on the wall, he just did not realise how close the wall was. Instead, he slammed into it within minutes of a 3–2 FA Cup quarter-final win at West Ham which was everything a typical George Graham game was not supposed to be. 'As soon as the new people came in I knew they didn't want an ex-Arsenal manager running the club. I thought that was small-minded but it meant I knew I'd be on my way sooner or later,' he said. 'And I knew it was coming to a head after that game at West Ham. I thought we'd played well and got a great result. I did the press conference then went up to the boardroom while I waited for the players to get changed and on the coach. But when I went in two of the board just ignored me. After a big win, away from home. I knew that was it for me. It was a Sunday game and I'd given the players the next day off, went to the training ground and then David Buchler, who was one of the directors I didn't know, came in and sacked me. I was disappointed in the way they did it. I don't know if there is a good way to sack a manager but you'd want it to come from the boss, the chairman, rather than one of his minions.

'The criticism I got most was over the style of play, the football we produced. But I care about winning first. That's the most important thing. You have got to be successful and win things. I would have loved to play exciting attacking football, scoring goals all over the place. I was renowned for being pragmatic, tough and solid defensively. That was my reputation. But it was the first thing any team needs to be able to do.

'I know that everybody at Tottenham looked at me through the prism of being "Arsenal's George Graham". Certain clubs have a reputation for playing attractive, attacking football but Tottenham had been in the doldrums for years and playing attractive football isn't that easy if you haven't got the quality. As a professional, you have to do what you have to do. We're not playing for fun, for a laugh. We're trying to win.

'I can understand the die-hard Tottenham fans and their attitude to me. I accepted it as well. Since the day I was sacked I've never been back to Tottenham or White Hart Lane. The club have said that I'm welcome to come back any time and I wouldn't have a problem in doing that but I can't sit in the directors' box at Arsenal one week and then turn up at Tottenham the next. When Spurs sacked me I thought: "I've got a choice now – either I get another big club, or I jack it in." I loved working on things on the training ground. There's nothing better than drilling the players on a set-piece during the week and then scoring from it on the next Saturday. When that happens, the players are delighted and I'm delighted. You can't replace that feeling, that satisfaction. But I wasn't going to go back down the leagues again. I know a lot of managers do that but I thought I'd worked hard to get to the top and I wasn't going to step down.'

Yet even after leaving the job, Graham copped the flak, the most destructive coming from Sugar, who demonstrated an avowedly vindictive streak, condemning the Scot in barbed tones: 'He's a coward who will not stand up and admit his mistakes. I got mugged into believing that this Adonis of the football world was the be-all and end-all in management, skills and tactics. In my time at Tottenham I made lots of mistakes. The biggest was possibly employing him.'

Graham, even with the benefit of hindsight, did not see any need to rake over old coals or have a go back at Sugar. That was all in the past. There was nothing for him to gain. Maybe it was down to the accumulated impacts of a 23-year playing career which led to two significant ankle operations and an arthritic knee. Chatting to him now, I suspected he enjoyed his bolt-hole in Spain more than the prospect of another London winter. And even with ample cause, he felt there was no point in harbouring a grudge: 'I thought I had a reasonable relationship with Alan Sugar,' he insisted. 'I didn't feel I ever had any problems with him. He gave me the job. We went to Wembley and won the League Cup. He must have enjoyed that as much as I did. That was wonderful for me and I still have the medal from that day in my cabinet.

'As a managerial spell it was a frustration, yes. I didn't feel I did as well as I should've done but it was very difficult for me to get players in or out so I was always fighting that situation and trying to move up the league with what I had which was always difficult. I wouldn't go as far as to say I had to manage with one hand behind my back, but I knew it was going to be difficult when I got there. I looked at the squad and felt too many were only there on their reputation. I realised pretty much straight away it was going to be a longer job than I'd expected when I took the job. But I always believe I left every club I went to in a better shape than I found it, including Tottenham.'

Graham has not been back since. In truth, few who do not know him will mourn that fact. The Tottenham fans, casting envious glances down the road to Arsenal, were desperate for a Messiah. There was only going to be one man who would fit that bill. Yet sometimes not even an affinity with and love of the club is enough, not when you are starting from so far behind. And it would take more than a decade and a half for Levy finally to feel genuinely comfortable that he'd found a manager capable of turning the tide of history.

7

OH WHEN THE SPURS . . .

Les Jeoffroy had not been to White Hart Lane for a few years. He started going as a kid, went on through his years selling commercial vehicles, then through nearly two decades driving a black cab around the streets of the capital, introducing his son Dan to the agony and the ecstasy – far more of the former, admittedly – of being a Tottenham supporter. But then, as he retired to live out in Biggleswade, he stopped going. Too expensive. Too much aggravation. Too late in his life.

Yet Dan sensed something was nagging at his father. So when Spurs drew Millwall in the sixth round of the FA Cup, the final FA Cup tie ever played at White Hart Lane, 117 years, one month and three days after Sandy Brown scored in a 1–1 draw with Preston North End in the first Cup game played on the site, he did everything he could to get two tickets. For one last time, they would go to White Hart Lane together. And on 12 March 2017, they set off. For a trip into their shared recollections but also for Dan to be taken on a journey into a past he had never known.

'It was a trip down Memory Lane, the journey I used to take when I was a boy,' explained Les. 'I wanted to talk to him, to let him know what it was all about, where it all began. So we started at Wood Green Station and walked past my dad's old greengrocer's. I could show Dan a lot of things he didn't properly know about, point out the places I'd lived, where things used to be. We walked down Lordship Lane, through Bruce Castle Park, Church Road and stood behind the North Stand, on what used to be Paxton Road but isn't any more because that's been taken up by the building works.

'I showed Dan where there used to be a kerb where I had to sit down and get my breath back after I was caught in a really bad crush in the last match in the 1970–71 season, when Ray Kennedy won the league for Arsenal.

'Dan was particularly keen for me to go to see White Hart Lane for the last time and I wanted to make that walk one more time as well, the one I did so many times when I was a kid growing up in Wood Green. The strange thing is that I think he was more emotional about it than I was. I was keen to do the walk, that was my idea, but of course when I got inside the ground it was nothing like it will always be in my mind, because it had already changed so much, over the last thirty years or so. Even over the last fifteen years or so, from when I took him as a boy, it's changed. I went inside, looked around and thought: "Where is the old bit?"'

There were no old bits any more. Even the seemingly famous piece of old ironwork atop the East Stand was a plastic replica. Not that it really mattered. Les said: 'My first game was Crewe Alexandra. Not the famous 13–2 game in 1960, but the following year. That was 5–1 and I remember Bobby Smith smashing a ball so hard that it hit someone next to me and they had to be carried away on a stretcher. I'd have been thirteen or so at the time. It was the first time I went and I was given a lift by some season ticket holders who parked on the Wingate Trading Estate. I went with them for that game but after that I began to go with my schoolmates. We had a legend then. We'd look up at the cockerel and tell ourselves it was filled with gold sovereigns. We were convinced that was true.

'My heroes were virtually the whole Double team. I idolised Bill Brown, but Peter Baker and Ron Henry too, then Blanchflower, Norman and Mackay, the whole half-back line, as well as White, Dyson, Smith, Allen and Jones. But in the Double season

I thought I was in danger of becoming a jinx. They hadn't lost a home game all season but I went to watch them lose to Leicester and then they drew with Wolves in the following midweek and lost at home to Newcastle. But the next game they beat Chelsea 4–2 on Good Friday.

'My dad got tickets for the FA Cup replay against Sunderland through Spitalfields market, where he got his fruit and veg from. I just remember we had to abandon the car because the traffic was too heavy and then had to pick our way through all the cars that had just been abandoned on Lordship Lane too, and shove through a corridor of people to get there. I remember 15,000 people were locked out with 65,000 inside and we smashed Sunderland. That cost us 2s 6d but we were all sitting on each other, pretty precariously. I've got a picture from that match, with Cliff Jones, Charlie Hurley and the Sunderland defence and with us looking at the camera. The headline from the magazine was "Spurs Sink Sunderland".

'And I was there for the Sheffield Wednesday game in 1961. We won 2–1 to win the league. Everybody sang "Glory, Glory" and there were 20,000 on the pitch. And also the Cup Winners' Cup tie against Rangers. That was an incredible night. We queued halfway down Paxton Road. The club said they were going to disperse people who were there before ten a.m., but we got there earlier than that, and there were thousands of people behind us in the queue.'

Glory turned, as any Spurs fan will tell you, to turgid disappointment. Part of that unrelenting misery did for Les. 'It was not always great, was it?' he said, smiling. 'I remember going in the doldrums years, when the chant was "We're shit, and we're sick of it". And we were crap, rubbish, for a long time. I'd see lads in the pub talking about the team and start to think: "I'm a bit too old for this now," so I'd not been for a few years. But doing that walk, seeing the places I used to see so much, brought back a bit of my adolescence. After the Millwall game we went to the Antwerp for a good old-fashioned drink and a sing-song. It was a really lovely day.'

It probably helped, too, that he saw the 458th, 459th, 460th, 461st, 462nd and, when Son Heung-Min drove through Millwall keeper Tom King to complete his hat-trick in the final minute, 463rd FA Cup goal Spurs scored in their 199 Cup fixtures at White Hart Lane.

Football, of course, is about the players. They are the stars. The heroes. They are the ones who walk out onto the stage with the spotlight trained on them. Who take the bouquets and the accolades but have to dodge the brickbats. Yet without the supporters, like Les, who come in hope and expectation, week after week, month after month, year after year, there would be no superstars. It is the supporters who make it special, who create the atmosphere, make a stadium into something bigger, greater, transform four stands around a green patch of land into a living, vibrant amphitheatre. It is the fans, too, who would feel the passing of White Hart Lane more than the players, for it had been part of their lives as they grew from child to adult. Whose stories made the Lane more than just a place, made it a real, genuine, theatre of hope and belief. Young and old. Black, white. Men and women. Each of them had their own stories, their own back-catalogue of reasons that this place would always be special.

I've known Mike Collett for nearly a quarter of a century. For most of that time he was the Football Editor of Reuters, the international news agency. He might not have been a familiar name to newspaper readers in this country but around the world he was known as one of the great football experts. Bizarrely, and entirely accidentally, we now quite literally lived around the corner from one another in south-west London. But like me, his heart resided in a tiny corner of N17.

Mike's voice was now strained and husky, the scars of a battle with cancerous nodules in his throat, a battle he thought he had won. He still had to sip water to keep his throat moist as we chatted about what the Lane meant to him: 'My dad didn't have much interest. He used to tease me that he was an Arsenal fan. When I was eight or nine I was aware that Spurs had won the Double and that they were a good team but it wasn't until the next season, when dad bought me the Cup final edition of *Football Monthly*, Charles Buchan's magazine, that I saw Spurs v. Burnley on the front and liked the Spurs kit.

'I watched the Cup final and they were my team but I wasn't fully aware of what it meant. But one afternoon I was at home, on my own, watching the football results. Bob Danvers-Walker or Len Martin, or whoever read them out, suddenly said: "Tottenham Hotspur 9, Nottingham Forest 2." I leapt off my armchair: "Yes!!! Tottenham Hotspur, they're my team." And that was it. The deal was struck. September 1962. Spurs 9, Forest 2. The day I became a Spurs fan for life. Nine years old.

'The first game I saw was in 1964. I was eleven, and it was Spurs versus Sheffield United. Twenty-second of August. Jimmy Greaves, of course, was the first player I saw score for Spurs. That, for me, was so fantastic, because he was my all-time hero. Frank Saul got the other goal. But that was the first time I went.

'What I remember, from being a kid, was that there was what was called "the old press box", which was in the East Stand, not the West. Maybe that came from when the West Stand was being built initially. Who knows? But it was at the top of the East Stand. And it was there that I saw that game against Arsenal in 1971. My uncle, Harry, had a season ticket in the old press box. I'd never actually been there and I wasn't sure how he got it but it was doubtless through some nefarious character.

'But that day, I'd have been eighteen, I left school early to get to the Lane. By five p.m. it seemed like there were 100,000 people there. It was absolute insanity. I was with my mate Lawrence – who's dead now – and said to him: "We'll never get in paying at the gate; but I've got an idea." I knew that my uncle used to use a little doorway that was in the East Stand, an unmarked doorway, where he showed his tickets for the old press box and got in that way. So I told Lawrence about it and we decided we'd give it a try. I was going to tell the doorman about my uncle, that he'd already gone up and he had our tickets by mistake. We'd ask the doorman to ring up to the press box to see if my uncle was up there with our tickets, get him down and then try to blag our way in.

'So we did that, got in through the door and into a holding area, a pen, with a wire or metal doorway. Next to that was a two-person lift that took you all the way up to the old press box. He listened to our story and bought it, but told us he'd rung up and hadn't got through, but that there was another phone in the lift and that we had to wait there while he went to try to see if he could get through. But he left the door open and we scarpered through the gap, up the stairs and bang, we were inside. There were at least 50,000 people still outside but we saw the game. And then the next season, for an FA Cup tie, we ended up with legitimate tickets for the old press box, so I did see a game from there as well! The teams looked like Subbuteo players from up there.'

As with so many Spurs fans, the European nights had a special fascination for Mike. One in particular: 'It was the Uefa Cup quarter-final against Cologne in 1974, when I stood in front of The Shelf. We won 3–0 but it wasn't the match itself. I was cheering so much when we scored one of the goals that I jumped up and down. I had my keys – my house keys, my car keys, everything – in my pocket and they fell out but I didn't notice.

'I'd parked my car, an Austin 1100, miles away, on the other side of Bruce Castle Park. I went for a drink afterwards and it was only when I got back to the car that I realised I didn't have any keys. I worked out what had happened and decided to go back to the ground. By this time – it was maybe an hour or an hour and a half after the final whistle – I was shitting myself. I was thinking: "What am I going to do?" So I got back to White Hart Lane. There were still some people around and I explained what

Erection of the Spurs Cockerel, 1909.

Arthur Rowe explaining his Push and Run philosophy during a White Hart Lane training session ahead of the 1950–51 season.

Bobby Smith and Jimmy Greaves denied by Benfica keeper Costa Pereira during the 1962 European Cup semi-final second leg, 5 April 1962.

Jimmy Greaves wheels away in delight after scoring past Nottingham Forest goalkeeper Peter Grummitt on 30 September 1962.

Alan Mullery celebrates with the Uefa Cup:
his last game for Tottenham, 18 May 1972.

Bill Nicholson opening the gates at White Hart Lane on
1 January 1974 – he was entering his last year as manager.

Glenn Hoddle opening the scoring at the Paxton Road end with a penalty in the 2–0 win over Nottingham Forest on 16 August 1980.

Graham Roberts holds the trophy aloft after Spurs had beaten Anderlecht 4–3 on penalties in the UEFA Cup final second leg at White Hart Lane, 23 May 1984.

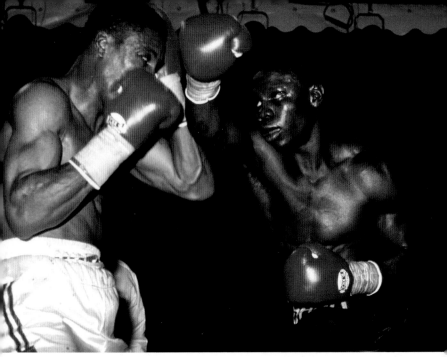

Chris Eubank lands a right on Michael Watson during their titanic WBO Super-Middleweight title bout at the Lane, 21 September 1991.

Osvaldo Ardiles (c) with his coaching staff, including former player Steve Perryman (l), circa 1993.

I thought had happened to one bloke outside the West Stand and he let me in. I went inside and of course the ground was deserted. I walked across the pitch, the deserted pitch, to the other side and the East Stand. I looked around, under all the rubbish and somehow found my keys. There were no fences in those days, just the little low railings and I stepped over them, walked back across the pitch, stood in the centre-circle of White Hart Lane and just thought: "This is absolutely one of the most magical moments in my life." There was one floodlight still on. The other three were off so the shadows were quite long. I will never forget that. It was just beautiful.'

Games can be beautiful too. Including, for Mike, the 5-0 'revenge' win over Arsenal in 1983, pay-back for Liam Brady's masterclass a few years earlier. But it is the little things that you recall as much as the matches. For me the whole reason that football was football, something that transcended the matches and meant far more, was encapsulated by the crunch clash with Everton in 1985. Spurs had crushed Howard Kendall's team 4-1 at Goodison on the opening weekend of the season but the original return fixture in January was postponed by a brutal winter snowfall.

The game was rearranged for Wednesday 3 April. It was must-win for Spurs, and not far off it for the Toffees. In the sixth form, but with my university place already effectively confirmed – even I was going to get the two Es at 'A' Level which were all I needed to secure my offer at Oxford – I bunked off early and walked the mile and a half to the railway station in Wickford, the dormitory town in the Essex commuter belt where we'd moved from our old home in Walthamstow in 1976. It meant I arrived, via Liverpool Street, in plenty of time to take my spot on the right-hand side of The Shelf, about level with the edge of the penalty box. It was to prove a typical Spurs evening in front of more than 48,000. Two sloppy goals, Paul Miller's misdirected header slapped home by Andy Gray before Trevor Steven robbed rookie left-back Mark

Bowen to waltz round Ray Clemence. And while a thunderbolt from Graham Roberts gave us hope, it was extinguished when, somehow, Neville Southall managed to turn Mark Falco's point-blank header over the bar, right in front of where I stood. As I left, turning right, heading for the staircase, there was a father and son standing there. The dad, wearing his Spurs scarf, was a picture of despair and dejection. But his boy, maybe nine or ten, wearing Everton blue, had a smile as broad as the Mersey. Even in my anguish, I saw that for what it was. The reason we all love the game.

And also why the end of the Lane was a poignant thing. Mike said: 'I think I've been in every single part of the ground. All the stands, upper and lower. I stood in the old Enclosure in the West Stand. Stood in the boys' section below The Shelf, when I remember paying 1s 3d, before they got rid of the boys' section. I have a picture of me standing at the front of The Shelf, 1968. The sun shining on everybody and you can see me and my cousin in the front of The Shelf. So I've sat or stood everywhere it's possible to be in that ground. And I feel it's actually my home from home. And I will miss it terribly.

'When I'm there, I always feel as if I've only just left. It's like when you have a conversation with a really close mate. You might not have seen each other for a week, even a month or two, but you don't need to say "Hello", you just pick up from the last conversation. When I'm at White Hart Lane it's like picking up a conversation. Like I've never been away. Those two or three weeks haven't really happened. I'm just back. It's so familiar.

'I feel as if I know every piece of brickwork. I hated it when The Shelf disappeared. I didn't always stand there but I remember that if you were in the West Stand, for a three p.m. match in March or April, the sun would shine through the corner – this was before the roof was joined up – and The Shelf would literally glow gold in the sunshine. I used to look at that and think it was one of the most beautiful sights in the world. I'd think: "My God, that is so beautiful." The way the sun was shining, filtering through the gap in the stand, was fabulous.

'So it is going to be very emotional. I'm a bit of an anorak. I have records at home that I've kept since that first game. Chelsea in January was my 800th match at White Hart Lane. By the end of the final season it will be 812. I know how many times I've seen the first team, the reserves, the youth team. I know the records.

'I'd get there at one p.m., because when they opened the gates all the boys would run up the stairs to try to get to the front of The Shelf. If you got there, you were made. And you'd stand there for two hours before the kick-off. And if you weren't able to get to the front of The Shelf, you'd run to get behind the first crash barrier behind the front. That was massive because nobody could be right in front of you there either.

'I was allowed to go by myself from thirteen for Saturday afternoon games, fourteen for night matches. But only if I went with friends. I lived in Hendon. It took an hour to get there on the 102 bus from Golders Green. I'd get off at the Edmonton Angel – that's long gone – and walk down the High Road.

'For me it was about watching Jimmy Greaves, because he was just a marvel. I was there when Jimmy scored that fantastic goal, that famous goal, against Newcastle. It was astonishing. It still takes my breath away. I didn't see the goal he got against Leicester, which only the people inside the ground saw, one of the greatest goals he ever scored, because there wasn't a single TV camera. I was too young for the one against Manchester United, but I saw Newcastle.

'I remember being very aware of the atmosphere when it was still a standing ground. I was able to judge the attendance within a thousand or so. I could tell how cramped it was. From The Shelf or the lower side I'd say 26,000, then read the papers the next day and it was there or thereabouts. But you knew if it was a big match because from two p.m. or two-thirty onwards the singing and chanting was different. You didn't have music playing. The atmosphere was created by the fans. And if you were playing Arsenal, Chelsea, United or Liverpool – never really West Ham then – it felt different, palpably so.

'As a kid, up to my early twenties, I'd go with my mates. Then my son Ryan was born in 1986. The first game I took him to was at Fulham in the Football Combination, the reserves, on a Tuesday afternoon. He was eighteen months old. The first game I took him to at the Lane was in 1991, the week before the Cup final, but also against the same opponents, Forest. We drew 1–1. And I had the period of going with him when he was a young boy. That changed the dynamic, taking my boy to the Lane and until he was fourteen or fifteen I felt that I was looking after him. Then there was the period when there was more equality. And now we go as adults, father and son. We'll stop off at the Bell and Hare, although it's now called No. 8, or meet at the ground. It's quite an emotional thing for me. It's not overwhelming but if I'm there first and see him coming up the stairs, I still see the little boy, the little five-year-old I first took all those years ago. That's a lovely feeling.

'Even through the dark days of the nineties – and they were pretty miserable, because we were miles behind Arsenal – I always went there, every single time, thinking: "This is going to be the turning point, when we'll score the greatest goal I've ever seen." And to this day I've never left early. I've never left before the final whistle. Neither has Ryan. I used to say to him: "We've got to stay to the end; we might score the greatest goal ever. And if that means getting home twenty minutes later than you might have done, it's worth it." So the labour of love is still there.

'There's a group of us now. Me, four mates and Ryan. We've got membership but two season tickets between us. And every June or July, just after the fixture lists come out, we meet up to draw the games we'll go to, seven each. And when they come out, we'll argue and see if we can swap. But that's fantastic, always a great night. And after the game, we always go to the Barca café, on the way back to Seven Sisters Road, for a cup of tea. We've been doing it for donkey's years.

'For me, what's so fantastic about the new stadium, whatever it's called, is that the journey to the ground will be the same. Because that is part of the experience. That journey. It's intrinsic to the event, the match, the day.'

Others had been going for far longer than Mike. Morris Keston was, and for plenty of older fans still is, Mr Tottenham. He made his first trip to White Hart Lane in 1943, part of a London still suffering from the bombing raids of the Blitz. And, in a football sense, he had his own near-miss.

Now in his 90s, Morris, who was the ultimate superfan long before the concept took firm shape, remained as sharp as a tack. He said: 'I was eleven or twelve and my friends were driving me mad to go to football. I wanted to go to the pictures. We were living in Clapton but my two cousins said they'd take me to a match. Arsenal were sharing White Hart Lane then because Highbury had been requisitioned to be an air raid patrol centre, but they were playing at Chelsea – Spurs were at home to Palace – and they were each going to go to a different game. I asked which was nearer to Clapton, went to White Hart Lane and the rest is history. But if I'd gone to my first game a week later I'd have been an Arsenal fan and changed my life completely! I had a lucky escape.

'It's not as if after one game I thought: "I'm going to come here every week" but I started to go more and more. I missed the push and run title season because I was on National Service in Egypt but when I got back out of the Army I started to write up notes on every game I saw in an exercise book. I ended up with six of them, all full. It became something I just had to do. And it became a sense that I was expected to go, to a match everywhere. I'd pay one shilling to stand in the enclosure in front of the directors' box. Then we'd give the guy a penny to let us climb over his turnstile for a better view. It wasn't until 1960 that I got a season ticket. I used to go everywhere with England, too, but it wasn't the same thrill. I'd always rather see Tottenham than anyone else.'

Keston became pals with the legends of the game. Not just his Spurs heroes but also George Best, Bobby Moore, Geoff Hurst and others. He became a confidant of many, organising testimonials, making approaches to potential managers (all, very much, off the record – but it has always been a game in which deals have been done, often shrouded in slightly questionable behaviour). It was the game that mattered most, though.

'We'd go to the ground two hours before the start to get in,' he recalled. 'For a night game I'd turn up at four-thirty in the afternoon, to make sure I got a place on the halfway line. I used to love the games under lights. The atmosphere for the Górnik game, which was the first European night, was incredible. You heard the roar of the crowd. And I don't care what you say, nothing you'd get today could be as loud as that sound. You just wouldn't get that sound. You'd hear "Glory, Glory". There'd be the Enfield Town Brass Band on the pitch. I will miss being able to look around, to point to the places where I used to go. That is nostalgic.

'I'd rather things stayed as they were. The stadium is pretty good, although it needs tarting up. White Hart Lane, for me, is a real football stadium. I feel the same way about Goodison Park, too. Then again, I guess they were both designed by Leitch. But they're football stadiums, not pieces of tin put together, real grounds. Of course the ground I first went to has already been rebuilt, more than once. The big change was the West Stand. At the start I was against that as well but I came to accept it had to be done, even if a lot of that was about the Centenary Club and the lounges. As far as I'm concerned, the prawn sandwich brigade are the last people you need at football. You want to go and be with the same people every week. You don't go to watch football for the food. If you're at a game, it's fish and chips, steak or roast beef, even in the lounges.'

Maybe not roast pork, though, even if the bacon sandwiches in some of the less-expensive parts of the ground are renowned. The

Jewish connection has been an intrinsic part of the Tottenham and White Hart Lane story. As Martin Cloake and Alan Fisher pointed out in their terrific *A People's History of Tottenham Hotspur* the area around Tottenham Hale had become a Jewish enclave by the early part of the twentieth century, the refugees from Russia, escaping the pogroms, swiftly moving on from their original East End staging posts. There were thousands who arrived. My family, from a long line of rabbis, ended up in north London in the 1920s, albeit by a rather unlikely route via Latvia and Sunderland – they thought they were going to New York but were instead dropped off in Gateshead – when the decision was taken to anglicise the family name from Lipschitz to Lipton.

Spurs rapidly became a critical element in the lives of those working-class toilers. My family was just one for whom football was part of the cultural assimilation. It was necessary too. Reading Hansard reports of the Parliamentary debates of the time, the scale of anti-Semitism from even government representatives appears both shocking and scandalous. It passed without much comment. Nevertheless, Tottenham's identity as a 'Jewish' club grew. It was estimated that by the mid thirties up to a third of the fans at White Hart Lane were Jews. A remarkable figure, which made the decision to host the 1935 friendly against Nazi Germany even more astonishing. Even then, the fixture caused anger. Protesters, led by the Trades Union Congress and desperate to prevent the match from taking place, stated: 'We regard the visit of the German team as an effrontery, not only to the Jewish race but to all lovers of freedom.'

Despite that, on 4 December the swastika was unfurled over White Hart Lane, the German team giving a Nazi salute. At least, unlike in Berlin three years later, England did not pay similar fealty and the flag did not last long before a fan climbed onto the roof of the West Stand to pull it down. But after England's 3–0 win – a Jewish boycott did not prevent a crowd of 55,000, with 1,000 police on hand to quell the disturbances that brought 14 arrests – FA president Sir Charles Clegg, who raised a toast to 'the leader Adolf Hitler', claimed the game had helped cement friendship between the two nations and criticised the TUC for supporting and encouraging the protests: 'This is the first time the TUC have interfered in football. I hope it will be the last time. Before they start to tell a sporting organisation what to do and how their members should behave, they should see that their own members, who are responsible for rowdyism, are kept under proper control. These TUC people seem to forget that football is a sport. They will never succeed in dragging politics into the great game of football.'

Even after the war, and for many years, there was talk of an 'unofficial apartheid' between the club's Jewish supporters and its Gentile directors. Mike Collett, who admits he grew up with a crush on Irving Scholar's elder sister, who lived near him in Hendon, said: 'In my eyes, as a young teenager, Arsenal was the Jewish club, not Spurs. We got the *Jewish Chronicle* at home and every Rosh Hashanah, for at least the previous two or three years, there was a message from Arsenal saying Happy New Year. But it was only later, maybe around 1966, that I remember seeing a message from Spurs. If you look at the demographics, there were as many Jewish Arsenal fans as Spurs ones. And only five per cent of Spurs fans were actually Jewish.

'When I was a kid, the West Stand was full of Jewish season-ticket holders. They would go to the match, watch Spurs win 5–0 and still spend most of the afternoon moaning. It was horrible. I'd rarely sit there but when I did I disliked it. I preferred the East Stand or the Paxton Road.'

David Pleat also drew a distinction between the different elements of the White Hart Lane supporters. The son of a family of anglicised immigrants said: 'The thing that made White Hart Lane special was The Shelf. Pat Nevin tells me that the first season he was at Chelsea, when he came down from Clyde, he used to go to Tottenham to stand on The Shelf. Other players at other

London clubs would come to watch Tottenham play because the club stood for football and the ground was part of that. Everybody admired Tottenham. Chelsea were nothing. Arsenal were a big side but a bit dull. But people enjoyed watching Tottenham. The Shelf played a big part in that.

'When the atmosphere was good, it was something else, and most of the time that came from The Shelf as well. The fans there started the noise and it reverberated round. It echoed round the ground. But it wasn't a raucous stadium. It wasn't a Portsmouth or a Stoke, where it's just about making a noise. It's not like that. The fans aren't like that. It was as if some of them came so they could admire, in a quiet way, the quality of the football we tried to play. For some of them it was like going to the opera. They'd sit quietly, watching the movement evolve. Mind you, the fans could go the other way as well. Part of it was the Jewish element. I know they're emotional people and have a lot to say, all the time. And if we lost a last-minute goal, they'd disappear. It was unbelievable really, but it was what it was. You can make all the excuses in the world about the traffic, and how hard it is to get away from White Hart Lane – and they did, I tell you – but honestly, if we were losing with ten minutes to go, they were so upset. They weren't horrible people, at all, but they were so disappointed because it meant so much to them and they'd leave the ground.'

The Jewish identity has never been diminished. Indeed, it actually intensified, as a direct result of the anti-Semitism directed at Tottenham – Jew and Gentile alike – by rival fans through the late 1970s, 1980s and afterwards. Sick chants. Hissing to replicate the sound of the gas chambers in the Holocaust. Nazi salutes. But it was the response that was a surprise. To take flags displaying the Star of David to matches was one thing. Like many Jews, my father proudly wears one of those round his neck. But for many, myself included, to hear Spurs fans self-proclaiming themselves as 'Yids' and members of the 'Yid Army' remains troubling and complicated. And when the club was enmeshed in controversy in 2013, after the FA and Metropolitan Police agreed that any use of the 'Y-word' would be prohibited at football, irrespective of the context, with a number of Tottenham supporters arrested for breaching Section Five of the Public Order Act, following complaints by the grandstanding Peter Herbert of the Society of Black Lawyers, the White Hart Lane Board eventually decided to back the fans.

Max Radford, a lifelong fan who spent a significant part of his childhood in Israel, said: 'It's quite an emotive subject for a lot of people. Views are really polarised and there is a lot of debate. My take is that I've experienced the ugly side of it but since the fans have adopted it as a badge of honour rather than the other way round it's completely changed the nature of it. I'm Jewish and I sing it as loud as anybody. I'm proud and it's quite clear how we feel that by using the word in that way we've taken the sting out of it. It's all about context and how you use a word. If it is said as a positive, it's completely different. It's reclaiming the word and about context. Two people can call me a Jew. In one context it's something I would be proud of. But in another context, using the same word, it's completely different.

'I use Yiddish terms. My family and friends do. It's all about context. I would hate to see it removed or banned as was threatened, because I genuinely feel that what we've done with the word has changed the context. I think if you ask the majority of the younger generation of fans, that's what they would say. They don't see it as derogatory but a word they have adopted for the positive. I completely understand the other side and people who have experienced how aggressive anti-Semitism was, especially those whose families suffered in the Holocaust, would be opposed to it much more. But I look at how things used to be compared to how they are now, when some opposition fans were outright racist and anti-Semitic and used it against the club and fans because of the management and ownership of the club and the Jewish supporters.

'But we've now taken it as a badge of honour and completely flipped it around. We now don't get anything like the same level of anti-Semitism from opposition fans. If the authorities tried to step in now and ban us from using the word in the way we do, and enforced that, it would be worse. The animosity would be worse. I don't think banning it would help.'

Mike Collett, though, disagreed: 'I find it incredible, to this day, when you get hundreds of fans singing "The thing I love most is being a Yid". The singing of a song like that, by people who aren't Jewish. For me it's extremely ironic. I know the argument, that it's appropriation of the language. A bit like the hip-hop group NWA, who did "Straight Outta Compton". But they *were* black. It's really, really weird for me that so many sing the song, that they are proud of being "Yids", when they're not Jewish. They're the furthest thing from really being a "Yid", from knowing what the word means, the derogatory derivation, as it's possible to be. I don't see it as the word being reclaimed.'

For most, though, it is just about the football, what the Irish call 'the craic'. And the anguish. Radford returned to London in time for the greatest of the Spurs near-miss campaigns. 'I came back for the 1986–87 season and one of the first games was the League Cup semi-final replay against Arsenal,' he said with a pained expression, as the memory resurfaced.

'We had never been behind at any point in the tie. One thing about that game was that I caught the ball when someone shot miles over the bar. But the second thing was that it was the first time I had ever seen a grown man cry at a football match. At half-time there was an announcement about Wembley tickets and travel but we somehow lost and I looked around and saw people bawling their eyes out, adults. It felt so humiliating after that stupid announcement.

'Yet I remember the euphoria when Danny Rose thumped home that volley right at the start of the Arsenal game in 2010. The noise and atmosphere that night was exceptional and I just wonder if we will still get that kind of atmosphere, that intensity, in the new stadium.'

Alan Fisher, an author and blogger as well as a social worker, put it simply: 'I can't remember being anything other than a Spurs fan. The first game I saw was in 1967, Spurs 2 Sheffield United 0, and I've been going regularly ever since – I think I've seen over ninety per cent of the home games since then.

'I was eleven or twelve, living in Ealing. My dad wasn't interested in football. He had a sweet shop and the only time it closed, normally, was on a Sunday afternoon. For him to take his football-mad son to this alien place he had never been to and never wanted to go to means it will always stick out in my memory. He had to make an arrangement with my mother and someone else to look after the shop, something he'd never do.

'So it was such an important day in my life. He must have known how much it would mean to me. It told me how much he cared for me, too, that he would make what was a big sacrifice for him at that time. I remember the experience of the day far more than the game. That has stayed with me ever since. We got the Tube to Mansion House and then hopped on a Football Special Routemaster bus. We went into the East Stand and climbed and climbed and climbed up, popped out into the stand out of the stairwell and then what I recall is the pure green of the pitch.

'It's probably a false memory because it might have been a mud-heap – it often was when you look back at film of games in those years. But that's where the stories come from. Those stories, your stories and myths are all part and parcel of being a fan. I remember the noise of the wooden seats when everybody stood up if something happened. The culture of the stand, the friendliness of everybody sitting next to each other, even though they only saw each other every second Saturday.

'But that is what football does – it brings people together. And it still does now. We go with our friends, our kids, pass on the stories. It's not just about the result of the game. It's about being there.'

Fisher was also in the crowd to see Greaves's goal against Newcastle. For him, like so many of his generation, the striker, whose incredible Spurs goals record is unlikely to be surpassed, remains the greatest player to ever have worn the white shirt with the blue cockerel. For others, though, Greaves is just a legendary name, not flesh and blood. Sean Walsh, who writes The Tottenham Way blog, said: 'The first player I remember was Robbie Keane. I loved watching him do his cartwheel when he scored – you knew it was going to be a good day. I don't think you could call him a legend but he had a cult status and he'd get a huge reception if he came back to watch a game. He was a good player in a very ordinary team. And of course he had a fantastic partnership with Dimitar Berbatov. It was a joy to watch them every week. I loved the silky arrogance Berbatov brought with him.

'People talk about the "dreadful noughties" but for me they weren't dreadful. That was when I started to come. Even when Arsenal drew 2–2 to win the title in 2004, we still had the comeback, Jens Lehmann giving away the penalty, Jamie Redknapp scoring, so they didn't beat us as well. I remember being four years old and getting a set of Spurs pyjamas and my first game at White Hart Lane, against Manchester City in 2006. It was everything I thought it would be, and more. It took my breath away. It is a special ground.

'The game I'll remember most was the 2–2 draw with Arsenal in 2016. There was that spell after Francis Coquelin's red card, when Toby Alderweireld equalised, and there was just such a sense of expectation, which came to fruition with Harry Kane scoring such an outrageous goal when he had no right to score from so far out on the left. There wasn't a normal cheer when that went in – it was a scream of disbelief that you could feel. At that moment I really felt we were going to go on and win the league. And that's a moment that will always live on with me.

'I sit at the Park Lane end. I like the atmosphere, the chants and the noise. This season we've all been trying to keep the fact this is the last season here a bit subdued. We didn't want it to seem like a final season. Once we knew about the move to Wembley for the Champions League, that there would never be another European night at White Hart Lane, that was a sad thing. The closer we got to the United game the more emotional it got for everyone. I certainly felt it building up and it became something the fans talked about more and more as the clock counted down.

'We were seeing the new stadium grow in front of our eyes, every week. I walk past the new stadium on my way in and it's impossible to avoid. Daniel Levy has done a good job in letting us see what is happening, and what he wants from the new stadium, especially that idea of a wall of sound at one end, is exactly right. The good thing is that we know we are coming back to basically the same place. And it will be fantastic. But it won't be what we remember. We'll lose some of that nostalgia and mystique.'

Even the younger fans recognised it. The White Hart Lane volume of Tottenham's history was closing: 'I've got mixed feelings about what's happening,' Fisher said. 'I'm proud of the way the new ground is going up next door. I've been critical of Daniel Levy in the past but I think his motives are genuine in that he wants to build the new ground in Spurs territory.

'I'm one of those supporters who has a sense of place. Yes, that changed with Wembley for Europe this season, and will again when we move out there for the year while the stadium is being finished. But for a few years I had a season ticket which gave me admission to the Enclosure in front of the West Stand. In those days you could walk round and I always went to the same spot on the left of The Shelf. And for over a hundred years, every single Spurs fan has walked the same streets, walked down the High Road. That is such an important thread. For all this to be going on at a time when there is such a bond between the players and the fans is really important. There was a gap that was allowed to grow over a decade or more, but I feel there's something very different in the air now.

'Saying all that, and knowing that the move has to happen, I'm not going to be able to cope with it very well. I was struggling with the thought of the last game at the Lane for months before it actually happened. I'm a football fan. Every match, before kick-off, I look at the players and look around me and at the stands, especially before a big game. I look at my kids and still think it's a privilege to be there. So when it stopped, even though we knew we'd be coming back, it was hard.'

One voice. Echoed by thousands.

8

CAPTAINS, LEADERS, LEGENDS

There are, in essence, two kinds of captains in football. Those who lead with their minds and those who do so with their bodies. Few combine both. But while European managers and players do not understand the very British obsession with on-field leadership, there is no doubt that, at White Hart Lane, the identity of the bloke who called heads or tails at the coin toss always mattered.

Perhaps that is entirely because of the legendary status of the best of captains, the men who led the winning teams that wrote their own chapters in the history of the club. From Ron Burgess, no more than a name from the past to all but the oldest of supporters, onwards, they represent a golden thread, an inheritance that rumbles through the years.

Unquestionably, at the apex, the man who most led by precept and example, stands Danny Blanchflower. He may not have been born a Tottenham man – indeed, he initially thought about leaving when he was dropped by Bill Nicholson. Nobody, though, embodies the ideals, the ethos and the vision of the Double side more than the Ulsterman, who was able to articulate the manager's ambitions and interpret them in words, often in poetic, romantic imagery. Blanchflower's place in the White Hart Lane story is unquestioned. He was an immortal, untouchable. Morris Keston, enshrined in his own place as the most famous of Tottenham fans, agreed. 'Danny was a god to the other players,' he said. 'I remember one night we went up to Blackpool and were about to go out for the evening but as we left the hotel Danny was outside. He said hello, asked where we were going and then said: "Could we have a chat?" It was about nine p.m. We sat down and didn't get up until half past one in the morning, just with Danny talking to us. I can't imagine Wayne Rooney holding court like that . . .'

Yet it was, arguably, the member of that team who was more robustly physical, flesh and blood, thunder and lightning, whose legacy was carried further by those who succeeded to the captain's role. If Blanchflower remains the spirit of Tottenham's greatest age, Dave Mackay's influence, his status as a leader, impacted most on the men who followed in that leadership position. It was Mackay who laid down the template of the Spurs skipper, whose approach to the task galvanised supporters and successors alike. And like the Scot, those who wore the demands of on-field leadership were determined to give their all for the club that became an enduring part of their lives.

For Alan Mullery, it was imperative that he live up to his predecessor when he was elevated to the role in 1968. When we met to turn back the clock, the memories tumbled out of him: 'In those days the dressing rooms in the West Stand were closer to the corner flag, not in the middle of the ground like they are now. As you started coming up the stairs into the tunnel, which was quite tight, only a couple of yards across, the fans on the far side could see some movement and suddenly that roar would go up. It's quite something when that noise, 50,000 of your own fans, hits you like that, a huge thing. Then the tannoy would start up with "McNamara's Band" and "Glory, Glory", with everybody joining in. It was pretty awe-inspiring to have that.

'When I started, Dave Mackay was the skipper and he'd lead us out, with a ball in one hand, and always do the same thing. Just as he came out onto the pitch, Dave would boot that ball fifty yards up into the air – or it seemed that high anyway! – and sprint after it before catching it on his left boot. The crowd would just go crackers, the roar got louder. He did it every match but it always took my breath away because I'd never seen anybody do something like that to get the whole place going. But that was Dave, what he was about, the sort of character he was. A wonderful, wonderful player. Hard as nails but such a competitor and footballer.'

And a player whose reputation endured. Steve Perryman joined Spurs as a 16-year-old, in awe because he used the same training facilities as Mackay and Greaves, saw them walking out onto the pitch that he was to grow to know equally well, if not better. Perryman's impression of the demands of the Tottenham captaincy were forged by those early years. 'In the dressing room in the old West Stand we came out into a narrow corridor,' he told me. 'But it was so narrow that, even though both dressing rooms opened out into it, you couldn't go down the steps at the same time. So one team would go down and then have to wait for the other one.

'Now, of course, the teams come out together but it wasn't the norm then and it wasn't even possible at White Hart Lane. Whenever we were ready to go we'd walk out and for me, to walk down those steps at the front of the team as captain, did mean so much. I had that image, still, of Dave Mackay, booting the ball in the air, sticking out his chest but I wasn't quite as confident as that. If anything, I was a bit shy, wanted to make a shy entry. I wasn't a shy player, at all, but I was always a little shy before the ball was kicked.'

Like Mullery and Perryman, Gary Mabbutt also felt he was the inheritor of a proud tradition. 'It was a special thing to lead the team out onto the pitch,' he said. 'I loved the fact that I was the first one to be seen, to hear the roar, to have that adrenalin pumping through me as I led the team onto the pitch. The first time, when I was asked to do it, I remember thinking to myself: "How many great stars in the history of this club have done what you're about to do?" and thinking of people like Dave Mackay, Danny Blanchflower and Steve Perryman. I just hoped I'd be able to do it numerous times. And it was as special as I hoped it would be, every time. My routine was to carry a ball with me and then, as I actually walked onto the grass, to drop it and half-volley towards the goal. If it went in the net, the crowd would all cheer, if it missed, I'd get an "Ooh!"'

The Lane, though, was not just a place of examination for those who walked onto that piece of turf. For those, like Perryman, who grew up at the club, the stadium itself, it had a greater, more life-defining significance. He did not come from Tottenham territory. Ealing, in West London, was closer to Brentford, QPR, Fulham and Chelsea.

'I'd been a district schoolboy up to the age of eleven but then I went to a grammar school and I dropped out of the football scene because we didn't play competitive games at our school,' he said. 'You weren't allowed to go to trials even, so I dropped out. But then we had a change of sports master, when the regular one went away on a refresher course. The new chap came in and for some reason, I still don't know why, put us in for the Ealing district trials. We played our first game against Harrow and won 9–1 and that afternoon Charlie Faulkner turned up at my door.'

Ah yes, Charlie Faulkner. In Hunter Davies's classic account of his year in the heart of Nicholson's camp, *The Glory Game*, Faulkner is described as '58, and very dapper with a cigarette holder, suede shoes and a sparkle of gold teeth'. He told Davies: 'I don't know why I chose Ealing. Perhaps it was just because it was near my home. I didn't know any of the players but Steve stood out a mile. While he was playing I rushed around trying to find the teacher but he wouldn't give me Steve's address or any details. I was supposed to go to Leicester for a league match but I cancelled it. Steve was too promising to miss. I eventually got his address and went round to his house at one p.m. His brother Ted opened the door and said: "Hello Mr Faulkner; I saw you at the match this morning. We had a letter from you last year when you worked for QPR." We waited more than a year and both Bill and Eddie thought we'd lost him. Steve wanted to go to QPR, his father preferred Tottenham and his brother thought he should go to West Ham. When he eventually decided, I took him to the club, got out the form and signed him myself.'

It is an account that, 50 years on from 1967, still tallies with Perryman's own recollection: 'Charlie told us who he was and that he should've been at a first-team game but explained to myself and my older brother that he'd liked what he'd seen and felt he wanted to come and see me. He invited me to start training and so I was going across London twice a week for the next year. Because I hadn't signed forms, I was allowed to visit other clubs. I went to Arsenal a couple of times, Chelsea, QPR. In the end thirty-odd clubs wanted me. I didn't want to leave home. I looked at all of the options but the difference at Tottenham was the feeling of warmth. I felt it when I walked behind the stands. That was the big draw for me. Not the glamour side of the club. It wasn't about that. I just had the feeling that it was a nitty-gritty work place where I could go to do my job, where I could improve and make strides in my life. I ended up turning down the chance of a sixth-form education. In fact, I actually left school at fifteen to take up the apprenticeship I was offered.

'It wasn't the natural thing for me to do, the path I expected. That was going to be university. My brother went to Brunel to study and when I told them what I was doing the teachers went berserk. But for me it was going from one education situation to another. It was where I was going to learn to play football. It wasn't that it was "a dream" for me. I just knew that somebody wanted me and I thought it would be interesting to take that chance.'

Perryman was a kid in demand, and from the outset he was treated as a precious gem to be cultivated, cut and polished. 'I joined in the summer of 1967 and I'd only been at the club three or four days when I was asked to take part in a kid's TV programme explaining the life of an apprentice professional. The opening shot was me surrounded by Gilzean, Greaves, Jennings, Mackay and Cyril Knowles. It was an unbelievable experience, something I couldn't quite live down. Some of the other apprentices had been there for two or three years but I was put up for it when I'd just left school. First impressions always stay with you, so my memory of White Hart Lane starts with that first impression. The key for me was that I felt welcome there. All of us were trying to do a job but it felt right.'

Even so, it was still a school of hard knocks: 'It wasn't always enjoyable but that apprenticeship, the things we had to do, meant I got to know every corner of the ground, the whole of the stadium, all the inner workings of the place. There was a boardroom, called the Oak Room, in the old stand before that got knocked down. We had to clean that. And we had to take all the rubbish across to the incinerator they had in the East Stand. It wasn't somewhere that was flash, glitzy or glamorous. It was a place of work, the place where you had to do the right things to get your career going. But you knew that if you could do it right, then all the good things could come later. That was Bill's philosophy.

'He was right about what the stadium had to mean. It was there for a purpose. It was going to house our supporters who would, in turn, take us on a journey. They didn't need padded seats. They weren't coming to see players have fights in the tunnel but what they expected was players ready to go on the pitch and be players. We would train under the stand, an indoor gym we played in and loved playing in, when we'd get smashed against the wall. Eventually that turned into a ball court with astroturf and a viewing gallery but you still couldn't chip the ball high. But that was the place where Jimmy Greaves and Dave Mackay did their work. It ended up becoming the car park for the directors. But it was a down-to-earth, non-glitzy, working-class place. A place to perform and play, a place where you could give the fans success and glory, what they demanded.'

Perryman's memories were echoed by Ray Evans, one of his team-mates in the 1974 Uefa Cup final defeat to Feyenoord: 'I probably have to go back to when I first signed there on schoolboy forms at thirteen. I remember going down to Cheshunt at the weekend, being driven there, but two nights a week going to White Hart Lane after school. Everything about that stadium meant something. I remember we'd have to take the equipment from the Lane to Cheshunt, up the A10, on a flat-back truck. It wouldn't be allowed now but in those days it was just what you did. For me the stadium was so many things. Yes, it was the ground where the first team played, but it was also, once I'd signed as an apprentice, my practice ground. Where I had to go to work. I remember the balls hanging down on a rope under the West Stand that we had to jump up and head.

'There were a lot of us, young kids, all dreaming of playing for the first team, for Bill Nicholson. Some of us made it. Steve Perryman, Tony Want, me, John Pratt – John and I made our first team debut in the same game, at Arsenal – but also so many others who were "going to be" stars and didn't manage it for some reason. Good kids, just like us. Some played elsewhere, some just drifted out of the game. Each season that passed if you stayed in the apprentices you grew more senior, moved up the pecking order.

'But Steve is right. The Lane was our office. It was where we worked. We'd be there soon after nine a.m., start training at nine forty-five or so, walk out into an empty stadium. There'd just be a few groundsmen and maintenance staff walking around. But you'd get to know every one of them by their first names, nicknames. And you'd see the first-team coaches, people who'd played for the club, recognise what it meant. Not just Bill but Eddie Baily too, Cecil Poynton. They'd played there as well, they understood and knew the history, what the club represented. So to feel part of that history, every day, was fantastic for me, as a local lad, who'd grown up just down the road in Edmonton. And then I was playing for the first team. I remember that first game at the Lane, against Newcastle in 1969. I came out of the tunnel, onto the pitch. Even now, looking back, it's hard to explain to somebody else, to relive that feeling, that moment. But for me it was about the emotion as I walked out of the dressing room, down a few stairs, into the narrow tunnel and then up the stairs into the daylight. It was a dream come true for me.'

But dreams did not come true out of nowhere. Perryman said: 'Tottenham was a down-to-earth place. They didn't give you anything that you didn't earn. It didn't matter where you came from, you all had to work as hard for everything. But it was right, it was fair. I didn't deserve to be treated any differently to any of the other lads. I got into the first team at seventeen. There were lads of twenty-two who were still in the reserves but they were happy that I was getting on. I didn't ever feel any jealousy. It was a proper place, with a good ethic, led by good people.

'People think if you pass the ball that's enough. But it's about moving for the next ball, so your team-mate can play a through ball. If you don't and it goes out of play, that is the sort of thing that really grates. Everybody has to be a player. And it was all backed up by that stadium. I've been there in November when it was getting dark, the last one left inside, taking the rubbish to the far side because I'd done something wrong. That was my punishment. I'd look around me and think: "This place is so alive every Saturday but so dead now." I could still feel the ghosts of the past inside, around me. I felt pride just being there, that drove me on every day. It was just a proper place to work. When I went to any of the other clubs that I might have signed for I didn't feel that.

'I spent nineteen years there but from the first year I felt that special feeling, that sense of it being somewhere that had that effect on me. That dictated that I couldn't have gone to any other club. I wanted to be there. I would've signed for nothing. If you were at Tottenham you were going to be brought up the right way, especially under Bill. He had done it before, he'd won European trophies and knew what to do. For me, White Hart Lane was a place where dreams were made true. And that made the supporters loyal, more loyal than anyone else, the most loyal. When the team isn't winning trophies, they are the most loyal. It was a place where we all came together but it was something that was led from the top, from the manager. When you are at a club like Tottenham they expect you to win all the time, and rightly so. As far as I was concerned it *was* the best club in the country.'

Three decades on, another totemic skipper, albeit of a team that was slowly emerging from the fallow years, Ledley King, spoke equally evocatively of that fierce bond with the supporters, the life-blood of the club, and the game. King said: 'I joined Tottenham as a fourteen-year-old and worked my way through as a player. It's been such an important part of my life. I have an amazing relationship with the fans. They sang my name from the start, even before I'd done anything. And they still do now. I have such appreciation for the fans and the support I had, even when I was injured. They kept me going because I loved that feeling of hearing them.'

And even those who did not grow up and learn their trade with Spurs in their blood came to feel the same instinctive, tribal relationship with that patch of north London earth, the stands that surrounded it, and the passion it engendered Mullery, who remains adamant that his proudest moment, as a boy from Notting Hill, was not marking Pele in the 1970 World Cup but to be part of the 1967 FA Cup-winning team, said: 'Every game we were there to win. And if we didn't win, we were expected to ask ourselves why we hadn't. But it was worth that. I was there, every other week, playing in front of 60,000 people at White Hart Lane, a place that meant so much to so many people. The effort was worth it for that feeling, looking around at all those faces, seeing how desperate they were for us to do well.

'When Spurs came in for me in 1964 it was a life-changer. It was a big move at the time. People might not remember it now given the way the game has moved on and the money that everybody has to spend but I went to Spurs for £72,500, which was a record fee between British clubs at the time. My wages nearly doubled, too. I went up from £20 per week to £38. It might not sound a lot now, I know, but for me, then, that was big bucks.

But the big difference was the attitude. Under Bill it was simple – every week we *had* to win. There was no other choice. If we lost a game, it was terrible. We knew we'd let each other down, Bill down, the fans down. And if we lost to Arsenal, blimey – it was like a morgue for the following week until we went out and won a game again. Fulham were never going to win the league or get to a Cup final – although of course, when I went back, we did get to the Cup final in 1975. Fulham was a club where everybody loved each other. If we won, it was great. But if we lost, there was always another game the next week. But the moment I walked through the door at Spurs it was another world. So, as far as I was concerned, Fulham was fun. But Tottenham was business.'

Yet the business was failing. Slowly, almost imperceptibly for a while, but failing. 'When I joined, the power of the club was known,' Perryman said. 'Good players wanted to sign for Tottenham. When he was leaving Blackburn, Mike England wanted to come to Tottenham. Bill didn't even have to be a great salesman, because of the history and tradition of the club and the aura of the Double side. Spurs didn't just have to go and sign big name players either. It was a club that made players into big names. Pat Jennings and Cyril Knowles were pretty much unknown players when they signed. But the further we moved on from the Double era, the more other clubs were able to catch up in terms of what they could pay and offer you.

'So from Spurs being one of three big clubs, there were now ten or so and that means you're not going to sign as many good players.

'In 1977 we were relegated. We led the club to relegation, which, in truth, had been coming for a few years, when we had a player like Alfie Conn sitting on the ball in that game against Leeds two years earlier, when we won to stay up. You just don't do that. But I could sense that feeling between us and the fans even on the day we were relegated. We lost 5–0 at City and it was not pleasant, horrible. But on the last day of the season we played Leicester at home and won 2–0. The supporters showed what the club meant to them. If we were going to continue playing for them we had to understand that these people felt they deserved to be back in the top division. They deserved better than we'd given them. It's easy to show support when a team is winning but they showed it when we were losing. It was a wonderful place to learn about yourself, too.'

Traipsing around the Second Division, with games at Eastville and Field Mill, at Boothferry Park, Meadow Lane and the Goldstone Ground, was not what Spurs were supposed to be about. And it showed in their inconsistency, putting nine past Bristol Rovers – Colin Lee scored four on his debut – but tasting defeat at Hull and Charlton, and as the pressure really started to tell, losing three out of four from the start of April. Suddenly, one more slip would mean another twelve months of second-class status. 'It was a Wednesday night and we had to win,' Perryman said. 'Hull were already relegated but they promised beforehand that they would make us fight every inch of the way. They did, too. It was a physical, irritable game, miles away from the football we'd played for most of that season. But it was still 0–0, in a game we had to win, with five minutes to go. We were flinging bodies madly into the area, John Duncan clashed with their keeper after a corner and I stabbed home. Hull thought it should have been disallowed for a foul. They might have had a point. But in that atmosphere, it would have taken a brave referee to disallow it.'

Promotion was the platform for Keith Burkinshaw to change the face of the team, his flit to South America rewarded with two pearls, Osvaldo Ardiles and Ricardo Villa. It was to kick-start a new era which brought three trophies, another final, and two other runs deep into European competition. As for the captain, Burkinshaw recognised a kindred spirit: 'For me, Steve was the one who understood the team. We had it all together. He would ring on a Sunday and we'd talk for a couple of hours about how the team had done on the Saturday, the preparations and what we'd do for the following week. We'd talk for ages. He was tremendous for the club. He understood how I looked at football. He was my captain and a big influence over the rest of the players. Everyone looked up to him. He was the best captain I ever came across. I used to say him: "When you are out on the field, if you see something that can improve the team, do it without coming to the sidelines and if it comes off, fantastic." If it didn't I took the blame. That's how we were.'

Among those who followed Perryman over the parapet and into combat was Graham Roberts. Raw-boned, physical, with a style and determination that captivated the supporters. He got them and they, 100 per cent, got him. 'Every time I walked onto that pitch it was different to me, unlike any other stadium,' the former England centre-back said. 'Yes, I played in my way. But when I was wearing a Spurs shirt, waiting to go out and then running out down the tunnel and onto the pitch, I felt that I owed everybody, needed to give them more. I would look around the ground, see The Shelf, the fans in the Paxton Road and Park Lane ends, everybody standing, all creating that unbelievable atmosphere. And I still feel that way now, even though I last played for the club over thirty years ago.

'My first home game for Spurs was against Arsenal. I came on as a substitute in a League Cup tie and the first thing I did was to tackle Kenny Sansom. You might say I let him know I was around! We won that one, 1–0, so it wasn't a bad way to start. I had grown up in Southampton. I'd actually played at White Hart Lane once before, for Portsmouth in an FA Youth Cup tie, which we drew before losing the replay. But I'd barely been there before I met Keith Burkinshaw and he sold the club and his ambitions to me. I was close to going to West Brom, pretty much eighty per cent there, but Keith showed me around the ground, explained what it meant, told me what I could do for him and the club – and it just felt the right place. It was, too. And for me it's been like that ever since, a truly special place.

'I guess the fans identified with me because of the way I approached every game. They could see how much I cared every minute. I always gave everything, a hundred per cent, every match.

'It didn't always come off, of course. One of the worst nights was a League Cup quarter-final against Burnley. We went one up and everybody expected us to cruise it but I ended up scoring two own goals and we lost 4–1. It was horrible. I think anybody else who'd had a night like that would've been crucified but instead – and I still can't really believe it – they clapped me off the park. They forgave me, instantly. When that happens to you, as a player, you only want to give more back, to let the supporters and the club realise you get what it means to them. I think it was because they saw a bit of themselves in me – that if they'd been given the chance I had, they'd have played with exactly that intensity, because of just how much it meant to be playing for Tottenham.

'By 1985 I was the captain. That was the year we should've won the title. In fact, if we'd beaten Everton at home I'm convinced we would've won it. We were supposed to play them in January, when we were absolutely flying, but even when we did play the game in April it came a few weeks after we'd had our first win at Anfield in seventy-odd years. They went ahead after a mistake by Paul Miller, which Andy Gray scored from, then Mark Bowen got caught out by Trevor Steven but we kept going, even though Neville Southall was incredible for them. I finally managed to beat him with a thirty-yarder into the top corner and we really went for it. But Southall was amazing and the save he made from Mark Falco, when Glenn picked him out, was the hardest thing to take. It was a brilliant save from Mark's header and won them the title.

'It still hurts because we should have won the title that year, but instead finished third because we had so many games to play in quick succession. It all caught up with us. I remember towards the end of that season we barely had time to train. It was game, rest, maybe one day a week training and then matches. It felt like we were playing every two days.'

One of Roberts's lieutenants that season, and a future Spurs leader, was Mabbutt, who like the rest of that 1980s team saw White Hart Lane quite literally rebuilt around him. His Bristolian tones have not been softened too much by more than a third of a century's association with north London. Mabbutt said: 'I joined in 1982 just as the West Stand was being completed. Time flies by so fast and it still seems like a modern stadium to me now but the capacity is only 34,000 and that is so small in comparison with the other teams in the Premier League. White Hart Lane will always have a special place in everyone's hearts and I was lucky to play there so many times. I have been associated with the club for a long time now and it has a magic about it.

'Sometimes Spurs fans can take a while to warm to a player but I was fortunate. I was a bargain-basement buy, nobody had heard of me, but I played in the Charity Shield, started against Luton the following Saturday, scored after five minutes and won the fans over. And what amazed me, from the very start, was the fans. Spurs had a first-team squad full of international players, big name players, but suddenly there in the side was Gary Mabbutt from Bristol Rovers, someone whom they'd never heard of in their lives, and they just gave me everything. I got on the end of Glenn's free-kick and headed it in. It was the first league goal of the season, so it meant something, and the bond was made. From that moment until this day my relationship with the Spurs fans has always been special, wonderful. Every time I go back, it's the same.

'People tend to forget that I went to the club as a box-to-box midfielder, a bit like Bryan Robson at United, John Wark and Graeme Souness. My job was to break things up and then be the one joining from deep. That season I was actually the joint top scorer in the league with twelve, level with Steve Archibald. Of course after that I got moved around a bit, although most of my time I was at centre-back. There were a lot of games. Over the years, fighting for a European place, beginning seasons when everybody, the players and the fans, believed we were going to win something. From my first game at White Hart Lane I had those expectations. I always felt there would be a full house and an electric atmosphere.

'People ask me about different memories of being in the ground and it's difficult to pinpoint one or two moments when you were the club captain for eleven years and played there for sixteen seasons. I played six hundred and nineteen games for the club and still go most weeks, so White Hart Lane has been part of my family for thirty-four years. My final game was the last match of the 1997–98 season against Southampton. It was my last game but also Jürgen Klinsmann's. Neither of us played another game. It was time for me to quit given the numerous injury problems I'd been having but the fans were absolutely amazing.

'My name was sung by the whole ground and I couldn't have asked for or expected anything more. It was tough coming off the pitch for that last time, knowing that I was never going to play again, after sixteen years at the club, in front of the fans I'd become so close to over those years and the relationship I had with them. The respect was two ways, from the fans to me but also from me to them, but it was still a hard day for me, knowing that it was the last day in my life I would be on that field as a Tottenham Hotspur player, the captain of the club I'd grown to love. Very, very sad. It's one of the few shirts I've kept.

'To see White Hart Lane suddenly being put in the shadow of the new stadium over the past few months meant it started to dawn that we were in the last handful of games that were going to be played there. The important thing is that the routine will be the same. It literally is a move next door.

'For years fans have walked up the High Road, either from Seven Sisters at one end or White Hart Lane station. So the fans have those memories and always will have. The thing that unites all of us who played there is our own special memories, and it's the same for the fans, who will remember the games they saw, big ones, but also the matches that nobody else will recall but they do because they should have been doing something else, or their child was born that day. Those are the things that are signposts for our lives and that's what the stadium means for people. Everybody who has spent time at the ground is a part of its traditions and history. And before too long, everybody will start to build their own memories of the new stadium too.'

They will, doubtless. Although they will only augment the old memories, not supplant them. That is particularly true for those who played for the club. Roberts still finds it tough to talk about the end of his spell at the Lane. 'The day I was told I wasn't wanted any more was one of the hardest days of my life,' he told me. 'It was December 1986 and David Pleat had taken over as manager. A few months earlier he'd told me I wasn't really wanted any more and that I could find myself another club but I wanted to stay. I wasn't going to just walk away from the club I loved, not like that.

'The following season, despite what he'd said, I was in the team up until December. We were due to play Chelsea in a night game, but he rang the house and told me I wasn't playing and that I'd been sold to Rangers. I've got to be honest, I've never spoken to him since, not once. I have no time for him. I'd been at the club for seven years and for it to end like that wasn't right. I would never have treated him like that if the roles had been reversed.

'A few years later I remember coming back to play against Spurs, for Chelsea. I was captaining them after they'd been promoted back into the First Division. Spurs were a decent side, with Gazza, Steve Sedgley and Gary Mabbutt. We beat them 4–1 and I made the second for Kerry Dixon. But I couldn't celebrate any of the goals, not one of them. I just couldn't do it. Bobby Campbell was our manager and he had a right go at me, told me I should've been setting an example, running around celebrating. But I just said: "I can't do it; not here. This is my home, a club I admired and played for. There is just no way I'm going to celebrate beating them." I left a long time ago, stopped playing twenty-odd years ago, but ever since, every time I go back – and I'm lucky to work at the club on match days now – I feel like I want to be out there again. All the time. On that pitch. Being part of it, what it means.'

Roberts' words demonstrate that he absolutely understands the depth of feeling that Tottenham stirred in the supporters. But one can only imagine what it was like to be part of a family that was involved with the club for more than half a century.

9

BLUE AND WHITE HART . . . LINE

From parent to child and on to the next generation. It is the tale of supporting a club, passed through the family tree. A common bond between people who share strands of the same DNA. Many supporters will talk about their father or mother taking them for the first time, making that journey along the Tottenham High Road. Seeing the stands, or the lights breaking through the scudding clouds, illuminating the teeming rain.

But it is not only supporters who can feel part of that line of family succession. It can also apply to those who pull on the famous white shirt. Les Allen scored the goal against Sheffield Wednesday, on the evening of Monday 17 April 1961, which secured the first leg of the 'impossible' Double, the most important of the 27 he claimed in that remarkable, unprecedented season. Team-mate Terry Dyson, in his autobiography, *Spurs' Unsung Hero*, recalled the key moment in understated terms: 'Danny [Blanchflower] was standing over the ball waiting to take a free-kick and told Maurice [Norman] to move into the penalty area. He found him, Monty [Norman's nickname] headed into Les' path and Les volleyed it in for his 23rd in the league.'

In all, Allen scored 61 goals in 137 appearances over a six-year spell, although he was eased out of the side and his role as Bobby Smith's partner by the arrival of Jimmy Greaves. Yet when Allen moved on, joining QPR and being part of the side which shocked West Brom to win the first Wembley League Cup final in 1967, before later managing the Loftus Road outfit it was merely the close of the first chapter of a remarkable Tottenham family story.

Between Les, his son Clive and his nephew Paul, they amassed 642 appearances for the club, bagging 173 goals, spread over 34 years. And that was not the end of it, either. Clive spent a further six years on the coaching staff, first under David Pleat and eventually working as Harry Redknapp's strikers' coach, while his younger brother Bradley still combines his media duties for BBC Radio London with his role alongside John McDermott in the club's academy set-up. Clive and Paul are still involved as match day lounge hosts.

That makes 58 years and counting. More than merely an engagement with the club, a stay, a spell. For the Allens, Tottenham is their club. Their home. Their place.

Les, nearing his 80th birthday and living in Essex on the fringes of London, does not get along to the Lane too much any more. But his memories of his time there, playing under Bill Nicholson, were the inspiration for his sons and nephew to play their roles in the club's history.

Clive, the astonishing, prolific, 49-goal spearhead of David Pleat's 1986–87 side, said: 'I did think it was my destiny to play at the ground, yes. From an early age. When I was young my dad would take me to games. I remember walking along the High Road with him, going to big matches, with the floodlights already on, and him being stopped by the fans, because they wanted to talk to him about the Double team. They'd talk to him, of course, but then turn to me: "Do you play, son?" I'd always say yes but it would then be: "If you're half as good as your old man, you'll be a player."

'To hear that about your dad is incredible and to grow up as I did, with Spurs supporters saying that to me, just told me I had to be a big Spurs player, that it was something I was meant to do. It built that affiliation with the club and the ground.

'One of the things I remember from those days, growing up,

and as I started to play seriously, was him telling me a few little things about his time at Spurs, under Bill Nicholson, what Bill had said to him and that team, how they had worked and the quality of the players they had.

'So from my early years I was hearing all these things from dad. How he scored four goals in an FA Cup tie and walked into the dressing room feeling pretty pleased with himself, only for Bill to say: "You might think you did well, Allen. But you should've got six!"

'I was really lucky because he could dip into those memories, to tell me the experiences he had been through as part of the best team Spurs have ever had. It was a great education for me. He talked about Dave Mackay, the best player he had ever seen, someone who could do everything. He said how wonderful John White was, talked about the ability and quality of the players in that team, the way they worked and how tough Bill Nicholson was. For him, just having a team of winners was never enough. He wasn't satisfied with that and he let them know it. I heard that from an early age and it made a real impression on me.'

Bradley, ten years Clive's junior, echoed his sibling: 'I think that the message and the meaning of the club from those Glory, Glory nights was passed on for twenty, thirty, forty years. There are people still going to the ground this season who can remember those nights in the sixties and they are passing those memories on to their grandchildren.'

For Paul, who was to play alongside Clive in Pleat's side, the glory was initially even more reflected. 'I suppose for me it started with my dad Ron, who was Les's older brother,' he said. 'When I was a young boy he was always talking about Les and how proud he was of what he had achieved. I was brought up being told about the Double side. So I knew a lot of things about the players, the history they made, what they achieved. And he'd always talk, not just about Les, but also about Dave Mackay, who was his favourite player.

'My first recollection of football and wanting to be a football player, trying to grow up and achieve it, was in 1970. Les was manager of QPR at the time and they played Derby, with Dave Mackay playing for them. My dad took me and that whole experience meant so much.

'I've always had an affiliation with Tottenham because of what Les achieved there. My dad made me aware of that and what he had done in the game. When he became a manager, going to that live game, that was the catalyst for me thinking I could do it. I started eating, drinking and sleeping football.

'Les was quite an unassuming man, even in those days, in terms of what he had achieved. But I still get very proud when I go back to White Hart Lane now and see the photographs of the Double team, the side that won so much and did what people thought was impossible. I think about how massive that was, history created. And I think about what an amazing atmosphere it must have been for Les and the others. It was truly incredible.'

All three of the Allen boys wanted to follow in Les's footsteps. Two succeeded, while the other might have done. Clive, the eldest, had the first chance to make the impression he craved: 'My biggest early memory was when I was fourteen and I'd been selected to play for London Schools against Bristol Schools, at White Hart Lane. Mark Falco was in my team, Gary Mabbutt was playing for Bristol, although he was a year younger than us.

'They hadn't checked before the game and realised just before the start that the team strips clashed, so we ended up wearing the Tottenham youth team kit. It was the biggest night of my life. I was fourteen years old, wearing the Spurs strip, at White Hart Lane – and I scored a hat-trick. That was absolutely fantastic. Mark scored as well and it was an incredible experience. It felt so right, just right. I knew that it was what I was supposed to do for real at some stage. I was at home, playing in the biggest stadium I'd ever played at in my life, scoring three goals and wearing a Spurs shirt. It couldn't get any better than that.'

Actually, it could. Although not before Clive did a tour of the capital. Starting at Loftus Road, he then moved to Arsenal and was famously traded for Crystal Palace left-back Kenny Sansom without playing a competitive game for the Gunners, before returning to QPR. There, he played for Terry Venables against Spurs in the 1982 FA Cup final, although an injury sustained in the original tie meant he missed the replay, settled by Hoddle's early penalty. But in 1984, Spurs, who had seen Keith Burkinshaw quit, suddenly needed a man to lead their line.

'Terry went to Barcelona and took Steve Archibald with him,' Clive said. 'Peter Shreeves had just taken over from Keith Burkinshaw and I got a phone call. I'd been at the club as a schoolboy, training with Peter and I'd known him playing for the QPR youth team. I picked up the phone and he said: "You know where the ground is; I'll see you in the morning." That was the Wednesday night and on the Thursday morning I was at White Hart Lane to sign. There was no need for negotiations. I was going to sign for Spurs. It was where I wanted to be.

'What I found inside the ground when we played was that there was a real buzz. It was absolutely incredible. I'd been at QPR, playing in front of maybe 15,000 or 20,000, and I was used to that, so it felt a huge step up. One thing Peter said was: "No disrespect to QPR Clive, but there you can play [well] one or two times in four matches and they'll be happy with you. Here it's three or four, at least! That's what we're looking for." That stuck with me. We *had* to go out to win. We were Tottenham. It was a different pressure and I loved it, absolutely loved it. I felt at home from that Thursday morning, as I knew I would. It was just right. I scored twice on my debut at Everton, a great way to start.'

Within 12 months, there was not just one Allen in the Spurs squad, but two. Paul had made his name and reputation in 1980, the youngest player – and winner – in Wembley FA Cup final history when West Ham's white, claret and blue ribbons bedecked the famous trophy. He was also robbed of the chance to become the youngest scorer when he was hacked down by Arsenal's former Spurs stopper Willie Young as he bore down on the Wembley goal in the last few minutes.

Paul said: 'I had been to White Hart Lane for games with my dad. I admired Hoddle and Ardiles. I remember going to games with my brother, who wasn't a Spurs fan but used to go with friends from work, and we'd stand on The Shelf. I did that when I was playing at West Ham. I was there for the Feyenoord game, when Glenn just destroyed them, including Cruyff. He was just magnificent. I saw a few games that season.

'My first game at Tottenham and first experience of playing there was when I was sixteen. I'd done reasonably well in the youth side at West Ham and for whatever reason – I guess there had been some injuries and they wanted to reward me for what I'd done in my first season – they included me in the squad for Steve Perryman's testimonial. As soon as I turned up at the ground I realised it was something special, the history of the ground, the fans, everything. I remember coming out from the right-hand side of the old stand, up the stairs and through the narrow tunnel. They had signed Ardiles and Villa the year before and I looked around and thought: "This ground is amazing; it's something special." I managed to get on as a sub for ten minutes, my first involvement in professional football, as a first-year apprentice, a taste of first-team football. And the following season I played there in the FA Youth Cup.

'So when I had the chance to go there, with Les's history, I knew it would be something special. I wouldn't say I thought it was my destiny, not like Clive. But when I had the chance I was always going to take it.

'I walked in from the car park and thought: "This is where I want to play my football." I didn't question it for a second. I walked in and met Irving Scholar. The players weren't there because they were in Australia, but I was sold on the place from the instant I walked in. I saw the bust of Bill Nicholson, everything about the club. I wanted to be part of it. The chance to play with Clive was an incentive as well. We'd never played with each other before, so that was something I wanted to do. I arrived in 1985, for £400,000, and although we finished that season quite well, David Pleat came in.'

The rest is writ large in Tottenham history. For Bradley, on Spurs' books as a schoolboy but who forged his career at QPR, Charlton and Grimsby, scoring twice in eight appearances for the England under-21 side, it was a glittering, illusory glimpse of what might have been for himself, too: 'My first game at White Hart Lane was for Havering versus West London Schools. They had Frank Sinclair and Eddie Newton. We played the first game at Craven Cottage and the return at the Lane, the first time I'd played on the pitch.

'I don't think I played there again until I went back with QPR in the early nineties. But I remember going to watch Clive play when I was seven or so. It was strange to be going to matches and seeing your brother playing. I had followed him around. He had more clubs than Jack Nicklaus. I remember him scoring a hat-trick for QPR at Birmingham on his debut. I saw him at Palace, two spells at QPR, then Spurs. I would go to watch Clive when he started there and was there when he had that great season, scoring forty-nine goals. I remember some classic games in that season at White Hart Lane. That was probably one of the best Tottenham teams in terms of the style of football they played. They were put together by David Pleat and should've won something because it was a team with some fantastic players, with Clive being clinical up front. For me, in my childhood, watching that was an inspiration. You felt a sense of occasion. And I still feel that now.'

Clive's goals, 33 in the First Division, 12 more in the League Cup, 4 in the FA Cup, adding up to his remarkable tally from 54 appearances, won him nothing except the twin accolades of being named PFA Player of the Year and Footballer of the Year by the

Football Writers' Association. But it was his role as the cutting edge of a tactical formation which ripped up the status quo that Spurs fans still discuss in awestruck tones.

In fact, as Pleat admitted to me, it was not his intention to play with a five-man midfield and a lone frontman. He had begun the season playing an orthodox two strikers, with Tony Galvin, so often Hoddle's out-ball, operating on the left flank. And he had also been considering a heretical decision.

'If I'm honest, a hundred per cent honest, I had thought about the system,' Pleat said. 'But I actually stumbled onto it. Galvin got injured. Then Graham Roberts left the club. And with Ossie Ardiles, I was wondering and thinking that maybe it was time for me to move him on, that he'd had his time at the club and he didn't have a part to play. To give credit to Irving Scholar, he said to me: "Have a look at it first." I did and could see what I'd missed before, that we could use Ossie as the link man. He was perfect in that role, nicking the ball, laying it off. Paul Allen was my ferret in the middle. Waddle was the brilliant wide man. He wanted to play in Hoddle's position and I had to persuade him that we had to let Hoddle play there. We played Villa at home in the January, smashed them 3–0 again – they were a poor side that season – and after the game Waddle came up to me and said: "I'm not enjoying this." I tried to explain to him what was happening, that, yes, he was playing out wide, but that he was playing brilliantly, the team was too, and that the football and what we were trying to do meant it was working. He lived with it and then Hoddle got his wish to go to Monaco – although only after he broke an agreement to go to PSG under Gérard Houllier – and so I wanted Waddle to play in the middle the next season. And of course it was a great season, no question, with the system, the five midfielders supporting Clive. I thought our football was mesmeric.'

Mesmeric and effective. Although not without a hiccup at the very outset, at Oxford United's homely, tight, almost square Manor Ground – now the site of a private hospital – on 22 November

1986, where I stood as one of the visiting fans on the exposed Cuckoo Lane terrace.

Clive said: 'On the Friday morning, the day before the game, David called us together and said: "This is the way we're going to play. Any objections?" Ray Clemence piped up and told him: "We tried that at Liverpool and it didn't work." But David was adamant. "It's what we're going to do. And whatever happens, win, lose or draw, I will take responsibility. This is the way I want to move forward, because I think it will work."

'After twenty minutes we were a goal down. David Leworthy, who had come through the Spurs system but had been sold to Oxford, scored for them. We looked across at the dug-out, waiting for David to change it, because it didn't seem to be working. But he didn't react at all, showing us he believed in his ideas. I scored one and Chris another before half-time, and we each got one in the second half as well. We won 4–2 and never looked back.

'We went on an incredible run – fourteen wins in nineteen and just three defeats. It was amazing, absolutely amazing, but it was a system that suited the individuals we had. Having the extra man in midfield took all the defensive responsibility away from Hodd.

'People looked at what we were doing and didn't believe it was going to work. They looked at me playing on my own up front, Chris on the right but joining in, Paul in the middle, Glenn playing free. But it was just perfect for us. Glenn was never a real midfielder and that system allowed him to play as what they call a "false nine" when it's Leo Messi doing it now.

'The best game, for me, was West Ham on the Boxing Day morning. Steve Hodge came in from Villa to make his debut. We just ripped them apart. It finished 4–0 but it could've been eight or ten. We played the best football of the entire season that day. I still remember it vividly. The memories are so sharp and fresh. We had some fantastic days.'

From the right side of midfield, Paul, now employed by the PFA, was one of the grafters among the craftsmen. Not that he cared. 'In terms of the football we played, that was the highlight of my career. The only sadness was that we had nothing to show for it.

'It was football in the real Tottenham tradition. We were entertaining, open, expansive. We thought we had it all. If you look at that team – Ray Clemence in goal, Richard Gough and Gary Mabbutt, the five of us in midfield, plus Tony Galvin, Chris Hughton, and Clive scoring so many – it was a really fantastic side. Not only the way we played but the amount of goals we scored, well over a hundred. I remember we smashed United 4–0, beat Liverpool home and away, beat Everton, who ended up as champions, 2–0 at home, with Clive scoring both goals. We beat West Ham 4–0 in the league and then 5–0 in the League Cup. There was a great atmosphere within the group. We felt we could go out and win every game. We were that confident and so creative, while Clive was just a magnificent goalscorer. The balance and blend in the side was just great.

'But the sadness was that we didn't do what we should have done. Chris Waddle was ready to take over from Glenn even when Glenn went to Monaco and I felt what we were developing. If we could have kept that group together a bit longer, we could have achieved so much, won so much. But Glenn left, and over the next few years Chris and Clive did too and we went into a transitional period for a while. But on the pitch, being part of that team was the most exciting and rewarding season of my career as a player, even if we won the Cup in 1991 to make amends for what happened against Coventry.'

Clive moved to Bordeaux, sacrificed, as Venables, now back in the country and installed as Pleat's successor, attempted to land Gary Lineker, but Paul played 370 games over eight years before leaving for Southampton in 1993.

It was in the ten years before the Lane was knocked down, though, that all three Allens returned to the fold. Clive was the first: 'I quit in the mid nineties and was working as a pundit in the media and working with the England youth teams, coaching them. But Pleaty brought me back to the club. Glenn had left and David knew I wanted to coach. He said: "I know you want to coach, so come and join us. There's only one way to find out if it'll work and we'll see where it leads us." He asked me back to take charge of the reserves, and I did that until Harry Redknapp came in and he promoted me to the first team.

'For me that was a great natural progression because I had insight into the young players after working with them for the previous three years. I was there for six years on the staff and in that time I think it's fair to say the bond between the fans and the club began to be cemented back into place. They'd had a hard few years but suddenly started to have something exciting again. Harry gave them that fast, attacking, adventurous football, the sort of football Spurs fans have grown up to expect and want from their club.

'We had the players who could play that way. The best night I experienced was Inter Milan in the Champions League. The atmosphere was awesome, incredible and the performance was as well. Luka Modrić ran the game in midfield, Gareth Bale was sensational. It was just a pleasure to be there and be part of it, because we had some fantastic players all over the park. I loved working with Rafael van der Vaart. He was a magician and I had a rapport with him. He was so good at scoring in the big games. Luka was always something special – as he's shown at Real Madrid since he moved there – and Gareth was one of those talents you get once in a decade, if not once in a century. He had so much natural ability, pace and strength. He was just a boy when he joined the club, a level behind, but he became a real man, developed into a great, great player. I thoroughly enjoyed every minute of that night. It was an experience you could never forget or want to. It all gelled together and they showed the ability they had, playing at the top of their games, at the highest level.'

Bradley was also at the ground that night, only some 15 yards or so behind his brother, in the commentary booth. 'You don't get that vantage point at any other London stadium,' he agreed. 'You are so close to the pitch, the benches and the technical areas that you can really see what is going on and observe the managers and coaches, what they are trying to do tactically, close-up. You also notice what you can't see on television, the camber of the pitch.

'Harry's team, which was built around Modrić and Bale, was a special team, maybe the best eleven I've seen at Spurs. I was in Milan and saw Gareth's hat-trick there, so I knew what he was capable of. With some players who are going to make it at the highest level, there is that moment when everyone sees what is there. With that performance you just knew that it had come for Gareth. He was unplayable that night. The atmosphere was electric – it was truly brilliant. To see them pull the defending champions apart like that was very special.'

Each of the Allens felt sad about the end of the Lane. And also a sense of rising excitement at what was to come next. Clive said: 'I wanted to make sure my grandson, who is three, could come to his first game before the end of the season so that he is able to say, in the years to come when he's older and grown up, that he went to White Hart Lane, the old stadium, and saw a game there, before it became the Super Stadium. I think it's that important for everybody.

'To see it all come to an end at the Lane will be tinged with sadness for me. I was there for ten years in total, as a player first and then on the coaching staff. That's a long time. I got to know the little things about the stadium over the years and it's sad that those things have gone.

'But what I do like about the new stadium is the way it is being built now, surrounding White Hart Lane. I look at what I see going up so close by and think the ground is just sucking the Lane into the new arena. So because of that, because it is just, literally, next door – or even part of the same site, not even quite next door – I don't think the spirit will be destroyed. I keep telling myself that and I believe it's right. The new ground is progression, not the end. Just the next stage. That's how I feel about it.

'I didn't expect to shed any tears. But at the same time it has been my life. It is the stadium I've known since I was a kid, the one I grew up with, where I was a fan, where I played and then where I went back as a spectator again, working in the press box or as part of the match day staff in the boxes and lounges. So there was a sadness, of course. But at the same time there is the excitement about it because I know the club is moving forward and going in the right direction. The mood is better in the ground, now, this season, than it has been for a long time. What's even harder to believe is that they don't even give the left-back stick any more, and they always used to do that!

'And what we're seeing, what is making that more the case, is that the fans can see the work the club is putting in to develop their own young players. It's what they've always wanted to see again, because it's what the club was always about. But they think that the next stage will mean Spurs don't have to be a selling club, which they had become over the years. The future is fantastic and the fans are making themselves part of that. They've become a big part of what the club is doing.'

Bradley, rightly proud of his impact on the developing talents of Harry Kane, Josh Onomah, Cameron Carter-Vickers and Harry Winks – 'both Harrys are humble kids who have been well-educated and are grounded in what the club means' – as well as Ryan Mason and Andros Townsend, agreed the foundations were already in place: 'The chairman wants Tottenham to be a club that does everything properly, to retain the links with the past and the historical days, the great period with that great team. Even this season, when the corner between the East Stand and the Paxton Road end has gone for the building work, the atmosphere has still been amazing. It has been great.'

And Paul, too, felt that sense of family. Not just from a personal point of view, but among those who flocked to the Lane throughout the last, eventful campaign. He even thought they had become more supportive, less . . . well, less old Spurs: 'In terms of the fans and them being critical, I'm not so sure it's too different from any other club. Expectations were high, yes. But I always felt they were a very knowledgeable crowd. And I also felt that, particularly in the really big games, they were a real strength to us as a team. Yes, they were very, very passionate. But knowledgeable too.

'They did show their disappointment at times but so did we as a team and as players. I still felt they were very loyal to us, home and away, they just wanted us to do well and would do everything they could to help us.

'I've been back working at the club on match days for a few years now so I have mixed emotions. The first thing, for me, is that it is fantastic the club are going to stay in the same location. This is the site where all my memories are, as a player and a fan, so even if the ground is moving and changing completely, it's still, basically, in the same place.

'It's sad because this ground, these stands, this pitch, are where I've got so many fantastic memories. But most of us realise that we need to progress as a club. With what the club is achieving it is a great time to be a Spurs fan, on and off the pitch. From a personal point of view I'm really excited. Every time I come to the ground I look over and the new stadium has grown, developing more and more. And I think about what the future holds for Spurs, because I want the club to do well, and the move will help the club achieve that.

'When I look at the team and the club now, I see something special building. We've had some great times over the years and I've been going as a fan for ten years now. In that spell we've had some great sides and great moments but in the last couple of years, with so many young players coming through and developing, it has been great to watch.

'We sometimes take Harry Kane a little for granted because

he's scored so many goals but we forget he's still a young man. I love the humility Harry shows, on and off the pitch. He is so driven and I know he cares about the club. And I love watching this team, the athleticism and power, the work-rate on and off the ball. I know I'm biased, of course but most neutrals enjoy watching them at the moment and I see the camaraderie, that they want to play for each other, the potential in the group, with the next generation already coming through in players like Harry Winks. I'm really excited about the future.'

He is not the only one. And it would not be a shock if there was another Allen along in a few years to keep this remarkable family affair going.

10

THE ENTERTAINERS

Some players are born to play for certain clubs. They are a natural fit. A fish in water. And at White Hart Lane there was always a craving for a special kind of player, the type of talent who would, as they say, put bums on seats – and make them stand up at regular intervals. Rival supporters might have mocked our pretensions. They often did. For a decade or more, talk of Spurs being about more than just a football team, an idea, was justifiably the stuff to provoke derision when they went most of the first decade and a half of the Premier League era finishing between ninth and fourteenth.

But there is no doubt that Tottenham supporters love those players who can do what they themselves could barely imagine, and make it look as effortless as hanging up their coat when they got in from work.

English football has produced many mavericks and free spirits. Those from abroad have been welcomed too. Yet arguably, some would suggest unquestionably, nowhere has embraced the concept of individuality – sometimes to the cost of the team – more than White Hart Lane.

That was why Danny Blanchflower's talk of 'Glory' had so much resonance. He was not creating something new, merely giving order and structure, in words, to a concept that was already built into the DNA of the club and its supporters, a lust and desire for that extra excitement which the most gifted can bring, the ability to make every supporter shake their head, not in despair, but in joyous disbelief.

Nicholson brought in Greaves, not only the greatest scorer in Tottenham's history – and whose European top-flight scoring record was only broken by Cristiano Ronaldo in 2017 – but also a player whose quality would make even rival fans swoon. There were more than 30,000 at Home Park, Plymouth, to see his first outing in a Spurs shirt, in a *reserve* match, in 1961. The headline on Ian Wooldridge's match report in the *Daily Mail* was 'YES, IT WAS REALLY HIM'. The peerless Wooldridge, with whom I had the pleasure of sharing the odd glass of gin and tonic during my fledgling days on the *Mail* in Derry Street, described Greaves as 'the Unregistered Prodigal' and wrote that 'Twenty-three cameramen crouched, four newsreels rolled, 12,907 necks craned' to see Greaves score twice in a 4–1 win. Clement Freud, later to become a Liberal MP and television personality, was sent to the South-West for the *Observer* while in the *Express* Clive Toye suggested: 'It might have been a visit from minor royalty. Or Marilyn Monroe. Or Krushchev. But it was not. It was Jimmy Greaves back in English football.'

Nicholson also signed Alan Gilzean, another showman, who formed deadly partnerships with both Greaves and Martin Chivers. And so the bond between the White Hart Lane fans and the stars they adored continued down the years: Hoddle and Ardiles; Gascoigne and Waddle; Klinsmann – a signal of intent in his first season, as he represented Alan Sugar's determination to turn Spurs back into a force, but of desperation in his second incarnation, as the relegation rocks loomed large, but delivering with quality and endeavour on both occasions; Ginola; and Gareth Bale. And in the final couple of seasons at White Hart Lane, with the torch being carried by a new generation in Dele Alli and Christian Eriksen, as well as the home-grown scoring prowess of Harry Kane, that sense of destiny, of romance, was rekindled, brighter and more intense than for many years.

It is a conveyor belt running across 70 years or more. For many, it started with a player who is often overlooked, Tommy 'The Charmer' Harmer. A player who made his debut the season after Rowe's 'push and run' side won Spurs' first title, and who was sacrificed when his old team-mate Nicholson recognised he needed the different talents of John White to help complete the jigsaw puzzle which was to bring the club's greatest success.

The peerless Brian Glanville, in his elegant obituary of Harmer shortly after his death on Christmas Day 2007, at the age of 79, suggested he 'would doubtless be described today as a cult figure; a very special footballer, even a maverick, a triumph of mind over matter and skill over strength'. If ever there was a description to sum up what Spurs fans want to see, it was in those words from one of the masters of football writing. Even if Brian is an Arsenal fan, a 'Gooner'.

And for me, and those who started to watch Tottenham in the 1970s, there is nobody who encapsulates that vision more than Glenn Hoddle. Football fans always want to have a playmaker who can destroy the opposition. But amid the fury and chaos, where some are merely geometry teachers, Hoddle was a nuclear physicist. Forget splitting defences with a ball. You felt he could have split the atom.

Hoddle was everything a Spurs player should be. Languid and with utter panache, capable of mesmerising feats, a scorer of brilliant, breathtaking goals, a passer unsurpassed. And Tottenham through and through, with every essence of his body. Born into the club. Nurtured by the club. And running it too, both on and off the pitch.

For Hoddle, Tottenham and White Hart Lane represented more than fate. It was, as he confesses, his 'destiny' and one he embraced with an understanding, an innate consciousness, of what the club means and stands for.

'The style of football Tottenham played was made for me and I was made for Tottenham,' Hoddle said. 'Over the history of the club, before and since I played, the club wanted players coming through who were Spurs lads and that made it more special. A lot of people want to go and be entertained. I always had a fabulous relationship with the fans. I was a player they wanted to come and watch, and it was a pleasure for me to play for this club because it has always been a technical club. The fans want players who can do things that are out of the ordinary and make a difference. That's the style of player they have always loved, from John White and Danny Blanchflower, even before that, right through to now.'

Growing up on a Harlow council estate, deep in the heart of Spurs territory, the meaning of the club was brought home to the young Hoddle by his father Derek. Hoddle said: 'I was a Spurs fan from the age of eight, when I first came to watch a reserve game against Leicester, under floodlights. I was a fan from then onwards. Apart from my family and kids, it means everything. It's been in my DNA since that first game. That was the first time I'd been to the stadium, and seeing that green grass, under the lights, that was it. I was a Spurs fan from then on and regularly went to the games. If you're lucky enough to go out and play for the youth team or reserve side at White Hart Lane, that's special. But it's even more special to run out as part of the first team. That was a very proud moment for me and my family.'

By the age of 11, Hoddle had been placed on the club radar by Chivers: 'Roy Evans and myself were invited to go along and present a trophy in April 1974 to Harlow Junior Boys. One young lad ran the show – he was a joy to watch. I went back and raved about this young lad I'd seen that Sunday. He was aware of space and of people coming at him because he had the ball.'

Those talents were to grow. Hoddle said: 'I used to go to Spurs from Harlow as a twelve year old to train and get back at ten p.m. You wouldn't get that happening today. I grew up quickly doing that, I tell you, but I had that love for the club. I wanted to be a footballer. I joined the staff and even then I was as passionate as any Spurs fan could be. I felt that this ground was my home. I had to look after it. That was my job. So I had to clean the dressing room and the boot room.

'One day Gary Hines and I were told by Johnny Wallis we had to clean the cockerel. We looked at him and I said: "Yeah, all right – you're having a laugh aren't you?" And he just said: "No, there's the polish." We had to go back over, behind The Shelf. There was a ladder we had to go up, onto the roof, and polish the cockerel. You wouldn't dream of it these days with all the health-and-safety stuff. It was a beautiful, glorious summer's day. It should've taken us an hour but we came back six hours later, red as beet-root because we'd been up there in the sun . . . but we polished that cockerel and were proud to do it. It was one of those things that stayed with me every game I played there. I'd run out down the tunnel and on to the pitch and every time I'd go out for the warm-up I'd look up at the cockerel and think about that day I'd had to go up and polish it. That kept my feet on the ground.'

While Spurs were suffering in the aftermath of Nicholson's exit from the manager's office, Hoddle was being readied to be unleashed upon the game. He had made an appearance off the bench in a 2–2 home draw with Norwich at the start of the 1975–76 season. 'For my first game at White Hart Lane the pitch suddenly looked so much smaller,' Hoddle said. 'It was because I'd been playing there in the youth team and the reserves, when there was a very sparse crowd. I couldn't believe it when I got out there with 40,000 people. It just looked so much smaller than normal. It was incredible.'

Few outside those at the Lane that day were aware of the young-ster. That changed on 21 February 1976 at the Victoria Ground, Stoke. Jimmy Greenhoff put the home side ahead before John Duncan diverted Jimmy Neighbour's cross home to level. And in a perfect start to what was to be a Tottenham career full of memorable moments, the first of a series of long-range stunners. 'Martin Chivers was a hero of mine as a kid coming through, and players like John Pratt had coached me as an eleven or twelve year old, so for me to be playing with them, for the first team, was sensational,' said Hoddle. 'As the ball came out to me I remember Pratty saying: "Hit it Hod." It was on my left foot and I just struck it. It flew off my foot beautifully and went past Peter Shilton. It was like it was a dream. I thought: "This isn't happening" and then suddenly Martin was giving me a cuddle because I'd scored. That was something special.' Less special was Hoddle's nervy post-match interview with ITV commentator Hugh Johns. Floppy-haired, with a shirt lapel wide enough to park a small car on, the 17-year-old midfielder mumbled: 'I was pleased with the goal and the performance, until the last ten minutes when I gave a few balls away.'

More than 40 years later, Chivers said: 'Of course I went over and jumped on him. I knew it would be the first of many.'

Hoddle knew he had to prove himself all the time, especially in the mid 1970s when English football, frequently played on bottomless pitches, energy-sapping quagmires which seemed designed to level things up for the cloggers, was all about physicality and brutal tackles. Hoddle said: 'I was very shy as a kid and wasn't that loudly spoken. I was told I had to become more arrogant. A few games later Martin [Chivers] said: "You're going to get yourself to the level that's near the top. I can see it." Getting there is one thing. The hardest thing is to stay there.

'I forced myself to be as perfect as I could be on my left and right foot. That's what I had to do. It was about doing that work. What you put in, you get out. Football for a while wasn't my game. It was playing in the air, all 4-4-2 and lamping the ball. You didn't have time to pull it down. It was a different game to modern football. I had to show character, that I could cope.'

He had to cope with adversity, too. In his first full season as a first-teamer, Hoddle started 39 of Tottenham's 42 First Division games. But the team under Keith Burkinshaw was simply not good enough and finished bottom of the league, relegated for the first – and only – time since 1935. 'The year we went down hurt, a lot,' he recalled. 'I remember we lost 5–0 at Maine Road and I was in tears. It was my club, we were part of a team that had taken them down and that really hurt. So I learned the hard way. And the success we had meant ten times as much because of what I'd experienced getting relegated first.'

From early on, Hoddle was clearly cut from a different cloth, but the sniping was to continue throughout his career. That he only won 53 England caps looks even more of a waste of his talents now than it did three decades ago. 'To say I was a luxury player was garbage,' he argues, powerfully. 'I believe the real "luxury player" is the one who keeps giving the ball away and doesn't use it. I smile about it now and it made me laugh when people called me lazy. But it was just the way it was. People talk about character, but what is character? Is it tearing around at a hundred miles an hour? It makes me laugh.'

Steve Perryman, Hoddle's first Spurs skipper, agreed: 'The game wasn't conducive to his style. It was a very aggressive game in those days but Glenn just drove through it with his confidence. He just moved through it.'

Not that it was just outsiders who questioned Hoddle's application. Peter Shreeves, Burkinshaw's No. 2, remembers the criticism inside the camp, too. He said: 'You could see Glenn putting backspin on the ball on a concrete floor. When we signed Archibald and Crooks, he said: "When I get the ball, don't worry about controlling it because I'll do that for you." He used to play it a yard in front of them and it would come back to them. They couldn't believe it and had never seen anything like it. Glenn was extraordinary but the others would say: "He's a lazy bastard that Hoddle, Pete." And I'd say: "You get bonuses for wins, don't you? So keep giving him the ball." He had to fight against that all his career. He never got the caps he should have done because of that.'

Promotion after one season in the Second Division came with Hoddle, now the heartbeat of Burkinshaw's team, contributing 12 goals. And the summer of 1978 brought a step-change with the arrival of Ardiles and Villa, who saw in Hoddle a kindred spirit. Ardiles said: 'Glenn was always a god at Spurs. In fact, Glenn *was* God. He was Maradona without pace, an incredible talent. Ricky and I had a South American way of playing. So did Glenn. I felt Glenn was the one speaking the same language as us. He was the most gifted English footballer I played with, the greatest passer of a ball, a magnificent talent who could win a game just like that.'

Ardiles was a close-hand observer of many of Hoddle's finest moments, goals of consummate quality. The former England manager said: 'I wasn't a great goalscorer. But I scored some great goals, which people remember. The volley against Manchester United was my personal favourite. I played a one-two and before I knew it I was in the air and volleyed it home. There was another against Forest in the same season when the ball never touched the ground from the keeper and then Chris Jones' header. And the chip at Watford . . .'

There were plenty of others. Drilled in with either foot. Placed with precision. Deftly converted as he made his runs late. Burkinshaw saw the mixture of Hoddle's vision and Ardiles's energy as being central to his plans. 'We'd go to places where it was difficult to play the football we wanted to play – along the deck and with good movement. It wasn't always possible because some of the pitches were mud-heaps. The team was built around Ossie and Glenn. I wanted to see intelligent passing, intelligent movement, trying to play the football that I knew the spectators wanted to see. Glenn was usually our best player. Glenn was the best technical player I came across. One of my biggest disappointments was that England never really gave him the credit he was due. I think they should have picked the team around him. He was such a gifted player and fantastic for us.'

Under the manager's guiding hand, things were changing. Spurs were about to enter an era only bettered by Nicholson's Double-winning side. Looking back, Hoddle said: 'Keith took the club down, but they saw something in him. Maybe they would've sacked him if we'd not come straight back up, but we did, and then Ossie and Ricky were signed.

'I remember all the ticker tape before the Villa game. Maybe everyone thought the ticker tape was enough to win the game, like it had helped Argentina in the World Cup. But we lost 4–1 instead. We had the midfield but it wasn't until Keith went out and bought Steve Archibald and Garth Crooks, with Mark Falco there as well, that we had the strikers we needed. Mark was a terrific goalscorer who could come on and make the difference, affect the game and in big games, but who didn't have the consistency to do it every game. But then we had the whole jigsaw. We had the creativity and style we wanted to play and we were able to progress.

'It was a wonderful time. To win things, yes. But it was also the way we played. We looked forward to playing. I knew I had good players around me and I thought we were going to win every time we went on the pitch. And we had that for a few years. Keith didn't have much skill when we played the eight-a-sides. When he joined in, we took the piss out of him. But what he couldn't achieve as a player, he wanted his team to do on the pitch. He wanted us to express ourselves and play that way. He wouldn't change his philosophy about how to play. There was balance in the squad. Irving Scholar tried to change things off the pitch but he fell out with Keith and Keith left the club. Who knows what could've happened if he'd stayed.'

Who knows indeed. Instead, Hoddle's final three years as a Spurs player were about near-misses. Two third-place finishes, the last eight of the Uefa Cup before the Heysel disaster saw English sides banned, a League Cup semi-final replay defeat to Arsenal, having never trailed at any stage over the three games until extra time, before losing the 1987 FA Cup final in his last Tottenham appearance. There was also a farewell goal to savour at the end of that season, in a 3–1 home win over Oxford: 'If you wrote a story, starting with my joining the club at eleven and then in my last game scoring with a goal like that, getting the ball on the halfway line, dribbling through their whole defence, taking it round the keeper and sticking the ball in the back of the net, it was just perfect. It was the way I could say: "I'm going to Monaco but this is for you." You couldn't have written it any better than that.'

Actually, contrary to Hoddle's own recollections, that was *not* his final game at the Lane. He has forgotten the 4–0 win over Manchester United played on the Bank Holiday Monday afternoon nine days later, one of two more league matches he played in before the end of the season. He could not forget that Wembley date with Coventry, though. 'The Cup final was my last game for the club and it was a really hard one for me to swallow. For it to end like that was terrible, the worst feeling I had in football.

'I'd have loved to have won more. But there are a lot of players who had trophies coming out of their ears, but would people talk to them about their careers?

'The way I played football, I affected people. I wanted to emulate Bobby Charlton and George Best, and people saw something in me that made them want to play football and want to support a club. That's as important to me as any medal. If you can do something people think is special, that they admire and remember thirty years later, that's as good as winning any medal.'

By that final season, Hoddle had been joined by another player who represented the essential style of Tottenham. Unlike Hoddle, Chris Waddle grew up wanting to wear the black-and-white stripes of Newcastle. He was, however, another genuine working-class hero, hewn from Tyneside's coalfields, who picked up a few bob in a sausage factory while making his initial steps at Tow Law Town before breaking into the first team under Arthur Cox at Newcastle. It was there that he first appeared on Tottenham's radar. Still a man who loves to discuss football, Waddle said: 'I grew up in Gateshead and had five years at Newcastle where my career developed. When it came time for me to leave, and I knew it was going to happen, Tottenham was where I wanted to go. It was a club I had always admired because they were about entertainment, and that was my game, too.

'As a player I just wanted to entertain, so I believed it was going to be a good fit for me, especially when I looked at the players who were there, Glenn and Ossie in particular. I thought I could play with them, could see myself playing with those players. It looked like a team that played my style of football, so when I knew I was leaving that all came into my mind.

'I think I'd made an impact the previous season. We went to White Hart Lane and lost 3–1 and people remember we played in that silver-grey away strip that season. I scored our goal, even though we lost, but it was a game where I had played well, and I was later told they'd had a look at me that day and decided they wanted me if I was ever available.

'There were other teams who were interested but Tottenham came in heavy and it was where I wanted to go, even though it was a massive change for me from living up in the North-East. But it was where I wanted to be and the football reasons made it quite an easy decision for me. Going to Spurs was a different level for me, too. I knew it was a step up. I had to get used to London but I couldn't have asked for a better club, a great club.'

It took a while for Waddle to convince the Spurs fans that he was worth the wait. 'The first six or seven months I didn't enjoy so much. It was hard for me to settle in London, a big change, and I needed to meet some friends and find places to go, so getting used to a new life was hard.

'I couldn't help but learn from playing with Glenn, Ossie and Steve Perryman and it was great to pick up that experience and knowledge, something I'd never previously had. It was the perfect place for me to develop my game. Peter Shreeves signed me but the results were a bit mixed and Pleaty, who had done so well at Luton, got the job. I think he always wanted to go to Tottenham and he had the players he wanted to work with, players who were ideal for the club.

'When we switched to the 4-5-1 it was about finding a way to get the best out of the players we had. If you look at the Premier League now, most teams play with just the one striker but at the time it was a shock. I remember we did it for the first time at Oxford, when we won 4–2, and people were reacting "Wow!" and asking what had happened to the game of football. But it made sense for us to do that with the players we had.

'If you have good players you can learn from them – I learned a lot – and you can play any system. Playing that way suited Glenn, because it gave him a free role, he could go where he wanted to go. I started on the right but had the flexibility to go inside and Clive Allen was just absolutely deadly in the box. But it was for the other players as well. We started that season with Tony Galvin on the left but brought in Steve Hodge, Paul Allen would go box to box all game, Ossie was so clever, he had the guile and craft to find the passes nine out of ten times if you made the right runs, while Richard Gough and Gary Mabbutt were terrific at centre-back. So there was a great balance in the side.

'The question David had to answer was "How do we get the best out of these players?" and the only way, which he recognised, was to play with one striker up front. It worked. Glenn was in the hole, free to do what he wanted and because he was such an intelligent player other teams found it hard to pick him up. And if they did, it meant I'd be able to go free and into the spaces, then Ossie with his little through-passes would find me. Teams had to come up with a way of stopping us and we would go onto the pitch expecting to score a few goals. The centre-backs were excellent, Ray Clemence was a top-class keeper, but I guess the weakness was at full-back.

'Even so, I still feel it was the volume of games that killed us, more than anything else. That team should have won a couple of trophies. It's a huge shame we didn't win anything but I put it down to playing too many games in too many competitions. We finished third, lost in the League Cup semi-final replay and got to

Wembley in the FA Cup and if we'd focused on one or two of them I'm sure we'd have won something. But by the end we ran out of legs a bit. I'm not going to take anything away from Coventry. That was their day but all the games took their toll. It was really difficult for us.

'When I go back to White Hart Lane the first thing people talk about, straight away, is the '87 team. If you think about it, that was a team that didn't win anything, and there have been plenty of Spurs teams that did. But that is the team they want to talk about.

'What they say, looking back now, is: "We're not bothered about the fact you didn't win a trophy; the football was worth the admission money. In fact, we'd pay double the price to watch football like that again." But that sums up what Spurs means and what White Hart Lane has always been about. We pleased lots of people and for me that's the biggest compliment you can get as a player – that you made the people, the fans, the supporters, excited. That's the Tottenham way. Being part of a team that played in that tradition, a team that played the Tottenham way, makes me feel warm still.'

Not that the fans were always so complimentary, even when the team *was* winning. Waddle said: 'It's fair to say the home fans could be a little bit impatient, to say the least. I remember that all right. But they knew what they wanted.

'I remember the last home game of the 1986–87 season, when we played United and were 4–0 up. The game was won and we played a bit of keep-ball. Normally you'd expect the "olés" for that, when you're just proving you're in total control, but we got slow hand-clapped for doing it. It just struck me what the fans wanted, expected – it was about entertainment, all the time. In some ways, Newcastle was similar. The fans there would take 5–4 every week and I think Spurs fans have the same outlook. They want to be excited, entertained.

'The expectations were always high because of the history of the club, but it wasn't just about winning. It was about winning the right way, by playing the sort of football they could talk about in the pubs and when they got home. Of course they demanded the players gave everything, the old "110 per cent". But what they really wanted was to see them doing it with a swagger, with a bit of style.

'One of the things that really surprised me when I joined the club was just how much other teams and their fans were so desperate to beat us. It seemed that it meant that bit more to all of them to beat Tottenham. Maybe they felt we were a bit flash, a bit too cocky. I don't know. But it was the same everywhere in the country, and especially in London. Every game was like that.

'I know I scored some good goals there, from long range, some twenty-five yarders, and a nice one against Arsenal. It was four great years for me. For those four years I gave everything, entertained the fans and scored a few goals. I still look for Tottenham's result and I've always had the utmost respect for the club and what it stands for in terms of football. I like to think that if you drew up a list of players and asked which ones were "Tottenham players", who were part of what the club means and is about, I'd get a tick by my name. I loved being there. It was a great time.

'When I think of Tottenham I think of a club that has the manner, the arrogance – in a good sense – that all good clubs need to have. My son is twenty-two and he said to me at the start of this season: "Are you going to take me to White Hart Lane? Because I've never been there." I wanted to go back before the end of the season and show my lad what it was like, at least so he can see where I played for those four years.

'It is a special club, a special ground. There are some truly great players who have played on that pitch over the years and the atmosphere was always different, crackling. But I love what the club is planning. It looks like a spaceship but if it all works like they plan it to, that's the future. People from outside London, I don't think they understand how big Arsenal and Tottenham are. But both of them can fill out 60,000 grounds, no problem.

Tottenham are as big as anybody and will get the chance to show that when they move.'

Waddle, of course, was not the only Geordie genius to make his mark on the Lane. But where Waddle floated past opponents, Paul Gascoigne was happy to destroy them with his brilliant, intuitive footwork, his balance and strength and his mesmerising quality. For three years, under the tutelage of Terry Venables, he was the crown (and clown) prince of English football, although only after Irving Scholar, perhaps because of that snub by Alex Ferguson four years earlier, pulled out all the stops to land him.

Ferguson had decided he wanted Gascoigne after a game against United in which the maverick 'absolutely tore apart' his midfield trio of Bryan Robson, Norman Whiteside and Remi Moses. Indeed, Gascoigne had given Ferguson a personal assurance, on the eve of the United manager's departure for his summer holiday, that he would come to Old Trafford. But Scholar struck, offering to buy a house for Gascoigne's parents. It was the deal-maker, leaving Fergie spewing and seeing him write a letter to tell Gascoigne what he made of the choice. 'He caned me. He couldn't believe I'd turned down the biggest club in the country.'

But along with Scholar's instincts for a deal that would get the transfer over the line – he offered a £2 million fee and wages of £4,000 per week – Spurs could bring something else. Gascoigne said: 'We played against Spurs and I scored two goals. My boots were Hummel at the time and they were owned by Spurs. At the end of the game Terry came over to me and said; "At least you've got the right boots." When we started to talk about a move he said: "If you come and sign for me I can guarantee you that within ten games you'll be playing for England." That was all I wanted to do, to play for my country. And he was right, too. After eight games for Spurs I was joining the England squad.'

It was another perfect fit. Venables made Gascoigne the focal point of his team and the Geordie delivered on the pitch, while being a constant fuzz-ball of nervous energy off it. With the benefit of hindsight, of course, his OCD and hyperactivity might have been diagnosed earlier. As Gary Lineker, a team-mate with club and country, pointed out: 'If you were going to be in a hotel with him for a month, that would be enough to drive anybody mad.'

But Gary Mabbutt, who played with both Hoddle and Gascoigne during his remarkable Spurs career, knew that his club had a diamond. Mabbutt, who remains a close friend of the troubled Gazza, said: 'Glenn and Gazza were fantastic players, who could grab a game by the scruff of the neck and turn it your way. He was a fantastic player and we saw the best of him at Tottenham. In 1990–91 Paul was absolutely outstanding, and even if it's impossible for one player to get you through a season single-handed, Paul definitely got us to the final.'

He did, too. While Paul Stewart scored the only goal in a scrappy third-round win against his first club, Blackpool, Gascoigne then took over. Two goals against Oxford, another pair of beauties at Portsmouth, the first a stunning header, the winner after some twinkle-toed brilliance and an edge-of-the-box shimmy, before he wriggled through the Notts County defence to score the come-from-behind clincher in the last eight. Which brought a semi-final showdown with champions-elect Arsenal. Tottenham fans still recall Barry Davies's commentary as Gascoigne lined up a 35-yard strike at David Seaman's goal. 'Is he going to have a crack? He is, you know!'

But Gascoigne's self-destructive streak was to resurface time and again and the repercussions of his maniacal lunge on Gary Charles in that FA Cup final resonated throughout the rest of his career. Maybe knowing that chairman Alan Sugar had decreed he needed to be sold in order to balance the badly listing books tipped him over the edge. Possibly. Although it might just have been the importance of the game and the chance to win the first winners' medal of his career. Mabbutt said: 'He was always totally hyped up and over the top but even more so that day. In the warm-up he would ping the ball at the band in the middle of the pitch. They stood up – and he did it again! I thought he was just being Paul but those two challenges at the start of the game were awful. He got carried off and Terry gave us the team talk at half-time. He said Gazza was in hospital, seriously injured. But that he'd got us to the final and if we played the same way we'd lift the Cup. We went to see him the next day and take him his winner's medal. He said he'd cried when he saw me lifting the Cup and asked the surgeon if he could go to the party.'

It was to prove Gascoigne's last appearance in a Tottenham shirt, even if his £5.5 million move to Lazio was delayed by 12 months as he recuperated from his cruciate ligament operation. Gascoigne himself said: 'Playing at Spurs was one of the best times in my life. I wish I had never left and had stayed for another two years. We had a great bunch of lads and an unbelievable manager. I loved it as a person and as a player.'

Nearly a decade later, the next free spirit arrived at the club with Gallic charm, flowing hair and a body to die for. David Ginola was never going to see eye-to-eye with Kenny Dalglish when the Scot was appointed to fill the void left by Kevin Keegan at Newcastle, and the £2.5 million fee Spurs paid to land him in 1997 was always going to be popular with the White Hart Lane fans. Ginola was a showman from his toes to his fingertips, extravagant and thrilling in possession, but not exactly a player who would naturally dig in and fight when the team was on the back foot. He was, in many ways, an unlikely signing for Christian Gross, although he flowered under the demanding hand of another arch-disciplinarian, George Graham. Not that their personal relationship was harmonious. Although Graham insisted to me that he was grateful to Ginola for his contribution as Spurs won the League Cup, David Pleat said: 'George didn't like Ginola. I think he was a bit jealous of him.'

Ginola himself spoke fondly of his time at Tottenham: 'White Hart Lane was always a place where I felt I belonged.' He had no doubts, either, about why he was sold to Aston Villa in 2000.

'George Graham didn't want me any more. He said to Alan Sugar to put me on the transfer list. I think I had become too big for him. I had just been Player of the Year. I wanted to end my career at Spurs. I was thirty-two. I could still play at my best, and I had been working hard to be at this level. I didn't want to leave. But he substituted me in thirty-six of the seventy-nine matches I started. He would always look for the negative things to say about me, trying to put me under pressure. I tried my hardest but Graham would always give me hassle. He would single me out and crit- icise something in my game, so that I lost the respect of my team-mates.'

But not that of the supporters, the thousands who came to the Lane to watch Ginola bring them a taste of magic dust. He was another link in the chain of great players that runs through the years. And even during the last season at the Lane, as Pochettino's side ran Chelsea all the way to the line, the fans still recalled what Ginola and the other entertainers from the past meant to the club. The yearning for 'Glory' remains a Tottenham bedrock. It is not just enough to win. They have to win with style.

11

KING TO A KNAVE

The only two managers to win the title for Spurs had both played for the club. Arthur Rowe and Bill Nicholson each understood what that shirt meant, what White Hart Lane was all about, why the cockerel needed to crow. It was perhaps no surprise, then, that a succession of former heroes wanted to be the next ex-Tottenham player to make the transition to the dug-out, to follow in the footsteps of Rowe and Nicholson.

Yet why were none of them able to do so successfully? Why did each of them find the manager's office a far harder place to perform than on the pitch? There was no specific reason why Terry Venables, Ossie Ardiles or Glenn Hoddle lasted far fewer months than they wanted. Why Steve Perryman and John Gorman, loyal assistants both, struggled to see their ambitions fulfilled. But there were threads which ran across all their reigns. Issues that undermined them, brought angst, frustration and eventual departures when things initially seemed so bright.

Then again, nobody ever suggested it was easy managing Spurs. Not even the best of men, the most successful of those who occupied that most isolated and exposed of roles. It is a club where boardroom tensions have always had a part to play.

Venables needed to be convinced to return in the first place. David Pleat may be of the opinion that Irving Scholar had gone behind his back to see if 'El Tel' wanted the job but the man himself did not skip and jump down the High Road. One of the intermediaries in the initial talks was Morris Keston, who said: 'When they had to sack David Pleat, Irving Scholar came to my house. He said "Do me a favour – ring your mate." Terry said to me: "Look Morris; I didn't get a good reception there as a player. I don't feel I want to go back." But I persuaded him.'

Venables did seem the perfect fit. His spell at Barcelona had proven his coaching acumen, honed at Crystal Palace where he put together the 'Team of the 80s' and brought George Graham in as a youth team coach, then further developed by taking QPR to the 1982 Cup final meeting with Burkinshaw's Tottenham. Winning La Liga at the Camp Nou may not seem much of a feat now but Barcelona had waited 11 years for the title they celebrated in 1985 and it was only a combination of nerves and a desperate penalty shoot-out that prevented Venables from adding the European Cup to his collection 12 months later. When he was sacked by Barca at the start of the 1987–88 season it was only going to be a matter of time before he returned to the game and Pleat's unfortunate managerial demise brought the offer that he eventually accepted.

It was seemingly the perfect appointment. England's most engaging, sparkling and tactically-proficient young manager was coming to a club which had been third the previous season and was already boasting real quality in Chris Waddle and Clive Allen and, by the start of his first full season, Paul Gascoigne. Scholar, though, insisted he was never entirely sold on the man he had appointed, being wary of his outside interests, the ones touted as 'baggage' by FA chiefs when they announced Venables would not be retained as England boss just a few weeks before Euro 96. Indeed, to listen to the ex-chairman, he was wary from the outset. Scholar said: 'At one point I told him: "Do me a favour Terry, you concentrate a hundred per cent on football, and you won't go wrong."'

Not that everyone was sold on Venables' football judgement, either. Pleat, of course, had an understandable axe to grind but his verdict held water: 'After I left, if you look at the record of the subsequent three years, the club didn't do as well under Venables as they did under me. He got knocked out of the FA Cup at Port Vale and brought in players who, for me, just weren't Tottenham players. Van den Hauwe was one, and I thought Terry Fenwick was just a cynical defender. Gary Lineker and Gascoigne got Terry out of jail to an extent.'

To an extent indeed. The pressing financial issues that forced Scholar to leave had begun to affect on-field matters too. Waddle was sold in 1989 without ever having a training session alongside new recruit Lineker, and even as the inspirational Gascoigne guided Venables' side to the 1991 FA Cup final, his sale to Lazio was being agreed. Scholar took out a secret loan from Robert Maxwell to keep the club afloat before resigning, while keeping his share capital, in October 1990. And when Gascoigne's impetuosity and reckless Wembley lunge on Gary Charles meant the move was off for a year, Alan Sugar bought out Scholar's controlling stake, shunting Venables up from the dug-out to the role of chief executive. It did not take long for internal fissures to open up. Scholar recalled: 'I went to a game and we lost 3–1 in Nottingham. We're watching the game and Nat Solomon, one of the directors, apologised. He said to me: "If I'd known then what I know now, it would never have happened. You warned me and told me." Tony Berry, another director, said the same thing. Three weeks after I left I predicted what would happen. I said: "The first year will be the honeymoon; the second will be the divorce." And that's exactly what happened.'

History proved Scholar right on that one. Behind the scenes, Venables' relationship with Sugar was unravelling, quickly, although it took two fraught years for the dam to burst, in dramatic fashion. In the meantime, Venables had been forced to return to a managerial role when Peter Shreeves' second spell at the helm proved a bust. Among the arrivals around that time was a coltish teenager from Portsmouth named Darren Anderton. 'My head was in a bit of a spin,' Anderton said. 'I was being told that

Tottenham and Liverpool wanted me. The accountant said he acted for Terry and that I was top of his list for the summer. Then I got the call from Jim Smith, my manager, to say a fee had been agreed, apparently £1.75 million. I asked what I had to do and he said I had to go and speak to them. He said: "Terry Venables will make you the player I believe you should be." And I signed that day. Terry was an amazing guy, a lovely fellow.'

But not a businessman. Venables surrounded himself with a series of questionable associates. Among those was Eddie Ashby, Venables' financial adviser from 1991 to 1997 and who was subsequently jailed for violating bankruptcy laws and debarred from being a company director following a string of business failures. And, it was to transpire, Venables was not a man who could possibly co-exist with the streetwise but strictly straight down the line Sugar, who claimed the so-called 'dream ticket' was a living nightmare because Venables refused even to attempt to comprehend the requirements of the money man. Sugar was adamant that with debts of £11 million he had told Venables there was no money to spend – and that he then returned from holiday to find £2 million had been lashed out to bring Gordon Durie from Chelsea. Sugar was to subsequently brand Venables an 'ostrich' and 'totally out of his depth', suggesting he was clueless about the rules and regulations of the Stock Exchange and financial accounting concepts. Boardroom disagreements swiftly became all-out rucks and Sugar's offer to buy out the £3 million investment Venables had made as part of their joint takeover, for a 22 per cent stake, was rejected out of hand.

Thursday 13 May 1993 saw the Football Writers' Association's Footballer of the Year Dinner at the Royal Lancaster Hotel next to Lancaster Gate Tube station. Instead of pictures of Footballer of the Year Waddle – now back from France at Sheffield Wednesday – dominating the back pages when they were printed that night, the headlines were all about Venables' imminent sacking. It was pretty obvious who the source was. The next day, Sugar's casting vote as chairman – Venables' close friend, lawyer Jonathan Crystal, was among the rebel directors opposing the move – saw the manager sacked, although by 6 p.m. an injunction had been granted which saw him reinstated.

Two days later, Sugar explained his thinking, making clear the sacking was not about football. 'Nobody is questioning his ability as a football coach,' said Sugar. 'It was a very sad day and everybody involved regrets deeply that it has come to this. All I can say is that if he had different people around him, and not particularly restricted to this Mr Ashby, but to other people, we would not be having this argument.' Pointing to his share offer, with Venables having borrowed much of his £3 million investment at the punitive interest rates of the time, Sugar added, caustically: 'Every businessman in the world would like to be able to recover interest on loans they took to go into business ventures but regretfully, in the cruel, harsh world, that is a dream.'

A battle royal was under way. The majority of Fleet Street sided with Venables, who cultivated the media with his outgoing personality and ability to weave a tale, plus his coaching acumen. That approach had won him many friends, who both respected his footballing wisdom and thoroughly enjoyed his company. But Sugar, too, had his champions. It was a vicious fight, with a sting in the tail that was to have repercussions that lasted for more than a decade, forcing football to confront – and then scuttle away from – its dark side.

The High Court battle might have started with a victory for Venables but a month later Court 35 brought the game into chaos as Sugar's allegations over the 1992 transfer of Teddy Sheringham to Spurs from Nottingham Forest were aired, bizarrely by Venables' legal team. In an affidavit read out in court, Mr Sugar claimed brown paper envelopes had been ferried to motorway service stations, because Venables had told Sugar that then-Forest manager Brian Clough 'liked a bung'. The court proceedings also brought reports of the £58,000 in cash paid to former Arsenal skipper

Frank McLintock for his part in the proceedings. Venables and McLintock strongly denied the accusations that a bung had been paid and both have always maintained their conduct was entirely above board. An inquiry into the allegations that Venables bribed Clough was subsequently dropped by the police. The CPS told Venables and McLintock that no charges would be brought. It all took place against a backdrop of abuse from Spurs fans, fiercely in the Venables camp, as were his players. An unsightly mess, but when Sir David Nicholls refused to extend the injunction that had, temporarily, kept Venables in his job, Sugar was victorious. Not that you would have known it as he was smuggled out of the court by the judge's entrance after one irate fan had screamed: 'You'd better take him out the back door or honestly he'll die. We will murder him.'

Venables, a man the supporters had wanted to stay and bring back the glory days, was gone, with a hefty legal bill too, which saw him eventually accept Sugar's earlier offer. His career had many more twists and turns to come. Yet getting rid of Venables was not the end of Sugar's problems, with the next departure from the club being skipper Neil Ruddock, who had been the leader – with Sheringham at his shoulder – of the internal protests.

Despite initial denials by Sugar that he was contemplating it, within weeks he had appointed the manager of West Brom, Osvaldo Ardiles, whose own place in the club's history was already legend. Yet instead of cementing that reputation, the little Argentinian was to become another victim, his footballing integrity coming up slap bang against the new realities of life in the lower reaches of the Premiership, as the top flight had been re-branded 12 months earlier, and a chairman who looked at the bottom line before everything else.

Ardiles' time as a Spurs player brought a number of highs and lows, but it was events that were entirely outside his control that ended up scarring him most. Just 11 months after parading round Wembley with the FA Cup, a trophy won by that stunning goal by his close friend Ricky Villa, Spurs were closing in on a return visit. Then everything changed. Ardiles said: 'What happened in 1982 was the worst time of my life, as simple as that. Everything was going so well, so beautifully, I was playing the best football of my life. And then the country I was born in was at war with the country that had adopted me. If it wasn't for the Falklands War I might've been the best player in England, the Footballer of the Year, that season. But then it all came crashing down because of the Falklands.

'Everything in my life started to fall apart. I felt I could never go back to England. To be in the middle of it was hard. I was being asked what I liked about England. If I said I like playing there, I was called "pro-English" but at the same time I was being criticised in England for supporting Argentina's claim to the Falklands. I felt bad in Argentina, bad in England, bad everywhere. I felt I could never go back to England.'

For Ardiles, things went from bad to worse when his cousin José, a pilot, was shot down and killed. 'Mentally my world was turned upside down,' he said. 'I immediately requested a transfer from Tottenham. I couldn't see how I could continue playing in England, so I went to France. I joined PSG but my football suffered. I couldn't believe how badly I was playing. Football had always been relaxing for me – I just wanted to have the ball but I became a really bad player. It was a complete disaster. I've never played so badly. Even the basics were proving difficult. I just couldn't play. The most obvious thing for me to do was to go back to Tottenham.'

Whether the welcome he received in N17 would have been quite so warm had the Union Jack not still been flying over Port Stanley is up for debate. But Ardiles remained at the club for another six years, playing under Keith Burkinshaw, Peter Shreeves, David Pleat and Venables, before brief spells at Blackburn and QPR culminated with his arrival at Swindon, where he was soon appointed manager.

From the outset, it was clear Ardiles would manage as he played. He introduced a midfield diamond, guiding the Wiltshire side through the play-off to promotion. Yet within days they had been relegated two divisions as a result of financial irregularities. The repercussions for the club were immense and by the following February Ardiles had moved on to Newcastle – rapidly replaced by Kevin Keegan on Tyneside – and then West Brom, before Sugar came knocking.

It was a call he could not resist: 'I always felt the love with the fans.' Yet this time things were rocky, despite having his old skipper Steve Perryman as his right-hand man. Spurs began the 1993–94 season with a bang, Sheringham scoring the only goal at newly promoted Newcastle, but things degenerated swiftly. 'That year was a disaster,' Anderton said. 'Ossie started well then Teddy picked up an injury and was out for four or five months. Ronny Rosenthal eventually came in but he wasn't Teddy. Luckily Teddy came back and we escaped relegation.' Only just. It was not until the penultimate game of the season that goals from Vinny Samways and David Howells secured the victory at Oldham that kept Spurs up and effectively relegated the home side. If that was bad, worse was to follow, although neither Ardiles nor Sugar were responsible. Those financial misdemeanours under Scholar, involving the transfers of Mitchell Thomas, Chris Fairclough and Paul Allen, saw Tottenham initially deducted 12 points, fined £600,000 and banned from the FA Cup, although Sugar somehow won that legal battle with the FA. His response, too, was emphatic, signing Germany's star striker Jürgen Klinsmann and Romanian World Cup duo Ilie Dumitrescu and Gica Popescu.

Spurs still had some home-grown talent in the form of Sheringham, Nick Barmby and Anderton, but even they couldn't avoid the heroic failure that followed. 'Everyone talks about the "Famous Five" and it was all right if you were in that five,' Anderton said. 'It was the "Shit Six" it was difficult for. Colin Calderwood's joke was that it was the Shit Six at the back who were the problem.

But it wasn't the fab five going forwards, it was eight. It really was madness. Ossie would say: "We win the ball back, and we all go. Colin, Sol, Stuart Nethercott, not you. But the rest, we all go." It was great fun to play in and training was so enjoyable but teams worked it out very quickly. It was a shame it didn't work. Ossie was a great guy and an incredible footballer, even then in training. People talk about Glenn being unbelievable in training but Ossie was right up there.'

Ardiles was tight-lipped when it came to talking about working for Sugar, although he hinted at his deeper feelings: 'He was famous. He had to appear that he was sacking people and wasn't afraid of anybody. But he was very supportive of me at Tottenham. That's the real truth. He supported everything I wanted to do and he was very good for me. He wasn't nasty at all. Yes, I tried the Famous Five. And he said: "You're fired." It was a very emotional day. I'd spent eighteen months working very closely with him. We had a lot of battles together, with the FA, and other clubs. We were very close. So it was very emotional when he had to say goodbye.'

Perryman, though, was less inclined to pull his punches. Still deeply involved in the game – he even missed the final day at White Hart Lane in May 2017 because his Exeter side were involved in League Two play-off action – he was critical of Sugar: 'Alan Sugar wasn't a football man, at all. He tried to build a different place with a different ethos. A lot of the football spirit left under him. There were too many excuses and I didn't feel people were as proud of the club as they could be. There were too many excuses for the players not performing.

'One of the biggest mistakes I ever made was going back to work there. It was not a mistake to be Ossie's assistant and it wasn't that I wasn't happy to be back at Tottenham Hotspur, but to work for Tottenham Hotspur at that time, it was a completely different place to the one I'd joined and played most of my career for. It felt that football wasn't the priority any more, where the game didn't rule. It wasn't a good place to be.'

The chairman may change, but sometimes the problems remain. For Hoddle, like Ardiles, there was no way he could refuse the offer made by Daniel Levy, in March 2001, barely a month after the ENIC group, headed by Joe Lewis but with Levy as his chief executive, had bought out Sugar. Hoddle was still bruised by being prematurely (in his view) forced out of the England job. In 1999 he was made to resign after an interview in *The Times* in which he was reported as saying those born with disabilities were being punished for their sins in a previous life. Although Hoddle insisted he had been 'misinterpreted', he had made similar comments in a Radio Five Live interview the previous year. Hoddle's fate, though, was sealed when the then Prime Minister Tony Blair went on the ITV *Richard & Judy* show to say 'it would be very difficult for him to stay' if he had indeed made the 'very wrong' statement. Hoddle then caused animosity at Southampton when he walked out on the south-coast side to rejoin the club of his youth. And found it was not what he thought it would be.

'I'd turned Tottenham down once, when I went to Chelsea. Alan Sugar came to me at the last minute, but I'd already given my word to Chelsea,' said Hoddle. 'But when they came in again I probably made a big mistake. I let my heart rule my head because of what the club means to me. I wanted the job so much.

'You need to feel the confidence of the board. I had a problem with the politics of the club at the time. It should've been the happiest place I managed but it was the most unhappy because of the politics that got in the way. I was told that David Pleat had to stay as director of football. He wouldn't have been my choice, to be honest.

'There were players I wanted to bring in that got blocked. The club wasn't in the financial position it is now. I didn't have the money I needed. Tim Sherwood and Gus Poyet were free transfers and that's what the budget was. I tried to get in Samuel Eto'o, who was only twenty-two, and Fernando Morientes for £10 million and they were blocked, which was disappointing. But as a manager you've got to get on with it.'

More critically, Hoddle found himself immersed in a fight not of his making, between Levy and the club's prize asset, Sol Campbell. One of the reasons Levy had sacked George Graham to give the job to Hoddle was that he had nurtured Campbell and made him a key part of his England side during his spell in charge of the Three Lions. The chairman believed a relationship existed between them and that it could help to persuade the defender to sign a new deal. As, in truth, did Hoddle himself: 'The problem with Sol Campbell was his agent, not Sol. I had him round my house for a meal with my family, trying to convince him he should stay. He gave the club his word he was staying but I could sense there was a problem and the agent was getting in his ear.

'I did feel let down. It was a difficult decision for him. It wasn't one I particularly liked but he made it and there was nothing I could do about it. It wasn't about him leaving – I left but that was after thirteen years, when I felt it was time to go abroad. I didn't go to Arsenal. There's no rights or wrongs when it comes to joining rivals. I didn't like the fact that he went there . . .'

Nor did the Spurs fans. They never forgave him, although Campbell's departure opened the door for a home-reared central defender who became as popular as his predecessor was reviled. Every Spurs fan will tell you about Ledley King. That he only had one knee but was better than John Terry. The former England defender himself recognised good and bad in his new manager: 'I enjoyed playing under Glenn. He brought in Dean Richards and we played with Chris Perry in the three. That was Glenn's way of getting as many attacking players into the formation as he could.

'So there were the three of us, attacking full-backs in Reto Ziegler and Steven Carr, Anderton, Poyet and Sherwood, Sheringham and Les Ferdinand. It sounds like a really good side. It just didn't perform like one. We probably had a lot of older, experienced players. Quite a few of them were in the last chapter of their career. Old players can be stubborn and stuck in their ways and Glenn found it hard to control some of the egos in the squad. There was talent but differences with Glenn. He was still a young manager. He was still one hell of a player even then – and that maybe didn't go down as well as it might have. I loved it but some of the older players saw it differently.' Anderton, one of those older players, said: 'Glenn came in and played the way Glenn plays, trying to beat them by playing good football. But we weren't good enough to do that.'

Hoddle and his No. 2, John Gorman, did agree with Anderton that the make-or-break day for his reign came under the roof of Cardiff's Millennium Stadium in February 2002. The Scot, who remains an engaging and friendly man, happy to laugh over talk about the charity match at the Lane in which he absolutely destroyed one particularly clumsy journalist turned right back (now the author of this book), said: 'I came back with Glenn and it was tough for us because the expectations were too much. The truth is that we were a long way behind the very best. In the first year we came tenth, when we'd been in the top four at Christmas, and while we felt we'd started to move things forward, the board weren't happy. We felt we'd started to play some good football. I still think the critical game was the League Cup final against Blackburn in Cardiff. If we'd won that – and we should've done, given the chances we had and the penalty we should definitely have got – I feel we'd have really been able to bring things forward with those young players. So I feel if we had beaten Blackburn and got into Europe, especially on the back of smashing Chelsea 5–1 in the semi-final, and if we'd been given the resources other managers since have had, it would have been a different story.'

Anderton added: 'Beating Chelsea in the semi was one of the best performances as a team in my time there. It was a great night, the only time I beat them in twelve years. Then we went to Cardiff, we were massive favourites and didn't perform.'

The issue, insists Gorman, was the old one – money. 'We could only deal in free transfers, with the exception of Robbie Keane,' he said, echoing Hoddle. 'I'm still proud of that, how we brought in Ledley King, Simon Davies, Matt Etherington, Anthony Gardner. I was doing work I was proud of. We got in Hélder Postiga, who was only a kid, and he was crucified but most of the others were on frees: Gus Poyet, and Teddy coming back. The other killer game was United at home, when we were 3–0 up at half-time, playing brilliantly, but then collapsed in the second half.

'Glenn was a fan as a young player. I think we both ended up feeling the same way – that it's hard to be in charge of a team that you love so much. I started off a Celtic fan but from the moment I first joined Spurs as a player that changed. I felt something and became a Tottenham fan, which I still am to this day. It might seem a bit trite, but, once a Spurs fan, always a Spurs fan. The stadium is a special place to me, still. It was when I was a player. I remember when Keith signed Ossie and Ricky and how the atmosphere was just electric. Glenn left England thinking: "If only" and it was the same with Spurs. He could have really done something with that club if the money had been there. When you have the talent Glenn had, and the passion for the club, he just needed those last few ingredients. He wanted to play football the right way, the Tottenham way, but you have to win games as well.

'The end came quickly. We hadn't started the season that well but it was only September. I remember we lost at home to Southampton, with James Beattie scoring a hat-trick – thanks James! Of course, Glenn had come back to Spurs from there, so it hurt to see them celebrating like that, but it still was ridiculously early in a season to make that decision. I still feel that if I'd had the same role as Chris Hughton, just a member of the coaching staff rather than being Glenn's assistant, I'd have been allowed to stay. But as it was, with my title, I had to carry the can along with the manager.

'Despite all that and the feelings of regret, Glenn still loves the club, will always be a big fan and that won't change. He loves the way they're playing now, too. He doesn't have any bad feelings towards the board, either. He accepts that's what happens in football. He'd just love to have had that chance again, in different circumstances. But he is and remains a fan. That will never change with me either. We both wanted to improve the players as individuals, even if the team wasn't winning as much as we'd have liked.'

Hoddle does appear to have mellowed towards Spurs in the intervening years. His work as a pundit helped and the love he had for the club remained, as was evident from the reception he received after the final game at the Lane, responding to chants of acclaim and love that were as heartfelt then as they were when he was the brains and artist of the team. He understood, too, that Levy had adapted his way of working within the club set-up. Hoddle said: 'Over the years Daniel has evolved. He's a very good businessman and made some very shrewd moves for Tottenham on that side.

'We wouldn't try to run the business side because we wouldn't know how to do it. For a while I felt like telling him: "You need to trust the people you put in and employ to do the job, get behind them and give them everything." He needed to let the football people run the football side of the club, trust them and back them. Which is what he is doing now. Daniel is good for the club. He's taking it forward and I would trust him. He's the right person.'

Many Spurs fans thought Hoddle could have been the right person. As others before felt that Venables or Ardiles could be. But it was not to be for any of them, for a variety of reasons. Regrets are part of football. And it is not only the supporters who carry them for years and years.

12

TAXI FOR MAICON

For years, they had dreamed of a night like it. When the cream of Europe would be laid bare and destroyed, brought low at the Lane. And even when it did happen, plenty of those who were there could not quite take it in, despite the fact that some could close their eyes and recall another Spurs side felling European giants, with an intellectual playmaker and a fearless, fleet-footed Welsh flier on the flanks. In 2010, though, the beating heart of the side was a quiet Croatian, not a Belfast boy who spoke with a romantic cadence. A little will o' the wisp schemer named Luka Modrić. And Cliff Jones's role was filled by a callow lad from Whitchurch named Gareth Bale. A pair who were to end up winning the Champions League three times in four years, playing for a club that wears a famous all-white strip. But, of course, for Real Madrid, not Spurs.

On the evening of 2 November 2010, it was like watching fantasy football made real. Of all the chants that reverberated down White Hart Lane over the years, during all those great European nights, surely nothing was as mocking, as evocative, as powerful as the one that marked Bale's evisceration of the Brazilian who was supposed to be the best right-back in world football. 'Taxi for Maicon, Taxi for Maicon, Taxi for Maicon, Taxi for Maicon.' Repetition after endless repetition. Just as the match saw the same story told time and time again, just in different forms of humiliation, beaten on the left, the right, for pace, for thought, for intelligence, for class. A night that was, without question, the high-water mark of one manager's reign. A night that will never be forgotten by those who were there to see it. Or the thousands that will tell their friends and family that they were there, even though they were not.

Yet the story of that Champions League campaign, the first and last to be played out in N17, did not begin when the draw was made in Monaco two months earlier, or even when Tottenham squeezed past Young Boys Bern to reach the group phase. Nor did the ambition of the club end when Real Madrid and the 'Big Bad Portuguese Wolves' José Mourinho and Cristiano Ronaldo came to town five months later. For even as that flame of mixing with Europe's greats once again flickered, with breathtaking illumination, only to fade away too swiftly, it was lighting a long-running fire that burned away in the background, igniting the club's ambitions. And while Harry Redknapp's side ensured his time in the dug-out will always be recalled for the positives more than the frustrations, that run brought a sense of direction and clarity to the grand plan and vision for the club that had been whirring away in Daniel Levy's brain for the best part of a decade.

George Graham. Glenn Hoddle. David Pleat. Jacques Santini. Martin Jol. Juande Ramos. Six managers in the space of seven years. An ever-changing cast-list when, just down the other end of the Seven Sisters Road, another club was proving the model of managerial consistency. Each season of Spurs failure made worse by the successes just a few miles away, feelings heightened by the snowballing triumphs of Chelsea, the club Roman Abramovich had chosen to invest in after turning his nose up at Spurs in 2003.

Hoddle's sense of being prevented from doing the job he wanted to do remains as clear now as it was when he was sawn off on the day two giants collided at Old Trafford in September 2003, Martin Keown's 'gargoyle' leap above Ruud van Nistelrooy after the Dutchman's late penalty miss a signpost and symbol of what was to become Arsenal's 'Invincibles' campaign. Pleat, in turn, knew he was a sticking plaster, a temporary solution, as Levy sought a trailblazing manager for the new era. But he was determined to leave his stamp, telling me: 'I'm proud of some of the players I brought to the club in that season. Robbie Keane and Paul Robinson, Jermain Defoe too.'

Defoe remains the most popular of Pleat's signings. He was missed when he was forced to send his apologies and not attend the final game at the Lane, instead needed on Wearside for training. His bond with the club and the ground remains a strong one. 'David brought me to the club and it was amazing to know he wanted me,' Defoe said. 'He came up to me and said: "I've never seen anybody else who shoots like that with no backlift." He got me to the club and allowed me to start scoring goals for them. At that time I was really close to Mitchell Thomas, who was at Spurs in the 1980s. Mitchell told me what the club had meant to him as well, so when I got the phone call to say there was a deal for me to go to Spurs I said: "I don't need a contract." I just wanted to sign. The wages, the terms, didn't matter. I just wanted to play for the club, to go out there, get on that pitch, in that stadium, and score goals.

'I was lucky because I felt that relationship with the fans from day one, the first time I went to the ground as a Spurs player, even before I'd actually kicked a ball for the club. I signed too late to play in a midweek match against Manchester City, but I couldn't believe the reception I got when I came onto the pitch before the game. Then I made my debut the following weekend against Portsmouth and the reception was unbelievable again. I felt a connection, with the fans and the ground, straight away. When people say "some things are meant to be" I think they're right. Good things happen at the right time and I just believe that at that point in my life I was meant to play for Tottenham. To score all those goals, especially at that ground. It was supposed to be a big part of my journey. It was an amazing time for me in my career and I love that stadium and what it means.

'Tottenham was a place that took hold of me. Growing up, I wanted to play for that club. I told my family it was supposed to happen. That I was meant to follow in the footsteps of Jimmy Greaves, Martin Chivers and Gary Lineker – Jürgen Klinsmann too. Then Glenn Hoddle, Chris Waddle and Gazza. There were all those great goalscorers who had played there before me but I felt it was right from day one. As soon as I had the chance to play for that club I had to take it, I needed to be part of it. But I scored on my debut and everything took off from there.'

Defoe was to go on to score 143 goals in 363 appearances across two spells, to stand behind only Greaves, Smith, Chivers and Jones in the all-time Spurs scoring chart, with 90 of those coming at the Lane. Yet the club was still struggling to make its mark and towards the end of that 2003–04 season Levy wanted the great Italian manager Giovanni Trapattoni to take over, perhaps seeing him as a more sophisticated version of Sir Alex Ferguson. He then switched his sights to the young emerging manager of Porto. But José Mourinho's touchline slide at Old Trafford, after his un- heralded side knocked Manchester United out of the Champions League in 2004, caught the attention of another London club, for whom money was no object. Instead, Levy ended up with the manager of France, Jacques Santini, whose copybook was blotted before his arrival as Les Bleus slipped out of Euro 2004 at the same stage as England.

More critically, Santini was not comfortable speaking English, and his tenure ended after barely five months. Ledley King said: 'His English wasn't great and he found it difficult. But at that period we thought things were going to go in the right direction and it would be a good chapter. I felt it was my time. I was captain, playing at the back and trying to push things forward. I saw poten- tial in the team. We were difficult to beat and you could see where we were going. Then one day he was gone. It was a shock. The day before a game we were going to travel. We were called into a room and he said he was leaving.'

In truth, it was a necessary move, and Levy already had the replacement on his staff. The chairman had employed former Denmark midfielder Frank Arnesen as his first sporting director, part of a drive towards the European model he was determined to introduce at the club. Arnesen, in turn, had engaged former West Brom midfielder Martin Jol as Santini's unlikely No. 2. But where the Frenchman struggled to communicate, blunt-talking Dutchman Jol was on the players' wavelength. King said: 'Martin was already at the club and was more suited to the job. Santini maybe felt Martin was undermining him. They saw the game differently. Martin had great English and it was a difficult situation. Not that we had any problems with Santini but we enjoyed Martin. It felt like we moved up a level with Martin. I felt we could take the club forward. He was a very passionate man. He wasn't scary but you knew there'd be trouble if you upset him. He was fun to play under.'

Fun and, very nearly, successful. Ask any Spurs fan about their worst afternoon and they will more than likely mention 'Lasagne-gate' pretty swiftly. The day when Tottenham needed to match Arsenal's result on the final day of the 2005–06 season to secure fourth place and the golden ticket to the Champions League big time, all on the day the Gunners were waving goodbye to Highbury. King wasn't playing that day but will never forget the trip to Upton Park: 'I wasn't playing and I arranged with Jermaine Jenas and Paul Stalteri – we were all injured – that we'd meet at the training ground and go over to West Ham. We got there and suddenly all we were hearing was "Did you hear about the players not being well?" It wasn't until we got to the changing room that we could see how sick they were, that the players had no life in them at all. There was no atmosphere. It was really sad because it was such a big game for the club and they didn't get the chance to have a proper go at it. It was a bug of some sort – it wasn't the lasagne after all.'

Spurs lobbied the Premier League for a postponement, but

Jol's team were forced to play, losing 2–1 and seeing the prize slip through their fingers. With the league's top brass all enjoying the boardroom hospitality at Highbury that afternoon, and seemingly uninterested in even listening to Tottenham's entreaties, the decision bred a rift between the Spurs hierarchy and the Premier League that was not entirely repaired for the best part of a decade. 'The game should've been cancelled,' King said. 'I don't know how we got enough players to play. It was unbelievable that they played at all. They looked really ill. They couldn't play like that.'

It was Jol's 'Sliding Doors' moment. Issues with his strikers, particularly Dimitar Berbatov and Robbie Keane, began to emerge. A year later, another fifth-place finish was not good enough. Jol, though, seemed to believe it was. After Spurs finished the season with a 2–1 home win over Manchester City, the Dutchman went on to the pitch, took the proffered microphone and declared: 'We are the best of the rest.' It was a comment that infuriated Levy, whose ambitions were now far higher than scrapping around for the high-table leftovers. And in August 2007 director Paul Kemsley and secretary John Alexander were spotted meeting Sevilla coach Juande Ramos. Tottenham tried, unimpressively and without any conviction, to claim it was wrong to join the dots. The manner of Jol's exit was about as poor as it could be. The Dutchman was sitting in his dug-out seat during a European tie with Getafe when he received a text confirming what the press box sat behind him all knew – that he was going to be sacked at the end of the game, with Ramos coming in.

'It was strange,' King said. 'I wasn't playing. I was behind the bench and someone texted me to say he'd been sacked. I was sitting behind him. I went in at half-time and said to a few people: "What's this?" There was a funny atmosphere but in the second half the fans knew something and it seemed that Martin was the only one who didn't. He went into his room and came out fifteen minutes later to say he was leaving. I felt helpless as a player because there was nothing I could do. He had a belief in my ability.

He allowed me to think I could be the best I could be. Nothing too technical – just a sense of belief and the way he treated me as a man. I started to get confident in my role in leading the team.'

Ramos had won the Uefa Cup in 2006, his Sevilla side destroying Steve McClaren's Middlesbrough 4–0 in Eindhoven. The following season, with Spurs forced to play a game at Chelsea on a Saturday lunchtime, having controversially lost 2–1 to Sevilla on the Thursday night, he completed their last-eight exit with a 2–2 draw at the Lane. And, initially at least, King said the players thought they were getting the real deal: 'Ramos couldn't speak English. We'd played his Seville team the previous year so I was looking forward to him coming. But the first thing he said was we all had to lose weight. He rubbed everybody up the wrong way with his approach. He seemed to just think we were all fat, without even looking at us. The only player who didn't have to lose weight was JJ [Jermaine Jenas]. He didn't have to lose any. He said the Sevilla team weighed a hundred kilograms less than us. But we did have Paul Robinson and Mido . . .

'Even so, we started off with trust in him because he'd proved he was really good in cup competitions. After the first leg of the League Cup semi-final against Arsenal we were really confident. The 5–1 was magical. Nothing was going to stop us. We just battered them. He knew the big teams well and we prepared well for them. Our downfall was against the lesser teams. Ramos seemed to think we'd just beat them. But his attention to detail with the big teams was great.'

And it wasn't long before his relationship with key players started to unravel, including, to the disbelief of the majority of Spurs fans, with Defoe, who later admitted to being bruised by the way he was shovelled out of the door to Portsmouth, managed by a certain Harry Redknapp. Defoe said: 'I didn't get on with Juande Ramos and didn't agree with his methods. I didn't think he was good for the football club. I love the club, really love it, and he didn't. He might be a good manager but if you see someone coming into the club you love who isn't good for it, that hurts. I was part of the club before him and felt when I took him on I was being protective of the club. There were a lot of things he did I didn't agree with and a lot of the players had the same opinion. I just felt this person is not right for this club; the club deserves somebody better. It was as simple as that.'

Ramos was to have his moment of success. Spurs' first visit to the new Wembley for the 2008 League Cup final saw a comeback victory over a Chelsea side still coming to terms with the departure of Mourinho, Jonathan Woodgate's cheekbone rebounding the extra-time winner past Petr Cech. But after that victory parade under the Wembley arch, Ramos lost his grip. Spurs only won six of the next 26 games in all competitions, with the Spaniard's apparent fixation on the Europa League at the start of the next season, playing the hampered King in that competition rather than in domestic football, utterly mystifying. Out went Ramos, his coaching staff and director of football Damien Comolli. In came their antithesis. 'We wanted to give Juande Ramos as much time as possible,' Levy said, justifying his decision. 'But there comes a time when you know you've got to make a change. I wanted him to do something drastic, something people weren't expecting. I needed to change the team around. I knew only one person who could do that and that was Harry Redknapp. Once he decided he wanted to come I went about agreeing everything with Harry and Portsmouth.'

Redknapp was known as a boyhood Arsenal fan. Yet he trained with Spurs as a kid, under the guiding hand of Tony Marchi, and he recalled meeting Bill Nicholson when he was 12 years old: 'He was a legend, the greatest manager of all time. He was a very serious guy. I spoke to Steve Perryman recently and he said if you got a "well done" out of Bill it was a miracle.'

Redknapp was mocked for constantly claiming during much of his reign that he took over a team 'that only had two points from eight matches'. 'I'll be honest,' he said. 'My missus could've kept that team up. The bloke from the pub up the road could've done that. With Bale, Modrić, players like that.'

Speaking during a recent podcast recording, he added: 'Daniel won't like me saying this but I met him eighteen months earlier, when Martin Jol was still the manager. I asked why they wanted to get rid of the manager. I said I didn't feel it would be popular or a good move for me. They're not going to be overexcited about me taking over from him. They won a few games and it sort of died a death. We [Portsmouth] played in Braga in the Europa League in the October. On the Friday morning I was on the coach to come back to the airport and got a call from Daniel, who wanted to meet me. That night I went to see him at his house and then took over for the Bolton game on the Sunday.'

The impact was instant. A 2–0 win over the Trotters proved it was about the manager more than the players and a stunning and remarkable midweek 4–4 draw at Arsenal, opened by a special goal from David Bentley and closed by Aaron Lennon's last-gasp leveller, confirmed the change of mental focus. King saw the change in philosophy take root: 'Harry understood what it was all about in the Premier League. He simplified things, made it easy, played players in their positions. It was common sense. I started playing in the league games, when I'd been in the cup games under Ramos. From the moment he came in, we clicked. It can be psychological and mental. We played differently.'

By January, although Spurs were still perilously near the drop zone, Redknapp had no doubts that he'd keep the team up. That didn't stop him from persuading Levy to get out his chequebook for a new striker, and not any old one. 'The day I left to go to Portsmouth I got messages and texts telling me to "come home",' Defoe said. 'They don't say "come back to Tottenham", like your mum doesn't say "come to mum's house". It's "come home", always "home". And that's what it was like with me and the Spurs fans. Soon after I left I got a phone call from a friend. He said: "Listen to this" and I could hear, in the background, the Spurs fans singing my name. So when I got the opportunity to come back, I knew I had to do it.

'Of course there was a connection between me and Harry. I'd known him from being a kid at West Ham, and when he left Portsmouth to go to Spurs I was happy because I knew he would be good for the club. And it wasn't just my opinion.

'There had been a lot of whispers and then the phone rang and Harry was on the other end: "JD, will you come back?" It was within a few days of him taking over from Ramos and I just said: "Make it happen please." I then got a call from Daniel Levy, who promised me he'd make it happen, that I was coming back. I didn't want them to pay as much as they did, £18 million, to get me back. I didn't want the club to have to spend that much money. I was at Portsmouth for less than a year and I didn't think it was fair for Tottenham to have to pay so much. I had nothing against Portsmouth but I just wanted to be back playing in a Tottenham shirt. It was the only place I was really happy. When I came back I walked onto the pitch again and I couldn't believe the reception I was getting second time around. I had to pinch myself. I couldn't believe it.

'I'd really enjoyed working with Harry at Portsmouth and we have a great relationship but when I got to Spurs I could see the change in him in just a few weeks. He suddenly realised he was at a really big club, a massive club, for the first time. He knew he was under more pressure but the way he went about his business was brilliant. Nobody should ever try to take away what he achieved at Spurs. Look at what he did – two top four finishes in four years, never out of the top five. That proves what a good job he did and how good he was for Tottenham. He was the one who took the club into the Champions League.'

Redknapp set the bar high – for himself and for those who followed. Robbie Keane had returned from Liverpool, while Honduran midfielder Wilson Palacios brought vital grit and re-solve, before the murder of his brother by a kidnap gang had an immediate and understandable effect on his performances. The much-travelled Pascal Chimbonda, too, helped improve a squad and, crucially, Bale, the most talented of the lot, came out of his shell. Ever since that season, Redknapp has had to contend with claims that he was willing to shift the Welshman on, not least because of Bale's status, among some fans, as a jinx when he did not taste victory in his first 24 games in a Spurs shirt. Rumours of a loan deal to Nottingham Forest or a proposed £3 million sale to Birmingham were loud and persistent, although Redknapp was later adamant that he had no intention of selling him: 'He was never going to go on loan. I always rated him. I was at Southampton when he was there. I went to see Tottenham against Fulham when I was with Portsmouth and he was fantastic. They were winning 3–1 and drew but he was absolutely brilliant and I thought he had the ability to become what he became.

'It's absolute rubbish for anyone to claim we were going to loan him out. He was always going to be a big player. I'm not saying I knew he'd be as fantastic as he became but he had everything. He could run, shoot, dribble, head it. He was the full package. Where does he play now, for Real Madrid? He plays where he wants to. You free him off, giving him no fixed role or defensive responsibilities, and let him go. When he was stuck on the wing no right-back could stop him. You could try and go wide to mark him, but he had the freedom to go inside, pick up the ball and run at the heart of teams. He was fantastic.'

While a penalty shoot-out defeat at Wembley by Manchester United had prevented Spurs from retaining the League Cup – Ramos's win remained, as the Lane was turned to rubble, the club's last trophy – the direction the team was moving in was positive. The following summer, Peter Crouch, who had begun his career in the Spurs youth ranks alongside King, returned to the club. An opening weekend victory over Liverpool set the tone, four straight wins representing the club's best top-flight start since the 1960s. 'We had a good pre-season,' Redknapp said. 'There was confidence around the place and we all felt we could have a real go at it. I saw us as a team that could qualify for the Champions League that year.'

The belief grew as the season wore on. An FA Cup run added to the mood, especially when Spurs drew Portsmouth in the FA Cup semi-final, a club in turmoil – with boss Avram Grant having to dig into his own pocket to pay the training-ground staff – and beginning their precipitous plunge to League Two and the brink of financial disintegration. It would surely signal an end to a bad run of Wembley losses and result in a final with Chelsea. It was not to be. Spurs dominated possession, with countless efforts on goal and 20 corners. But they still managed to lose 2–0. 'I don't know what happened,' a nonplussed Redknapp said seven years on. 'We had seventy-five shots but we missed chance after chance and they stuck their chances away. It was a low night.'

It was a case of here we go again. Next up, over the course of the following seven days, were Arsenal and Chelsea, both at the Lane. Manchester City, embarking on their relentless spending spree after being taken over by the investment arm of the Abu Dhabi royal family and determined to demonstrate their ambition, were four points ahead in the battle for the crucial fourth spot, and while Spurs had two games in hand with six to play, the odds had shifted markedly. Even the fans had steeled themselves for the disappointment of falling short once again. For the normal. For Spurs. 'The players knew the importance of our response,' Redknapp said. 'Getting into the Champions League was all-important. They were two massive games.'

In truth, nobody could have imagined what was to follow in those frantic few days in April 2010. Indeed, for the best part of six years, which included loan spells at Bristol City and Sunderland, before he turned himself into a first-team fixture under Mauricio Pochettino, most Tottenham supporters believed Danny Rose would be remembered for just one swing of his right boot, three minutes into the game against Arsenal, which sent Łukasz

Fabianski's punch arcing back over the Gunners' defence and the Polish keeper to hit the back of the Park Lane net. 'When it dropped I went: "No Danny!" Redknapp said. 'Then I went: "Yes Danny!" It was a fantastic goal. I used to say to Danny when he was a left winger with the England under-21s, that he was a left-back – but he didn't want to play there. I said he'd play for England at left-back. When you're stuck out and being marked it's different. He's got pace and power and aggression. He's a fixture in the England team now.'

Back to back wins, Bale scoring in each game, altered the mode and mentality, among players and fans alike. Even so, there was still one huge task. Redknapp and his side travelled to City on 5 May, four days before the end of the season, a point ahead in fourth, the final Champions League spot, with two to play. Redknapp was counselled to be cautious, to play for a draw. He did not listen: 'We had a go. I played two up front, two wingers. I said: "Let's go for it, we can cause them problems." It was a great night, fantastic, one I can never forget.' Certainly not, although many will most recall Bentley's big mistake, interrupting Redknapp's post-match TV interview to dunk him and his suit in a vat of water, rather than Crouch's close-range header. It hastened the England winger's Spurs demise. More crucially for the fans, it was an invitation to dine at the top table for the first time. All Spurs had to do was get through the door by beating Young Boys Berne in the Champions League play-off round the following August. They'd be playing on a plastic pitch, but, at least so Redknapp believed, they were up against plastic opponents. 'Clive Allen went to watch them and told me they were so average,' he said, allowing himself a smile now. 'When they got their third I turned to him and said: "I thought you said they were fucking useless!" Maybe it was meant to be that way. After all, Nicholson's team had been four down at Górnik Zabrze in 1961. Three was comparatively easy. Defender Seb Bassong pulled one back before the break, Roman Pavlyuchenko another afterwards, and at 3–2 Spurs were back in the tie. At the Lane, with the fans bang up for it, Crouch scored a hat-trick, Defoe the second, and the 4–0 victory meant that Tottenham were back in the hat for Europe's elite competition, being drawn with the defending champions Inter, as well as Werder Bremen and unlikely Dutch champions FC Twente. They'd be trying to win the European Cup, that most famous of trophies, for only the second time, and the first time since Nicholson's men had reached the last four against Benfica back in 1962.

On the eve of their opening game with Werder Bremen, I, along with the *Telegraph*'s Jason Burt, sat down with Levy in the lobby of the Spurs team hotel in the North German city. He had pulled off a deadline day swoop, taking Dutchman Rafael van der Vaart from Real, a symbol of his ambition. And it was clear the chairman saw that coming night as the vindication of all he had put into the club. In the light of what has transpired since, his words have even more resonance. Levy said: 'Tottenham is a huge club. We have more than 30,000 people waiting for a season ticket. We deserve to be in the Champions League. Our history dictates that but it has taken us a long time to get back. It's something special. But it's not about me. It's about the club and the fans.

'The club isn't Tottenham without its history. The history of this club is so important. I don't think we'd get worldwide recognition without our history so I think it's vital. It's a combination of factors. We have a huge following around the globe. Everyone, in a way, expects us to be in the top four or certainly contending to be in the top four. We have a great player base and a fan-base that is the size of a top-four club. Yet we haven't been here for such a long time. We should all be proud. We are, believe it or not, one of the smallest clubs in terms of stadium capacity in the Champions League. We don't have the income of some of the other clubs. So I think we have done well.

'We all want to stay there but we all have to be realistic. There are only four places in England and there are seven or eight clubs competing. There are probably two clubs you could say are guaranteed to be in that top four. You then have two places for six clubs. One has to be realistic. The odds are stacked against you. But what we won't do is jeopardise the club to challenge to be one of those two. You can't run the club on the basis of being in the Champions League. Often people say you just need an extra player. It doesn't work. It's about the team. I like to think it's important to run the club in the right way. It's not just about today. It's about the future generation of fans. You have to protect the club. If I'm honest you have to put it into context. We will make £15 million from being in the group stages of the Champions League but look what we spent on players. You could buy one good striker. You have to remember it's not a gold mine and we are suddenly going to get all this money. Harry has done a great job but the success of a club can never been down to one individual whether it be a player, director, manager or money. It's a combination of factors that all come together and, as ever, there will always be an element of luck.'

The following day Spurs squandered an early two-goal lead to draw but two weeks later they were far too strong for Twente. And so, for what was to prove to be the first of two visits in that campaign, to the San Siro. After 45 minutes, some of the travelling supporters were thinking about heading out. Spurs were four goals down and a man short, after keeper Heurelho Gomes was rightly dismissed. Horror-show stuff. 'Tim Sherwood was with me,' Redknapp said. 'He came in and said: "You might as well take Bale off; you've got a game on Saturday." It was probably a sensible thing to do. But I said: "No, I'm going to attack them!"' Barking? Some would have thought so. Had Inter scored a fifth, it might have been a record-breaking night, for all the wrong reasons. But, from nowhere, Spurs found a different dimension. They started to give the ball to Bale, who eyed up Maicon and ate him for dinner, scoring one five minutes into the second half and two more in three minutes as the game entered stoppage time.

It was Spurs who walked off feeling like winners, even though they had lost. Their mindset had been transformed, as was to be proven in north London two weeks later. Redknapp said: 'If it had lasted another ten minutes we might have won it.'

And it meant that when the teams lined up for the return group game, there was no inferiority complex, just a determination to make Inter pay for their complacency. The game-plan was simple. Let Modrić control the middle of the park, allow van der Vaart to find spaces – and give the ball to Bale. From the outset, it was an unequal contest. Bale had Maicon on toast, turning the Brazilian into an inanimate object, hapless and helpless. He played a role in van der Vaart's opener and then set up tap-ins for Crouch and Roman Pavyluchenko in the second half. It could have been more, too. Cliff Jones, who knows more than most about thrilling wing-play, could barely believe his eyes. 'Gareth was unstoppable that night,' said Jones. 'There was an expectancy every time he got the ball. That was one of the greatest performances any Spurs player will ever produce. I'd take a little credit for when he started scoring headers. I'd tell him to arrive later and come across the defender – that's what Bill Nick told me, I was passing it down the generations.'

Redknapp conceded he expected a more trademark Italian approach from Rafael Benítez's side: 'I was surprised. It was amazing after Bale had given him such a torrid time in the first game. Maicon was rated the best right-back in the world and Gareth destroyed him. I found it strange that they left Maicon out there with nobody in front of him. There was all the space in the world. He was left exposed by Rafa. The bloke in the pub could've set them up better. He hung him out to dry that night – and Gareth took him to the cleaners. At White Hart Lane the atmosphere is fantastic on nights like that. The crowd is on top of you, the place is jumping, it's intimidating for the away team, they turn up and suddenly they find it's all tight, that we're getting straight after them, winning tackles and challenges.'

Up in his box in the West Stand, Defoe was rubbing his eyes in disbelief – and frustration. The striker had helped Spurs reach the Champions League but was then forced into a watching brief. He said: 'I came back from the World Cup. We'd just signed van der Vaart and I had a good beginning to the season. I scored a hat-trick against Bulgaria but then got an ankle injury in Switzerland the following midweek and was out for two months. I was at the stadium for the Inter Milan game, watching what Gareth and Luka did to them. It was an unbelievable night, just stunning. What Gareth did to Maicon, such an experienced full-back who was being rated as one of the best in the world, was just something else. To be there and see that was fantastic and even though I was disappointed not to be on the pitch it was just great to be there and feel part of the atmosphere and see what Gareth did, close up in front of me. It was absolutely mental.'

For Bale, it was what he needed: proof that he had what it took against the very best. He said: 'When we were trying to qualify for the Champions League, it was so we could test ourselves against the best players in Europe. When we got in and got drawn against Inter Milan, the reigning champions, it was a chance to test ourselves. It was a great atmosphere that night. For me personally, when I played so well in the group stages and then the knock-out stages, it really gave me that belief that I could compete with the best. Since then I've kept growing and have the confidence that I can compete against the best and beat the best.'

A home victory over Bremen and a draw in the Netherlands saw Spurs top their group, although the demands of the Champions League were taking their toll on domestic form, despite a stunning victory at Arsenal from two goals down, sealed by Younès Kaboul's header. The dropped points in the league were to prove costly. When European combat was resumed, Redknapp and his players were back in Milan for the first leg tie in the knock-out phase, this time to take on the red and black of AC at the San Siro. On this occasion, rather than a goal glut, it was a single strike, scored by Crouch, that was to prove decisive, being the only goal of the tie, as Spurs went toe to toe on the pitch and in the technical area, with Redknapp's assistant, Joe Jordan, refusing to be intimidated by Massimiliano Allegri's pocket Rottweiler, Gennaro Gattuso. 'I'd watched them and felt we could give them problems,' Redknapp said. 'We felt we'd keep it tight and hit them on the counter and that's what we did, Aaron Lennon getting away down the right and Crouchy putting it away. That was a fantastic night. And we saw it through with an unusually defensive display from a Tottenham team in the home leg.'

They did, even if it was a nerve-shredding affair, William Gallas's first half goalline clearance proving critical and tie-winning. Next up, Real Madrid and Mourinho. Things did not go to plan. Bale was hampered by injury, Lennon cried off in the tunnel and after 14 minutes Crouch saw yellow for the second time in an act of self-inflicted harm. 'Crouchy getting sent off destroyed us,' Redknapp said. 'It would have been hard enough with eleven men, let alone ten. Lennon wasn't well, he didn't feel good and couldn't play. But I'm sure we could've given them a game and caused them problems if we'd been at full strength. Even as it was we were still in the game at sixty minutes. But we ran out of legs a bit.' There was no way back from a 4–0 loss and while the performance in the return was better, Gomes dived over Ronaldo's shot to hand Real the only goal of the night. It was to prove the last European Cup goal the Lane would ever witness, although not the last time the club from the Lane was to earn the right to play for the biggest trophy in football.

Having been in charge of a magic-carpet ride, giving his side the chance to lock horns with some of European football's most prestigious names and prove Tottenham were not out of place in their company, Redknapp did not take any blame for finishing out of the top four at the end of that season. Indeed, when Levy stood firmly behind his manager the following summer, blankly refusing to even contemplate letting Modrić leave for Chelsea, who were waving huge sums in front of the Croatian, their bond seem strengthened. Spurs began by shipping eight goals in two games, losing 3–0 at United before being thumped 5–1 on home soil by City, but the deadline arrivals of Emmanuel Adebayor – who had scored two for Madrid against them a few months earlier – and Scott Parker from relegated West Ham saw Spurs find their feet and form, losing just once in five months and winning 15 of their next 19 games, when they were on the wrong end of a truly desperate refereeing display at Stoke by Chris Foy. In January, victory over Wolves would send them top, for 24 hours at least. They drew, and then travelled to the Etihad. Two down and suffering, a quick-fire brace from Bale and Defoe brought them level. Then, Howard Webb, rated the best referee in the world but an official Redknapp was convinced had a downer on him, missed Mario Balotelli's blatant stamp on Parker's head. Defoe was a stud's length away from turning in Bale's cross before Balotelli won it from the spot in added time. The subsequent three-match ban the Italian received for the Parker incident added insult to injury.

It was at this point that the relationship between Redknapp and Levy began to unravel, on two fronts. The chairman and other Spurs directors had been constant presences in the public gallery at Southwark Crown Court as Redknapp was cleared, after a three-week trial, of tax-evasion charges relating to his time at Portsmouth. Yet even as Levy joined the post-trial celebration party, events on the other side of London were taking place that were to have a marked effect. England boss Fabio Capello quit the FA in the wake of the storm over the decision to strip John Terry of the captaincy following his clash with Anton Ferdinand, seemingly opening the way for an approach to Spurs for their manager, seen by the majority of fans and media alike as the most eligible English candidate. And, at the same time, Redknapp was badgering the chairman to spend more money.

Five years on, Redknapp insisted that suggestions he took his eye off the ball because of his England ambitions were fanciful. It was a point of view, though, that was strongly held by the Tottenham hierarchy. Redknapp said: 'I wasn't crazy about managing England. I just loved managing that team. When Roy Hodgson was announced I thought: "That saves me a problem." I was managing Tottenham and felt lucky. I never had a meeting with anyone even though I was red-hot favourite. Roy said he wouldn't go for an interview because he felt I was sure to get it.

'But in the January I think we had the belief we could do it, that we could win the title. We needed to bring in one or two to make the difference. If we'd had a go, it was there for us to do it. We needed bodies and two top players. But at that time Daniel didn't want to do it. We took Ryan Nelsen and Louis Saha, two free transfers. You need bodies and that was all they were. I haven't got the statistics but we ran into a few injuries and I didn't have enough quality. It wasn't about England. We were short and if we'd brought in two we could've won the league. In the situation we were in we could've gone and got a couple, pushed the boat out, and that would've made the difference.'

History is normally written by the winners, not the losers. Despite surrendering third place to Arsenal, Spurs were still fourth. Enough, in every single year since 2002, for a spot in the Champions League play-off round. But Uefa, having allowed Liverpool to enter the competition as a team 'without national status' in 2005 following their triumph in Istanbul when they finished fifth in the Premier League, had altered the regulations to confirm the holders would automatically be entitled to defend their crown, but that no country could have more than four representatives in the competition. Given that the rules were revised soon afterwards, you suspect Spurs should have readied their lawyers. As it was, given the way Chelsea had stuttered and stumbled their way to the final, losing manager André Villas-Boas on the way and finishing sixth, below Newcastle, Redknapp probably assumed they would run out of luck against Bayern Munich, especially with the Germans playing in their own stadium, and that fourth place would be enough to secure the final Champions League place for the 2012–13 season.

The rest is history. Painful history for Spurs supporters, and for Redknapp: 'I went over there cheering for Bayern. I was only concerned about Tottenham. Bayern smashed them but missed chance after chance. At the end, after the shoot-out, I walked round the pitch with the Chelsea fans singing "Thursday night, Channel Five" at me. That wasn't a lot of fun. It knocked me for six. I was pretty gutted. I just wanted to get home.'

Within days, Redknapp was not just out of the Champions League, but out of Tottenham too. His attempt to call Levy's bluff over a new contract could not have been more poorly timed, and with the Spurs board blaming the manager for not taking chance out of the equation by ensuring a top-three finish, his time was up. Levy had chosen, bizarrely, Villa-Boas, leaving a crestfallen Redknapp to wind down his car window one last time and declare: 'I had four great years. All you can do is leave a club in a better shape than you found it and I think that's what I did. The people who follow Tottenham had a lot to smile about in those four years, a lot to be proud of as Tottenham fans. I will never forget the fans and how they treated me. They were absolutely amazing. I would like to be remembered as someone who had time for everybody. I enjoy talking to people. I have time for everybody. I just want to be a decent person.'

Time softens even the deepest blows. Five years on and Redknapp was happy to take up the invitation to dine with Levy before a Spurs Premier League game at Bournemouth. There was no point in dredging up any hard feelings, especially as the fans who felt Redknapp had let them down now recognised his part in altering the football world's perceptions of the club. Redknapp said: 'It was a great time in my life. To stand there and watch some of the football we played, it was scary. The way we moved the ball round the pitch was incredible. And we had some great lads, like

Michael Dawson, a great professional. It was a fantastic time in my life. I loved every minute of it. I was fortunate to manage such a great club.' It could have been for longer, of course. But Redknapp made a real difference. Taxi for Maicon!

13

TRAGEDY, TEARS . . . AND TOUCHDOWNS

White Hart Lane was, first and foremost, a football stadium. It was devised as such when the club outgrew its second home in nearby Northumberland Park. It was rebuilt on a number of occasions as the demands of the supporters, changing times and evolving laws demanded, the capacity first rising, then falling. The successor ground to the north of the old stadium can hold almost double the capacity of White Hart Lane during its last campaign. But Spurs did not feature in every game there. And other sports took place under the shadow of those stands.

In all, between 1902 and 1988, 12 FA Cup semi-final matches took place in N17. It is fair to say few of them were memorable or remarkable, other than for the two sides involved. The first saw Southern League Southampton beat Nottingham Forest 3–1 in front of a crowd given as 30,000, with two goals from Albert Brown, the 'Tamworth Sprinter', among 25 goals he scored in his sole full season for the club – including seven in a single game against Northampton before leaving for Queens Park in Scotland. Brown's renown as the fastest player in the game brought him fame, too. Two months before that semi, Liverpool's England winger Jack Cox, a speedster himself, laid down the gauntlet. The *Nottingham Evening Post* reported: 'Jack Cox, of Liverpool, has issued a challenge to run Albert Brown of Southampton, 120 yards. Brown is willing if terms can be arranged.' Sadly, there is no record of whether the race ever took place.

Oddly enough, there was another FA Cup clash between the two teams at the Lane, this time in 1963 – a second quarter-final replay after the teams had drawn 1–1 at the City Ground and 3–3 at The Dell. An astonishing Monday afternoon crowd of 42,256 was there to see Saints win 5–0. Les Jeoffroy, then not quite a teenager, recalled him and his pals making the short trip from Wood Green: 'We all became Saints fans because they were the southern club.'

While there were other more regular semi-final venues, White Hart Lane was on the FA's map. There were more games before the outbreak of the First World War, with Newcastle attracting 33,000 as they beat Swindon in 1910 and Liverpool's 2–0 win over Aston Villa in 1914 watched by 27,474. There was also one game between the wars, when Swansea Town, as they were then known, had an estimated 710 fans from *Cardiff* in their ranks, among 25,476 inside, as they were taken apart by Bolton.

A 24-year gap followed before a remarkable series saw Chelsea and Arsenal clash four times in the space of two years. Arsenal had shared the Lane during the war although it was very much neutral territory both in 1950 and again in 1952. In aggregate, the four matches were watched by a staggering 259,768 supporters, with Arsenal's Freddie Cox scoring in all four games, as the Gunners won both replays. It was familiar territory for Cox, who had joined Spurs in 1938 and spent 11 seasons on the White Hart Lane books before moving to Highbury, scoring twice in Tottenham's run to the semi-finals in 1948. That attendance total may well have been higher, too, had the 1952 replay not been scheduled just two days after the original meeting. The post-war attendance boom was still at its zenith when more than 63,000 packed in to watch Luton draw 1–1 with Norwich in 1959, although the crowd of just over 55,000 to watch Chelsea hammer Watford on what was little more than a sandpit with a bit of grass on the outside edge in 1970 signalled where the game was going. By 1986, with Liverpool outlasting Southampton in extra time as they closed in on their Double, the crowd was down to 44,605 and while

Wimbledon's meeting with Luton two years later was never going to be the hottest ticket in town, only 25,963 attended.

And, of course, other 'neutral' matches, too. With Highbury still out of commission in the aftermath of the Second World War, some 54,620 turned up at the Lane to watch Arsenal lose 4–3 to the touring Dynamo Moscow on a Wednesday afternoon in November 1945. Some 23 years later, Graeme Souness came to the attention of Spurs with his performance in a schoolboy international in N17, while in 1981 non-league neighbours Enfield staged an FA Cup fourth-round replay against Barnsley at White Hart Lane, the furthest the north London non-league side have ever progressed in the competition.

It was not just club football either, with England playing home games at the ground five times between 1933, when France were downed 2–0, and 2001, during the £757 million Wembley rebuild. None of the other games were anywhere near as contentious as the 1935 clash with Nazi-era Germany, in which the club's Jewish connection and global politics took centre stage and brought wider issues into the equation. But Stanley Matthews did score a hat-trick as Czechoslovakia, soon to be annexed by Hitler's territorial ambitions, were beaten 5–4 in 1937. And four years after the war, with Alf Ramsey earning the third of his 31 caps on his home ground, two late goals, including a fluke for Billy Wright when his pump forward from halfway was caught by a gust of wind to deceive the Italy keeper, stole victory over the world-champion Azzurri – admittedly, there had been 12 years since the last tournament – in front of just under 72,000. The last of those England games, and the only one in which England suffered defeat, was soon forgotten, too. Just 17 days after losing to Holland at White Hart Lane – the stand-out moment was David James lasting just four minutes as a half-time replacement after he was clattered into by Martin Keown, sustaining a knee injury that kept him out for three months before he returned to the West Ham side in time to lose to Spurs at Upton Park – Sven-Goran

Eriksson's side performed rather more impressively against Germany in Munich. And five years later, Brazil beat Wales 2–0, with a coltish 17-year-old named Gareth Bale, then in his first season as a Southampton first-teamer, making only his second appearance for the Red Dragons, in front of 22,008.

Of all the other sports staged at White Hart Lane, boxing had the longest, and most infamous, association with the stadium. In 1922, White Hart Lane put on what was described by Pathé News as 'London's first open air boxing contest', with 7,000 said to be in attendance to see 'Bloomfield defeat Lloyd' and 'Seaman Hall beat Rossi' before Jim Smith proved too good for Pat King in a bout for the 'Dockland Settlement Championship'. The grainy seven-minute footage is notable for the fact that there is no referee in the ring as the fighters slugged it out, although the majority of the action caught on camera belonged to what was titled a 'Famous Comic Boxing Match', between Wally Pickard and Joe Bowker. The pair performed a variety of exaggerated moves, moving around the ring in slow motion and taking a series of bizarre falls, with an advert visible by the corner of the ring, imploring those present to 'Smoke Smith's'. Proof that entertainment fashions are transient, I suspect.

Other fights followed. In 1942, with London still braced for the regular bombing raids, some 30,000 crowded in to watch Pilot Officer Len Harvey defend his 'World, Empire and British' light heavyweight crown against RAF Sergeant Freddie Mills, at 22 some 13 years the champion's junior. The fight lasted barely four minutes, as Harvey aged visibly in the space of less than two rounds. He was knocked through the ropes and onto the apron, left as little more than a punchbag after a left hook put him down for a count of nine, and then finished off with a flurry of combination blows. Mills, the newsreel stated, got the belts he wanted, but also 'no jankers for hitting a superior officer'.

Colin Hart, the veteran boxing correspondent of the *Sun*, was only seven years old for that one. Three years later he was listening on his crackling wireless when Bruce Woodcock knocked out Jack London to win the British Heavyweight title, and by the time Joe Bugner took on Frank Bruno in 1987 he was part of the British boxing establishment. Bruno was Britain's most loved boxer, his opponent a man who revelled in the label of 'the most unpopular man in British sport'. That was a little harsh. The Hungarian-born Bugner's 'crime' was to win a contentious points verdict over Henry Cooper in 1971, a defeat which pushed the older man into retirement and a post-boxing career as a TV personality and Brut salesman. Bugner always felt he got a raw deal: 'I never wanted to be the man who ended Henry's career. I had no idea that was to be his last fight. What happened to me after that fight was worse than being crucified. Even the Kray twins got a better press. I was blamed for something I had no control over. Even one moronic Labour MP called for me to be stripped of my title, stripped of my assets and sent back to wherever I came from. I was a twenty-one-year-old kid and my mind was totally fucked after that. I had another twenty fights in England after beating Henry and the re-action from the crowd was bloody painful every time. In the end, I was chased out of my own country.' Bugner portrayed himself as a media victim, categorising himself alongside other 'targets' such as Daley Thompson, Ian Botham and Nick Faldo.

Originally Bruno, who had just been stopped by Tim Wither-spoon in his second shot at a world title, had been due to face Canada's Trevor Berbick, who pulled out 11 days before the scheduled fight on 29 September with a back injury. But Barry Hearn – whose Matchroom stable was to become the dominant force in British boxing, although his impact to that point had been on snooker, with many of the game's top stars, including the relent-less Steve Davis, cruelly dubbed 'Interesting' by the puppeteers of *Spitting Image*, in his camp – then made his first foray into the fight game.

Hearn rang Bugner, who was on his own comeback at the time but now waving the Australian flag, out of the blue. The chance to make his mark proved too good to refuse, although Bugner and Hearn did not meet until the boxer touched down at Heathrow. Bugner and Bruno had previously traded insults. Now they could exchange blows. And so the fight was set for 24 October, with estimates of a gate in excess of 40,000, income of £3 million predicted and a purse split earning Bruno £450,000 and Bugner £250,000, with the younger man's pot including 35 per cent of the gate receipts. The crowd was boosted by Hearn's vow that it would not be screened live on television. He cleverly, though, failed to reveal his plans to do a deal with ITV to show it 'as-live' an hour after the first bell.

The mutual disregard between the two boxers was evident in the build-up. Bugner publicly predicted a first-round knock-out and encouraged the criticism and the brickbats. 'Calling me the most unpopular man in the country is a wonderful line,' he said, as the fight came closer. 'That's why we're coming to Spurs, because we're going to fill the place. And when I knock him out they're going to like me again. I'm here to do a job. The twelve years' difference will make sense because I'm going to show Bruno for the inexperienced man he is. Bruno is a C-class fighter who may have just been promoted to B-class. I'm an A-plus fighter. As far as I'm concerned, I've got the strength, the size and the ability to beat him. I heard in Australia he called me a chicken. Well, this chicken has come to roost.'

Bruno hit back: 'His strong point is his mouth. He's got plenty of mouth. I've been waiting five years for this, all the slagging he's done. I'm not Muhammad Ali. I've not got a big mouth and I'm not going to shout off about what I'm going to do. I've got myself mentally fit and body-fit. I will go and do a good job.'

There was even a manufactured row in the build-up. It was announced that both men wanted to box out of the blue corner. Neither would back down, so the 'only way out' was a coin toss. A toss that, of course, had to take place on 18 October, six days before the fight, and just before kick-off in the north London derby against Arsenal, won 2–1 by the visitors. Bill Nicholson threw up the coin and the heads call meant Bruno was the winner.

Everything pointed in the younger man's favour. At 25, he was in his prime. Bugner looked, and was, a very different type of athlete, almost two stones heavier than Bruno's pure muscle and with an extra seven inches around the waist.

Under a red-and-white striped canopy, and with the atmosphere frenzied, Bugner's efforts to intimidate Bruno by using his head failed to pay off. As the fight wore on, the crowd turned on Bugner, with Bruno's superior reach keeping him in control and in round eight the home-town hero unleashed. A right and a series of blows brought a standing count and Bruno kept on coming, with the towel being thrown in as the bell rang, although only after referee John Coyle had stopped the fight.

Four years later, another contest at the ground became a national talking point. The late 1980s and early 1990s were the golden period for British middleweights and in Nigel Benn, Chris Eubank and Michael Watson there was a cast-list of heroes and anti-heroes. Eubank, from Brighton, with his lisp, his haughty manner and his showmanship, was happy to play the villain, even more so after his first meeting with Watson at Earl's Court earlier in 1991 had ended with a controversial points win that saw TV commentator Ian Darke state: 'That's astonishing. I would go as far as to say Michael Watson has been plain robbed. There's no way Chris Eubank won that fight.'

'The Rematch' was nailed on for 21 September, with 22,000 spectators, mainly around the ring as the terraces were filled only by stewards. Colin Hart said: 'Plenty of people thought Watson had won the first fight, so the return was natural and there was a great deal of anticipation that it would be a good contest. Nobody was quite sure who was going to win it.

'Before the fight there was a lot of bitterness between them. There had been plenty of trash talking and inside White Hart Lane there was a nasty atmosphere and a rivalry between the two factions. While there was no crowd trouble before the fight there was a lot of animosity. It was really nasty. I think it was something to do with the islands their families had come from in the Caribbean. It wasn't the first time. When Maurice Hope fought Sterling it was Antigua versus Jamaica and that was the animosity that played out that night.'

Inside the ring, it was a cracker, with Watson edging ahead. Then, with just 17 seconds left in the penultimate round, Watson's stunning right stopped Eubank in his tracks. He went down, seemingly beaten. Hart said: 'Eubank was put on the deck by Watson and everybody, myself included, thought: "That's it – he'll never recover." But instead he somehow got back on his feet and came out to hit Watson with a tremendous uppercut.'

It was a stunning punch, dredged up from deep in Eubank's boxing soul, Watson's head smashing against the bottom rope as he went down. The bell allowed Watson to return to his corner where he sat on his stool with a glazed look in his eyes, staggering to his feet for the round, where he struggled to even make enough of a forward move to touch gloves. 'When they came out for the last round, it was obvious that Watson was still impacted by that punch,' said Hart. 'The referee stopped the fight because he couldn't defend himself. They went back to their corners and then all hell broke out. People were climbing into the ring and Watson was lying there for several seconds, with nobody able to attend to him.'

Eubank, basking in his victory, unaware of what was about to develop, said: 'I want him tested to see if he has something in his blood because he was so strong.' That comment was condemned by former world lightweight champion Jim Watt, who was ringside, but as the analysis continued, with scrapping among some members of the crowd, Watson collapsed in his corner and slipped out of consciousness.

Hart said: 'When they did clear the ring to take him out, they took him to the wrong hospital, one that didn't have a neurological unit. They wasted all that time and by the stage he got to the right hospital, where they could get a scan of his brain, and he had the surgery there, they'd missed what they now call the golden hour. If the doctors can get to people in the first hour after something like that, there's every chance they will make a recovery. Michael was in a coma for weeks and weeks. On the Sunday morning, as it became clear what had happened, I was at the hospital. I had to sit down and write the story, to say that Watson was close to death.'

Seemingly inconceivable, but true. Watson was indeed taken by ambulance to the North Middlesex Hospital, less than a mile from the ground but which had no specialist unit, before being transferred to St Bartholomew's in Smithfields in the City of London, where he was seen by consultant Peter Hamlyn more than two hours after the blow was struck. Hamlyn said: 'He had two procedures in the early hours of the morning to remove blood clots and then a variety of other procedures designed to keep the pressure in his skull down while we drained excess fluid from the brain. Michael was closer to death than anyone I've ever operated on.'

Incredibly, he survived, although severely impaired and with his brain function reduced. His voice still slurring, he said in 2015: 'I remember being in complete control. I had him everywhere I wanted him. I visualised myself being world champion. I was just waiting for that moment. What happened changed boxing. That's where the blessing lies. My life is all about love and forgiveness. To overcome adversity and the odds. I've been through the darkest channels, a man who couldn't talk or walk. But I'm a fighter, here to give people hope where there is no hope. If I can do it, you can do it.'

Watson was correct. 'The aftermath, of course, was that the British Board of Boxing Control went bankrupt because Watson sued them,' Hart said. 'They brought in new rules and regulations to make the sport as safe as it could be. Of course, accidents are always going to happen in a sport like boxing but as a result of what happened anaesthetists are now always at the ringside, the nearest neurology unit is given advice that boxing is going on just in case of an emergency and the promoters and organisers must know how they'd get the boxer to the hospital as quickly as possible. Those are the regulations that not only saved Spencer Oliver's life when he went into a coma after a fight at the Albert Hall but ensured he made such a complete recovery that he's now a boxing pundit on Sky. So there was a lot of good that came out of it. Other boxers did benefit. But it didn't make me consider quitting. The only time that happened was when I was with Johnny Owen in Los Angeles. He was knocked out and I saw him being put in the ambulance, with blood coming out of his ears. When I saw that I knew it was nasty and serious. The doctors pulled the plug on him after six weeks. I thought then: "I can't write about this sport," but someone shook me up and told me that there would still be boxing and fighters, whether I wrote about it or not . . .'

Of course, not all the non-football stories had as much impact. When Daniel Levy announced that Tottenham's new stadium would include a retractable pitch and two separate tunnels and dressing-room complexes, with the artificial second surface designed to host American Football games in order to accommodate the possibility of the new ground becoming the home of a future National Football League franchise, some scoffed. But others recalled that the game had been played at White Hart Lane in the past.

In 1991 the World League of American Football was formed, ostensibly as a finishing school for potential NFL recruits. It included three European-based teams, Barcelona Galaxy, Frankfurt Dragons and London Monarchs, who played home games at Wembley for two seasons before the League was suspended. In 1995, it was relaunched, this time with six European sides, including the Scottish Claymores, but with London moved around the North Circular to White Hart Lane. Various sources claim the

White Hart Lane pitch was actually too small, measuring only 93 yards rather than the required 100, but that special dispensation was given by the WLAF.

That, though, is not quite how Jim Ballard, the starting quarter-back that season, remembers it. Ballard, drafted onto the practice squads of the Cincinnati Bengals and the Buffalo Bills, and who moved to the Claymores in 1996, played in the Canadian Football league for Toronto Argonauts and Saskatchewan Roughriders before moving to play in the indoor, short-sided Arena League and then moving into coaching. Speaking from his home in Canton, Ohio, and as genial and polite as most US sportsmen, in my experience, tend to be, Ballard said: 'The one thing that I recall was that they had to cut the yardage in the end zones. So the pitch was the normal length, a hundred yards, but instead of each end zone being ten yards deep they were only seven yards. As a quarterback, that made a difference as it meant I had less space to work with in terms of being able to throw into the end zone. It made pass completion a lot tougher. The crowds in the World League had started to fall away by the time I came over, although when we played in Germany we'd get up to 40,000 still. From memory we had reasonable crowds, though.'

An average, in fact, of 16,343 that season. Not bad. Ballard said: 'For me it was a great opportunity. I'd played for a Division Three school, the lowest college level, so I was used to playing in front of only four thousand fans anyway. So, as a guy who hadn't played at a big school it helped me catch up in terms of the speed of my game, plus I had an unbelievable mentor in Brad Johnson.

'If I'm honest, I really didn't have an understanding of the fran-chise of Tottenham, what it was, nor that the supporters viewed the stadium as hallowed ground, that it was so historic. I didn't have an idea, really, probably because I didn't, and still don't, follow soccer, the English leagues or the teams.

'I thought we might establish the roots of the game in the UK.

We thought that once people understood the game they'd find it entertaining. What I remember most is living in an old police barracks in Charing Cross. It was pretty grim. In fact, it was so bad that the next year they condemned the building.

'What I feel is a shame and sad is that there isn't a development league for the NFL any more, in the way the World League was. But I'm not surprised to hear that the new Tottenham stadium is going to host NFL games, because the NFL want to make inroads in Europe and expand their reach, even if it's a continent which pays far more attention to soccer. When the NFL plays games in London, they do very well, so it makes sense to have a big stadium that can host more games.'

The Monarchs were not the only team playing an American sport to call the Lane 'home'. A glance through the annals of the British Baseball Federation show that, for three years starting in the summer of 1906, Tottenham Hotspur were the leading force in the game in this country. Crowds of up to 2,500, who paid a mighty 5s for a season ticket – eight games in that first campaign – watched a team that had been formed by director Morton Cadman, who had played for the first team in the 1890s and later skippered the Spurs reserve side, and John Cameron, captain, manager and secretary of the 1901 FA Cup heroes. It seems fair to assume that chairman Charles Roberts, whose 45-year spell at the helm will surely never be matched, and who had lived in Brooklyn earlier in his life and played as a pitcher – although not, sadly, despite the mythology, for the famed Dodgers – would have been keen, too. One of Cameron's players from that victory over Sheffield United, Irishman Jack Kirwan – who was to become the first manager of Ajax – also featured on the diamond when they beat the Nondescripts 16–5 at the Lane to be crowned National Champions. That feat was repeated two years later, Leyton Orient beaten 6–5 in the final, with a team including Alf Whyman, who had scored nine goals over three seasons for Cameron's side in the Southern League. Grainy photos from the time show a side wearing dark – presumably navy – tops with Hotspur in white emblazoned across the chest.

That was many years ago. Far more recently, another man is reminded every day how he so nearly made his final step on that pitch. Fabrice Muamba grew up in north London, going to school in Walthamstow after his family fled their home in Kinshasa in what is now the Democratic Republic of Congo. Signed by Arsenal as a teenager – he started two League Cup ties but never made a Premier League appearance – and capped by England at every level from Under-16 to Under-21, Muamba spent two years at Birmingham and, a month short of his 24th birthday, was in his fourth season at Bolton when he arrived at the Lane for an FA Cup quarter-final match on 7 March 2012.

Three minutes before half-time, with the score standing at 1–1, the crowd realised a Bolton player had collapsed, for no apparent reason, near the centre-circle. 'It was a normal match and suddenly I felt dizzy,' Muamba subsequently recollected. 'My sight started to become difficult and if I tried to focus I saw double. Then I lost control. I was lying there and could hear the guys screaming "come back". Then it was just "bang!" I was gone.'

White Hart Lane chief paramedic Pete Fisher was one of the first to react. He said: 'I'll always remember that night. It's tattooed in my memory. It seemed like a normal Cup game, on a Saturday night. We were sitting like we normally do. Then all of a sudden I looked across and saw Fabrice fall to the floor and start shaking. We're all experienced paramedics and we just knew there was something seriously wrong. We knew straight away that we had to act.

'There was no chance to do anything else. The Spurs medical staff were already over there, with the Bolton doctor, and we were very close behind them. Everyone knew this wasn't a normal case of a player falling down having hurt themselves in a challenge. There was a sense of shock everywhere, instantly – or so I'm told by everybody else. But if I'm honest, I don't remember any of that.

All I remember is focusing on Fabrice. Not just me but the whole team around him. That's what everyone did.'

Bolton club doctor Jonathan Tobin was among those suddenly having to respond to a crisis. He said: 'The physio, Andy Mitchell, saw him go down. I was focusing on the goal mouth. Andy got there first and he was face-down. He turned Fab onto his back and Fab started making a respiratory effort but it was clear something major had happened and we started trying to resuscitate him. It was forty-eight minutes from the time he collapsed until we arrived at the hospital and another thirty minutes at the hospital without a muscular breath. Andy never panics but I could hear that edge of nervousness. He knew it was something big. I was running over thinking: "Oh God." But as soon as I realised he'd had a cardiac arrest I clicked into auto-pilot. You know you have things to do. When I heard the crowd chanting his name, I felt the hairs on the back of my neck stand up.'

Mike Collett, sitting at the front of the Upper Tier of the South Stand (Park Lane end) with his son Ryan, recalled: 'The crowd, all around the ground, picked up on the chants from the Bolton fans and started chanting Muamba's name . . . This went on for some time while Muamba was being treated. Finally he was carried away, and maybe some twenty minutes later the announcement came the match was being abandoned.'

Dr Andrew Deener, a consultant cardiologist at the London Chest Hospital, was at the game using his nephew's season ticket. As the players began to realise what had happened, with referee Howard Webb and Spurs' Dutch star Rafael van der Vaart among those ashen-faced onlookers, he jumped into action: 'I saw a player had collapsed on the pitch and it soon became very clear he was extremely ill. I could see people doing CPR. Something twitched in me and I knew I had to go and help. My brother told me to go. There were two young stewards who didn't want to know but then there was an older one, who we knew and he said: "Okay." I said: "This is what I do. I'm a cardiologist – it's my job to help resuscitate people who have had heart attacks" and he led me down.'

Still on the pitch, the other players, from both sides, were left in shock. Tottenham striker Jermain Defoe had seen many great days at the Lane. This, though, was one he would never forget for very different reasons. 'I walked over and could see him just lying there,' said Defoe. 'I could see it was his heart and that he'd just collapsed. I remember him lying there with his hand in the air. I got goose bumps and thought: "He's gone." To be there, to witness something like that taking place out of nothing on a football pitch, was very hard. Obviously it was something I never expected to see or experience. I'd never seen anything like it and for it to be Fabrice, someone I knew well, made the whole thing even tougher.

'I was there, standing on the pitch, as close as anyone while he was fighting for his life. You just forget why you're supposed to be there. Suddenly none of that mattered, football didn't matter. I didn't want to be there. None of us did. None of us could even think about going out to play the rest of the match. We couldn't have played.'

Collett added: 'What I remember most is that everyone left the ground in near-total silence. Walking down the steps, along the concourse, took about five or six minutes. Everyone was walking slowly, in a state of shock. No one said a word to whoever they were with because everyone thought he was dead. It was the eeriest but most respectful thing I have ever experienced at a match, not just at White Hart Lane, but anywhere.'

Away from the spotlight, Deener and Fisher had work to do. And fast. The paramedic said: 'Initially Dr Deener wasn't allowed to do anything because we didn't know he was a doctor. It was only once we were on the back of the ambulance, away from the stadium and the car park, that it was confirmed by Harry Redknapp's doctor friend that he was a doctor. Then he was allowed to get involved. He was ferried off straight away.'

The consultant added: 'I offered to put an intravenous line in but they felt we should get him off the pitch as soon as possible. Pete said to me: "Let's get him off." We got him into the tunnel and gave him some shots and once we got into the ambulance we were able to do more. Once we got him in the ambulance I was able to get into his femoral vein with a few shots, with Jonathan and Pete taking it in turns to give him cardiac massage, which was effective. The decision to take him to the London Chest rather than North Middlesex was a joint one between the three of us. But he'd still had no spontaneous cardiac output for seventy-eight minutes. That was really unusual, although we'd cooled him down to try to preserve his organs.'

Muamba had been defibrillated twice on the pitch, once in the tunnel, 12 times in the ambulance and 20 times at the hospital. Fisher's job was over. 'It was only afterwards, when I got home, that I realised the immensity of what had happened,' he told me. 'Did I think we'd lost him? I wrote a coroner's statement. That's how much I didn't think we were going to get him back. Traumatic? No. It was what we do. We're paramedics and that is our day-to-day job. It's the norm for us. The un-normal side was watching it back on TV, seeing the fans clapping and chanting for him as we were taking him off the pitch.'

Incredibly, Muamba recovered. Dr Deener is still somewhat stunned by the turnaround: 'He woke up on the Monday, two days later. About half an hour afterwards I went to see him. I asked him his name and he told me, whispering: "Fabrice Muamba." I said: "I understand you're a good footballer" and he replied: "I try!" That was a moving moment, there were tears in my eyes. After what he'd gone through, that was phenomenal.'

Within days, Muamba was pictured smiling in his hospital bed. His football career was over – although that was not confirmed for five months – and he had an implantable cardioverter-defibrillator fitted. On 8 November he returned to N17, receiving a standing ovation from supporters when he walked back onto the pitch he had last left on a stretcher. His return came during the interval of a Europa League tie with Maribor. Back inside the stadium, he said: 'I was nervous. I hoped I wouldn't collapse again. I just wanted to be there once, to give myself closure. It wasn't easy to go back to that spot, to be where my dream was taken away from me. It seems unbelievable even now. All I wanted to do was play football. But I'm glad I did it. It meant I could get on with the rest of my life.'

It was not just a moment for Muamba. Defoe, chatting after a training session at Sunderland, said to me: 'It took a long time for me to get over that. I kept thinking about Fabrice, about what I'd seen. I went to the hospital to visit him, spoke to his family. People know I have a strong Christian faith and try to be positive, but when I was told he was recovering and was going to be all right I felt amazing.'

14

THEY ALSO SERVE . . .

'Welcome to White Hart Lane, the world-famous home of the Spurs . . .' These are the words every Tottenham fan – and visiting supporter – has heard for more than four decades. And for 20 years the pre-game routine, as the players head out from the tunnel to start the nervous, edgy, intoxicating few minutes before kick-off, has been begun by Pete Abbott, sitting in his cluttered, dated, dilapidated and primitive eyrie perched high in the corner between the East Stand and the Park Lane end of the ground.

Pete has had plenty of other jobs at Tottenham too, including as a training-ground regular, interviewing players and managers for official club publications, through the misery era, and he has been a familiar voice as a newsreader on stations such as talkSPORT over the years as well. But Spurs is his first love. And like any Spurs fan, manager or player, he recognises his place in the line of succession.

As we looked down on the pitch through the large glass window, with Pete running through his pre-game order, he conceded the years had flown past but also taken their toll.

'Amazingly this is now my twentieth season doing this. And I can't believe that either,' he said, with a chuckle. 'I've done seven hundred games or so. I've been here, doing this, longer than Willie Morgan was. And when I was a kid, coming here, he seemed like he was always here.'

Ah yes, Willie Morgan, with his distinctive voice throughout my youth, who would play the latest top 10 hit and casually mention the High Street record shop where you could pick up your own copy. Presumably he got his for free. 'So there was Willie Morgan, then Gary Stevens for a few years. Then they got some girl in to do it, who didn't last very long. She claimed she was some sort of Polish princess and also had a job as a Barbie lookalike, a full-size human Barbie doll. Although maybe she was still more lifelike than Paolo Tramezzani . . .

'I suppose it's right to say I've become part of the fabric of the place and that every Spurs fan knows my voice – although I've never thought of it like that. From that point of view it's just a job. But because it's a job here, it's not just a job – it's always been far more important than that. I always pride myself on trying to do the best I can, especially if I'm being paid to do something. But I try and make it that little bit extra here because this is Spurs, this is my club, I've been coming here my whole life.

'As long as I've been here this is where the [announcer's] box has been. I don't know where it was before that. I'm not sure I'm going to miss this room. Look at the state of it. It's a tattered cubby hole. I can play whatever music I like. The only constant is "Glory, Glory" before every game and at the final whistle if we win. Otherwise it's been left down to me. But I'm always conscious that I'm not here as a fan. That this is work. Of course, I do swear at the ref and stuff, but not as much as I would if I was "a real fan" paying to sit here. Then I'd be doing a lot more. Then you can relax, watch and enjoy the game. I try to watch and enjoy as much as I can but there's always things coming up that I've got to get ready for.'

Pete was one of the invisible army at the Lane. Even during the final season, with the north-east corner removed to make way for the huge concrete pillar that is a major part of the new stadium, 31,000-plus were officially present for every Premier League. But behind the scenes, not counted in the attendance figures, were another 1,350 match day staff. Caterers, turnstile operators, gatemen, waiters and barmen, in the ticket office and the car park – people whose lives had become just as intertwined with White Hart Lane as any of those who paid to get in or the stars on the pitch. They included the men and women who tiptoed round the paying guests along the narrow corridors behind the East Stand, a design that must have been just about as easy to navigate as the lower decks of a Second World War submarine, especially with piping hot food to be delivered on time. If you looked at the plans for the 61,000-capacity structure that would one day dwarf its predecessor, with its broad, open walkways inside the ground, you could see that the Lane, for all its history, was simply not suited to twenty-first century Premier League football. Or even close.

But it is people, flesh and blood, more than mere brick and ironwork, that really make a ground special, that give context and integrity to the widely held idea of a stadium as having meaning. Take Alan Pegg, whose first visit to White Hart Lane was in 1962. Alan, who got his initial job at the club in 1990 by accident, 'handed an orange bib' when he came to a game with his brother, is now the senior steward in the players' tunnel. He saw a few scrapes and clashes over the years. And he also 20 managers, including the odd caretaker, come and go.

'I've always been a Spurs fan,' he said, soon after arriving in his spot from his home in Enfield. 'If you cut me open, I'd bleed blue and white, I would. The proof that I bleed blue and white is that fourteen years ago I had cancer of the oesophagus. I needed a fourteen-hour operation to have it removed. They say that when you're under anaesthetic you think of the things you love most. And when I woke up, my wife was there, and the first thing I said to her was: "How did Spurs do?" They'd beaten Man City 3–2 at Maine Road, just before Christmas. That's what it means to me. Unfortunately, my first love is Spurs. And my second love is my wife! And she knows that, has done ever since I met her.

'My boy is now twenty-eight. He's one of triplets. My wife used to look after his sisters and I bought him a season ticket and brought him over here. And for a few years, I had to apologise now and again for making him a Spurs supporter, although not so much now. When he was very young, Nick was standing outside and Kenneth Wolstenholme came walking by. So I said: "Ken, say it to him", so he said: "Some people are on the pitch, they think it's all over" and Nick said: "He really sounds like that man . . ." It's the little things like that that you remember.'

Alan, who admitted he was already preparing to shed a tear or two on the Lane's final day, loved watching Mauricio Pochettino's team and felt the respect of Harry Kane and his comrades for the job he undertook. But he grew up watching Greaves, Mackay and Smith – 'Those days were a little bit special' – and he got to know Gascoigne too. He also got to know the managers, and not just the Tottenham ones.

'I'm responsible for the security in the tunnel, although I do become a little bit of a gofer for the players, but that's natural,' he said, his north London accent as strong now as it had ever been. 'Because I'm the one who is looking after the tunnel. We do those things.

'I enjoyed all those nights when we'd beaten them lot up the road, Woolwich Wanderers. That's really nice. Once Mr Wenger wasn't allowed on the touchline. He was on one of his bans. It was a League Cup tie. Unfortunately we got thrashed that night but my job was to take Mr Wenger up to the director's box, because he wasn't allowed to be in the dug-out.

'When we got outside, he's three years older than me, so I said: "There's a lift there, Mr Wenger." But he said: "Oh, it's okay, we'll take the stairs." And he literally ran up the stairs, four floors, with me running behind him. And when he got to his seat, he was fine – but I felt I needed some oxygen!

'Originally I was on the track, making sure people didn't go onto the pitch. Then I was looking after the away managers before they had the fourth officials who have to look after the technical area and make sure the managers don't misbehave. That was very interesting, dealing with the likes of Gordon Strachan. He wasn't so bad. But a few were. Terry Burton, who used to be with Wimbledon, he was a little bit lively. And I used to have many rows and problems. Gordon Strachan would scream in my face because there was nobody else for him to scream at, so he did it at me! Then he'd go away, come back, sit on my lap and apologise. One day one of the assistant managers was swearing away. I'm pretty sure the manager was Joe Royle, and he'd obviously had enough of it because he came over, pointed at his own assistant and said: "He's swearing – throw him out!" You had the supporters behind them complaining, so it was down to me to say: "Can you keep the language down?" and when it's someone like that you can imagine the response I got.'

As for the home bosses, Alan had plenty of memories of them too: 'I've always found every manager I worked under down here was very good. They all had their ways. Even Christian Gross. I liked him, he was a nice person. I'm not saying he was the best manager in the world . . . but Santini, he lasted five minutes. Jol was a fantastic manager for us, a really nice guy, but he used to call a spade a spade. If he wanted something, he'd tell you, good and proper. And you had Harry with his funny ways. He was someone who'd come in and just talk for twenty minutes about what he'd done the night before, as if he was one of us.

'I got to know Glenn as a player and as a manager. He was the king of this place when he was a player. And it became a lot tougher for him when he was the manager, most definitely. If you speak to anybody who was here when he was manager, they all appreciated what he was trying to do. But it didn't work out and the hierarchy felt they had to change things. But he was God down here. It was nice to be able to speak to him as a manager. He was more or less the same but doing a different job. I do sometimes think back at the number of managers we've gone through. There have been times when I've thought: "He's the right one" and then it didn't happen and they disappear. But Poch is a really nice guy and doing so well for the team.'

That sense of the club moving in the right direction during the 2016–17 season was shared by many who had lived through the worst of Spurs times, the years when the only constant was inconsistency, the only nailed-on certainty abject disappointment, as Spurs fell behind not only Arsenal but also Chelsea, fuelled by the investment of Roman Abramovich.

Danny Frost, who worked alongside Alan, once dreamed of being a player himself: 'I used to play in the youth team down here, when we used to train here at the ground, underneath the West Stand. We never had the facilities they've got now but Bobby Smith and Dave Mackay were training underneath the stadium.' It didn't happen for him, though. Like nuns, many are called, but few are chosen.

For Barry Staines, the senior steward in the South Stand, whose job it was to look after the away fans, it remained a labour of love, even after 25 years. His first game at the Lane was to see Nicholson's team put nine past the Icelandic minnows of Keflavík in the Uefa Cup in 1971, sitting above the Paxton Road terrace. 'I remember the goals . . . ish,' he said. 'I do remember how cold it was.' Given that it was a September game, maybe it wasn't quite as cold as he thought?

Barry saw things change over the years. 'We used to turn up in our jeans and trainers, were given a bib and told: "Away you go." Now, for a three o'clock kick-off I'm here by nine in the morning. I open up the stands and the turnstiles, go round the stands and check all the areas, the stairwells and catering bars. Then we change the segregation line, making sure that's in the right place, because it moves depending on the allocation for the away fans.

'Then we have our security briefings.

'That has changed as well, the briefing I give. When I first came it was pretty basic: "There's a bib; you're going to stand there." And that was it, really. But now it's very different. We tell the stewards they have to stop the fans from standing up in their seats, to be on the lookout for the sort of chants we don't want to hear, the offensive stuff. We also talk about what the away fans have been like in the past, what they might do, so we're aware of that.

'Personally I don't watch the games. I have to be on view. You can't do it. It's not part of the job. You could argue I've got the best spot in the house but I only get to feel what it's like and see bits and pieces, not what's actually happening. For me I'm here for the fans and their safety. After the games I finish shutting off the South Stand, then go over to the East Stand, into the press room and help out there. So I get back to Enfield and home by about half seven.'

Barry was just one of those who was responsible for the smooth running of match days. And like many of these secondary players on the grand stage, his view of the action was often partial or even completely different from the thousands who paid to get inside.

Although he did not know it at the time, 28 January was a landmark day for Darren Baldwin, the club's 'head of playing surfaces' – senior groundsman in old money. Due to the demands of the television companies, the FA Cup fourth-round tie with Wycombe, won in trademark dramatic style as Spurs twice trailed before nicking a 4–3 win in injury time, was the last game staged at the ground to kick off at the once-traditional 3 p.m. on a Saturday. It was the final time he had to arrive at 7 a.m. to remove the heating lights from the side of the pitch before double-cutting the grass, marking the pitch, putting up the portable goals and the real posts, the protective nets for the warm-up, testing the Hawkeye goal line technology system and turning on the sprinklers, all by 1.45 p.m.

Speaking on his way back from the ground a few months later, Darren, who had to forsake his Arsenal support – 'I was more of a Pat Jennings fan really, I moved with him' – to woo his wife, and who used to work at Highbury, recalled how his 21-year association might actually have lasted just a matter of weeks.

'My first memory was surviving an interview with Claude Littner,' he said, with what felt, even over the phone, like the sort of shudder every *The Apprentice* wannabe goes through when Claude's name is mentioned. 'He was chief executive at the time and obviously a good friend of Alan Sugar. It was July 1996 and I was an assistant groundsman at Arsenal. He phoned me and I remember the conversation, because he kept on with: "Why do you want to come to Spurs?" I tried to point out that he'd phoned me up but he must have asked me that question ten times.

'I've had a fantastic career here but it nearly never happened. As early as 6 December in my first season, we played Liverpool at home. Steve McManaman took a shot from miles out, it was bobbling through to Ian Walker, hit a divot and flew over his shoulder and into the net. I was stood at the North Stand, leaning on a wall by the disabled section. And if the wall wasn't there I'd have fallen over. The blood drained out of me.

'The next morning I got a call from Claude. "Come and see me," he said. I only had to go up three flights of stairs to his office but it was the longest walk of my life. I was convinced I'd be blamed and that would be that. But Claude asked what I could've done to prevent it and I told him the truth – nothing. That it was a newly-laid pitch, in the early days of its life, and that it was impossible to avoid things like that happening.'

That particular bump is long forgotten by most, Darren excepted. Every match, he wanted perfection from his pride and joy, viewing events on the pitch with his attention focused on something completely different to the fans, who just wanted to see Tottenham play well and win. Despite this, he still realised what made the Lane a ground apart from the norm: 'The biggest and the unique thing about White Hart Lane is the atmosphere.

'Even though I've been here for twenty-one years and am going grey, now at the back end of my career, the hairs still stand up on the back of my neck when the teams walk out in front of a full house. Even the Millwall Cup tie in March 2017, the noise when they came out was incredible. When you're in one of the stands, you only really hear the sound around you and it bounces back. But for me, standing in the middle of the pitch, I hear the whole stadium. It's difficult to describe but when I'm stood there, in the centre-circle, as the teams come out of the tunnel, there is no other place I would want to be. To be there, in the very middle of that atmosphere, is unbelievable.

'It is a bit strange on a match day, though, because while everybody else is watching the game, I'm not. We'll talk afterwards and someone will say: "Didn't Moussa play well?" and I can't answer because I haven't watched it. I spend the whole game watching the players' feet, to see if they're slipping, or watching the run of the ball, to make sure the pitch isn't too dry. And sometimes I decide to water the pitch at half-time because what you want to do is produce the friction that allows the ball to move more quickly. So I don't really watch the game, just the surface.

'This season has been one of the easiest for me because of the building work that knocked down the corner between the East Stand and the Paxton Road end. Before that, because the whole ground was enclosed, it was a very difficult environment in which to grow grass. We do have the artificial lights but with the north-east corner gone it was, quite literally, a breath of fresh air for the pitch. I had an airflow in the stadium and that's made a big difference to the playing surface. Technology has changed and come on a long way in my industry. I've seen the introduction of hybrid pitches. There was undersoil heating before that, of course. And there has been huge development in how you renovate a pitch at the end of a season. That's changed dramatically. We have the artificial lights and the blowers on the side of the pitch to help the grass dry out.

'When I started there were four of us full-time plus six match-day staff. Now there are thirty-eight of us, if you include the staff at the training ground. We even have landscape gardeners and a kitchen garden where we grow the vegetables for the restaurant.

'Spurs have always wanted to play football, good football, going back to the eighties and before that. My brief was always to create a surface where they could play that football. I take a lot of pride in my work. If the pitch isn't right, I take it personally. I've had many sleepless nights and stressful periods because it hasn't been right, and at times been poor. You live that. Even this time, with the synthetic touchline we've put in, which was a test, a trial for the new stadium, there have been issues. When Jan Vertonghen turned his ankle as he went out of play in the West Brom game, he was in tears because he knew he'd be out for a while. I'm not saying it was because of the artificial strip but that night I went home and I was in a bad mood. My wife asked me what was wrong and I just said: "Jan's got injured." I took it personally.'

Darren was not the only one to be concentrating on something other than the football. Pete Fisher, the club's chief paramedic on match day, was an intrinsic part of the Fabrice Muamba drama. But even on a normal match day, sitting next to the dug-outs at the tunnel entrance, barely a dozen yards from the pitch, his view was an oblique one. He said: 'I'm a Spurs fan. Being a paramedic has opened many doors. We were invited to come down here and provide pitch cover and medical cover for the team. As a fan and as a paramedic, that works perfectly.

'We've been here for ten years now. I think when we first started we were watching the games. I think everyone does that. But now we're watching for injuries. There has been many a time I've had to go home to watch the match because there are so many bits you do miss through injuries and knocks to players.

'There's been some fantastic moments here. European nights, Champions League, "Taxi for Maicon". Of course I didn't join in. Very professional! We've had some wonderful times here. It will be emotional for everyone when it's finished. I've been a Spurs fan all my life, been here through thick and thin. But it will be a new chapter. I'm not sure if there will be tears but it will be

Alan Pegg, White Hart Lane tunnel steward.

George Graham shows his frustration as Arsenal score their last-gasp equaliser in an FA Carling Premiership match at White Hart Lane on 18 December 2000.

The view from the White Hart Lane press box.

Ollie with his ticket on Bill Nicholson Way before his first
Spurs game, against Stoke, 9 November 2014.

Mauricio Pochettino hugs Harry Winks after the youngster scores a debut goal in the 3–2 win over West Ham on 19 November 2016.

Harry Kane scoring the last Tottenham goal at White Hart Lane in the 2–1 win over Manchester United, 14 May 2017.

Paul Jiggins hard at work in the White Hart Lane press box.

Rainbow over the East Stand as players and former players parade after the final game at White Hart Lane, 14 May 2017.

Pitchside on the author's final visit to White Hart Lane, 14 May 2017.

The shape of things to come as work continues on the new stadium, July 2017.

emotional. The atmosphere that you get in here with the fans behind the team is amazing.'

An emotional connection with the club is a common thread among those for whom the Lane was a place of work, with memories as strong as any other fan. Steward Barry Staines said: 'I was a fan. I went as a boy to the training ground at Cheshunt, with my granddad. The family has always been Spurs fans. My dad, granddad, going back.

'For me it's Glenn Hoddle. I loved Ricky and Ossie, the excitement when they came over. I was up in The Shelf for their home debut, all that ticker tape, all the excitement, off the back of a great draw at Forest. And they lost 4–1. Typical Spurs! We always do it the hard way.

'I've found it very difficult this season, especially when fans came in and thought it might be their last visit. As we got nearer to it there were more and more fans saying the same thing. So it's been mixed emotions, really, thinking of the stadium we're going to get and working over there, because that's going to be an amazing experience, but at the same time there is that sadness at losing such an iconic place.

'Every time I've come here this season, walking to and from the train station on White Hart Lane, I've looked up at what's going on, the work that's taken place since the last time, and thought: "It's grown again." At the beginning of the season we'd talk about it and it was: "We've got a while yet." And I'd say to people: "It'll be here quicker than you realise." And now it's happened. But it's great. It's going to be fab.

'The thing I will always remember and take with me is the intimacy, that feeling of closeness to the action and the atmosphere.

'You could argue I've got the best spot in the house but I only get to feel what it's like and see bits and pieces, not what's actually happening. I'm here for the fans and their safety. But the atmosphere in some of those games, when I'm standing down at pitchside, looking up, that's been: "Wow!" Inter Milan, for example, that was one of the greats, a special, special night. Incredible. You felt something. At the end of the game, with everybody standing up singing, I could feel the hairs on the back of my neck standing up. That was emotional. I couldn't actually join in the singing about "Taxi for Maicon" but inside I was laughing so much.'

Back in his box, Pete Abbott, another of those for whom Hoddle was the greatest player and hero, knew exactly what Barry meant. 'My first game was 1971, against Everton. We won 2–1, Chivers and Gilzean,' he said, eyes slightly glazing over. 'If I'm honest, all I can actually remember is that we got a throw-in we should never have got, and I was so excited about that. I was only nine. I was sitting up here, above The Shelf. And it was a long way up when you were nine. Mind you, it's probably a long way up now, too.

'The most amazing game I ever went to here was against Hull in 1978, which I've always thought was probably the most import-ant game in the club's history. We'd been relegated the previous year. It was the last home game of the season and if we didn't win we wouldn't have gone up. We did win 1–0 in the end but it was the most extraordinary game I've ever seen. I've never known ten-sion like it. In the previous few weeks we'd lost at Brighton, lost at Burnley, been beaten 3–2 at home by Sunderland after scoring in the first minute. We'd really ballsed it up and it was down to us needing three points from two games, when it was only two points for a win, and our last game was at Southampton, who'd overtaken us and hadn't lost at home all season. So we knew if we didn't beat Hull that was it.

'We didn't look as if we'd ever score and then Steve Perryman scored, about nine minutes from the end, and that was it. I've never seen anything like it because it seemed like the whole crowd came on to the pitch, because it was just that release of emotion that had been building and building throughout the game.

'Since doing this, sitting behind that pane of glass, the Wigan game, 9–1, was the only time I've lost count of the score and had to check with other people. There were a few 4–4s as well. There was the one against Villa, in the 125th anniversary game and then the same season against Chelsea, when Robbie Keane equalised and then Dimitar Berbatov missed a great chance to even win it in the last minute. They beat Reading 6–4, when Berbatov got four.

'The high-scoring days stand out. Mind you, the performance against West Brom in January [2017] was something special. I can see why some are already comparing it to Feyenoord and Glenn killing them, when there'd been a bit of a war of words before the game with Cruyff in the build-up, and Glenn was just absolutely brilliant, the best forty-five minutes I've seen of any game.'

For Darren Baldwin, the countdown to the final game was a tough one: 'I'm a big lad. I'm forty-five now and quite thick-skinned. But if there's anybody in that stadium on the last day who doesn't have a lump in their throat, they don't love football. It's a grand old stadium and it's been part of my life for twenty years. And we will walk out of there and have only a limited time to salvage our stuff before we hand it over to the demolition team, shut the doors behind us for ever and know we can never go back. So that will be an emotional day for me and the others. I'm one of the five or six longest-surviving people at the club, living through the change.

'There will be a feeling of emptiness, I know. My two daughters are now massive Spurs fans. I guess it's for them, as well. The next generation will not know anything about White Hart Lane for themselves, only what they are told. But it's like the young players at the training ground. When we first moved from Chigwell, the kids then could compare the two, they understood what they had and realised they were lucky to be in the new environment in Enfield. But we needed to make sure the next bunch, who hadn't known Chigwell, realised how lucky they were too, how they were part of something that had been going for a long time.'

Something that came to an end on 14 May 2017. When, for the final time at the Lane, Pete Abbott made his traditional pre-game welcome and then took to the microphone in the box for his last message to the fans. 'I've been coming for forty-six years, and the whole ground has already been rebuilt once over that period,' he said. 'So while everybody is talking about moving to a new stadium, we already have done once, in that this *is* a new stadium compared to the one that I first came to, because every single stand has been rebuilt.

'When I first came it was mainly terracing and The Shelf, with those wooden bench-type seats that clattered when they went up and down, only the four floodlight pylons in the corners and the white wall round the ground.

'Every time I look at the new stadium I think about moving in there and realise it's getting that little bit closer to this place coming to an end. But I don't know, I just . . . for me it will be the same as every other game. I'll do exactly the same things. There'll be some other things at the end, presumably, yet to be decided. But otherwise it will be doing the game as I've always done it. And hoping I don't make a mess of it.

'I suppose all of us have that feeling of it being part of us, part of our heritage, part of what defines us, because this is the only home we've ever known. We've been here for so long and while the other ground is just over there, a hundred yards away, it's going to be a completely different place. So we will miss this. On big nights, this place is an amazing ground. Even sitting behind glass, as I do, you can't hear everything but you can sense the atmosphere. I remember the 5–1 League Cup semi-final against Arsenal. The noise that night, from everywhere, was unbelievable. So it's things like that.

'But that's all just memories. And you can take your memories with you. There are a lot of memories here, good and bad. But even though the ground isn't going to be here, that doesn't mean the memories disappear. You just take them on to the new one.'

15

MR CHAIRMAN

Ogres come in many forms. In football, they are often the mythical beasts who reside in the boardroom, reviled and detested. The ones who are blamed when things go wrong. The easy targets. Victory, they say, has a thousand fathers. Defeat is an orphan. And the chairman is always responsible for the state of the orphanage.

Of course, the most common complaint, the one trotted out by fans, players and managers alike – frequently to provide a smoke-screen for some other failing – is that the chairman, the board, do not get what the club is about. That they are businessmen, primarily, not football fans.

At Tottenham, even in the good times, the directors have always been the bad guys. They might have been aided and abetted by managers who treated the money as if it were their own, but there were few positive words said over the years about Charles Roberts, at the helm for half a century, Fred Bearman, Sidney Wale, Arthur Richardson or Douglas Alexiou, let alone Alan Sugar or Daniel Levy, even if the current chairman appeared to be turning things around because of the scale of his vision and his ambition for the future of the club.

Morris Keston, whose support of the club had lasted 74 years and counting by the end of the 2016–17 season and who had seen nine chairmen in command, said: 'The Spurs board was always a bit tight. They missed out on Tommy Lawton because they wouldn't stump up the money to get him. Every time there was a change in the board you'd tell yourself the next lot would be different, but they never were. They were always the same, from Fred Wale onwards. I always wondered if some of them would have preferred the club to play behind closed doors and have no supporters.'

Nobody suffered from the view that the board did not care about the club or the fans more than Irving Scholar. He was blamed for many things over the years: for forcing out Keith Burkinshaw, who damned him in the eyes of many with the alleged throwaway comment he made as he walked out of the club for the last time; for the demise of The Shelf; for trying to make Tottenham a genuine commercial entity and therefore more than just a football club; for negotiating with Robert Maxwell; for selling out, eventually, to Alan Sugar.

Scholar defiantly pleaded guilty to some of these charges. He believed he was a prophet without honour, a man ahead of his time who saw the shape of things to come and was castigated for being far-sighted. For him, the triumph of the Premier League, the financial behemoth that is viewed with jealousy by the rest of world football, which has made multi-millionaires out of kids but also enriched many of the leeches who prey upon the game, was all the justification he required.

He did not shy away from his role as one of the Big Five, when he, along with David Dein at Arsenal, Philip Carter at Everton, Martin Edwards at Manchester United and Noel White at Liverpool, sat down with Greg Dyke, then head of ITV Sport, at London Weekend Television's headquarters on 16 November 1990 to discuss, in effect, the transformation of English football, the meeting that was, eventually, to result in the creation of the Premier League.

Nor did he feel a need to defend himself. He was proud of being dubbed one of the 'Men Who Changed Football', as the quintet were styled by the BBC 11 years on from that fateful meeting. But he was equally emphatic in pleading not guilty to some of the other charges made against him. And as for the chief complaint, that he was never a real supporter, he had nothing but scorn. His commitment to the club was made clear by all those hours he spent as a kid, as a young man and then as a Monaco-based property developer and business executive, travelling the length and breadth of the country to watch the team he always loved.

Scholar was into his eighth decade but nothing could diminish his Boy Scout-like enthusiasm. Life in Monaco had been good to him, the regular tennis matches on the clay keeping him fit and active. And wearing his smart burgundy roll neck, as we met at the upstairs bar of the Ivy Club in London's West End, he looked far younger than his 70 years. There could be no doubting that he was a man at ease with himself, who had built a successful life on the back of his energy and business savvy. And below the surface, the enthusiasm of his youth shone through. You can take the multi-millionaire out of Hendon, but it's harder to take Hendon out of the multi-millionaire.

Many supporters and ex-players still point the finger of blame at him, seeing him as being central to the problems the club had to deal with, and its less than spectacular success on the pitch, over the quarter of a century. Yet it did not take long for any barriers to be dismantled. Talk about Tottenham, about what the club means, and any wariness is replaced by infectious excitement. Maybe it was a need to prove that he was not what he was represented as being, but Scholar came alive when he talked about his love affair with the club, the one that started long before he ever dreamed of being the chairman.

Indeed, the more he relaxed, the more the young Scholar came out, with the Yiddish inflection of his youth, slipping out instinctively. 'If you say that people don't understand that passion, that it was only business, that couldn't be further from the truth,' Scholar said.

'The first game I saw was in 1952. An uncle took me to see Spurs versus Cardiff. I used to go home and away, which was unusual. It wasn't like it is today. Then people would have season tickets for Spurs *and* Arsenal, would go to White Hart Lane one week and Highbury the next. I know it sounds crazy but it's true. Now people travel up and down the country every weekend but in those days very few people used to travel away.

'But from the age of thirteen or fourteen, a friend and I would go up and down the country. My parents didn't know I was going to football, only that I was out all day and would come back in the evening.

'One day they were sitting in the car park waiting for me, because they'd found out what I did. So I was ordered into the car and told off: "As long as we know where you're going, and who you're with, that's okay; but we want to know where you are." That was understandable, and so from that moment on it was official.

'We'd go up and down on the train and there would be very few fans. There were four or five older men, in their thirties, people like Morris Keston and his friends, and they'd see us going as kids, sitting there on our own. One of the most vivid moments for me was a game at Wolverhampton. The team used to travel on the train. I was sitting there in my seat, with a big rosette on. Bill Nicholson went past me. He turned, ruffled my hair. It had been touched by the Hand of God. I didn't wash it for a month . . . He was sensational, a wonderful man.'

Scholar's reverence for Nicholson and his great team was undiminished. If anything, it had grown stronger and deeper. He talked wistfully of the day he cleared space on his table in the directors' lounge to spend a couple of hours talking with the architect of Tottenham's greatest side: 'It was like going to Heaven.'

'My favourite from that team was the late great John White,' he said, turning his attention to the players. 'He was one of the finest midfield players to have worn the shirt. There was the great warrior Dave Mackay, who was the kind of player that every manager dreams of. Danny Blanchflower was the real brains of the team and Cliff Jones the quickest player I've ever seen and one of the bravest.

'The following season Jimmy Greaves, the greatest goal scorer I have ever seen, joined and promptly scored a hat-trick on his debut against Blackpool. If you were there in December 1961 to see his first, a magnificent bicycle kick from about twelve yards at a corner, you would never forget it. He went on to get two headers and I don't think he ever did that again in a Spurs shirt. These are the memories of a fourteen-year-old that are as fresh today as they were on the day they happened.

'There are so many. The Glory Glory Nights competing in Europe, when the Tottenham roar at the Lane was at its loudest. The battle cry of "Glory Glory Hallelujah" still brings a lump to my throat and a tear every time I hear it. The many great games over the years, the debut of my hero Alan Gilzean at home to Everton – the G Men had arrived [Greaves and Gilzean]. The First King of White Hart Lane was born.

'My very first season ticket was in the East Stand. When we knocked it down I had that seat taken out. Block D Row D Seat 117. That was my first season ticket. But I stood until 1962, 5 April, Benfica at home. I got there really early, went in the boy's entrance, Upper Shelf, great. Until I was getting crushed and had to move. That was a great game. There were three goals wrongly disallowed. Bill Nicholson was never someone who liked to say too much but he always felt that, when that draw was made, the winner would win the European Cup. And he was right.

'I then moved from the East Stand to the West. I saw nearly every game. In the season we were relegated to the Second Division, out of forty-two league games I saw forty-one. I was really upset when I had to miss Hull away, because my cousin wasn't going and I had nobody to go with on a Tuesday night. My wife said: "Let's go out then." But later in the week he rang to say that the second goal for Hull had been a little dodgy. I said: "I didn't see that on TV," thinking there had been a snippet on the local news. Silence. "You didn't bloody go, did you?" And he said: "I rang to tell you but she picked up the phone and said she'd kill me if I told you." He went, I didn't, and it was the only game I missed all season.'

Of course, most fans only get to see the players, their heroes, from a distance. A few get invited into the elite, the inner sanctum, getting the opportunity to walk into the boardroom as a guest and rub shoulders with the movers and shakers, and sometimes even the players. But Scholar went much further, although he maintained, vehemently, that his involvement only came about because of his fears over the financial burdens the club was taking on. With the official bill for the new stadium pushing £800 million, an eye-popping sum, it was unsurprising that some supporters feared Spurs might be making a similar mistake, irrespective of the board's assurances that they would take no risks over the club's future by mortgaging themselves to the hilt to fund the next home. After all, Arsenal struggled to cope with the repercussions of spending £325 million on their new home. While nobody thought Daniel Levy would risk making a damaging financial over-commitment, previous boards made similar promises. Maybe Scholar's private concerns that history could end up repeating itself had validity?

'What had happened was, I'd read about the West Stand, how there were problems but they were going ahead with it,' he said. 'I went to a couple of meetings when they were trying to sell boxes and I just felt: "Hang on; where's the money going to come from for them to do this?"

'And I went to a lunch, because I was at the time using the same contractors who were doing the stand. They stuck me opposite Arthur Richardson, who was the chairman at the time. We were just chit-chatting and I asked him about the stand. He said everything was fine but I looked into it and felt there was going to be a problem and that the only solution would be if they started selling players, which frightened the life out of me, because we'd seen what had happened at other clubs in the past – and since.

'I could see that there was going to be a major problem and that they were going to be saddled with the largest debt in football, which they were. It was unheard of in those days. Carrying big debt was unheard of and my fear, as a fan, was that the only way they were going to get out of this was to sell off all the players. That was total anathema to me.

'So I spent the Christmas of 1981 getting together all the information I could from the public sources. What was very interesting was the way the company was set up in 1898 – that they offered for sale a share issue of 8,000 shares. When they stopped in 1905, they had actually sold 4,892 shares. In the thirties, around 1936, there was a gentleman called Mr Berry who was very unhappy about the way the club was being run and he tried to buy some shares and do some form of takeover. On the statute book, Berry v. Tottenham Hotspur 1936 is *the* case, the precedent case in corporate history of how companies and directors have the ability, without any reason whatsoever, to refuse the transfer of a share from one person to another.

'I found out all that and went to see a leading barrister called Robin Potts QC. I said it was 1982 and that precedent from the thirties couldn't still be right, but he said: "Yes, it is good law. But they can't actually stop you buying the shares." That seemed odd. I couldn't see how I could buy the shares if the club were allowed to stop me. He explained that I could buy the shares but had to sign a proxy in the name of the person I'd bought them from, so the shares were kept in their name, which is exactly what happened.

'At no time did the board ever know how many shares I had, because nothing had changed in the shareholder's list – everybody was still there. I got the list of shareholders, approached them, even if they had one or two shares, told them I knew they had that holding and offered them a price for them. Within the first week I had a number of letters accepting the offers. I was really shocked because I hadn't expected that. After all, I had gone to most people on the list. But one person I didn't approach was Sidney Wale, the former chairman, whose family had been involved since the forties.

'Eventually I was approached, out of the blue, by Geoffrey Jones, who was the Secretary of the Club. After we'd talked all round the houses for a bit, I said I had to go and he said: "Sidney is upset you haven't approached him yet to make him an offer for his shares!"

'I didn't know what side he was on but found out afterwards there was a lot of ill-feeling between him and the board over the building of the stand, because – and he was an accountant – he felt the club couldn't afford it. He felt he wasn't being treated with respect. Then I spoke to him, made my proposal, we agreed the deal, and that put me in a very strong position. So that was it.'

Suddenly, the outsider, the raider, was in the ascendant. Now it was about applying the final touch, completing the boardroom coup. Scholar said: 'I had about thirty-five per cent, probably enough to do it. I'd made no direct approach to the directors, but then it leaked out when the club doctor, Brian Curtin, gave a speech and said there was going to be a big change. I got a phone call telling me it was about to hit the papers and then they came to me and offered me a seat on the board. It took about two weeks for it to go through, and that was it.

'The capital value of the whole of the company was about £1 million, with a deficit of over £5 million. Within two weeks, Doug Ellis bought Aston Villa for £600,000. At that time, football was not a sport that everybody wanted to be involved in.

'Douglas Alexiou was Sidney Wale's son-in-law. I met and liked Douglas, who had experience as a director and we made him the chairman. Shortly afterwards, I was in America and got a call from Paul Bobroff, who I didn't know at all. He said he had a chance of getting fifteen per cent from the family of Fred Bearman, who had been the chairman in 1961, which I had tried to get before. Paul said: "If I buy these shares, can I come in with you?"

'I said he had to ring me if he ever got them. He did and spent a lot more per share than I had done. He then rang me, and I made the biggest mistake ever. He said he had the shares and was happy for me to take them from him at exactly the same price he had paid, in exchange for a seat on the board.

'I thought to myself: "Here am I, getting involved in something when I don't even know what's what, because I haven't looked at the books yet – and someone wants me to own fifty per cent of that company about which I don't know much, except for the big debt."

'It was a heart-ruling-head moment. Because I was living abroad I felt it would be good to have someone in London who had an interest, so I decided to leave it as it was, with him keeping his shares. In retrospect it was a mistake.'

The kid from the terraces was now the boss. 'It was a feeling of total obligation, absolutely. That's exactly what it was,' he added, smiling at his memories. 'I know this sounds crazy, but it's true. At that time, if they lost, I thought it was my fault. If they won, it was down to the manager and players. That, when you think about it, is obtuse.

'My dream in those days was that we would lift the Holy Grail, the European Cup, and get revenge for Benfica. That was so important for me. And the other thing was to keep going forward, taking the club up. We needed to change things. The biggest change was the introduction of closed circuit TV in an attempt to eradicate hooliganism.

'What was most difficult for me was making that move from being a fan to the director's box, getting used to it, learning how I had to behave. When I first got in I was still jumping up and down every time we scored a goal. That's what I'd always done. But you're looking around you and see nobody else is doing that. So you learn. It's a huge responsibility but if you felt you were going in the right direction and working together to make the best of things, that's good.'

Had Scholar merely been a titular, understated chairman, he might not have become such a divisive figure. But that, in truth, was never likely. Scholar and his lawyers found a way round FA regulations which prevented paying part-time directors or issuing unlimited dividends to shareholders. The Football Club became a subsidiary of Tottenham Hotspur plc. And in November 1983 shares in the new company were floated on the Stock Exchange. Each share was priced at £1.08 and the offer was oversubscribed four times. But the price fell to 90p per share on the first day of trading and took another three years to get close to the original offer price. He also oversaw a diversification – one that was to prove catastrophic – into the sportswear and leisure market as Tottenham bought the Hummel kit manufacturers. Asked if he thought he'd pushed too hard in retrospect, there was only certainty: 'Not at all, not at all. Football was lagging way, way behind. It needed to be pulled up and be modernised in a serious way. When I got involved it was completely different to today. In those days, most of the owners were football fans, one way or another. We all had a common aim, a similar feeling for it, to try and do what we could do to make each club better than it was. If you win, it's great. If you lose, it's not so great.

'Today it's all foreign owners, chief executives, all that stuff. But then it was more to do with individuals working together. We had meetings, lots of meetings, discussing lots of different things. When I look back on it now, it was all the groundwork for the future to go forward.

'We were the first sports company in the world to go public. It was nothing to do with regulations – it was about raising money to pay off the debt. It raised £3.8 million to pay off most of the debt, while the existing shareholders put in another £1.1 million. That effectively covered the debt, but we weren't out of the woods.

'As for the Hummel deal, it had never been done before. Football wasn't that popular at the time, as a result of the hooliganism holding the game back, so we were advised that we had to find other streams of income. If we had a season that wasn't as good as we'd hoped, we wouldn't be reliant on football income and would still be able to bring in income. We changed a lot of things. I was fed up seeing kids walking up and down wearing baseball caps and American Football shirts. This was anathema to me – why weren't they wearing football shirts for our teams?

'I was determined we were going to break that mould. I brought in a chap called Edward Freedman, and we worked very hard to change things. Edward did a fantastic job, an excellent job. He's a really good guy, and we're still friends. When I left, he felt he couldn't work at Spurs because he didn't like the new regime and he was approached by Martin Edwards. A few years earlier, Martin was concerned by Manchester United's merchandising and there was talk of Spurs taking it over. That sounds laughable, now, but it's absolutely true. Edward was invited up, in 1992, because they were wondering if they needed to buy our services on merchandising. This was at the start of the Premier League, remember, when the two clubs had identical revenues despite United having a much larger fan-base and capacity.

'Later on, Edward had a meeting with Martin in Manchester, about something completely different, and Martin offered him the chance to go to United, where he changed everything at a club that was commercially way behind at that time. United are now in a different league – way ahead of everyone. The Glazers have brought American ideas into United and done an amazing job commercially.

'But we were the only club in the First Division who didn't have a shirt sponsor when I got involved. I kept on asking the commercial department why we hadn't done anything. Mike Lewis, who was the commercial manager, got fed up hearing me ask about it. He got into lots of negotiations with various people but it never quite worked out. Then we drew Bayern Munich in the Uefa Cup. Mike Rollo was a young man we'd just employed in the commercial department as Mike's assistant. He said he'd had some ideas about sponsors for the game. He approached Holsten, and they sponsored the match. Everyone had a good time and Mike Rollo asked if they'd think about going on the shirts. Two days later they asked: "How much?" we gave them a figure and it was done. Mike Lewis couldn't believe that Mike Rollo had done it just like that. And we knocked out Bayern Munich and won the Uefa Cup!'

Gary Mabbutt, who played the first half of his 16-year Spurs career under Scholar's reign, said: 'Irving Scholar had a vision, similar to the way David Dein was thinking at Arsenal or Martin Edwards at United. There were a lot of forward-thinking owners at that time and, looking back now, they were proven to be correct. A lot of things were changing in the early eighties and they were trying to bring about those changes in football as well.'

In 1985, the year after that Uefa Cup triumph, the future of the ground became a pressing concern, with Scholar and the board vastly under-appreciating the opposition to what were seen as plans to change the whole feel of the ground by rebuilding the East Stand and replacing The Shelf with executive boxes. It was a campaign that saw Haringey Council become a battleground as Tottenham were out-thought by the fan lobby and protest group which took the name 'Left On The Shelf' and the acronym LOTS.

Their tactics included a mourning wreath at the final home game of the 1985–86 season, and a fast-response unit which saw the club out-manoeuvred. It did not help that the club risibly claimed that police fears of 'rowdiness' were a legitimate reason for pushing ahead with the rebuilding scheme. LOTS and other fans were able to demonstrate that the claims were palpably manufactured.

Chris Waddle thought that the changes begun by Scholar took away some of the home advantage Spurs were handed by the unusual design feature of that elevated East Stand terracing. 'The ground felt very different to me when I first walked out there, because of what I was used to at Newcastle. The focus for all the fans there was the Gallowgate, the big end behind the goal where all the loudest fans, the ones who made the atmosphere, who sang and chanted, would congregate.

'That was what I expected, but at White Hart Lane it was different, because the loudest fans were all on The Shelf, running all the way along that stand. Even now, that would seem a bit strange, because normally the noise comes from behind the goal – either from the loudest home fans or the away supporters – but it made White Hart Lane somewhere unlike most other grounds. Manchester City had the Kippax, but there weren't too many like that.

'That made it interesting. It was a good-looking ground that had extra character because of the layout and design of the stands. Normally I'd think it was an advantage to have the noisiest fans behind the goal, but it was something I grew to really like, too. I missed it when the ground changed.'

Waddle's belief that the Lane lost something when The Shelf disappeared was echoed by one of Tottenham's greatest servants, Steve Perryman, even if he accepted the reality of footballing evolution. He said: 'I think you come to a point where progress is needed. Tradition and all that is a great thing but eventually if the dressing rooms are not quite right and the shower area is out of date, then it makes sense to build new stands, although they can never have the same class as the old buildings. A new stand might be glitzier but it will never have the same background. At the same time, progress has to happen. The big shame for me was that The Shelf came down. That affected the atmosphere, no doubt about that. That was a proper area to watch the game from and people used to leave home early just to be able to go there. That was not the case with the West Stand, rebuilt in the early eighties, which took away some of the character of the ground but didn't really harm the atmosphere in the way knocking down The Shelf did.'

At the mid-point of Scholar's reign other incidents emerged that were to cloud the future. When Spurs signed Paul Allen (£400,000 from West Ham), Mitchell Thomas (£275,000 from

Luton) and Chris Fairclough (£387,000 from Nottingham Forest) over successive summers they made 'loan' payments to the players not disclosed to the Transfer Tribunal, which were never intended to be repaid, meaning the fees they paid were lower than they would have been. These were among 40 offences of malpractice to which the club would offer guilty pleas nearly a decade later, costing them, initially, a record £600,000 fine, a deduction of 12 points (for the season which would see four teams relegated as the nascent Premier League was reduced to 20 teams) and a year's ban from the FA Cup. Quite how Alan Sugar and his lawyers overturned most of the punishment is still hard to reconcile.

Nevertheless, it was over the bricks and mortar that the then chairman took most stick. For about the only time in our long conversation, Scholar went on the defensive. He knew it was not his finest hour. 'I didn't decide it had to go,' he said. 'It was the natural progression. The stand was built in 1934, by Archibald Leitch, whose handwriting you could see everywhere years afterwards – Ibrox, Goodison, Tynecastle, Vicarage Road and other places.

'But his actual design, originally, was to enclose the whole of the ground. I thought there must be a way of having a standing area in the middle part of the stand, between the seats. Originally, that middle tier of seats was still a standing area. So The Shelf was still there and there was standing in that area. But it only lasted a few years because of Taylor.'

The Taylor report, launched in the aftermath of the Hillsborough Disaster, did indeed end the days of terracing but it is hard to imagine, even now, that Scholar really initially envisaged what was mockingly described as 'The Ledge' in his plans for the stand. And when, despite the protests, the building work began, there was more humiliation for Scholar and his board when the club was refused a safety certificate for the opening home game of the 1988–89 season and the game with Coventry was postponed with just a few hours' notice.

'Was I embarrassed?' he said. 'Of course I was. I was there until God knows what time the night before trying to ensure it would be done in time. We had a huge contractor. I was told everything would be fine and they let us down. Afterwards they were extremely apologetic. It was supposed to be Gazza's debut – and he ended up making it at Newcastle instead.'

LOTS reported 'an air of bewilderment, disbelief and anger' from those hundreds of fans who turned up for a match that was not going to take place. Scholar was chastened and bloodied and while he had appointed Terry Venables as his fourth full-time manager they had an uneasy relationship, which was swiftly to descend to levels of bitter and lasting hostility. More crucially, the figures off the field were not stacking up and Scholar, against all his business principles, found himself injecting £3 million from the Football Club funds to keep Hummel afloat, while the debt to Midland Bank soared to £10 million out of a total owed of £12 million, including around £1.1 million to Barcelona following the signing of Gary Lineker.

As Spurs fans celebrated the acquisition, dreaming of what a front trio of Lineker, Gascoigne and Chris Waddle could do to defences under Venables' management, financial realities were having their impact in the background. Lineker signed on 23 June 1989. Within six days, the troika were being broken up, without even having a Spurs training session together, much to Waddle's lasting disappointment.

The former England winger, now a familiar voice as a TV and radio pundit, and still as strong-willed off the pitch as he always was on it, despite the criticisms he regularly faced, told me: 'I would've been happy to stay at Tottenham for the rest of my career. Me and Gazza had been pestering Gary to come and join us at every England squad. I'd sold him the idea and given him a promise that I'd be the creator and he'd score thirty or forty that season if he came back from Barcelona. I think I talked him into the move and I was really excited about the idea of the three of us.

'I'm pretty sure we'd have won a few things and I'd have loved to have had the three of us in the same team. I know we'd have sold out most stadiums up and down the land to come and see us and it would've been so interesting to see what we'd have done together. That would've been a Tottenham team with a different dimension.

'But within a week or so of him signing, I'd left. That was a move that came really quick, a real surprise to me. One day I was at Wimbledon, watching the tennis in a hospitality box. And forty-eight hours later I was signing for Marseilles. I got a phone call telling me to go to the ground. Out of nowhere I was told that the deal was done and it was happening. Apparently Marseilles came in and Spurs put a price on my head, £4.5 million, which they didn't think they would match. But they did. The Tottenham board were shocked that they were willing to pay that much and the club felt they had no option but to let me know and go and talk to Marseilles.

'I'd always wanted to play in the European Cup – the Heysel ban was in place so there was no European football for English teams for five years – and playing abroad had always appealed. I'd spoken to Glenn about Monaco and he said Marseilles was even more fanatical about the club. I was used to that intensity of support from Newcastle and Tottenham so I thought I'd go, but at the back of my mind I was thinking that if it didn't work out I could come back to Tottenham at the end of the season.

'It was a shame that I didn't even get the chance to say goodbye to the fans. By the time I came back with Sheffield Wednesday it was a bit too late. At the next England game in the September I walked into the reception at the hotel. Gary was standing there, looked at me and said: "You wanker!" I said to him: "Mate, I really didn't know it was going to happen." I was all a bit defensive and then I said: "Hold on, you left Everton for Barcelona, didn't you?" And he smiled and said: "I'm joking. I'd have done exactly the same thing . . ."'

Scholar's solution to the deepening off-field problems was to turn to a controversial politician turned publishing giant, also the owner of Derby County and effectively, through his family, Oxford United, who was asked to underwrite a rights issue to clear the debt. Given what was discovered about Robert Maxwell's business dealings and corporate theft after he slipped off the side of his yacht in November 1991, some 18 months later, it was a decidedly narrow escape for the club. The problems kept coming. But there was a potential solution to the ever-expanding debt – selling Paul Gascoigne. This was, of course, exactly the sort of transfer decision Scholar had been worried about when he first got involved with the club a decade earlier. Yet, out of necessity, it was now going to happen under his watch, unless he could identify a solution. That meant finding someone to whom he could sell the club and it felt like being caught between a rock and a hard place. And, in truth, it only put off the club's inevitable Gascoigne decision, rather than avoiding it.

'Put it this way,' he said. 'At the very end I had the choice to sell to Maxwell or Sugar. And I didn't sell to Maxwell . . .

'I went to him because it was difficult. We had a facility with the Midland Bank on an annual basis. The year had finished and we had to renegotiate another year and it took a long time. But the facility was renewed way before Sugar got involved, so everything was back to normal. But when a company gets into trouble, especially a football club, the first thing that happens is that bills don't get paid, salaries don't get paid. But that never happened. Not one salary was late.

'Those on the outside were making it sound worse than it was. And there were certain people on the inside doing the same because it served their agenda. And this was the time when the Premier League was being discussed and for that whole year the five of us were working very hard to create the League.'

It all added up to the beginning of the end for Scholar, who fell out with Bobroff after failing to inform him of his outline negotiations with Maxwell. Things were to come to a head in early 1991 when the Stock Exchange, citing concerns over the financial stability of the company, suspended trading in shares. Scholar was publicly censured by the Stock Exchange and resigned from the plc board while, for the short term, retaining his role at the club.

That soon ended, but Scholar's influence on football lived on. The Premier League is perhaps Scholar's true legacy to Tottenham and to the game, even if the timing of the new structure, which coincided with White Hart Lane being plunged into what many fans call 'the Doldrum Years', worked against the club he wanted to see as a dominant force. Without him, Dein and Edwards in particular, it might never have come to pass.

'Certain clubs had their agendas, others had different ones, but we were always trying to take it forward and improve things collectively,' he said. 'Look, I always felt if it was good for football, it was going to be good for us, and that's what was behind my thinking.

'Early on in my involvement with Spurs, each First Division Club, as they were at the time, got up to around £25,000 per season from the Football League TV contract. In early 1986 this rose to around £50,000 after we agreed the 10 Point Plan, which gave the First Division fifty per cent of the new deal and any subsequent one.

'I was involved as one of the First Division negotiators chosen by the clubs and my specific responsibility was television. I'd been on the League TV negotiating committee before, when we introduced the play-offs. And in the summer of 1988, while we were again trying to introduce greater reform, the first real major sea change took place when the First Division became autonomous, with their own exclusive TV deal with ITV, which gave each club around £600,000.

'This was the forerunner of the Premier League. It took a lot of hard work and total belief by the five of us. We were all totally convinced this was the way forward. All of us knew television would play a big part and that at last the clubs would sell the rights for a proper competitive price. Up until then we were being held back by the cartel which was run by the BBC and ITV. We even voted to black out football on television for the first half of the 1985–86 season, as we were so incensed at the broadcasters' refusal to come clean and make proper sensible offers at a proper sensible price.

'But at no time in our wildest dreams could we have envisaged the billions that would be raised from domestic and especially overseas Premier League TV sales. It just goes to prove that the faith we all had in our sport and clubs during all the dark days of our European ban, hooliganism and the television cartel was well placed. The Premier League has been the biggest sporting success story of the last twenty-five years and we are all very proud of being a small part of its creation. When you think today each club receives in the region of £100 million as a minimum guarantee, it puts a few things into perspective.'

It does. The sums are enormous and the success of the Premier League is incontestable. Yet Scholar is now an outsider. 'Do I have regrets?' he said. 'You always have regrets. There are things I might have done differently. But you can't change things now. You have to get on with your life.

'Who would ever have thought on 6 May 1961 that out of the two Cup finalists, the next one of them to win the League would be Leicester not Tottenham? Nobody would ever have thought that. If I'd said that to you on that day, nobody would have believed that.

'White Hart Lane has been such a big part of my life. It's the same for every fan and I'm no different to any of them. Like them, I've been going my whole life. It's the place where you feel comfortable, where you've had so many experiences, had good times and bad times, winning, drawing, losing, been lifted up to the sky and dropped through the floor.

'With a £400 million debt likely on the new stadium, is that the final vindication for me? I'm not sure about that! But these are different times. Interest rates are at the lowest level in seventy years. But vindication? No, I don't think so. Everybody who is involved contributes in one way or another. You have the baton, you pass that baton on and hopefully you'll be judged to have done a good job. But that's for others to say, not me. Someone once said to me I had more feeling for football than others. Yet there were some who wrongly accused me of only being about money. But I'm the last chairman who worked for nothing. Nothing. I didn't want a penny. To me it was personal.'

For all Scholar claimed that he was happy to be out of football, I wasn't sure I believed him. I felt he would have loved to come back, on a white charger, and have his time all over again and be the chairman of Spurs when they were the best club in the country, the best in Europe, and maybe even the best in the world . . .

16

'GIVE US 800 INSIDE AND
12 PARS FOR THE BACK . . .'

My first game at White Hart Lane was in October 1972, a 4–3 win over Stoke, standing on The Shelf with my father, peering down from that glorious high perch, with the most wonderful, splendid, perfect of views – especially if you were right by the front wall. And over the next 21 years I would go time and again, watching from all parts of the ground, as I grew from a boy to a man. Well, given my somewhat less than imposing 5ft 6in, maybe not quite a man . . .

I recall sitting in the upper tier of the Paxton Road end, to see the Uefa Cup ties with Cologne (quarter-final) and Lokomotive Leipzig (semi) in 1974, although my dad did not take me to the final against Feyenoord. I'm not saying I held it against him. But, yes, I held it against him. If we'd gone, Mike England's double would have been added to by Chivers or Peters, no doubt. We'd have won the Cup again. Definitely.

One of my clearest memories was of keeping Tottenham up in 1975. You don't remember it, I'm sure. Nobody does. Except me and, maybe, David Cecil Lipton. Spurs were in trouble. Big trouble. It was the first year after Bill Nicholson had left, relegation loomed, and it was down to me to save the day. We were in our lounge in Walthamstow, quite a big one because a year or so earlier we'd cut through the dividing wall. It was throwing it down outside, so it was indoor football. My dad was in goal, telling me that if I scored the next penalty Spurs would stay up.

If I missed, they would go down. Quite a big responsibility for an eight-year-old you might think, as I ran up, thumping low to my spring-heeled dad's left, pinging in off the inside of the radiator. In my mind, he gave it everything to keep it out. I suspected later that he didn't. But when Spurs beat Leeds 4–2 on Monday 28 April, two days after the end of the regular season, to send Luton down and keep us up – Chivers, back in the side after two months as an outcast under Terry Neill, was the star, although Cyril Knowles scored twice – I was not even moderately surprised. And I didn't even tell anyone it was down to me.

The following year we moved out to Essex, which changed my match-going routine. With my dad back on his home manor, running an insurance broker's by the Angel, Islington, with his elder brother, he would rarely drive me from home. Instead, I'd catch a train to Liverpool Street, to be picked up on Bishopsgate, the bottom of the A10, and then driven to N17. Still mainly behind the goal, although it was from the Park Lane upper that I saw Terry Yorath score what I remember as an absolute stunner to finish off Bolton in 1979, which was clearly a birthday present game as I turned 13 two days later. Had my father been observant, and my mother not Goyim, it would have sufficed as a Bar Mitzvah present too, such as the ones that all my male cousins got. But that's another story.

Soon after that, I started going on my own, and more regularly. It took two trains and a short walk from White Hart Lane station. The new West Stand was being built at that time, the building works more evident from The Shelf, which became my new home. The tiny kid with the scruffy knees grew, slightly. There was the merest hint of bum-fluff around the top lip and while games came and went, with some precious moments on the way, studying mattered to me as well.

My school wasn't the best, in truth. Indeed, through my time at Bromfords Comprehensive there seemed to be three main career options – the forces, the City or inside. Further education was not really considered to be an option for most, and if I had not been pushed, prodded and nagged by my English teacher, Mike Clamp, aided and abetted by the egalitarian vision of a nuclear physicist and academic from Melbourne named Neil Tanner, the college's admissions tutor who was at the forefront of a massive push to encourage state-school applications, I would never have even dreamed of applying to Oxford, let alone getting a place to read English at Hertford College in Catte Street, quite literally opposite the Bodleian Library.

Saying that, I still meet up with three schoolmates on a reasonably regular basis. One of them is currently the Military Advisor to the Political Director of the Foreign Office, another was Chief Executive of Global Transaction Services for RBS, while the third is head of Japanese Operations for Deutsche Bank, so maybe it was a better school than any of us thought. Or maybe I was just lucky not to end up in Wandsworth Prison, rather than just Wandsworth . . .

But even during my student days, the pull of the Lane was a strong one. A brief membership scheme, which promised a Cup final ticket and guaranteed entrance, saw me transfer my viewing position to the Paxton Road terrace, which was to be my home for the next five years. That my three years among the dreaming spires coincided exactly with Oxford United's spell in the top flight, allowing me to witness Everton blowing the title in 1986 (London Road stand of Oxford's Manor Ground stadium), Sir Alex Ferguson's first game as Manchester United boss (Beech Road terrace) and the debut of David Pleat's Spurs 4-5-1 (Cuckoo Lane end) was an added bonus.

It was during that period, when I was home for the 1985 Christmas holidays, that I saw arguably the greatest goal scored at the Lane that never was. The unlucky player, in an FA Cup replay against Oxford – after a pretty grim 1-1 draw in the initial third-round tie, which had given me the opportunity to make an unexpected and brief pre-term trip back to the city – was Chris

Waddle: 'I picked the ball up in front of the Paxton Road end, dribbled past everybody and scored, and it was given offside, even though I'd gone through the whole team on my own. I remember I said to the referee: "You can't disallow that – it's the best goal I'll ever score." In the old days if a player was in an offside position he could be given offside. The ref said he thought I was going to cross or pass it and so it was offside. He was never going to reverse his decision. But I was only ever going to do one thing on that run. I was devastated, even though we came back to win.'

Back in Essex the highlights of the game had been taped on our VHS machine. If you looked closely, you would have spotted, just to the right of the posts, two lads wearing sheepskin coats. I was the one wearing brown and my brother Trevor was in grey. And you'd also have seen both of us going mental at the ref. Even the eventual comeback victory did not reduce our sense of injustice on Waddle's behalf. More than 30 years on, it was reassuring to learn he still shared it with me.

Before long, the student needed to find a career. Despite initially being turned down for a junior reporting role on the *Oxford and South Oxfordshire Courier*, a letter in which I told the editor Frank Rawlins that 'although I accepted his decision not to give me the job, I couldn't accept the discourtesy of not letting me know' served to get me my first foot through the door, although that position lasted just six months before, along with the deputy editor, I was sacked for plotting to set up our own paper, a free-sheet for estate agents. Four months after that, however, I was offered a post with the West Riding News Service. Huddersfield was, for a Londoner (I always considered myself such, even though I'd not lived in E17 since 1976), foreign territory. The job meant court, council and general news Monday to Friday and Huddersfield and Halifax Town on a Saturday, with the towns' two Rugby League sides on the Sunday. Before long I was filing ten reports on a Saturday, all of different lengths and with different angles, for the national Sunday papers within an hour of the final whistle, including spending 25 minutes getting the quotes from gnarled old managers such as Eoin Hand, Ian Ross, Billy Ayre and John McGrath – those were the days of heavy regional editionalising. Papers were then able to target different areas of the country much more strongly. That is why a London-based Aston Villa fan, for example, would only ever get a small report on their team, unless they were playing one of the big sides, whereas the Midlands edition would focus on Villa. In those days, remember, there were only four pages of sport in most national papers. Now, I'm in charge of putting out up to 40 pages for Sunday and Monday papers, and often more than 20 pages midweek. With far fewer staff than were employed 30 years ago.

I decided that it was sport for me. And sport, for most newspapers, meant football. In 1993 I made the move full-time, becoming a sports reporter/sub-editor for UK News, a short-lived rival to the Press Association, serving the evening newspapers in the Westminster Press and Northcliffe stables and based in a classroom-sized office on the second floor of the *Leicester Mercury* building. So it was, on 23 October, 21 years after I first went to White Hart Lane to stand on The Shelf, that I timidly, anxiously, signed my name in the car park Portakabin that then served as the journalists' pre-match room, to watch Spurs play Swindon from the press box. It was the start, in so many ways, of the rest of my life.

I don't remember much of that game. I had a vague memory, which was confirmed as being unusually accurate when I looked it up, of Jason Dozzell scoring for Spurs, although no recollection of the soft penalty that was thumped home by Paul Bodin to level the scores. I know I joined in, at the back, as the 'Mondays', the daily reporters, grilled Ossie Ardiles. And I recall persuading Colin Calderwood to stop in the Mixed Zone area outside the West Stand to actually talk to me and me alone. It was big news, indeed, in the *Swindon Evening Advertiser*, I tell you. But, more crucially, it gave me my first taste of the best, and worst, press box in English football.

Best and worst? Oh yes. We were in the lower tier of the West Stand, and at that point in time on the immediate right-hand side of the tunnel, directly behind what was the home dug-out. So you had the perfect view of what was going on, the players giving each other a nudge and a josh, the manager or his assistant going loco at the referee, the linesman or the fourth official. But the camber on the pitch, far more pronounced than the television cameras could possibly show you in two dimensions, meant it was all but impossible to see what was happening on the far side of the ground, under the East Stand.

For a sense of theatre, nothing could compare to the 45-minute show when David Ginola was playing on George Graham's side of the White Hart Lane pitch during the Scot's controversial reign. When Spurs were kicking towards the Park Lane end, Graham would occasionally walk out to the edge of the pitch and bellow, almost for effect, knowing the chances of Ginola listening on the other side of the pitch, let alone responding, were nil to non-existent. But when Spurs were heading for the Paxton Road end, more often than not in the second half, it was a very different story. Graham was a jack-in-a-box, a constant presence, chivvying and harrying, urging and demanding, screaming and imploring. And because Ginola simply could not ignore a voice that went, whenever he drifted wide, virtually straight into his earhole, he was a man possessed too. A player transformed from decent into frequently unstoppable, to the extent that Sir Alex Ferguson never forgave either the PFA or the Football Writers' Association for making him their Footballer of the Year in 1999, a season in which, as the Laird of Old Trafford never failed to point out, United did actually win the Treble.

Graham smirked at the suggestion that he had played on Ginola's vanities. He said: 'With some players it's about coaching. With others it's about giving them their head to go and play. David was a free spirit. When he was on the pitch he just had to do what he did. You can only afford to carry one player like that. When a move broke down David wasn't exactly going to work back but I had to accept that for what he gave us.

'For me there were two games in particular when he won us the matches. And while I know that people say he always seemed to play better at White Hart Lane in the half when he was starting on the dug-out side of the pitch, when he could hear me, both of those games were away – at Barnsley in the FA Cup and Wimbledon in the League Cup semi-final. He was a player who caused you a lot of emotions. He was frustrating, yes. But he was also capable of being breathtaking.'

Of course, the press box was not always in that position and its location is one of the tales of the Lane itself. Brian Scovell, still going strong after more than half a century in a career which began at the *Isle of Wight Mercury* and brought 40 years on the 'Street of Shame', said: 'My first game was in 1959. I was working for the Press Association and I was sat right behind Bill Nicholson, where he used to sit to make his notes. [Nicholson had recently installed a phone system, allowing him to call his assistant, Cecil Poynton, in the dug-out.] I could look over his shoulder – but I couldn't make out what he was writing. It was a thrill to sit behind the man who was directing operations. He was on the right side of the press box, right behind the directors.

'The atmosphere in those days was electric. It was the finest of all time. Nothing like it has happened, before or since. There was a wonderful buzz all the way through games. The noise, the shouting, hearing them singing "Glory, Glory". For me, the atmosphere at Spurs in those days has never been bettered at any domestic game, ever. The enclosed roof above the terraces, especially on the East Stand, but also the West Stand which had its own enclosure at ground level, kept the sound in and that buzz lasted for ninety minutes.

'I can't remember songs about individuals so much. But of course you couldn't miss "Glory, Glory".

'After one of those games we were in the oak-panelled room that served as the press room – we called it the Oak Room, but that was actually the directors' lounge. It was very small and we were all huddled together. Laurie Pignon, who was on the *Sketch*, was calling out that he had too much work to do and that he needed a whipper-snapper to help him out. I'd never actually met him but I went outside to the telephone room at the back, picked up the phone and rang up Solly Chandler, who was the Sports Editor at the *Sketch*. I said I wanted a job and he told me to come round the next day at eleven a.m. I had all my diplomas and certificates but he said: "I'm not interested in that. Who do you know?" I reeled off a few names – Walter Winterbottom, Alf Ramsey, Stanley Rous – and after five minutes he said I could have the job. The offer was no better than I was on at the PA but when I told him that he relented and gave me ten shillings a week more, so I took the job.'

Scovell, like many of his generation, sat in four different White Hart Lane press boxes. Although Mike Collett, the long-time Football Editor of the Reuters news agency and a Spurs fan since 1962, thought there might have been another. Collett said: 'I can think of five different press boxes, if you include the "old press box" in the East Stand. I have a photograph of that one.

'When I first started working there, it was in the old West Stand. The box was fairly central, at a decent height. A much better view than now. You'd go inside to the oak-panelled press room at half-time, for sausage rolls and cherry cake. It was always the same and my mates used to take the mickey out of me because I'd endlessly go on about the cherry cake. There was also a designated working room, which was quite big but the press room itself wasn't. You'd just go there for a cup of tea. The working room was at the back. And there was a staircase, with a few stairs up to the press box. My first working game there was in 1973 or 1974, for Hayters. There I was, working at the Lane. I just felt: "This is amazing; this must've been here since it was built." And it was clearly purpose-built, too. It wasn't an afterthought or something that had been added on.

'It's an interesting exercise going to Spurs as both a working journalist and a passionate fan but I never had a problem separating the two. When I am in the press box I am a hundred per cent a professional journalist, totally cut off from my fan "self". I've never had a problem with that, same as when I am in the Arsenal press box. Absolutely no conflict of interest ever. In 1980, when the West Stand was being rebuilt, they had a temporary press box in the corner of Park Lane and the West Stand. I remember watching the 4–4 draw with Southampton on Boxing Day from there, sitting next to Cliff Jones, who I'd seen play in my first game at White Hart Lane in 1964. I was working for UPI then.

'After the West Stand was completed the first press box was where the directors sit now, in the upper tier. And then for the last twenty years at the Lane we were down in the low-level box.'

Reporters of a certain generation still call the last press box at White Hart Lane 'The Steve Curry Press Box' – in 'honour' of the reporter blamed for acquiescing with the decision. The man himself, a veteran of the *Daily Express*, *Sunday Telegraph*, *Sunday Times* and, as a colleague of mine, the *Daily Mail*, admits he was taken for a bit of a ride by the club. 'It was my fault,' Curry said, laughing. 'I was chairman of the Football Writers' Association at the time and I got conned by Irving Scholar. I was given assurances that we would have the same view as the old box, in the previous stand, but that it would be a little bit further back. Instead, it was right at the front.'

Scovell added: 'The West Stand had to be improved but I'm still not happy about the Steve Curry Box behind the dug-out. That was an absolute carve-up. Scholar took him out to lunch, they were drinking all day, and Steve agreed to put it behind the dug-out. I tried to say they couldn't do that but it was obvious what had happened. He'd realised that where they'd initially put the press box was a place where they could instead sell the seats for more, in the upper level behind the directors' box. So that's what happened.'

That sounds very, very Spurs. Like so many clubs, the bottom line was *always* the bottom line. If they could squeeze a few bob more out of every match, they would try. But Curry's experiences go way back to the time when Scholar was just a schoolboy fan himself. He added: 'The thing I remember about the first press box, in the old West Stand, was that one man was always there – Leslie Welch, who was known as "The Memory Man". He had this amazing, encyclopaedic memory, had been on radio and television for years, but was a big Spurs fan and a constant presence in the press box. He'd sit in the front row, in the right-hand corner, and was always there.

'You had a good view from there, too. But the press room was tiny, and I mean tiny. It was barely a cubby hole, and the press steward used to dispense the post-match drinks as if they were coming out of his own cabinet at home. He was such a Scrooge with the drinks. But the room was so small it was an impossible place to have a conversation. We were all shoulder to shoulder.

'What made up for all of it was to watch that team, the one that Bill Nicholson put together. They were a fantastic team, the real Spurs. I was a young journalist then and it was a great place to go, with a fantastic atmosphere.'

Most of those who have worked in that box first visited the Lane as supporters. Although not always as supporters of the home team. John Cross, my long-suffering partner in crime and successor as Chief Football Writer of the *Daily Mirror*, has never exactly hidden his allegiance to another north London side. He said: 'I grew up as an Arsenal fan and went to every single away game. Going to White Hart Lane was always my favourite ground, my favourite game of the season.

'Sometimes, if I'm honest, it was pretty brutal, the pushing and shoving, being squeezed and pushed from pillar to post, standing behind fences. But overall it was a brilliant experience, absolutely fabulous. The best night of my football-supporting life was the League Cup semi-final replay in 1987. People talk about 1989 and winning the title at Liverpool but for me I preferred that game at the Lane. It winds me up when you get pundits who don't understand the depth of the rivalry and say it's short-sighted for us to get hung up on finishing above or below Tottenham. But if you don't get that, then you're not a fan.

'As a kid growing up in London, if you weren't going to your team's away fixture, you would go to a random ground, and I always found that the atmosphere at White Hart Lane was really good. I really loved it and I'm so pleased the club is basically staying in the same place, even if they will be playing in a new ground.

'But from a journalist's point of view it's the worst ground in the country. You are near the bench and overlook the tunnel, which gives you amazing access. But that's outweighed by the smashed phones and laptops on the floor, because it's so compact and the working conditions are so poor. You can't even see the far side of the pitch. In that sense it's an absolute shambles, an absolute nightmare of a place to work.

'So it's a place of opposites for me – my favourite ground to visit as a fan and the worst professionally. But I can't think of another ground that has that same intensity. I love the place for all of that. In that regard I think it's heartbreaking that this has been the last season and it's come to an end because I don't think any new stadiums have as much soul or history as the old ones. For me there's a lot of sadness. It's a place where, every time I go, it brings back so many memories. It's such a great place with a fabulous atmosphere. The new ground just won't be the same. I feel a little bit of any club dies when it moves no matter how wonderful the new stadium might be.'

John was speaking as a football fan as much as a journalist. The *Sun*'s Paul Jiggins, Millwall to his core but who covered Spurs for most of the decade running up to the last game at the old Lane, had a different take on things. 'A lot of my colleagues complain about the position, saying that it's too low and you can't see anything,' he said. 'But what it does give you is a great insight and indication of just how strong a Premier League footballer is. When you see a ball go up to the halfway line and a centre forward hold it up, with thirteen stone of centre-half coming into the back of him and he still manages to hold him off while keeping control of that leather thing on the ground, without even looking at it, then you realise the skill and technique, and why they're out there playing on that pitch and I'm sitting here watching. It gives you that insight.

'You feel you're part of the action whenever you come here. You go to some stadiums, not just the ones with running tracks but even the ones that have stands close to the pitch, and you feel detached. But here, you always feel part of it.

'I think it's one of the best atmospheres, certainly recently. There was a time a few years ago when maybe the football wasn't as exciting as it could have been, when maybe the atmosphere was a bit flat. But Pochettino, after his first few months, when he started getting things into gear and the tempo came back, when Tottenham were playing fast and furious again, then the atmosphere was second to none. There are some characters around us too, either side of the press box. Don't get me wrong, sometimes they get on your nerves, but they're never boring.

'When West Brom played here in January 2017, Tony Pulis must have forgotten where we were all sat, just behind him. At one point he shouted out to his assistant: "Don't worry about complaining; you'll never get a decision here. They're a top-six club, remember." Then he shouted out: "Mauricio, you should be ashamed of your players, the way they're getting decisions like this." Then when he came up to the press room after the match, I asked him about it, and it was: "No complaints about the referee; no complaints about the way Tottenham played the game."

'It's a great place to analyse the benches and the fourth official and what they have to go through. Sitting where we do and watching that for ninety minutes, you really wouldn't want to be a fourth official! I'll feel an ache having to go to Wembley. But that's a different kind of ache. The fans who sit around us, long-time fans, will be emotional. That's great in football. There will be a bit of a lump in my throat, even if I'm a Millwall fan.'

I'm on the same page as Paul. Then again, you can never ask a Gooner for a proper assessment of football, can you? They have no soul, any of them. Just a bunch of south London interlopers.

Another who agrees with me about the sheer immediacy of that press viewing area is Gerry Cox, who runs the Hayters Teamwork sports agency, long a fixture of the London media scene and a regular bylined reporter in many papers. Gerry, like me, is Spurs to his bootstraps. He started to come to the Lane in 1968. On one occasion, he left early and missed Jimmy Greaves scoring a consolation goal against Manchester City – meaning he never actually saw his hero score for Spurs in the flesh. He normally stood on the terraces, although he recalled being bawled out by Warren Mitchell, who morphed into a Spurs-supporting version of Alf Garnett in front of his eyes when he and his mate showered the actor's seat with peanut shells when they sat in the West Stand for one game.

Gerry said: 'I started working here in 1987. Soon after I arrived at Hayters. I came to a game and watched it from one of the hospitality lounges because my wife, who was my girlfriend at the time, was working for Mike Rollo, who was the commercial manager. Reg Hayter, the founder of this company and who was a Fleet Street legend, had said to me: "Can you get into a game to do a trial report?" I watched the game and sent over my report the following morning, from a fairly routine League Cup win over Barnsley.

'On the team-sheet, it said Gary Mabbutt, only he didn't play. As the players were walking out, the girls in the hospitality department were saying: "Did you hear about Gary? He's not playing because he hadn't turned up for the team meeting. When they went to his house he was in a diabetic coma." So when I filed that in my match report the next morning, Reg rang back and bollocked me for not actually letting him know that night!

'If you asked me who my all-time hero was, I'd have to say Jimmy, because when I was growing up the only adults I was aware of, outside of my family, were The Beatles and Jimmy Greaves. Then, as a teenage fan, watching Spurs a lot, Hoddle was just by a mile the best midfielder I'd ever seen.

'I can remember seeing Gordon Durie throw his shirt at Ray Clemence and then being bombed out, and Tim Sherwood offering his gilet to one mouthy fan. You see a lot of stuff close-up. The stand-out memory, working here but also as a fan, was the 3–1 Inter Milan game. Gareth Bale was out of this world but he wasn't even the best player on the pitch because that was Luka Modrić. He came of age that night. That was seeing White Hart Lane rocking for the first time in years, a great match to cover.

'But there were loads of downs, covering Spurs. I worked at the club for a while doing Club Call. So I'd be in the tunnel as they came out and have to interview Venables. Gazza was off-limits at that time because it was the build-up to the World Cup, so most often it would be Lineker and Mabbutt. There was a little bet on between a few of us to get Pat Van den Hauwe to say anything, while Paul Stewart was fairly monosyllabic. Of course, given what emerged in 2017 about the sexual abuse he suffered as a kid in the North-West, we know now he had something of a dark history.

'That was quite the hardest thing I've done journalistically, by a mile, because it compromises you. Instead of doing the job and getting stories, good and bad news, you have to portray everything as great.

'When I was doing stuff for the club newspaper, *Spurs News*, during that Alan Sugar era, results were poor and you had to try to get five upbeat articles a month. And you'd end up ringing up players and asking them questions which they didn't want to answer, trying to get four hundred words out of them which you could stretch out to make a piece. And it was grim. You had to put your journalistic principles to one side when they'd tell you how "great" the spirit was when you knew it wasn't.'

Cox's recollection of Sherwood and his gilet, taken off and proffered to a supporter during the north London derby defeat to Arsenal as his brief reign stuttered to its inevitable conclusion in 2014, the darkest night before the Pochettino-created dawn, stirred another memory for me from the same game. By that season, the written press had been moved to the other side of the tunnel, with the radio stations and foreign media now taking all the seats immediately behind the home dug-out. But I was on the right edge of the rehoused press box, next to the tunnel wall, about ten rows from the front and 15 yards or so from the Spurs dug-out. Sherwood was apoplectic when a Spurs player went down on the far side of the pitch, screaming blue murder at the referee, the assistant ref, the fourth official and anybody else in the general vicinity. Desperate for confirmation, he sprinted into the mouth of the tunnel, awaiting the replay on the mini-monitor to prove he had been right, the officials wrong. Sky's match director, though, having judged the whistler correct, did not even bother to show the replay. Not that it stopped 'Tactics Tim', who sprinted back, rushed to the very edge of his technical area and bellowed towards the referee: 'I told you it was a foul. I've just seen it again. You got it totally wrong!'

I had returned to London as Football Editor, later Chief Football Writer, of the Press Association in 1996, after covering England and ghost-writing a column for some chap called Gareth Southgate, who had agreed to write a Euro 96 column for us, which then went to regional papers across the entire country (whatever happened to him?), and then spent four years at the *Daily Mail* before jumping ship to fill the void left by Harry Harris to become Chief Football Writer at the *Mirror* on the eve of the 2002 World Cup. It meant I spent far more time at Highbury, and then the Emirates, Stamford Bridge, Old Trafford, Anfield or The Etihad, being paid to watch the best teams in the land in order to chart the course of the title race and chronicle the clubs that filled the newspapers, dominated the airwaves and made the big stories, rather than devoting huge swathes of my working life to events in N17. Not that it ever prevented my first thought, wherever I was, from being: 'What's the Spurs score?'

And I even got the chance to play on the hallowed turf. It was 2002, at the end of the season, and I was invited to play in a press game. We changed in the visiting dressing room – I'd have preferred the home one, but you can't have everything – and even though I ran out into an empty ground, it was a moment I'll never forget. The fact that John Gorman then turned me inside out and back to front as I demonstrated why I was never likely to earn a living playing right-back was a mere detail.

I still witnessed some shockers from the other side of the touchline, in my normal press-box berth. Spurs were three up at half-time against Manchester United and then Manchester City, both under Hoddle, only to somehow conspire to lose. This was despite City having been reduced to ten men on the way into the tunnel in that FA Cup fixture when Joey Barton, not for the last time in his career, went loco at the referee. Against United, I was sat next to the Old Trafford press officer at the time, Diana Law, daughter of Denis. She was distraught at half-time, but, believe it or not, I was more concerned as the teams came out for the second half. She truly did not believe me when I said, with a prediction that sadly materialised: 'If you score the next goal, you'll win this . . .' Pure Spurs.

But there were also some truly wonderful nights and after-noons, when the hardest thing in the world was pretending I was a dispassionate observer rather than a supporter whose blood was pumping into overdrive. Indeed, one of my proudest moments was when a Spurs website labelled me 'clearly an Arsenal fan' for my report on their 5–1 win over Inter in the San Siro stadium.

One such example was Sunday 5 November 2006. Spurs had

not beaten Chelsea in 16 years and the big blue beast, powered by the super-ego of José Mourinho, expected another stroll at 'Three Point Lane'. When Claude Makélélé fired through a crowd of defenders from the edge of the box, for what was the second, and last, goal he was to score in his five-year spell at Stamford Bridge, normal service looked set to be resumed. But Michael Dawson, one of the nicest, most decent and pleasant-mannered footballers I have ever dealt with, headed an equaliser and in the second half Aaron Lennon, whom, it is fair to say, I would not put in quite the same category as Dawson (although given what we later discovered about his personal demons, his behaviour should be placed in a different context), sidestepped Ashley Cole to plant in the far corner to my right. Yet the thrill of the victory was enhanced by the situation and the assumptions that big games and controversies tend to instigate. Many Spurs supporters have always assumed John Terry said something he should not have done to Ledley King, given the mild-mannered Spurs skipper's angry reaction, before he was, mystifyingly, given a second yellow card and sent off by Graham Poll, helping Spurs to hang on to a victory that brought wild celebrations.

And I had a front-row seat for a moment missed by the cameras, too. In the first half, Paulo Ferreira, one of Mourinho's favourites who had accompanied him from Porto, had been given the runaround by an inspired Robbie Keane. At the break, the Portuguese was replaced by Dutch defender Khalid Boulahrouz but he fared no better against Keane, left dumped on his backside for the cross that was converted by Lennon. Soon afterwards, just 23 minutes into his appearance, the board went up and Boulahrouz was hooked. I will never forget the look of pure venom on the Dutchman's face as he stormed across the pitch, refusing to even look Mourinho in the eye until, almost as he passed the manager, he turned to his left and bellowed: 'You bastard!' Given that Boulahrouz barely featured for Chelsea again before being sold the following summer, it seems Mourinho did not forget, either.

There were plenty of other stand-out games, too. Only Spurs could lose to Portsmouth, the worst team in the Premier League by miles, in an FA Cup semi-final at Wembley on the Sunday and then promptly beat both Arsenal (Danny Rose's infeasible strike and some Gareth Bale brilliance) and then Double winners-in-waiting Chelsea in the space of the following seven days. That was just thrilling to witness in the flesh, partly because it was so unexpected. Equally intoxicating was Bale's wonder-night against Inter and then the gut-wrenching, nerve-shredding goalless draw against AC Milan in the 2010–11 Champions League run. I knew I had to compose myself and find a way of ignoring my emotional response in order to convey the facts, the consequences, the details and the meaning, in 750 to 800 words, within five minutes of the final whistle. And then do it all over again, normally with an extra reaction story featuring quotes from the key players and Harry Redknapp as well for the back page news line, within the hour. Working live, under deadline pressure, knowing I *had* to get it right, was the best part of my job, by a million miles.

Of course, it wasn't just press journalists who worked at the Lane over the years. There were the broadcasters, too, famous voices including that of John Motson, whose first visit to the Lane was in 1956, taken by his father to see their team, Boston United, lose 4–0 in the FA Cup. Motty, whose first job in journalism was as a reporter for the *Barnet Press*, of course had the facts and figures at his fingertips. 'My first game there working for television was against United in 1972. In my early years as a commentator we used to sit right out in front of The Shelf, pretty close to the pitch and we felt part of the atmosphere. It was a great commentary position because you got the crowd as well as the action on the pitch.

'There was a period when the Spurs fans wanted to be entertained and accepted that the team might just fall short. There were great players – Greaves, Gilzean, Lineker, Waddle, Gazza – who were capable of tremendous things. Gazza basically got Spurs to

Wembley on his own in 1991 and I was at most of those games.

'From the point of view of being a commentator, I remember Irving Scholar moving the box and it was a terrible view – because we were too high. It spoiled the experience because suddenly I felt more distant from the fans as well as from the action. But for the last few years the booth has been lower, on the platform used for European games. Once again, I have been able to experience that special atmosphere and really feel involved in the match.

'The great thing about White Hart Lane was how close the fans were to the pitch. You always felt they were part of the action. It seemed they did too. And that was why sitting in the middle of The Shelf was such a great commentating spot. Things changed slightly when the old Main Stand was rebuilt in the early eighties. But there was always a special feeling just before kick-off. "Mac-Namara's Band" would come on the PA and that was the "right, now it's happening" moment.

'For a long time White Hart Lane seemed trapped, behind the times, which is why the Scholar era was so different. They were the last big club to agree to perimeter advertising. But then it was a complete change. They were only the second club, after Manchester United, to expand and put in executive boxes. That seemed like a revolution at the time, a commercial step-change under Mike Rollo.

'But while it was a breakthrough at the time, the ground does look and feel old-fashioned now. It has caught up with some of the modern demands but is still lagging behind. The cockerel had to be moved when the stand was rebuilt. So did the press box, which used to give a view as good as the director's box. I think the end of a stadium brings more nostalgia and sentiment. That's natural. But on the plus side it won't be such a wrench for Spurs supporters as it has been for fans of other clubs who have seen their club move a few miles away. After all, Spurs are, quite literally, moving just a few yards.'

Words and voices are all part of the media. But what about the pictures, the images that help make a newspaper more than just a jumble of opinions? Richard Pelham delivered more back-page snaps for the *Sun* than most of us have had hot dinners. Lawrence Lustig, who like Dickie hailed from West Ham territory but saw the error of his ways in primary school and went on to follow the one true footballing faith, was similarly prolific in output for the *Daily Star*. Both loved the Lane.

Lustig said: 'We lived in Chingford. The boy next door, who was my hero because he was older, was a Spurs fan and I wanted to be like him. Of course, they were a great side then, so I started supporting them, and as soon as I was old enough I went to games. There was a bus from the bottom of the road, the 102 or 191, to the Angel in Edmonton and from there I'd walk down the back streets to the ground and go in the schoolboys' entrance. It cost me threepence each way on the bus, threepence for the programme and 1s 3d to get in.

'My football hero was Jimmy Greaves. Of course it was. He was everybody's hero. In those days you didn't have fancy replica strips. But one birthday my aunt bought me a white football shirt, sewed a Spurs badge on the front and the number eight on the back. There were others – Chivers, Jennings – but Greavsie was Greavsie.

'We all had our favourite places to watch games from. When I was really young I'd stand on The Shelf but at the Paxton Road end of it. That seemed to be populated less than the rest and because I was smaller the fact that the steps were higher at that end meant I could see more.

'Then, when I started there as a photographer, you could still work on the pitch, going onto it during the warm-up. You can't now. Everyone gets assigned fixed positions. I started work as a runner, a Saturday boy, at fifteen, running the film back to the photographers' room where they'd see what shots they had and get them back to the papers as soon as possible. In the September of the following season, I'd just turned sixteen and was sent to my first game as a photographer. At White Hart Lane. Spurs were playing West Ham and I was working for an agency. They said to me: "We need a picture of Bobby Moore." You've got to remember I was only sixteen and this was Bobby Moore, the man who had lifted the World Cup just six years before. I went on the pitch as they were warming up, approached him and, quite timidly, said: "Mr Moore . . .?" He looked at me. "Bobby. Call me Bobby." I was really nervous. "Okay Mr Moore . . ." "I said call me Bobby." "Yes Mr M . . . Bobby. Do you think you could kneel down?" He looked at me as I was about to take the shot. "I think you need a ball with this, don't you?" he asked. I nodded – and he shouted out to Geoff Hurst to throw him a ball. He knelt down and I took the picture. Then he said: "You might want to take another one because I might've shut my eyes." That maybe changed my life. If he'd told me to eff off I might never have worked at a game again.

'I hear younger photographers moaning about the conditions and the facilities today and laugh. When I started we'd get in by a little side gate. We weren't allowed near the press box so we went to the Enclosure in front of the West Stand. There was a little pathway between the Enclosure and the Paxton Road, separated by a small fence on either side. There was a bloke who'd wear a white doctor's coat who opened the gate and let us down the little alleyway onto the track round the pitch. We didn't get a programme. Not even a team-sheet. Or a cup of tea. You'd have to buy your own programme and sit by the side of the pitch, listen to the bad tannoy when they read out the teams and write out the changes on the back of the programme you'd bought.

'At the same time, if you wanted to go and photograph the team in training, you didn't have to ring the press officer to find out if there was any access. I'd have to ring Bill Nicholson and ask him. He'd tell me if I could come or not, but once there you'd be there for the whole session. And when they weren't using the pitches at Cheshunt they'd be at the ground, either on the pitch or in the indoor court behind the West Stand, and I'd go and shoot training there.

'I was gutted to be there, on The Shelf, the night Arsenal beat us to win the first leg of the Double. That was horrible. It was the one thing we had over them. They hadn't ever done it. But there just seemed to be Arsenal fans everywhere. It felt as if they outnumbered us.

'But the good memories include Alan Mullery scoring the goal to win the Uefa Cup. I was there as a fan and then twelve years later was there behind the goal when Tony Parks saved the penalty to beat Anderlecht. I kept calm. For about five seconds. I was at the *Star* at the time and got the picture but can't remember what I did after that. I do remember going round Tony's house the next day. It was in Chigwell somewhere, a very small flat backing onto the railway line. You wouldn't get a youth-team player living somewhere like that these days.

'In my mind, the ground was never empty. It was always a full house. Of course it wasn't. They weren't filling every space every game. If you look back, they were actually averaging 30,000 or so, when the ground could hold over 50,000.

'When you're working, you have to be professional. But I have to say, without being melodramatic, it was always special for me to go to work at White Hart Lane. I always loved it. I'd seen the whole ground change. There used to be four separate stands, different to what it is now and certainly to what it will become, but I honestly felt honoured to be able to work there.'

Pelham has his own White Hart Lane tales. 'I would've paid to watch Paul Gascoigne play football,' he said. 'And Gazza made me. They were 2–0 down in a game in 1991 or 1992, with two players sent off – Van den Hauwe and maybe Paul Stewart, I think. Gazza single-handedly ripped the other lot apart to get it back to 2–2. I was angry because I couldn't send back a new picture. The kit wasn't working properly. The next thing I knew I heard the motor drive on my camera going off. I looked round and there was Paul, standing next to me with his finger down on the button, letting every single frame go on my camera. They were great images that everybody used, of him with the camera, but it got me in the shots as well. And it sealed the relationship we had. When it was Spurs during the Gascoigne days, the picture desk would always send two photographers: one to shoot the game, the other to shoot Gazza.

'The Lane is a deafening ground. I can only work there wearing ear-plugs. It is one of those old, iconic stadiums. An amazing place and a great football ground. So often I'd come away from White Hart Lane and wouldn't be able to sleep because of the adrenalin from experiencing that atmosphere. And that's me talking as a West Ham fan. The stewards know I'm West Ham, so we can give each other a bit of stick, which I have always enjoyed.

'It has nice facilities and a good working room now but it used to be horrible. When I started in 1989 you used to get a cup of Bovril and that was it. You were stuck with the fans. The gate was a side entrance, round the corner. In the mid-eighties we were made to wear white bibs with Hertz on them, advertising bibs. We weren't happy, so Monty Fresco, who was *the* senior photographer at that time, went out and got us all some caps with Avis on them. I think we all got upgrades on our hire cars off the back of that.'

For all of those who worked there, me included, the end of the Lane does feel like a death in the family. Even those who were not Spurs fans felt its passing, although there is no doubt the old bird had a pretty good innings. 'When my nan lived down the road, I'd come and stay with her in the summer holidays,' Gerry Cox said. 'I used to walk down the road and stand outside. Some days it was so busy you couldn't get anywhere near the ground. There was no club shop. But it just had this magical feeling about it. And the smell, the smell of cigars. As you got near the ground you'd see the clock, and as a kid it was like seeing the sea for the first time. So leaving will be sad. But then you see the new stadium, and with the team going the way it is you realise this is really still

Tottenham. It's not like West Ham and their move – I really feel we dodged a bullet on that one. It might be a different stadium, but we're still here. We'll be sitting in the press room at the corner flag, so we'll not be far away from home.'

'I don't feel we're moving,' Lustig said. 'It's just modernising the ground. It's not like Arsenal when they left Highbury, or West Ham moving from Upton Park. We're *not* leaving White Hart Lane – we're just modernising the ground. I saw that gradual transformation over the years and this is a bigger one, just all in one go. The old stadium is coming down but it's still the same site for me, so it's not like we're not going to be at White Hart Lane any more. We're still there and we'll have a capacity that will be as big as it used to be when there were terraces all around the ground, all those years ago.

'What I like about this team is the stability, which helps to create a relationship between the fans and the players. For years it was a revolving door. Players would come and go and you'd struggle to remember they'd even been at the club. I could name the teams in the sixties, seventies and eighties. But during that period in the first ten to fifteen years of the Premier League I couldn't remember the one that had played the previous Saturday. Now the fans know the team and it's strengthening the bond between the supporters, the players and the club. Daniel Levy has taken a lot of criticism but he really wants to make a success of the club and not just on a financial basis. As a fan he wants a successful side.

'So it does feel sad. It's like losing an old friend. But, as I've said, it's not that old. I grew up with there being four distinct stands, with those pointed roofs. That was my White Hart Lane. My boys talk about "when the stadium goes" but I'm not having that. It's not going. It's just being modernised. It will be bigger but it will still be at White Hart Lane. That's it. As long as they put the cockerel up . . .'

17

HE'S MAGIC, YOU KNOW

The wilderness years hurt. Brief moments of hope, swiftly disappearing under waves of bitterness and dejection. For every glorious goal, there was a sickening defeat. For every spell when everything seemed to be heading in the right direction, the thudding reality of running into a metaphorical brick wall. Each change of management merely the precursor to another crushing disappointment. Doubts over the real intentions, the true aspirations, of the club welling up towards and then crashing over the parapet. As Daniel Levy went through a series of coaches, managerial models, ideas and a large cast-list of players, there were times when many of those who came, with hope in their hearts, to White Hart Lane began to wonder if those inner prayers would ever be answered, if they would ever really see a Spurs team capable of not just challenging, but beating, the big boys.

Yet the last two seasons Spurs spent at the Lane were, unquestionably, different. The team was arguably the best since Nicholson's Double-winners, and not just because of the quality, intensity and energy of the football. Nor did things feel different because of the arrival of a truly home-grown hero, Harry Kane, or even because of the growing sense that something special was not just on the horizon but was actually underway. While the unchallengeable proof of silverware remained tantalisingly out of reach, in spite of back-to-back campaigns that were statements of dramatic intent and determination, things felt very different.

And even if much of this was down to the young men under his command, everybody recognised the major contribution of the man who had made it all possible. It is witnessed by the new fans' chant that is a testament to the faith the fans have in the Argentinian who has made them believe again, and whose impact has been so clear and vivid: 'He's magic, you know. Mauricio Pochettino!'

However, when Pochettino's name was first raised, after the André Villas-Boas era collapsed because of the Portuguese manager's sheer intransigence just before Christmas 2013, the Argentinian was dismissed as being 'not quite ready'. Instead it was Louis van Gaal who was being courted to replace Tim Sherwood, whose limitations had been swiftly exposed. Thankfully for Spurs, being beaten to a target by Manchester United – a club against whom Levy harboured genuine resentment after being forced to sell both Michael Carrick and Dimitar Berbatov, as well as losing secretary John Alexander – was for once a good thing. It was a near miss that saw the board recalibrate their targets and eventually settle on the then Southampton manager.

The two seasons before that had been typical Spurs. Villas-Boas arrived, insisting he had learned from his Chelsea experience, when player power had forced him out by the February of his first season. To a degree, he was correct. At Stamford Bridge, he had alienated Frank Lampard, Didier Drogba, Petr Cech and, to a lesser degree than was claimed, John Terry. Arriving at Tottenham, he identified Gareth Bale as the key man and hitched himself to the Welshman for the ride. Rather than chaining Bale to the flank (Redknapp was constantly implored by Spurs supporters to remember 'Gareth Bale, he plays on the left'), he built his team around the stand-out performer, giving him a free role to play as and where he wanted, although he ended that season as a taller, swifter and more powerful version of the type of 'inverted winger' on the right of a 4-3-3 trademarked by Arjen Robben. Explaining the initial switch, Villas-Boas said: 'I had Gareth knocking on my door once, not crying, but he was complaining a little bit. He said he wanted me to help him to enjoy his football a little more. We had a good conversation. Hopefully it turned out well for both of us. From that moment onwards his drive, his passion and his ambition towards the height of elite football has been immense.'

Bale agreed. 'No one wants to be stuck on the wing where you get a couple of markers put on you to take you out of the game,' he said. 'That free role is fantastic. You can go for a wander and try and find the space to affect games pretty much for the ninety minutes. But I've also been practising my new role in training all season and working incredibly hard with the manager on tactics, so what we achieved was not by accident.'

Villas-Boas was confident in his players. That 2012–13 season was one which promised much and when Bale and Aaron Lennon scored in a 2–1 home win over Arsenal that saw Spurs open up a seven-point gap over Arsène Wenger's side, the Portuguese suggested the visitors were now in a 'negative spiral'. And when the Welshman produced a stunning last-gasp winner at Upton Park, the manager was gushing. 'He inspires people and he is a direct influence on every single player. Players like this take responsibility at key moments. He is tremendous.'

Yet despite Bale scoring 26 goals – a season tally that had only been exceeded at Spurs in the Premier League era by Teddy Sheringham and Jürgen Klinsmann two decades earlier – and earning 72 points, Spurs finished fifth. Behind you know who. And when Bale had the chance to follow Modrić to Madrid, the issue was only ever going to be the price. Levy, with Franco Baldini now installed as the third sporting director of his reign, opted to buy before he sold. In came Denmark schemer Christian Eriksen from Ajax, Spain striker Roberto Soldado, Belgium's Nacer Chadli, Brazil midfielder Paulinho, French midfielder Étienne Capoue, Romanian defender Vlad Chiricheş and Roma's Argentinian star Érik Lamela for a combined £109 million. Yet with Bale going for a world record fee – when the £3 million still owed on Rafael van der Vaart was written off, it amounted to £89 million – other sales meant Spurs actually made a profit in that transfer window. Balance sheets are one thing. Performance is another. And while the criticism that Spurs had 'sold a giant and brought in the seven dwarves' was unwarranted, the fact that only Eriksen and the injured Lamela remained at the club by the end of the 2016–17 season told its own story. Tottenham's results under Villas-Boas were initially okay. But there were too many stuttering performances, with the result that Villas-Boas went off piste in October, following a narrow home win over Hull, and broke football's 11th commandment – never criticise your own fans.

'We looked like the away team,' he said. 'We played in a difficult atmosphere with almost no support. We have a wonderful set of fans but they can do better. We don't need the negativity. Away from home their support has been amazing. We play with no fear and we need that atmosphere at White Hart Lane. We didn't have the support we should have done. There was much anxiety from the stands, the players had to do it alone. We spoke about it at half-time. I told the players that we would have to do it on our own. They had to dig deep and look for the strength within themselves. They also believed that it's not easy to play in this stadium when the atmosphere is like this.'

Unsurprisingly, it had precisely the wrong effect. Humiliation at Manchester City was followed a month later by a 5–0 home thrashing by Liverpool, with Villas-Boas resolute: 'I won't resign and I'm not a quitter. The only thing I can do is work hard with the players to try and get the results that we all want.' Levy wanted to give him more time. But he also needed his manager to show he could put his feelings aside for the common good. Villas-Boas was asked if he was prepared to allow Emmanuel Adebayor back into the squad. He refused. And was sacked.

Now Levy was in a bind. Behind the scenes, Tim Sherwood, who had impressed in his new role of director of development, was lobbying fiercely for his chance, even as Levy was beginning discussions with van Gaal. The former England midfielder, who happily agreed to bring Adebayor back into the fold, was handed the job. But only on an 18-month deal that was unlikely to ever be seen through to the end. To be fair to Sherwood, he beat pretty much everybody he should have beaten. But he lost to everybody who was half-decent and his public attack on Jan Vertonghen after the Belgium defender blundered at Stamford Bridge in a typically throw-the-towel-in display was a stunningly ill-advised and foolishly self-defeating act. Sherwood's touch-line behaviour, too, became increasingly comical. Those on the board came to a clear conclusion – they needed a manager, not a cheerleader. Sherwood, reading the runes, went on the offensive, sealing his fate in the process. 'We're taking out one of the best players in the world and replacing him with seven players who have never played in this competition before. How on earth did people think we would be title challengers or even make the top four?'

Two days after the season finished, Sherwood was dismissed. On 27 May 2014, a fortnight later, Pochettino was appointed. It was an appointment that made perfect sense for once, even if few could have imagined Pochettino having so marked an effect in England after the stand-out one of his playing career. I was in the strange surroundings of the Sapporo Dome on Japan's Hokkaido island on 7 June 2002 at the 2002 World Cup when Argentina's No. 4, hair flowing halfway down his back and wearing an Alice band, dangled out a left leg as Michael Owen worked the ball past him in the penalty area. The England man went down despite minimal contact – some of Hoddle's training from four years earlier in France had stuck – allowing David Beckham to exorcise the ghosts of his horrible moment of madness against the same opponents in Saint-Étienne in 1998, when the England man was sent off for the slightest of retaliatory kicks at Diego Simeone. It was a nightmare for Pochettino, appearing at his only World Cup, with the highly fancied *Albiceleste* back in Buenos Aires before the knock-out phase started.

The rugged defender, a farm labourer's son from the town of Murphy in Santa Fe province, was to have a lengthy club career. It started at Newell's Old Boys where, as a teenager, he became an early disciple of Marcelo 'El Loco' Bielsa, a vesuvial and erratic coach whose purity of footballing vision was unquestioned but who also deserved the label of 'flawed genius' more than most. At the age of 22, Pochettino left home for Spain, spending six years at Espanyol, where he lived under the mighty shadow of neighbours Barcelona. Three seasons in France, at Paris Saint-Germain and Bordeaux, preceded a return to Catalonia and Espanyol, before he retired in 2006.

Barcelona's second club was in his heart, but even those at Barcelona had noted his work with the Espanyol youth set-up. And when the Nou Camp hierarchy were seeking a replacement for Frank Rijkaard in 2008, despite his inexperience he was among the candidates who were considered, although the final shortlist for that job consisted of Pep Guardiola – who had himself not coached at a senior level but had a grounding and background within the club – and José Mourinho. He was eventually offered the chance to take over at Espanyol in January 2009 and accepted immediately, introducing the high-pressing philosophy, straight from the Bielsa playbook, that was to become his calling card. By the time he left the club in November 2012, he had begun to attract wide praise for his work, especially his determination to give young players a chance, as long as they committed themselves to his unstinting work ethic. However, his burgeoning reputation did not extend to England, and there was widespread indignation and disbelief when, in January 2013, he was suddenly announced as Nigel Adkins's replacement at Southampton. The doubts about Pochettino's suitability for the role were not eased by his initial insistence on using an interpreter for all of his media appearances, but on the pitch the improvement was immediately evident, and with English players to the forefront. Calum Chambers and Nathaniel Clyne had an effective 'job-share' at right-back, while the

Argentinian, operating in tandem with talent-spotter Paul Mitchell, also promoted Jack Cork, James Ward-Prowse, Jay Rodriguez, Rickie Lambert and Adam Lallana. Leading Saints to an eighth-placed finish in the league in 2013–14 on a limited budget quickly silenced his critics.

When he then took over at Spurs, Levy asked Pochettino to conduct his media dealings in English. It was something he was already prepared for as long as his own requirements were met. That meant change, on Pochettino's terms. Baldini left, with Levy now pledged to work alongside the manager, listening to his ideas and attempting to make them happen. Indeed, given Pochettino's involvement in the new stadium project, and his determination to redesign the entire club in line with his principles and vision, it was not unreasonable to draw parallels with what had taken place under a certain Monsieur Arsène Wenger at another club not a million miles away. After all the mistakes and missteps over the years, the direction and ambition of the manager and board at last seemed to be united. 'I wanted to have a project with a good team,' Pochettino said. 'We needed to show we were capable of competing against big teams in big games.'

It was not going to be an easy process. First Pochettino needed to assess the squad he had, quickly coming to two important decisions: to root out those he did not believe would accept his core philosophies and disciplinary code and to place his trust in youth. In this way, he began to build a new, more determined and focused Spurs. Back-to-back wins in August over West Ham – new boy Eric Dier slotting in a pass from substitute Kane with virtually the final kick of the match – and QPR brought some breathing space. Then, in late October, Pochettino's side were booed off as they trailed Stoke 2–0 at half-time, eventually losing 2–1. That game was equally noteworthy for the new manager biting the bullet and unleashing Kane in a Premier League starting line-up for the first time, after the young striker had been prolific in the Europa League. The Spurs fans, desperate for a new hero to cling onto, saw the fresh-faced frontman as the answer. He was, as the chant had it, 'one of our own', a Spurs fan who had himself watched from the stands. Three seasons later, with Kane having won back-to-back Golden Boots and scored 75 Premier League goals, it looked like an obvious call, but Kane himself admitted that he had to earn his place. 'I was young at the time. Adebayor and Soldado were here and they were first choice. I was working hard to try and get that spot. It didn't work straight away. I had to wait my turn and I wasn't in squads at times. I went to ask him what I could do better and what I could do to get in the starting eleven. He told me a few bits here and there, but mainly to keep working hard. I did, and I got my chance – I managed to go from there.'

That there was mutual respect between them was key. Pochettino saw a young man who had struggled to make a real impact on loan at Leyton Orient, Millwall, Leicester and Norwich but who was determined to prove he could score goals at the highest level. Kane, in turn, recognised the man who could help make that happen. Kane said: 'When I first met him, I knew he was a respectful guy. Straight away I knew he was someone I could get on with but only if I was working hard, respecting him and being part of the team. That's what he wanted. He wanted players who would put in extra work for him and he'd show them love back. That's what we've got now. We've got a good relationship, great respect for one another and I think he's one of the best managers in the world – not just tactically on the pitch but off the pitch as well, in the way he manages his players. He's a great manager to work under.

'A lot of the time he's calm, but he's very passionate. If he feels the problem isn't the game but is about our attitude, he'll just tell us we need to work harder or play harder. He's emotional. And that's what we want – we all feel the same. We all want to win. We've all got the same goal. He's got two sides to him. He's very respectful. If you respect him, he'll show you respect back. If you work hard for him, he'll give you his time. But he's ruthless if you cross him. If you don't want to work for him and you don't want to be a team player, you won't be part of the team.'

Nothing was achieved under Pochettino without hard work. The Argentinian, though, leads by example, driving in to Tottenham's stunning new training complex, tucked away between the A10 and the M25, before the sun has fully risen. Pochettino said: 'I arrive every day at seven to seven thirty and after that spend all day here. We train either single or double sessions and if it is a double session I'm still here at half eight at night. But even if it's only one session, I spend a lot of time here. I never leave before half seven. We have a monthly plan but then decide what we are going to do each week. What's important is all the information we get from the players, so we have different plans for the long-, medium- and short-term. You have to give that information back to the players. Each of them needs to be managed differently. I think the way we press high is one quality of the team. That's really good. When you don't have the ball you need to recover it quickly. And when you do have it, it is important to try and build from the back. Football has changed. It is not the same as it was thirty years ago. Now players are athletes and need to have individualised training. It's not enough to have just one session every day. But training is hard, I understand that. It's not easy but it's a good challenge for us to keep players at the same level.'

And keep them aware of their responsibilities, to themselves and the squad, too. They are required to dedicate themselves, each day, to the core tenets of his project and to a mutual determination to be a unit. 'I do ask the players to shake hands every morning,' he said. 'It is important to create a good dynamic. It's just respect to each other and showing how you feel in the morning when you meet. Small things mean a lot to create a real team. You feel your team-mates, you feel your people. It shows you're interested in people when you shake hands. When you watch someone you can translate emotion to them. What is important is to try to create a more and better feeling from the beginning of the day and start to work in a different mood.'

Pochettino swiftly separated the wheat from the chaff. Of the team that started his first Premier League game, at West Ham, six – Younès Kaboul, Kyle Naughton, Nabil Bentaleb, Aaron Lennon, Capoue and Adebayor – had left the club within two years. As had five of those on the bench – Michael Dawson, Soldado, Brad Friedel (although the goalkeeper retired to become a club ambassador in his native United States at the age of 44), Lewis Holtby and, in a painful but necessary decision which was about proving that nobody would be allowed to upset the team dynamic, Andros Townsend. The England winger, frustrated at a lack of playing time, took it out on Pochettino's support staff during a post-match warm-down. His card was marked. 'That was a private matter,' Pochettino said. 'But there are always actions and consequences. When you behave in the wrong way, there are consequences. Discipline is always important for me. I can understand players. We have a young squad and you can make mistakes but when you cross the limits it's important to stop that. I am always clear – I like discipline. That is important. We need to show respect to players but they need to show respect to my staff.'

He had shown a similar approach with Bentaleb, who was the fulcrum of the side when, inspired by Kane, they beat Mourinho's title-bound Chelsea 5–3 on New Year's Day during his first season with the club. He was to make it equally clear that Kyle Walker had transgressed when it appeared the England right-back's head had been turned by discussions with City's Three Lions players about Pep Guardiola and his club during an international break in March 2017. It is Poch's way or the highway.

But he was able to take that approach because the players, board and fans alike – not to mention Spurs' rivals – could see the influence he was having. And signing Toby Alderweireld in the summer of 2015 was another huge moment on the way to the team being recast as the best defensive side in the Premier League. Yes, Tottenham. No longer 'soft Spurs' but a hard-as-nails, physical side, with a cutting edge too. Spurs had signed Dele Alli from MK Dons in January 2015 for £5 million but allowed him to stay in League One for the rest of that campaign before joining full-time the following summer. Within weeks he was a regular, joining Kane in an England starting side that was beginning to be constructed around a core of Tottenham players.

'I was the one who pushed for Dele Alli, a hundred per cent,' said David Pleat, who was still used by Spurs as a talent scout. 'I had to use my powers of persuasion with the board and fortunately they respect me enough. I watched him several times. I saw the quality and was singing his praises when they decided to sign him. But he wasn't the same player then. At Milton Keynes he was going box to box from deeper. So the manager has done well with him, too, no question about that. Alderweireld was also a very good signing. I think there is more of a bond between the fans and the team now. But I think a lot of that is because the team is so good. The football they are playing is what they want to see from a Tottenham side. The manager has done so well to put this team together. He's looked at Eric Dier, realised he wasn't happy as a right-sided defender and moved him into midfield. Then, because Victor Wanyama has done so well in that defensive midfield role, he's moved Dier back into a right-sided centre-back in a defensive three. He's done well with Dier.'

Pochettino's predecessors could see what he had brought to the team. Harry Redknapp, who described Pochettino as being 'fantastic', said: 'I'm a great fan. I love watching them play now.' And Pleat added: 'The big thing is that he trains them very hard. I asked him about Ryan Mason a couple of years ago, before he sold him to Hull and when he was using him in central midfield. Until that season he'd never played regular games before in his life. In four years he never played more than two or three games without getting injured. So I asked him how he'd got Ryan fit and

Mauricio said: "Because now he trains harder." He believes the harder you train, the more you are able to resist injuries. The old-school view, including mine, was that the more you rest players, the more you take the strain off them and the more physicality you could get on a Saturday. But Mauricio has a very different approach and it's hard to argue against it. They have a good team, playing good football and I think the crowd really appreciate that. They like what is happening at Enfield as well, even if very few of the fans have been up to the training ground. While I was director of football there was always a lot of talk about that being the solution. It took a lot of discussion. There were three different organisations who had a stake in the fifty-seven acres on that site but now there is a marvellous training centre and pitches. And when Daniel Levy leaves, which is inevitable at some stage, especially given he's been at the club for fourteen years so far, he will leave a real legacy. I just hope they can crown it, before he goes, by becoming champions. That's what he wants and what I want. It would be the ultimate statement.'

It is Pochettino's ambition, too. Finishing third in 2015–16 was frustrating, especially as the late collapse allowed Arsenal to snatch second place behind shock winners Leicester. But he was not taken in by the 'Spursy' nonsense. Tottenham had not 'thrown away' a title race they were never really in. It was just that they had stayed in the race for far longer than all the other clubs whose budgets and squad depth vastly overwhelmed theirs. It was not Spurs who had failed, but Arsenal, Chelsea, Liverpool – who had finished above Tottenham just once since the start of the 2009–10 season – and the Manchester giants. Yet it made him even more determined to do better going into the last year at the Lane and beyond.

'Playing with passion and showing our quality is good,' he said. 'I'm proud the fans are proud of what we are doing and that they can see big things. What happened at the end of that season was an experience we had to learn from. It wasn't a physical problem.

It was mental. When you lose focus it is impossible to move your body. The message was that we must adjust everything – training and matches. We always need to remember that we started to play as boys, we feel passion and emotion. If you lose that passion and emotion it's not good. But we didn't play the way we wanted to play. I felt it in the body language and energy.'

Pochettino had recast the spirit and essence of the club, and captured the hearts of his players, who believed he would give the supporters what they yearned for. Skipper Hugo Lloris said: 'Fans live in the past. That's natural. But now they are talking about our team, this team. We're all working hard to bring the club up to the level to compete with the best teams in England and Europe. There's a real identity in the club now. The fans accept that and understand the way we play and are feeling very proud to see young players from the academy. That's really important for Spurs fans.

'He is very energetic but also calm. He is Argentinian and that idea of *grinta* [meaning determination or grit] is inside him. He wants to share it with the players. Football is about work. It's simple, really. Work not talk. When he arrived it was very difficult to understand why he wanted us to work so hard. But within a few months we'd started to improve our fitness and conditioning. Step by step he created a real atmosphere of work and you can feel it and see the improvement in the players and the team. The next step is to win trophies.

'You can't pretend to be a big club. The next level for us has to be winning trophies together. That would be a big reward for all the players and the manager, the big prize.'

Kane, too, has his eyes on the big prize. 'It wasn't one big high for me here,' he said. 'There were ups and downs along the way. I had some great coaches in the youth team and reserves. I had to work hard and be driven but it was something I enjoyed and it makes it special to be where I am now. But I have that connection with the fans. So when I'm on that pitch I want to give everything for them and the team. It makes you run a bit more and try a bit harder.

'That's my personality and ours. We want to work hard. White Hart Lane was an amazing stadium and there were so many good and great memories there for me. This season we played while the new stadium was going up in the background. I just want to be there and see what the finished project is going to be like. Everybody is looking forward to that. We will have one of the best sides in England. We have a great young manager and a young squad. It's about keeping the hunger and mentality and improving. Before him we were playing for Champions League places. Now we're trying to win the title. The manager has done what needed to be done. He had an idea in his mind of how he wanted to play and he knew he was going to get that from certain players. He brought some players in, he brought a few of us up from the youth team and he got the balance spot on. We've got a very young team, a very strong team, we're hungry and we want to win some titles and trophies.'

The ambition was strong and deep-seated, stemming from the manager and cascading through his players, with the supporters buying into it in a way they had not done for 20 years or more. Spurs under Pochettino were a very different team indeed.

18

A NEW HOME

With every passing step as you walked up Tottenham High Road, heading north from Bruce Grove Station, it became larger and larger. A gargantuan vision of concrete and steel. A statement of Tottenham Hotspur's ambition that, just like its predecessor, will be known as 'The world-famous home of the Spurs'. A venue fit for legends to be created afresh. Testament, indeed, to the sheer scale of Daniel Levy's master-plan. A suitable home for a club ready, after many years, to fulfil its destiny. This was a stadium for twenty-first century football, paying tribute to the past but grasping the corporate future at the same time.

A stadium, yes. Gleaming and modern. A statement from the outside but inside boasting a host of spectacular, unusual elements. A microbrewery, capable of delivering 10,000 pints an hour – enough to satisfy even the most rapacious of thirsts. High-end restaurants, with menus devised by some of London's leading chefs and culinary experts, to go alongside the outlets for the supporters fancying the footballing staples of pie and chips or those smoked salmon bagels that always taste better at a game. A tunnel wall made of glass, allowing those with the cash a unique insight into what goes on in those last moments before the players emerge into the hallowed arena, or in the first moments after they slip back down towards the dressing room. State of the art facilities. Seats that cushion your backside, invite you in – all a far cry from the clattering wooden ones of my childhood.

Like any new structure, it cannot replicate what is lost. There are no Paxton Road or Park Lane ends and there is no Shelf either. But a stunning South End is planned, with 17,000 seats, representing the biggest single-tier stand in Britain. The blueprint for that part of the new stadium was the Westfalenstadion in Dortmund. Another club embedded in its roots, fighting against the odds, aiming to achieve 'impossible' dreams. And if 'safe standing', the German model, was to be adopted by the Premier League – with the campaign growing up and down the land – then what could be better than a wall of Tottenham Sound, cascading the songs and chants around this magnificent new structure. And while the club was being coy about how it would name areas that will run in parallel with the four touchlines, maybe the Nicholson Stand on the tunnel side, the Blanchflower End to the north, the Jimmy Greaves Stand as the designated place where the loudest and proudest would make their new home? Although fitting, in my opinion, that would be for others to decide.

Yet while it all seemed so obvious in retrospect, so clear that White Hart Lane had to be replaced by this stunning beauty, which will stand proud as the floodlights illuminate the north London sky, it was not always so clear-cut that the move would go ahead. A project initially considered more than a decade before, it was revised, scrapped and then reconsidered, amid a campaign in which allegations of skullduggery and double-dealing were made.

Of course, the idea of Spurs moving from the Lane had been mooted before. Indeed, in December 1977, the *Daily Express* sports pages were splashed with a picture of the Tottenham and Arsenal boards sat either side of a long table as they discussed the idea of sharing a proposed 75,000-capacity home at Alexandra Palace. The concept did not seem as far-fetched then as it would now. After all, as Morris Keston recalled, the two clubs had shared White Hart Lane after Highbury was requisitioned as an air raid patrol centre during the Second World War, including the

Gunners' friendly with Dynamo Moscow in the immediate after-math of the victory over Hitler's Germany. Three decades earlier, Spurs had been tenants at Highbury as the Lane was used as a gas mask factory during the Great War. The Alexandra Palace plans included an exhibition hall and a monorail to transport fans from Finsbury Park, 'or even central London'. The grandiose scheme eventually died a death, as Greater London Council leader Horace Cutler, who was to be replaced soon after by a certain Ken Livingstone, cited the negative reaction of local residents and politicians as the reason he would block any formal proposals, adding: 'The probable social and environmental consequences of a stadium at the Palace are untenable.'

At that stage, the prospect of football becoming one of Britain's greatest money-spinners and image makers would have been utterly unthinkable. It was fears of hooliganism that had spurred many of the objectors to consider the idea of a shared ground, and things were to degenerate further during the next few years. But the advent of the Premier League altered many things and when Joe Lewis and ENIC bought Tottenham from Alan Sugar, the exponential growth of the national game was in full cry. In October 2005, just three months after London's upset victory in the contest to host the 2012 Olympic Games, Levy publicly announced the club might be interested in taking over the stadium planned for Stratford: 'At the moment it is going to be used for athletics. If that changes, then I'm sure they'll come and talk to us. There are only one or two clubs who could occupy it. We have the fourth largest supporter base of any English club and that is an independent assessment. And we are one of the few clubs that have sold every single seat this season. Chelsea had empty seats in the Champions League. I can tell you now that, if we were playing in Europe, I don't care who it would be against, this stadium would be full. The supporter base is not just large, it is very loyal.'

That comment was to be tested over the coming years, although initially Livingstone, by now London's first elected Mayor, pushed back at the idea of a football 'anchor tenant' post 2012. Levy and the board, looking enviously at Arsenal, sought alternative options. In November 2007 they engaged Tony Winterbottom, who had been involved in Arsenal's Emirates project, to come up with plans to expand the capacity of the Lane to 52,000. Talks with the FA and – ironically – West Ham about temporarily splitting matches between Wembley and Upton Park began but got little further. Meanwhile, out of sight of the supporters and the media, schemes were in hand, with the club incrementally buying up land and property around the Lane, focusing on the Wingate Trading Estate directly to the north of the stadium. And in October 2008, after months of rumour, the club officially submitted a planning application for a new 56,000-capacity ground on that block of land, a development including 434 new homes, a 150-room hotel and a supermarket. The initial cost of the 'Northumberland Development Project' (NDP) was an estimated £400 million, with Levy pledging to 'deliver the most fan-friendly stadium in Europe', including a single-tier end, modelled on Dortmund's Yellow Wall, by the 2012–13 season, while the club would continue to use the Lane during the process. 'Too often new stadiums are surrounded by empty, dead space and we did not want that in Tottenham,' declared Levy. 'We have embraced the opportunity to create something truly special for local people.'

In truth, few argued with the concept. The sheer scale of the financial divide between Tottenham and Arsenal was astonishing, the Gunners banking around £1 million more in gate receipts and match-day spending than Spurs for every home match. In an era of wage-inflation in football, when there was a clear and pronounced correlation between budget and success, Tottenham faced the inevitable process of withering away into inconsequentiality unless they made the step into the Brave New World. It was a plan that appeared to be welcomed by the local community too, with Haringey Council voicing outline support, as well as public backing from Tottenham MP David Lammy, himself a White Hart

Lane regular. And on 30 September 2010, a special meeting of Haringey's Planning Committee unanimously endorsed the proposal. It looked like a significant move. Instead, it was merely the beginning of a saga that would have many twists and turns, and bring the board into open conflict with many fans.

While Spurs had been officially all-in with the NDP concept, the club was growing increasingly concerned that the council backing was lukewarm at best, with an unwillingness to contribute to the costs of the project, despite the knock-on benefits for one of the most socially-deprived wards in the country. And in the hours before councillors had sat down to vote through the revised plans, Tottenham, in tandem with American entertainments giant AEG, owners of the O2 arena – previously the financially-stricken Millennium Dome, which they'd overhauled and turned into a commercial success – had submitted their own proposals for the Olympic Stadium site. Within a few days, the reach of those plans emerged. Rather than adapting the stadium that was still being constructed in Stratford, with talk of retractable seats, Tottenham would simply knock it down after the Games and rebuild a football-only site. It soon became apparent that the required 'athletics' legacy would be created by upgrading the run-down Crystal Palace facility in south-east London, making that a 25,000-capacity venue with the prospect of a temporary increase to 40,000 if it was to stage a major event.

Some believed it was a shot across Haringey's bows. Yet AEG boss Tim Leiweke signalled the serious nature of the plans as he hailed the proposals as 'logical', adding: 'I think it is a crime if you sacrifice having a perfect football stadium for convincing yourself you are going to do a track and field event every ten years.' At Spurs, there was no doubt: Levy was playing for keeps. The idea seemed not only cost-effective – it had dawned on people that the initial £400 million price-tag for the NDP was likely to snowball – but also sensible in commercial and sporting terms. Football was always going to be the cash cow to make the stadium viable. The demand for a major athletics venue was limited. Spurs believed that Livingstone's mayoral successor, Boris Johnson, had promised that it would be an open and fair contest and the club were convinced their proposal made far more commercial sense than the rival bid from West Ham.

Those close to Levy and the project team were confident that the Spurs chairman was deadly serious. By linking with AEG, he had a plan that made genuine sense, making use of the infrastructure and development potential of the Olympic site. Architects had sold Levy the view that retrofitting the Olympic Stadium was simply not going to work because the track would add to the distance between the seats and the pitch, adversely affecting the sight-lines for football spectators. Levy, initially, was only focused on the rebuilding scheme but eventually found himself persuaded of the necessity of the Crystal Palace element of the overall plan by Spurs board member Sir Keith Mills, who was himself keen to be chief executive of the Games Organising Committee.

Dissent, expanding to outright and vehement opposition from the supporters grew at a rapid pace. Some fans were outraged, banding together under the label 'We are N17' while more than 2,000 people signed a petition demanding 'Say No to Stratford Hotspur'. The message to Levy and his colleagues was clear on the placards, which read 'Spurs must stay'. Supporters, inside and outside the ground, used a series of matches in the 2010–11 season to give loud voice to their discontent. They were adamant as they chanted: 'North London is ours, north London is ours; Say no to Stratford, north London is ours.' Yet there were dividing lines. The majority though, could not bring themselves to turn their back on history and break the umbilical cord between the club and its community, even if few now lived in Haringey, let alone N17 itself. Fan and author Alan Fisher said: 'We should be proud that Spurs had never played a home game more than six hundred yards from the second lamp-post on the corner of Park

Lane and the High Road, where that bunch of school-kids decided they wanted to form a club in 1882. That's fundamental. And for over a hundred years, every single Spurs fan has walked the same streets, walked down the High Road. That is such an important thread. There is only one Hotspur. It's rare for a club to stay in one place and I felt it was tremendously important to keep that heritage.'

Levy felt threatened and undermined by the scale of the back-lash, calling a meeting with 'We are N17' in which he accused the protest group of 'trying to kill the club', an argument which found favour with some fans, who thought that what mattered was the good of the team and its ability to compete with their capital rivals on a fair financial footing, rather than maintaining the vestigial links with the streets around the Lane. For them, Levy's numbers added up – moving would prevent the club from accumulating the sort of debts that hampered Arsenal after they decamped from Highbury.

A number of other supporters recognised the economics of the argument being put forward by the club. They were, though, in the minority. Yet it was not the weight of supporter response that settled the issue, but cold, hard politics. Lord Sebastian Coe, the ennobled head of the Olympic Organising Committee and, of course, a former Tory MP and latterly chief of staff to Conservative Party leader William Hague, was already determined to be the successor to the compromised Lamine Diack as president of the International Association of Athletics Federations. He needed the athletics legacy to remain in Stratford. Levy thought that having Mills on his board gave Spurs credibility, as it suggested the club had a vision for the site that made sense for both the club and the taxpayer. During the latter part of 2010, the very existence of the National Sports Centre at Crystal Palace was under significant doubt amid a cash shortfall, and spending money to revamp and upgrade the existing facilities was something Tottenham believed they could sell to the government, national sports authorities and athletes. But even as the clock ticked down to decision day, in early 2011, the Tottenham bid team began to fear that Johnson, Coe and the Tory establishment, including No. 10, wanted a deal with West Ham, irrespective of other arguments. The East London club, now under the ownership of David Sullivan and David Gold, and run on a day-to-day basis by Tory peer Lady Karen Brady, was also backed by Newham Council, the local authority who would take ownership of the post-Games site.

While Tottenham's proposal still seemed the more feasible and cost-effective, they were undermined by their plan to demolish the existing stadium. And the skirmishing between Tottenham and West Ham became increasingly nasty too, with accusations of industrial espionage being thrown about. Leyton Orient chairman Barry Hearn – head of the existing Football League club closest to the Olympic site and who feared the repercussions of West Ham being able to encroach on 'his' territory – was among those infuriated by the cosy arrangement that he believed was skewed against his club's interests. Hearn's worries were that Orient's fan-base would be enticed away by the prospect of Premier League football being just around the corner. He argued: 'To have West Ham on our doorstep offering discounted tickets would seriously bring into question the survival of Leyton Orient.'

Despite that argument, in February 2011 the die was cast and the Olympic Park Legacy Company announced that West Ham was the preferred bidder. Spurs fought on, applying for a judicial review of the decision, before finally pulling the plug on the legal challenge that October. At that stage, the cost of converting the stadium to football use for West Ham was said to be £35 million. By November 2016, that figure had risen, ever so slightly. To the small sum of £323 million.

Nevertheless, the bid for the Olympic Stadium had brought about a sea-change in Haringey, with councillors aware they had been in genuine danger of losing the borough's crown jewel. Spurs went back to the drawing board, drafting new proposals for the Wingate Estate site, and at the same time both Haringey and the statutory London-wide authorities demonstrated that they were now willing to bend, with the Mayor's Office putting forward more serious plans for improved transport infrastructure, significant extensions at both White Hart Lane and Northumberland Park overground stations and an upgrade on the Victoria Line and Seven Sisters Tube station. An initial promise of £26 million of public money from the Mayor of London's budget was a sign of intent, while Haringey relaxed its demand for half of the houses on the development to be classified as 'affordable'. There were still significant obstacles to be overcome, but Communities Secretary Eric Pickles finally approved compulsory purchase orders, and a six-month battle with Archway Steel, a sheet-metal company based on the estate, ended in Spurs' favour.

Although Tottenham felt they had been treated shabbily throughout the Olympic Stadium process, there was now momentum behind the plans for a new stadium next to White Hart Lane. By September 2012 – when Spurs had originally expected to kick off in their new home – the first spade went into the ground as work began on Phase One of the development, the supermarket that would be run by Sainsbury's. New club offices, a high-tech complex on the northern extremity of the site named 'Lilywhite House', were also swiftly put in progress. Inside the high-tech office block it felt more like Silicon Valley than industrial north London.

Hoardings along the High Road hid what was beginning to take shape on the land behind the Paxton Road end, although it was clear that it was going to be a grand design. Issues remained, major ones, even as supporters gushed at the emerging artists' impressions of how the new stadium would look. Director Donna Cullen, one of Levy's most-trusted advisers, conceded she had lost count of the meetings she had attended with planners, councillors and protesters and the speeches she had drafted and delivered. The initial plans for the site had envisaged Spurs moving into a three-sided ground during that first season in their new home, which would still have a capacity greater than the existing stadium, and the final South End would then be built behind a temporary facade. But that was soon deemed to be infeasible and the club admitted it was looking for temporary accommodation.

Milton Keynes was first mentioned as one of the potential places for the club to decamp to, despite Stadium MK having a capacity of just 30,000. The Olympic Stadium was also briefly suggested, an idea angrily dismissed by Sullivan, Gold and Brady. That would have been the irony of ironies. But the main contender was always Wembley, of course, even though the FA were initially reluctant to consider renting out the national stadium to a club side. In March 2016, Spurs were informed by Uefa that the building works that were now being stepped up next door meant the Lane could not be used for Champions League matches in 2016–17 if the club qualified, because the venue would be unable to support the commercial, marketing and broadcasting requirements of the competition. Senior figures at the club wondered if they should announce this to the supporters before the Europa League clash with Borussia Dortmund, after defeat in the first leg meant that the tie was shaping up to be the final European game the Lane would stage. But it was agreed that to make the announcement while there was still the chance of missing out on the top four – Europa League football would still be permitted – would be premature and potentially a stick with which the club could be beaten.

There were other pressing issues as well. Levy and his directors were still concerned about the overall funding of the project and as late as February 2017 Levy sent a stinging email to Haringey Council and new London Mayor Sadiq Khan, alleging the club had been 'taken for granted' by politicians of all stripes 'for far too long' and suggesting the Mayor should be personally 'embarrassed' by his apparent lack of interest in committing to the costs of completing the infrastructure upgrades that were desperately needed for a stadium which had now grown in scale to a capacity of just under 62,000. There were doubts that the £26 million promised by Johnson five years earlier would be forthcoming, while the sale of naming rights for the new stadium, meaning it can be branded in the manner of Arsenal's 'Emirates Stadium' or Manchester City and the 'Etihad Stadium' was an issue that had still not been confirmed by the summer of 2017. Such things were important when the project was now expected to cost £800 million, double the original estimate.

But the plans themselves had been transformed from draft ideas on paper to actual concrete and steel. From the outset, Levy had a vision, a simple but determined one. The new stadium would not just be a home for Tottenham Hotspur but a genuine and iconic venue, and also the home of American Football in London. Levy was aware that the NFL's plans for global reach potentially included a side based in Europe. He wanted to make sure Tottenham could persuade those who ran 'America's Game' that they could feel at home in his corner of north London.

Levy had not hidden his desire for the stadium to mesh the best of modern design with the traditions and feel of the Lane. And also, critically, to meet the needs of the NFL, who added £10 million to the funding pot as proof of their intentions, with separate dressing rooms, capable of coping with the 40-plus team rosters for Gridiron, being constructed opposite the football facilities and a plastic pitch laid underneath the grass surface.

He made a point of going to the United States to sell his plans for the new stadium, making it clear that he wanted to take the best of American sporting design ingenuity – incorporating some of the features at sensational new structures being built for NFL, baseball and basketball teams – and bolt that onto his ambition for a ground that would amplify what made White Hart Lane a stand-out stadium even when its capacity had fallen to barely above 30,000.

'Playing football and NFL games wasn't possible on one pitch,' said Levy. 'The question was how to make the two fields work. So the grass pitch will retract under the South Stand. There were a lot of technical hurdles but we solved each one of them. We needed a company with the expertise of building an NFL stadium as well as one for the English market, the right team. So we looked at the Dallas Cowboys stadium and the Minnesota Vikings to learn from those owners.'

Levy explained that it was all part of the grand plan, a concept that had begun to be put into practice with the opening of the Hotspur Way training complex in 2013. 'We want success on the pitch and strongly believe that to have a sustainable club you have to have an academy that produces players for the first team. Then you have players coming through with Spurs in their blood. You tend to get more out of home-grown players than those you buy in. We weren't a club that could continue to spend tens or hundreds of millions so we had to find a way to build that production line.

'To have a stadium that was bigger than Arsenal's was not the sole driver! But we have a waiting list of 58,000 fans. We had to find a solution. Everybody thinks it's about more revenue and money although we will have a lot of debt to repay. But over the medium to long term it gives you greater financial security. And if you want to be a big club you have to have a big stadium.

'The first challenge was how to retain the atmosphere that exists at White Hart Lane,' Levy said. 'That needs a very tight bowl. We will be five metres closer to the pitch than in another stadium in north London plus we will have the only stadium in the UK with a single-tier stand, seating 17,000. We hope to recreate a bit of Dortmund in north London. I think it will feel even more raucous than White Hart Lane. That's our objective, not just to recreate the White Hart Lane atmosphere but to create an even better one. We wanted to do something very different for the area. It's a very poor area of London and needed regeneration. Just building a football stadium isn't enough. We needed to create something for the local community.'

Levy turned to architects Populous, whose successful projects included the London Olympic Stadium, the Emirates, Dublin's Aviva Stadium, Eden Park in Auckland, the MCG in Melbourne, and NFL and Major League Soccer grounds in the USA. The remit, as reported by Populous chief architect Christopher Lee, was somewhat 'mythical'. He said: 'It was really key that we recaptured that crowd feeling. The acoustics have to be right. If they are designed right, then the sound amplifies itself, so that the louder it is, the louder it gets, multiplying all the time. And that's what creates the atmosphere.'

The chairman and his trusted team were still embroiled in negotiations with the FA about using Wembley. Agreements between the Stadium and Brent Council over the number of full-house events staged in any year would have restricted Tottenham to only using the lower tier of seating at the national stadium, with a capacity of 50,000 but a lot of empty spaces above. Then there were discussions about the full capacity of the stadium being made available for some games, as long as agreement could be reached with Brent and local residents. But money talks. Spurs were going to bring millions into the area over their nine-month stay and the FA were aware that Chelsea were also keen on renting Wembley – after Spurs had moved back to Tottenham – for up to four years while Stamford Bridge was dismantled and rebuilt to hold 60,000. If they could get approval for more full-capacity events, they could charge more in rent. In the end, at a contested planning consent meeting in March 2017, Donna Cullen stood up in front of Brent councillors and said: 'Brent is the proud home of Wembley but we want to make it our proud home here as well. We need to create a vibrant home advantage in the stadium.' After three and a half hours of discussions, the club got the green light – the entire 90,000 capacity would be made available for 27 Spurs games in the 2017–18 season while the new stadium was being constructed.

Yet there were still concerns. Levy wanted guarantees that

the club would not be embarrassed by the contractor failing to complete the project in time for Spurs to run out at their new home in 2018. Three weeks before the Brent decision he told the Tottenham Hotspur Supporters Trust that there was still the possibility that the temporary relocation might be put on hold for a year 'should any major issues arise' at the new stadium: 'Tottenham Hotspur will not move away for two years, so all conditions must be right before we make the call to move this summer.' A few weeks later, he reiterated the point in a more public forum. 'Our performances on the pitch and the sight of our new stadium taking shape signifies an exciting future,' he said. 'We continue to focus on ensuring that the future of the club is protected at all times and therefore, while everyone is eager to know if this is our last season at the Lane, we shall only make the decision to de-commission our historic White Hart Lane when we have greater certainty on the delivery of the new stadium.'

It was a message of determination to the builders, forcing them to give him the cast-iron delivery promises he required, but it also meant the confirmation that Spurs would be moving out, while long-assumed, came a mere 16 days before the final game at the Lane that season.

Levy inspired those who worked to turn his vision into reality. Among them was grounds chief Darren Baldwin, who couldn't wait to get to work on the new plot of land that was to become his pride and joy.

'The last season was tinged with sadness because it was a place that was full of history,' he told me. 'But it was also exciting because of what we were doing with the new stadium and the uniqueness of that project. What helps, hugely, is the man behind it all. We have an immensely ambitious chairman. I just had to steer the ship as regards the pitch. But it was Daniel's vision and it was up to me, along with others, to make sure we implement that vision. Without his commitment, drive and desire, none of it could have happened.'

Baldwin explained: 'Getting the new pitch to slide under the stand so we could use the NFL artificial pitch was a challenge and we had to find a different way of doing things. The chairman's mission statement was to recreate the White Hart Lane atmosphere and then enhance it, and to have a pitch that is as good, if not even better. The two had to go hand in hand. We did so much research, so many tests at the training centre. We didn't leave a leaf unturned. We were going to make this right for Tottenham Hotspur so we could say that we wouldn't have done anything differently.'

Just as crucial as Levy's vision for the future was his understanding of what he was part of and his attempt to create continuity with the past. Steve Perryman admitted that he lost his love for the club after his fall-out with Alan Sugar but it had returned. 'It was sad to see Tottenham go in a particular way but now I genuinely look at what is happening and see a club that is back on track,' said the former skipper. 'I can see the old ethic back. Yes, business has to be part of it now. And why shouldn't it be? We are talking about a lot of money being invested and spent, so business has to be a part of it but it also has to be a football club and we are seeing a club that can put eleven men on the pitch who want to perform and can perform. I'm getting that vibe now.

'I spoke to Donna Cullen once and told her: "I judge a country by how it treats its old people; I judge a football club by how it treats its old players." And I know from talking to a lot of the former players that they feel they are being treated properly now.

'The club did lose its way a bit, under the previous regime, but it's back on the right way now. The vibe I get is that it is vastly changed and that's got to be for the good. Part of a club is to have everybody united. You need as many people pulling for you as you can get. A lot of people outside will be trying to shaft you and beat you and so you need people pulling for you. But if you have the old players all pulling for you, you have a chance.'

Perryman's sense of a club renewing itself without losing what made it special was one that echoed with the thoughts expressed by a large number of former club heroes, many of whom were to receive invitations to pay one last tribute to the place where they had made Tottenham history. A day for memories, tears and hope. A day that was going to mean so much, to ex-players, managers and fans alike. After all, if you want to say goodbye, you hope it will be on a high, with positive memories and excitement about the future in equal measure. And Spurs' last season at the Lane was to be one of the most memorable in the club's history. With a fitting ending, too.

19

THE FINALE

For one last time, they made the journey to this place. From north London and elsewhere in the capital. From Hertfordshire and Essex and beyond. Some from as far afield as San Francisco and other cities and towns around the world. For each of them, it was a final pilgrimage to a place of collective and personal worship. A chance to pay homage to the heroes of their youth, to applaud the young men giving them belief again and to prepare themselves for the bright new dawn about to break.

Not just a football match, then. Not on this day. Not on 14 May 2017. At each of the 2,532 previous Spurs fixtures (not including the hundreds of youth team, reserve and friendly matches) the focus had always been on the 90 minutes. That was not just the main event – it was the only event. Other sports, too, were about the feature, the headline, the top of the bill. Yet that Sunday in May 2017, with the fans kept outside until two and a half hours before kick-off, playing Manchester United, picking up the three points to complete a remarkable unbeaten season at White Hart Lane, securing the best finish in the club's Premier League history, the highest since 1963, was not an end in itself. It was the means to an end – to The Finale. The gateway to a final act on this hallowed stage.

It might not have been only a day about memories, about the chance to say farewell. It might have been a day of legend. Over the previous few weeks, something which had at first seemed infeasible, then unlikely, then a growing, if still barely credible, dream and, briefly, a tantalising possibility had emerged and gripped the minds of some supporters – to say goodbye in the grandest of styles, as champions for only the third time in the club's history. It was not to be, although coming so close was hoped to be a sign of things to come. Proof that it was possible, if you had a genuine philosophy, a shared ethos, an outstanding manager and receptive players, to not only compete with those whose resources and finances dwarfed yours, but even to surpass them.

Of course, not all of them. One peak remained out of reach, even in a season of rare brotherhood, a campaign in which Spurs appeared the most unified, cogent, unquestioned team in the Premier League. Nine Spurs wins in a row between 26 February and 30 April merely kept the dream alive, far beyond what should have been its natural life, attempting to place doubts in the minds of Antonio Conte's side. But Chelsea deserved their triumph, no question. They won more games than anybody else and lost fewer than everyone except Spurs. They took advantage of their light fixture load, a consequence of the previous season's internal melt-down and bloodletting. And they had no serious injuries, perhaps a direct result of playing fewer high-intensity games, not having the three-day distraction of European trips in the Champions League. But without Pochettino and his men pushing so hard, so brilliantly, without those young men in white shirts playing such fabulous football, the title race would not have gone on for as long as it did before the impossible dream was proven to be exactly that.

But what memories that final season and those last nine months at the Lane had provided. What joy. What sheer, unadulterated pleasure. The end of the 2015–16 campaign had been a disappointment, the lustre lost as the final-day collapse allowed Arsenal one more year of mockery, although that in itself made finally laying the ghost all the more enjoyable 12 months on, especially as Arsène Wenger's side were left to contemplate their first season outside the Champions League elite since 1997–98. But it was to prove to be the platform for the team to progress to the next level, a higher base-camp for another assault at the big prize.

The following season, Pochettino and his players knew there was going to be extra pressure and scrutiny on them, even if the pre-season spotlight fell elsewhere. Remember that 2016–17 was supposed to be about two men in one city – Pep Guardiola and José Mourinho rather Mauricio Pochettino and Antonio Conte – despite fans of Manchester United and their sky-blue neighbours spending much of the latter half of the campaign trying to rewrite history, to pretend they had never been genuine title contenders. Huge sums were spent by both clubs on squads that had already cost the better part of half of a billion pounds to assemble. Meanwhile, Tottenham's efforts the previous season were written off as being a similar aberration to the remarkable triumph of the Foxes, and it was widely believed that they would be cast into the backwaters once normal business was resumed. The title claims of Arsenal, Chelsea and even Liverpool were deemed by many experts to be far more realistic than those being plotted in Enfield.

Nobody passed that memorandum on to Pochettino and his players though. Or if they did, it was scrunched up into a ball and hurled into the bin. The Argentinian had brooded throughout the summer: 'The feeling after Newcastle was horrible. It is true that after a couple of months you move on, but it put me in a bad mood for the whole of the summer. It killed my holidays. Seriously. I went to Barcelona and the Bahamas with my family, but all the time I was in a bad mood. There was no time to assimilate the defeat at Newcastle because the season finished at the end of the game and I did not have the chance to share my feelings with my players the day after and kill them!

'Normally when you lose and you are upset with the players you have the opportunity to tell them how you feel on Monday morning when you meet them and have a big discussion and a big fight. But it was not possible because many of my players went off to the Euros. So I had to keep my bad feelings inside for the whole of the summer. Even when I was texting my players in France to wish them well I had to hide my real feelings about the Newcastle game.'

That pre-season was vital, allowing Pochettino and his staff to get their message across and stiffen sinews. There were a few early wobbles, including draws at Everton on the opening day, when Spurs were lucky to go in only a goal down at the break, and more than a little fortunately against Liverpool two weeks later. But crushing Stoke 4–0 in the Potteries provided a kick-start to the season, and despite the loss of Harry Kane to an ankle injury sustained in an accidental clash after he had netted his first home goal of the season against Sunderland, Pochettino's men put the first prong in Guardiola's overinflated sphere in September. Spurs simply swarmed all over City, giving them not a millisecond to think or compose themselves, the 2–0 margin flattering only to the losing side.

In fact, the evidence that the victory provided – that Spurs could cope, at that stage, without Kane – was illusory. While Chelsea were embarking on a 13-game winning streak, Spurs were held to draws at West Bromwich and Bournemouth, and by Leicester in N17, during a run that also saw them struggling to cope with the demands of Champions League football, with defeats at Wembley at the hands of Monaco and Leverkusen that ultimately proved decisive in their failure to progress from the group stages.

Kane returned – still not fully fit – to score the penalty equaliser at Arsenal on 6 November before beginning what was to prove a record-breaking, relentless run at the Lane, with his injury-time double to turn imminent defeat against West Ham the following week into joyous victory. Even so, despite outplaying Chelsea for the first 44 minutes at Stamford Bridge six days later on from that West Ham win and leading through a Christian Eriksen belter, Pochettino's men went down to their first defeat of the League season, before falling to United in mid-December, a result that left them in fifth place, ten points adrift of Chelsea and seven behind Arsenal, with people speculating that the Spurs bubble had burst.

Six straight victories either side of Christmas provided the answer, Dele Alli scoring seven in four matches. Pochettino had surprised many observers when he opted for a back three, with Eric Dier dropping into the defensive line and Danny Rose and Kieran Trippier operating as wing-backs in the Christmas romp at Watford. It swiftly, though, became apparent this was a dry run ahead of meeting, and beating, the challenge of Conte's pace-setters in the final match of the Premier League's holiday season schedule, on 4 January. Kyle Walker, whose relationship with the manager was to strain in the following months, and Rose pushed Chelsea's own wing-backs, Victor Moses and Marcos Alonso, into areas where they were not comfortable, Victor Wanyama monstered N'Golo Kanté, Eriksen schemed and plotted, and Dele took advantage with a brace of perfect headers that flew past the stranded Thibaut Courtois as the Lane celebrated a glorious and fully deserved victory over the champions-elect.

'We're coming for you', promised the massed ranks inside, and ten days later, against a West Brom side that simply did not have a prayer, they saw 45 minutes of sustained, remarkable and scintillating brilliance. It was arguably the best half seen at the Lane by a Spurs side since Glenn Hoddle's destruction of Cruyff and Gullit's Feyenoord, and was capped by the first of five Kane hat-tricks after the turn of the year.

In the final analysis, though, the next four matches proved to be more decisive. A fortunate draw at City demonstrated Spurs' powers of resilience as they grabbed a point from two down, Son Heung-Min demonstrating his increasing importance when he scored the leveller. Then a disappointing display, compounded by the injury that cost them the services of the rampaging Rose for the rest of the season, at doomed Sunderland meant two more points dropped. Kane's spot kick squeaked out a win over Mid-dlesbrough but a week later they slipped to only their third loss of the campaign when they never got out of the blocks at Liverpool. It left them still ten points off Chelsea, although up to third, ahead of Arsenal on goal difference, after 25 matches.

Kane had dragged himself off the treatment table to wear the armband in an FA Cup win at Fulham on 19 February, in which he bagged another triple, before claiming a further hat-trick in the first half as Stoke were smashed for four once again, making it eight in four games with two against Everton. But when he went down in agony, holding his ankle, minutes into the FA Cup clash with Millwall at the start of March, most people at the Lane that day feared the worst – that without their talisman, everything would disintegrate. After all, they had been conditioned into assuming that, when push came to shove, it would all fall apart, as it had so often over the previous 20 years or more.

Yet things *had* changed. In the autumn, Spurs had not been able to penetrate opposition defences without Kane. His replacement, Vincent Janssen, was game and willing but did not carry sufficient threat. Defenders were happy to let him drop deep to receive the ball, confident he could not hurt them, while he also lacked the physical bulk and power of Kane. It meant the support runners from the second attacking line in the 4-2-3-1 system – three from Dele, Son, Eriksen, Érik Lamela, whose season was truncated by a mystery hip injury, and flop of the campaign Moussa Sissoko – were more often than not unable to get beyond the front man. Now, though, things were different. The back three system which Pochettino tended to prefer enabled the Tottenham wing-backs to press into midfield. Pochettino had seemingly lost faith in Janssen, but Son, Eriksen and Dele worked as a trio, spinning around and off each other, while the physicality of Wanyama and Mousa Dembele gave Spurs dominance of the midfield battleground.

In those eight Premier League and Champions League matches without Kane in October and November, Spurs scored just six goals. They matched that tally against Millwall alone, but more critically they netted a combined 11 goals, shared between Son,

Dele, Eriksen and Dier – in wins over Southampton, Burnley, Swansea and Watford in the space of 20 days starting on 19 March, before Kane returned to first-team action, this time fully up to speed. Chelsea's lead was beginning to be shaved away. Three more wins followed, including a swatting aside of Bournemouth as if they barely existed. Then, when many thought Pochettino and his side would fall apart in the aftermath of the undeserved FA Cup semi-final defeat to Chelsea at Wembley on 22 April, an afternoon when the team that dominated and played most of the football were beaten by clinical opponents who took every chance they created, the response showed what this Spurs side was made of.

Eriksen scored a late winner at Selhurst Park four days later before next up Spurs had a chance to end 22 years of grief and hurt from the other end of the Seven Sisters Road, the last north London derby staged at the Lane.

As a series of must-score chances went begging – Dele missing from two yards out at the most and Eriksen volleying over when the net was gaping – some fans began to harbour doubts. But Pochettino and his players did not. They simply knew they were better than this Arsenal side and that the goals would come. And, of course, they did, two in three minutes. The opener came from Dele, who was first to react when Eriksen's run and shot was beaten half-away by Čech, before Kane, of course, teased Gabriel into a reckless lunge, picking himself up to find the bottom corner from the resulting penalty. Sealing the deal with a win that confirmed Spurs would finish above the Gunners and reducing the gap to four points with as many matches to play. How the fans celebrated, producing a wall of sound at the Lane. Two decades of jibes had been silenced. There was a growing belief that the balance of power had fundamentally shifted in Tottenham's favour.

Five days later, though, the blossoming title dream was to end. If it had ever really, truly begun. Spurs journeyed to what might have been their home in Stratford, aware that victory would leave

Chelsea brooding for almost 72 hours on a lead down to a single point. Instead, Adrián's lucky save from Kane's strike proved critical, and Spurs lost their composure and sense of certainty. And when Manuel Lanzini took advantage of a series of inadvertent penalty-box ricochets to fire West Ham in front, it never looked like a response would come.

The faces of Pochettino's players told a clear story. The manager knew it too, and with the pressure off Conte's men did exactly what they had to do, first beating a woeful Middlesbrough to take themselves to the brink of triumph before getting over the line at West Brom under the lights on a Friday night.

The title dreams were over, but it meant there was no edge on that final afternoon at the Lane and nothing to take away from the moment.

It was time for farewells, to days gone by and to a ground that had meant so much to so many. Because the gates were shut until 2 p.m., with only club employees and the media allowed inside the ground before that, it meant hundreds of fans milled around on the Tottenham High Road, taking their final chance to visit the club shop before it too closed for good, peering down the narrow entranceway through the gates at the West Stand, dropping in to their match-day pubs, cafés and restaurants for the last time before a 16-month hiatus. They wore their Tottenham shirts, too, an array of kits from down the years. The 1978 Admiral outfit. That purple away strip. Home kits of recent vintage as well as the 2016–17 season's three different versions. On the 259 bus from Seven Sisters, pretty much rammed nearly three hours before kick-off, there was a sense of excitement but no 'edge', no anxiety. One woman, wearing her 'The Lane' last-day scarf, said: 'I know it's too hot for it but I had to wear it. Today, I had to wear it.'

Inside the stadium, the ground staff, led by Darren Baldwin, worked on the pitch, watering it to ensure the surface was pristine and perfect. They checked that the Goal Decision System was working properly, and that the flags were placed on every home supporter's seat, along with plastic bags containing club-issued T-shirts to mark the occasion.

Even before the turnstiles cranked and clattered for one last time, it felt like a day that was more about the past than the present. As the minutes to kick-off counted down, it was still quiet in the stadium. To begin with, only a trickle of people arrived, before slowly turning into more of a stream, although not a flood by that point. The seats behind the Paxton Road goal were the first to begin to fill up, with supporters looking around and picking up the flags that were later to be waved with such gusto. They would have noticed the extra screen that had been erected in the northeast corner, while those close to the centre of the West Stand would have seen the fresh lick of paint that had been added to the tunnel area to spruce it up for the occasion.

Underneath the fibreglass cockerel, beak pointed to the north, the East Stand also began to fill up. What was clear, even with just a few hundred fans inside, was that the mood was going to be celebratory. This was more of a wake than any sort of funeral. It was going to be a chance for the supporters to think back on all those games they had watched, on all those days they had made the journey to this ground, on the players they had revered, and on the managers they had warmed to and castigated. On all those moments when the ground rang out with dreams of glory, and those when the mood was angry and miserable. For without an understanding of how low football can take you, there can be no real pleasure when it allows you to savour the joy of success. Many of those who walked in on that day had witnessed the end of the Nicholson era, when Spurs were still unquestionably a 'big' club, the ones who had gloried in Hoddle and Ardiles and seen the cups won by Burkinshaw's team. The supporters who had dreamed and hoped when Waddle, Gascoigne, Lineker, Klinsmann and Sheringham ran out in the white shirt and who had lived through Tottenham's Dark Ages – those long years when 10th place in the Premier League was the summit of the club's ambitions, when they were left flagging, a million miles behind the teams who used to be their direct rivals.

But not that season, and not with that Spurs team. It was the 23rd game Spurs had played at the Lane in 2016–17, in a ground that had physically changed during the course of the campaign as the void cut in the corner between Paxton Road and the East Stand was filled by one of the support columns that would allow the towering new monument to the club's ambitions to be completed. From August through to the start of May, the fans did not even once feel the misery and disappointment of defeat. The Lane had become a genuine fortress. Those first 22 games had seen 20 wins and two draws in all competitions, the last of those coming against Leicester back on 29 October. After that, perfection. A run of 14 straight wins, soon to become 15, with 49 goals scored and just ten conceded, three of those claimed by Wycombe Wanderers, of all teams. It had been a season of sustained excellence, of vibrant, remorseless, relentless attacking football, with stunning goals from Kane, Dele, Eriksen and Son. A sense of kinship had developed, a genuine bond between Pochettino, his players and the fans, made all the stronger by the realisation that after all those years of doubt and despair, things were going right. And that the players, too, understood what the club meant to the fans. That they got it.

Try explaining to your seven-year-old that it was not always like this, that the default position for any Spurs fan is the assumption that it will all go wrong. That, for most rival fans, Spurs are supposed to be a running joke, not a serious proposition. No, don't try. Don't even think about it. Let him enjoy the moment, this season, these players, this squad. Let him imagine, maybe live through, a period when Tottenham do not let you down. When they can be what you yourself always wanted them to be, what sustained your own faith when everything sensible urged you to cast it aside, to find something that might bring you succour and celebration.

As the fans started to arrive in larger numbers, the buzz of anticipation grew. Yes, this was their opportunity to say goodbye to the stadium, and to a part of themselves – the place where they had watched their heroes, where their parents and grandparents had watched their own favourites. People could be seen whipping out their phones and cameras to take one last photo to remember the old place by.

The club placards and hoardings remained in place: 'To Dare Is to Do'; 'It's been my life, Tottenham Hotspur, and I love the club'. Leon Vardon, a White Hart Lane regular since 1969, desperate for a photograph of Dimitar Berbatov as the Bulgarian walked around the perimeter of the pitch 90 minutes before kick-off, and determined to enjoy his day, spoke for so many as he told me: 'This team have given us a real belief again. But Harry Redknapp changed it. His team changed it. They made us think it was possible. Mauricio and this side have made it happen but I felt everything was geared to go forward after that Inter Milan game. I've not known how I was going to react to this day but I just want to enjoy it.'

And enjoy it they all did, on an afternoon that was to see four decades of Spurs heroes celebrated in song. Even the usual pre-game tribute video, a staple of recent years as the final act before the players left their dressing rooms and narrated by the late actor Roger Lloyd-Pack, had extra resonance. With background pictures of the stars of yesteryear, he spoke, in sonorous tones that captured the mood, of 'The flick, the trick, the thirty-yard free-kick,' adding: 'Great past, glorious future; what was, what is, what's next . . . daring to try, daring to win, daring to do.'

And as the players emerged from the newly painted tunnel, two lines walking out together for the last time, as the flags began to be waved from every vantage point overlooking the surface, and after Pete Abbott, for the last time, stated: 'Welcome to White Hart Lane, the world-famous home of the Spurs,' a cry of defiance went up: 'Come on you Spurs . . .'

Meanwhile, up in the West Stand, in line with the 18-yard box at the Park Lane end, the blazer-clad heroes of the past took their own seats, peering down on their successors, waving and acknowledging the cheers, signing autographs, smiling at the recognition they were being offered.

It was, even before the kick-off, a joyful place. 'We are Tottenham, from the Lane,' was the song of choice, as if to prove it was a day to revel in what the club meant rather than go through the normal match-day emotions of anxiety and tension. Everybody wanted to sing, to chant, to be a living, breathing part of the day. The noise was a huge element of the day, crucial to the experience. The fans wanted to ensure this was about creating a non-stop echo of sound. And while Tottenham could win nothing by taking the three points on offer – although victory would confirm a top-two finish for the first time in 54 years – in a way it meant so much more than the game. The chance to say goodbye to the old lady with a victory, to complete all those vigils down the years.

In turn, those in the stands sang their songs: the East Stand fans singing songs recalling the days when The Shelf was an intrinsic part of that side of the stadium; the Park Lane faithful ignoring the taunts of the travelling fans, whose claim that 'you only came to see United' had never been more utterly, gloriously, humorously wrong; the Paxton Road; even, for once, those in the West Stand, certainly in the lower tiers. And after a nervous, slightly tepid opening, the actors down on the pitch, the new Spurs, Pochettino's Spurs, responded in kind. They stayed true to their philosophy, the way they always played now – patient, probing, seeking to exploit their opponents by pulling them out of position. It was Dele's name that was being sung loud before being cut off and replaced by a roar of delight as Victor Wanyama rose unmarked to head home from Ben Davies' delicious centre after the sort of quick-thinking corner routine that had become a mark of the team's identity. Five minutes and 35 seconds in and the roofs of the stands were reverberating with an outpouring of delight, a torrent of sound.

It was the perfect start, with the derisive voices from the North-West, songs aimed at reminding the home supporters of United's previous successes, interspersed with the taunt that 'You nearly won the League' insufficient, on this of all days, to elicit anything more than a dismissive response. Not when Kane was bullying Phil Jones, pinning him with his physicality, forcing the defender to try and make a tackle he was simply unable to complete, before pulling away into the space he had created by his sheer determination, the expectation that he was just too good for his England team-mate, to the extent that Peter Crouch, watching from on high, shook his head in something akin to disbelief. Only the reflexes of David de Gea prevented the lead from being stretched further, Kane's mastery prompting the supporters to open up their songbooks again. And out came the words that have resonated down the years. 'Glory, Glory', of course, bounced around the stands, but also 'One Aaron Lennon', a chant of support in recognition of the former Spurs winger's fight against depression, which had only emerged weeks before. Then there was a reminder that, despite having just one knee, Ledley King was better than John Terry – the former skipper was unable to hide the smile on his face as those in his vicinity pointed in his direction. There were songs, from the early 80s, including the promise to the Scottish striker who was Burkinshaw's key attacking weapon: 'We'll take more care of you, Archibald, Archibald' and name-checks for Paul Gascoigne, of course, but also Rafael van der Vaart and Jermain Defoe. 'Teddy, Teddy Sheringham' rang out and 'Born is the King' for Glenn Hoddle, while the fans, absolutely correctly this time, also sang 'Spurs are on the way to Wembley'.

Pochettino had a job to do, despite the unusual mood. He stood in his technical area, urging his men on with small gestures. Nothing fancy or ostentatious. That wasn't necessary, because he knew what his team could do and understood what made them tick. He knew how to make his point, as he had done by omitting Walker from the starting line-up. He was preparing, at the end of one season, for the beginning of the next one, which made the identity of the half-time guest on the pitch, Harry Winks, somehow more pertinent. A boyhood Spurs fan, who had been picked out by Pochettino as his next 'project', a player who the Argentinian, his staff and indeed the whole club hierarchy envisaged would be a big part of the side in the future.

The same went for the man who was to score the final Tottenham goal at the Lane, three minutes into the second half, the first of a staggering eight he was to claim in as many days, as Spurs ended the season not just second, but as highest scorers, with the meanest defence and the winner of the Golden Boot in their side. It was not Kane's best of the season, but a goal that once again demonstrated what he had become – an instinctive, predatory marksman, flicking out a foot to divert Eriksen's driven free-kick into the roof of the United net. 'He's one of our own,' was the automatic response from every nook and cranny, a song that was unlikely to fade with repetition, at least not while Kane remains as the symbol, emblem and beating heart of the Tottenham side.

Party time. 'Everywhere we go, everywhere we go. It's the Tottenham boys, making all the noise, everywhere we go.' The sun was now hiding behind the clouds that had begun to mass, menacingly, before sending down their contents. The rain, though, could not alter the mood. Nor could Wayne Rooney's response from a couple of yards out, the 8,070th and last goal scored at the ground, 118 years after David Copeland scored the first, prevent the cheers and chants, the cascade of pride in the club and what it stood for. At the back of the West Stand, the old lady began to leak, another sign that it was time to go. As the last few minutes ticked down, with those final few kicks signalling the end of so much history on this site, the flags were being waved again. In unison and brotherhood, awaiting the explosion of emotion that was to greet the final whistle when it was blown by Jonathan Moss, a fraction of a second before Walker, now on for Kieran Tripper, could complete the last competitive kick on this piece of N17 turf.

During the next 20 minutes, there were moments when it might have all been spoiled. The pitch invasion was not aggressive, with thousands standing there just waving those flags again, but a torrent of bodies did go hurtling past the stewards, and things could have spiralled out of control. Many just wanted to say 'I was there', others to grab a piece of grass. Yet the players were engulfed as they tried to make their way to the sanctuary of the tunnel and dressing rooms. Abbott's voice from the PA box made no impact, but from pitch level the sterner tones of Paul Coyte, the long-standing pitchside match-day announcer, who has interviewed hundreds of half-time guests down the years, gently, but effectively, began to corral everybody back into the stands as the platforms and staging were laid down for the post-match presentation.

Former full-back Ray Evans, watching from his home 6,000 miles away in eastern Washington State, said: 'I liked it, a lot. I'd have loved to have been there. I was a bit worried about what it might be like and certainly wasn't sure if they'd be able to get all the fans off the pitch after the final whistle. But once everything was cleared and the ceremony started I did feel very emotional, even from over here. It felt right though.'

And so the scene was set for the last act. Some 12 months earlier, when West Ham closed Upton Park with a home game against United, the night had started with the away side's coach coming under attack from a hail of bottles and other objects, and finished with an assault on the senses, fireworks, explosions and black cabs.

Spurs were determined not to make the same mistake. This was designed to be the antithesis, an unofficial act of reproach, directed at those to the east. Understated, natural, a homage to the past, a celebration of the present and a signpost of what was to come. And that's exactly what it was, from the instant the giant screens switched on to reveal Sir Kenneth Branagh, sitting in a cinema, urging all those present to join him in 'celebrating the history of our great club' and 'the story of White Hart Lane'. In about seven minutes, Branagh, with a mix of photographs, newspaper headlines, flickering, grainy images and more modern footage, accompanied by the music of the times, whizzed through those 118 years. It was a montage of memories, with the crowd responding to Parks' penalty save against Ajax, Defoe's five against Wigan, Hoddle strolling from the centre-circle against Oxford and other unforgettable moments. But they responded with equal, if not more, fervour, to the pictures of Nicholson and Burkinshaw.

The fans cheered, too, as the 48 'legends' were invited to emerge from the tunnel and walk to the middle of the pitch. Some were familiar faces, easily recognised by all. Others, who had first walked out onto that field 60 years and more before, would only have been known by a few. It was a mix of the great, the good and the decidedly ordinary. But that accentuated the message, as did the decision to send them out in alphabetical order, starting with the three members of the Allen family who wore the shirt, Clive, Paul and Les, who was not going to let the crutch he needed for support prevent him making his final appearance at the Lane.

Some had been here many times since they'd hung up their boots. Others less so. But as the rain teemed down and brollies were handed out to them all, the cheers were loudest for Steve Archibald, Ossie Ardiles, Martin Chivers, Cliff Jones – now 82 but still whippet-thin, and who fairly sprinted out – Garth Crooks, Peter Crouch, Mike England, Mark Falco, Alan Gilzean, the iPhone-carrying David Ginola, milking the moment in trademark fashion. And of course for Glenn Hoddle, Pat Jennings, Robbie Keane, Ledley King, Gary Mabbutt, Graham Roberts, Teddy Sheringham, Paul Stewart and Chris Waddle, carrying through the vow he'd made to his son that he had mentioned to me a few months earlier. Coyte hailed each and every one of them as 'the great players who graced this pitch thousands of times between them; the Kings of White Hart Lane'.

It did not feel forced but rather natural, the tempo increasing with each chorus of 'Oh When the Spurs Go Marching In', performed by the London Community Gospel Choir, until it was almost too fast for some to keep up. Then Levy's pre-recorded message, recalling his first match, against QPR at the age of seven, describing the Lane's importance to fans from across the planet and explaining his role as 'custodian': 'When I'm gone there will be somebody else.' He then promised that the club's new home would retain the intimacy and immediacy of the old stadium before Coyte welcomed Pochettino and his side – 'the last Spurs team to play at White Hart Lane' – to join their predecessors, led on by Hugo Lloris as Levy clapped from his seat in the West Stand. Last out, the manager, hearing the chant screamed in his honour: 'He's magic, you know, Mauricio Pochettino.' Over and over and over again.

There were tears now – lots of them – and lumps at the back of throats. Maybe it was an over-the-top response. But it felt like a milestone for so many. It was a defining day in the future of the club. The afternoon when Spurs were to take the ultimate leap of faith – the belief that the club could not just build a glorious new edifice to its ambition but fill it week after week. To use the gleaming construction that loomed over the shoulder of the Paxton Road end as the springboard to all those hopes of what could yet be. As tenor Wayne Evans, accompanied by the Tottenham Hotspur Marching Band, flanked on both sides by the players of the past and with Pochettino and his squad standing in front of him, sang 'Glory, Glory, Hallelujah' dry eyes were in the minority, a feeling intensified as Coyte said: 'Now, as we say goodbye to our home for the past 118 years, let's celebrate the role it has played in our lives. The generations that have watched games together in these stands, passing the love of this great club to sons and to daughters; the sights we've seen and the experiences we will never forget. Finally, it's now time to say goodbye to the world-famous home of the Spurs . . .'

As the music stopped, the families of the players entered the scene. And behind the cockerel, above the East Stand, first subtly but then in glorious technicolour, nature's leaving present: a glorious rainbow, illuminated starkly against the blackened backdrop of the clouds, the sun glinting down on this place for one last time. The songs began again, as the players made a lap of appreciation, the old and the new together. Jennings and Gilzean were chatting away, while Kane walked round with his baby daughter. There were more tears as, from nowhere, people started singing 'Can't smile without you'. Walking around the pitch, his daughter in his arms, Kane told a television reporter: 'I said before I'd love to score the winning goal and for it to happen was brilliant. To see it go in was special. We are growing. We so badly wanted to win this game.'

Hundreds stayed for as long as they could, well after the players and their families had disappeared. They wanted a final look at the patch of ground which had provided so many memories. A look at those familiar stands, a selfie or just a photograph. While Cliff Jones, loosening his tie in the main West Stand suite, belted out 'It's a grand old team', one of the Spurs songs of the 60s, 70s and 80s, Pochettino was conducting his media duties: 'It was a very emotional game and ceremony. It's very difficult to describe. I'm a very lucky guy to share the history of such a club in such a special moment. I want to say thanks to all my players and staff. We are sad and disappointed that Chelsea won the league but there is nothing to regret. All we can say is that next season we will give our best and try to win the league.

'In life you cannot stay happy with what you're doing now. You have to improve, improve, improve. For us it's the same. I thought it was important that we learned from last season and at the same time improve. It was where we put more effort in, that mental area. Last season was tough. Our objective is to win so it wasn't enough but we were so close. It is a good platform for us to learn and try to win. Next season is so important for us and the fans. The aim is to win a trophy. We were talking a lot and we believe that when the new stadium opens the doors, it will help the club to reach the last level. That is our expectation, that is our idea. Because the training ground, the new facilities and the new stadium will put the team and the club in the last level in Europe.'

By the time many had read those words, the keys to the site had been handed over, and the diggers had ripped off much of the top surface of Baldwin's pride and joy. The seats had been taken out, ready to be transported to a dump site, and the preparation work for a dramatic and speedy demolition of the stands was under way. A day or so later, there was an emotional elegy from an unlikely source. Kyle Walker might have been preparing to leave the club but he wanted to say his own personal tribute, posting a message on social media: 'I know it's been an emotional place for me. It's had ups and downs. We've won some games and lost some games we should've won but the fans have always been there for me. I said at the start of the season: "Let's make it a fortress." To go a whole season without losing one game at home, that's a credit, not just to us as players and the coaching staff, but to the fans as well, because we're all in it together, we've all made it happen. There's been such great moments and memories for me. Some memories go in my memory bank. But there's lots of them and I don't think singling them out would be fair. There's a lot of memories and I could be going for a few days if I started talking about them.'

Walker was not the only one. Indeed, his was just one voice among the thousands who had made the Lane somewhere special. It was hard to believe, even as I slowly dragged myself away down those stairs, that I would not be coming back. That the next time I saw a ball kicked in that vicinity, it would be in the huge new structure I walked past the Paxton Road end to stare at. Even as I did so, there was a smile in response to the final tannoy message, warning those last few fans who were trying to take something tangible home with them, hoardings, signs or seats, that they were being captured on CCTV, watched by police in the 'spaceship' module which hung eerily between the Park Lane and West Stands.

Then I turned my back on the past to have one more look at the future. Peering up and up and up at the gargantuan but gorgeous concrete beast that will swallow its parent whole. There was time for a brief look back, from the beer garden of what is now No. 8 but was the Bell and Hare during the club's glory days, the venue for all manner of post-game celebrations involving Nicholson's players. The old looked, suddenly, so small. Impossible given how vast it had seemed to me back in 1972. The new so magnificent and enormous. Thank you, Daniel. Thank you, Mauricio. Thank you, Arthur and Bill, Jimmy and Danny, Steve and Glenn, Keith and Ossie, Gareth and Jürgen, Ledley and Chris, through to Harry and Dele, Toby and Hugo. Most of all, thank you to everybody who went through what I went through, who shared what I shared, who, like me, had been able to take the gift handed from their parents and pass it on to their own children. It had been one of the backdrops of my life. A constant place, no matter how much it changed, from that autumn day against Stoke, when I had walked in as a six-year-old, unsure of what it was my dad was introducing me to, all the way up to that strange, beautiful, emotional May early evening when, deep into my 51st year, I left for the very last time. A lifetime in which so much had altered, including, so many times over, the ground itself.

Then, just a few months later, it was gone. Levelled to the ground. But it was still there, in my heart and mind, as it would be for all of us who were lucky enough to go there. And, hopefully, a bit of me and my memories would live on in Ollie and Emma. The new ground would be a place for new stories. The songs would be sung again. The heroes of the past, present and future celebrated. It is a golden thread. But as I waited for the bus on the

High Road, preparing to be whisked away back into the heart of London, I knew it was not like any other day. I was determined to love and grasp the future. I wanted to believe, because you have to believe, that it would all be bright, brilliant, better. That is what being a fan must be about. Yet it could never, quite, be the same. And every one of us who was there that afternoon knew it. The place had captivated and claimed me. And even if it was no longer there, I could never let it go. Nor would I ever want to. Now, does anybody have a couple of tickets for Wembley I could buy . . .?

20

2017–18 POSTSCRIPT
WEMBLEY WAYS

Before the glorious new dawn, a season of limbo. On the plus side, it was one at the home of English football, rather than, as had been mooted at one point, close to the concrete cows of Milton Keynes. But moving, even in the short-term, to Wembley, brought its fair share of problems and doubts, for the players, club and fans alike.

After all, Pochettino's side had hardly made Wembley seem like a potential fortress in their final season at the Lane, when they had decamped for what was, at best, a testing European campaign, bringing four matches across two competitions and a single victory, over a decidedly woeful CSKA Moscow side. Add in the FA Cup semi-final defeat at the hands of Chelsea, when Spurs had done everything right except the small matter of turning their superiority into goals, and no wonder the big talk, fanned in truth by those who wanted to see Spurs suffer, was of the 'Wembley curse'.

Many of the experts, too, latched onto the ground swap as a reason to dismiss Pochettino and his men. They may have come third and then second, with more points across the two previous seasons than any other side in the Premier League, but that was suddenly transformed into some sort of fluke, a freak, completely unsustainable when the tight intensity of White Hart Lane was no longer an option.

Which made the irony of complaints from the very same rival

fans, eight months later, about the prospect of Tottenham having 'home advantage' in the FA Cup semi-final and final, all the more ridiculous. What happened to the curse you were so happy to go on about?

But at the same time there was an in-built sense of the unfamiliar for those who had made the Lane what it became over those three Pochettino seasons. A place rival sides did not want to visit, where they were often beaten even before they stepped off the coach or out of the away dressing room. It is, and always will be, the fans who make a ground more than just a building.

In truth, the Wembley experience was one of initial nervousness and frustration, swiftly followed by achievement. A series of genuine highs, when dreaming was renewed, punctuated by what were, in essence, only relative lows, certainly in the context of those long, long years when mediocrity was the summit of the club's genuine target.

And in the final analysis, Wembley was – as it was meant to be and as the fans had hoped – little more than a bridge between the past and the future. Not the most expensive one ever built, although in the final months before the club said their Premier League goodbyes, the Football Association had been attempting to sell the stadium for £600m up front plus a possible £400m extra in receipts, in order to plough back £500m into grassroots football. But certainly the longest. After all, there is no bridge that takes twelve months to cross from end to end.

For Alan Fisher, a regular fan for more than 50 years, it was the most dragged-out season in recent memory. 'As far as I'm concerned,' he told me, 'Wembley isn't wrong. But it's not right. The bottom line, and in some ways it's a positive, is that it has reminded me of just how much I love the team and the club. Spurs are playing and that's what matters. You have to get behind the team.

'From my point of view, Wembley is a great event ground but it's not a football club's ground. There's something about the place that makes it hard to generate atmosphere. It seems to suck the atmosphere and joy out of you, somehow. You are there and cheering them but it just doesn't feel the same. It certainly doesn't feel like home.

'The move has just reinforced how precious White Hart Lane was, whereas, at Wembley, you don't feel part of the game in the same way. Being a fan is all about that intensity, feeling part of the match. That's what White Hart Lane gave you. You were so close to the pitch, with steep stands, it felt very enclosed and immediate. The other thing is that everybody has moved from their normal seats, away from the people you got used to sitting near. That was always part of the match – the people you got to know, who you'd sit with every home game. That had gone, been disrupted.

'Moving to Wembley changed the match-day routine. Ours became antisocial. I got on the train from Kent, met my son and granddaughter in South London, went to the ground and then home again afterwards. We'd not gone to the pub or met up with anybody. That's a real shame and one of the reasons I was so looking forward to going back to Tottenham, going to my old haunts, meeting up with people.

'If you were on the train and saw some people you knew you'd greet them like old friends you'd lost touch with. People were shaking hands and hugging each other because you're so grateful to see a family friend.

'And Wembley itself is a bleak place. No matter how much they dress it up with designer outlets, hotels, new buildings, it still feels like an industrial estate with a football ground at the end of it. It's not like it was before, with that walk down Wembley Way and the stadium standing on its own at the end of it.'

Mike Collett, like Alan into his sixth decade of supporting the club, agreed. He said: 'I never believed in the Wembley curse for a minute but I started off very unhappy about going there, just the sheer trek of going to Wembley and the absolute hassle of coming home, compared to going to White Hart Lane. It was a half-day journey there and back to watch the match.

'It wasn't that I hated being at Wembley. I've been going there since 1962, when I was eight years old. I have that emotional attachment and I quite like going there, even if the journey was a nightmare. It never felt like home but I wasn't one of those who felt it was awful. It was still a chance to watch Spurs play at Wembley.

'At first, I thought Spurs were really going to struggle there, like most people did. I thought every team that played against us there was happy to raise their game and be inspired by playing at Wembley. After those early games which weren't too good for Tottenham, my worries and fears had grown. I thought it was going to be very bad, we were going to finish outside the top four, maybe sixth or seventh at best, that we might not even finish in the top half. But I was wrong. Instead of being inspired by playing at Wembley, some of the teams just came and parked the bus, they were overawed by it.'

And Spurs blogger and fan Sean Walsh, whose own White Hart Lane experiences were only a decade or so long, nevertheless took a similar view. Sean said: 'I don't think too many fans have enjoyed going to Wembley. It's such a nightmare to get there. The attendances went down as the season was winding to an end and that's indicative of the fans' apathy for the place.

'As a fan you got used to the twenty-minute walk from Wembley Park tube, even if you never felt it should take as long as it did. But you never stopped getting tired of getting out and back home, how long it seemed to take. I think to a degree the club will be fortunate in that having spent the year at Wembley means the fans will appreciate the new stadium even more – despite the prices.

'Going to Wembley is different because of the issues the fans have in getting there. If you get through the hardship, it makes the good times even better and that's how the fans have treated Wembley – as something to be endured before the good times start back in Tottenham.

'But I feel the players will have a sense of relief at going back to White Hart Lane as well, being surrounded by the fans as they arrive again, seeing that excitement much closer to them. That familiar feeling back again. I know that the players used to always go in a coach from the training ground to the Lane for home matches, passing the fans on the way. That is an underrated part of the match-day experience for them.'

Until 2016–17, the squad had driven themselves to the ground, parked up and then met in a players' lounge where they ate before a game. But that lounge was in the south-west corner, the first part of the stadium to be dismantled, which meant, for the last season, the lounge did not exist. While the option of creating another lounge was discussed, Pochettino felt the squad should instead try meeting at the training centre, eating there and then driving in on the coach to the ground. At Wembley, it was back to the previous routine, although the drive to the ground ended in Brent, rather than Haringey, with the players gathering in the East press lounge, just as they had during the European games in 2016–17. Inside the club, it was felt that it had helped acclimatisation.

Not that you would have known that in the middle of October. In that final season on home soil, Spurs dropped just four points from their 19 games. After three Premier League games at Wembley, they had already squandered seven. With the tannoy pumping out a drum beat, Pochettino's men repeated their Cup semi-final performance in losing to Chelsea, Hugo Lloris's late error fatal, while Burnley were allowed to snatch an equaliser in added time and relegation-bound Swansea kept Spurs out through 90 minutes of total defence.

One factor, which Pochettino had tried to make light of, was the size of the pitch. Whereas White Hart Lane's playing surface measured 100m x 67m, Wembley's is 105m x 68m, a difference of 440 square metres. That is a lot of territory and it meant Pochettino had to amend his tactics and approach. Within the club, there was an acceptance that it took a while to adapt to a different way of playing. Pochettino, too, got some stick when it was pointed out to him inside the club that he had initially moaned about the small pitch at White Hart Lane when he arrived at Spurs, and now wished he had the same sized surface. Football managers are never satisfied. Even so, until the November loss of previous defensive mainstay Toby Alderweireld to a hamstring injury that presaged other significant issues with the Belgian, Pochettino stuck with the back three formation of the second half of 2016–17. Back at Hotspur Way, Darren Baldwin and his groundstaff team had to adapt the training pitch from White Hart Lane dimensions to Wembley ones but Spurs appeared hesitant and uncertain.

While Pochettino's side have been notoriously slow starters – fingers have been pointed at Levy's seeming determination to take transfer negotiations to the 59th minute of the 11th hour – Dean Scoggins, in his 27th season of watching the club, recalled: 'This "Wembley curse" thing was hanging over everyone. You thought "this could be a disaster, we could go into the new stadium without any European football". If you'd turned round to me then and said we'd get to the FA Cup semi-final, win the Champions League group, eventually go out against Juventus but still finish third, every fan in the ground that day of the Burnley game would've bitten your hand off.'

Instead of crumbling, a narrow, edgy win over Bournemouth, which featured a stunning save by Lloris to prevent Eric Dier putting through his own net, a crucial goal from Christian Eriksen and a late chance missed by old favourite Jermain Defoe, was the springboard. Spurs dropped just seven more points in the remaining 16 'home' games. Within the club, there was a belief that things had already turned for the better. Pochettino agreed that the Bournemouth win was important but pinpointed the Champions League win over a Dortmund side that had been far too strong for his emerging team two years earlier as the critical moment, pointing to the 67,000-plus crowd and the result, which put the previous season's problems into the past, as a bonding moment. 'That's when we started to feel at home,' said Pochettino. 'The atmosphere was brilliant, the fans were brilliant, fantastic, and I think in that moment we changed to believing we could win, we started to feel like Wembley was home for us and I think that was the massive change for the team.'

Arguably as important was the home game after Bournemouth. Liverpool arrived at Wembley as Pochettino's bogey team. He had never beaten Jürgen Klopp either. But with Kane terrorising Dejan Lovren, and Son and Dele also scoring, the 4–1 win, in front of a short-lived record crowd for any Premier League game of 80,827, was a message of genuine intent.

As were the attendances Spurs were able to generate. When the idea of a season at Wembley was first proposed, there were many who dismissed the notion that Tottenham could attract the numbers to fill it. Yet those 19 'home' matches saw the Premier League record set on three occasions, with the tally for the Liverpool game surpassed by the 81,978 that saw Spurs beat Manchester United and the 83,222 for the North London derby triumph, settled by Kane's majestic header, over Arsenal. In total, 1,291,103 came through the turnstiles for the Premier League games alone, an average of 67,953 that was only surpassed by visitors to Old Trafford. And if you add in the domestic and European Cup attendances, a total of 1,739,982 saw Spurs at home, at an average of 62,142. Not including the FA Cup semi-final game with United, which attracted another 84,667.

Alan Fisher pointed out: 'What's really surprised me is seeing some of the crowds we've had. Not for the big games, but getting 60,000 or more for games against sides in the relegation zone, 68,000 for Huddersfield! That makes it worth taking a step back. For a team that hasn't won anything in ten years.'

Of all those games, though, the one that is surely destined to resonate for as long as anyone who was there remains alive was the meeting with Real Madrid, the most-celebrated club in world football and the two-time Champions League holders. The previous games with Real had been a one-way story. Three defeats, one draw, no goals scored. That sorry history had been ended with a superb 1–1 draw in the Bernabéu, featuring an outstanding display by Pochettino's protégé Harry Winks – yet there was a sense of nervous anticipation, matched by concern, ahead of the return on 1 November.

Nobody should have worried. Spurs were electric, captivating, mesmeric. And far too good for the team that were to end the season in Kiev, champions of Europe for a 13th time. This was Dele's night, the perfect response to the end of the Europa League red card ban from the previous campaign, which had forced him out of the first three group stage games. Dele stretched out a leg to prod Kieran Trippier's first-time cross before his deflected strike from 20 yards doubled the lead. And by the time Kane picked out Eriksen's run, with former Spurs man Modric trailing in his wake, for the third, everyone there knew what they had witnessed.

Alan Fisher admitted: 'That was a genuine glory, glory night. It was magical. The noise when Eriksen scored the third was something else. It felt like the concrete beneath my feet was going to shatter. The whole place was erupting, the canvas was shaking.'

Those around Alan were of the same mind. Dean Scoggins added: 'We thought the Dortmund game earlier in the group was the best experience we'd had in a home European game, in my lifetime. But Madrid blew it out of the water. It was sensational.' And Sean Walsh agreed: 'The Real Madrid game was the best atmosphere I've ever been part of. That will live with me for a very long time, 80,000 fans there, so loud and on the pitch everything felt right, playing the European Cup holders off the pitch, on the biggest stage. We were pinging the ball round them, even Moussa Sissoko looked a player, the fans chanting "Olé". Everything fitted into place.'

Maybe not 'home' home. But home enough, even if the atmosphere was surprisingly flat for the home games against Crystal Palace – not helped by a noon kick-off and effectively two pre-game Remembrance Sunday silences (one official, one by mistake) that deadened the mood even more – and Brighton. But, while there was a feeling within the club that coming to Wembley had a big effect on bottom half of the League sides, who were lifted by the chance to play under the Arch and given extra impetus, the sense of determination fostered by the Argentine allowed them to get through a dodgy late autumn spell. In previous years, that may have begun a tailspin of poor form, leading, inevitably, to questions about the manager.

A defeat at champions-elect Manchester City – when Pochettino's gamble to try to hurt Pep Guardiola's team backfired spectacularly as they were handed their backsides on a plate – left Spurs in 7th place with 20 games to go. The top four looked a long way away. Enter, when it mattered, the talisman of the club. Back-to-back Kane hat-tricks against Burnley and at home to Southampton, the latter taking him to a record-breaking 39 Premier League goals in the calendar year 2017 and making him the most lethal marksman in Europe over the 12 months, were the start of a 14-match unbeaten League streak.

That run, including those Wembley wins over United, which saw Eriksen score within 11 seconds of the start, and in what was to prove Arsene Wenger's final taste of the North London derby, was the undeniable proof that Pochettino's team were the real deal. There was also the delight of Kane's 94th minute penalty equaliser at Anfield, after he had missed an early spot-kick. As the Liverpool fans fumed, Kane told the camera: 'You don't give me two chances!' Pochettino loved the moment.

City were long gone, on course for a remarkable, unprecedented season of goals and points. But Spurs, the fans especially, still had dreams of silverware. They were not to be fulfilled, a fact that will continue to pursue supporters – and, while they do not like it, the manager and his players – until it can no longer be stated.

Juventus, the Old Lady of Serie A, had been drawn as Spurs' Champions League last 16 opponents in December. By the time the tie came round, expectation was even more feverish. Within ten minutes of the start of the first leg, Spurs were two down and seemingly dead. Yet by the time they walked off the pitch in Turin, Kane's brilliant finish and Eriksen's free-kick appeared to have transformed everything. Three weeks later, when Son put Spurs in front, the fans were thinking of the last eight. But Juve are European royalty. For three minutes, Tottenham blinked. Juve struck with the venom and bite of a cobra. Two goals. Pain, anguish and humiliation.

Yet not, despite the frustration, for the fans. For Sean Walsh, it was still special. He said: 'Growing up I never saw Champions League football. The one season we were in it I was too young and didn't have the money so I tried to make the most of it. So, despite what I think about the place, Wembley has hosted some of my favourite Spurs memories. We were the better team for a hundred and sixty minutes of that Juventus tie. But we have to learn from it. With the comfort of home we will feel more nights like that.'

Mike Collett added: 'After the first couple of months it began to feel a little bit more like home. The atmosphere in the United game was sensational but that was rare, to have a great atmosphere in the place. There were times when the atmosphere was very poor, and very rarely compared to White Hart Lane.

'I felt that for most of the fans it wasn't really until half-way through the season that we even started to talk to some of the other people around us, and even then it was just cursory stuff about the game. Because it was just for one year, people felt they didn't want to attach too much of an emotional tie-up to the place because you knew you wouldn't be back the next year. Okay, there were isolated periods in certain matches where it was our home stadium. But it never felt like our home stadium.

'Yet there were some great performances. Liverpool was fantastic, beating them 4–1 and the way we played. We murdered Southampton, smashed Everton, killed them, beating Arsenal and playing so well was sensational. Some of the football was fantastic and to actually see Spurs score at Wembley was still a magical feeling.'

It left the FA Cup, and the battle to secure Champions League football, for the first campaign back in N17. Off the pitch, though, there were grumblings, especially when the club announced its price structure for 'The Tottenham Hotspur Stadium' in March. While the bottom price season tickets were £795, just £30 more than the final season at White Hart Lane, top-priced seats were £1,995, with most categories of seats significantly more expensive than their previous counterparts.

The Tottenham Hotspur Supporters Trust voiced their anger, accusing Levy and his board of failing to take 'a great opportunity to cement the growing bond between fans and the Club, and to secure future generations of support'. Instead, the Trust added: 'The headline prices masked a different reality.'

While many fans knew they were never going to be able to afford the corporate comforts of the 'Cheese Room', they felt let down. Alan Fisher spoke for many: 'We won't be sitting in seats that are as good as the ones we had, and that's a loss. We're going to be in a slightly different place. I was always in the same spot, where the Shelf had been, Row 14, opposite the dug-outs. Sitting with people I'd got to know as part of the same Spurs family. I'd been doing that, in that part of the ground, for fifty years.

'To a degree, sitting there, we were protected from some aspects of the modern game. We still had an old-style football experience, close to the players, seeing the beads of sweat, the hope and fear in the players' eyes. I saw Gareth Bale turn from a boy to a man in front of me, saw him grow up and felt so proud. We all felt part of that family. That will stay with me.

'I will keep on telling stories of those games, that feeling, what the Lane meant. Now I'm going to be in the lower East Stand but level with the penalty spot. It isn't going to be the same. That part of the new ground is in the corporate section. Those seats aren't available even if you could afford them. Even with the seats I've got, those prices are a real stretch. But the ones a few yards along will cost £1,500, a fifty per cent rise on what I was paying.

'That's a lot of money and I am worried about the prices. If the team starts to slip, in a very competitive Premier League, people will start to question the money they are being asked to pay. The club say £995 for nineteen Premier League games – no cup ties – is "reasonable". But people are having to make choices. I really hope we're not going to end up like West Ham or Arsenal with lots of empty seats.

'But I don't *think* Spurs fans are like that. Being a Tottenham fan is about faith and loyalty, over time and generations. It's not about winning, even glory, because we haven't won anything for too long. We have 44,000 season ticket holders for a team that has won the League Cup once, in 2008, in the last twenty years. That's a testament to the loyalty of the fans.'

However, fans will pay the money for top football. By the end of the 2017–18 season, three months before the anticipated first game at the new ground, nearly all of the 42,000 season tickets had been snapped up, along with the 7,000 corporate seats. General match-day admission plus the 3,000 allocation for away fans would take up the rest.

And what mattered, most, was that those supporters knew they would be seeing Champions League football, too. That did not appear a question when, despite Kane only being fit enough to make the bench after the ankle injury he suffered in the win at Bournemouth, Eriksen's stunner and a Dele double secured Tottenham's first win at Stamford Bridge since 1990. The gap was extended to ten points when a victory at Stoke – overshadowed by the furore caused as Kane claimed, and was eventually awarded, the winner when Eriksen's free-kick travelled all the way in – was coupled with Chelsea being held at home by West Ham.

Wobble time. Losing to City at Wembley was no embarrassment. There was not a team Guardiola's side did not beat in the Premier League. But a stuttering performance at Brighton, where

Kane scored in a 1–1 draw even though he still seemed off the pace, was followed by a heartbreaking but deserved semi-final loss to José Mourinho's United, in a game which saw Spurs start like a traction engine to lead through Dele but end up completely out of steam and second best.

A twitchy win over Watford settled some anxieties but defeat at doomed but still fighting West Brom, coming as Chelsea reeled off three on the spin, saw the gap down to two points with two matches to go, although Tottenham were only a point adrift of Liverpool, in third, who had just one match left.

Newcastle, of course, had left Pochettino stewing at the end of the 2015–16 season, a 5–1 defeat which cost his team second place. They had been swatted aside on the opening weekend at St James' Park but this was about Spurs having to hold their nerve and for most of the first half it was Rafa Benítez' side, with nothing to play for but less to fear, who were markedly superior. Chelsea, at home to Huddersfield, had started 15 minutes earlier, meaning everyone inside Wembley knew what was happening.

And when Huddersfield scored, during the half-time break at Wembley, the mood altered. On a night for heroes, there was only one who could possibly emerge, with Kane breaking out of his mini-rut to steer a first-time right footer into the top corner. Chelsea equalised but could not find a winner. Spurs, just about, held on. And they were confirmed in the top four, for the third season running.

The celebrations were tinged with relief. But no less real. Dele and Eriksen danced a jig, the rest of the Spurs players hugged each other. And when they got back into the inner sanctum of the dressing room, Pochettino's first instinct was to call the entire squad to order. It was not a long speech but those in the room spoke afterwards of the 'goosebumps' as the Argentine told them: 'This is a big achievement, really big. Nobody believed we could do this, nobody thought we could do what we have done. They all said we could not play here and finish in the top four. They all said we would not be in the Champions League. But I knew we would. I knew you would. We deserved it. You deserved it. We have proved them all wrong.'

Four days later, as the sun shone down, Pochettino's team went through their final preparations. Leicester at home. On the Tube heading to Wembley, less than an hour and a half before kick-off, there was no excitement, no buzz, none of the fever or fervour that normally comes with the last game of the season.

But just as the final game of the 2016–17 campaign was less about the 90 minutes on the pitch than underlining the history of Tottenham, so the corresponding game on 12 May 2018 was all about being the means to an end: The Return. Even if, as we were to discover a month or so later, there would be one last Wembley game to come in August.

Twelve months earlier, on that last day at White Hart Lane, the match was about celebration, remembering the past and thinking about the future. This was with a season of dislocation and impermanence finally coming to an end. On that final day in N17, the chatter and nostalgia among so many of those travelling to the ground was impossible to miss. This time round, any of that was difficult to witness. It had been a test of endurance.

Not that it had been all bad. But Wembley was not the Lane. It could not be. It never will be. Indisputably world famous, it was still only the temporary home of the Spurs. It was probably right, too, certainly fitting, that there was nothing really riding on that final game of the exile season. Well, nothing that actually mattered. For a club like Spurs, this Spurs, the £1.9 million prize money difference between finishing third and fourth was an irrelevance. And with Uefa having revamped the Champions League for the benefit of the biggest money-generators, fourth was already guaranteeing automatic entry to the group phase of the next season's competition, one in which home, for Spurs, would, once again, for the first time since 2010–11, the year of Bale's emergence, be back in N17. Familiar territory, even if the actual bricks and mortar had changed out of all recognition in that long hiatus.

There was one bauble on offer, although with Kane having lost his fitness and form in the last few weeks of the campaign, if not his innate sense of where the goal is, it was actually unlikely that he would score the three needed to catch up with Liverpool's Mo Salah in the race for the Premier League's Golden Boot.

But for the vast majority of those who made that walk from Wembley Park, along Wembley Way, past the fluttering blue and white Tottenham flags that formed a path and towards the less than magnetic pull of the Arch and the stadium that stands beneath it, it was about what they believed was a final journey to the place they were desperate not to have to return to, at least until the business end of the 2018–19 season.

As Alan Fisher put it: 'For me the whole Wembley season has been part of the grieving process, of getting used to my loss. It's taken me the best part of a season to actually realise the White Hart Lane I knew has gone and I felt that loss acutely. There was a tiny sense of disappointment over the season for some fans. I didn't share that. I was quite sanguine about it. We played away from home all season, had one of our best Premier League seasons, certainly in terms of points. But for the last few games everyone was counting down the days before we go back. It felt that everything was on hold before we returned and could then start to go forward again.'

Dean Scoggins agreed: 'The atmosphere was different. It wouldn't be what I called as raucous as the Lane was, and when I was a bit younger and jumping up and down in the South Stand. It was very different at Wembley. It was family friendly and has been welcoming. I thought the club did a brilliant job in making it feel like home, even though it never was. And we had a year of going to the best stadium in the country to watch Champions League football.

'So I felt we had to embrace it. I've been one of the ones who has really benefited from the season at Wembley. We struggled to get a ticket for my dad, me and my son all together at White Hart Lane but at Wembley we could go whenever we wanted because it's bigger. At the same time, there was that yearning for home. I wouldn't want to have another season there but it's proved Spurs ARE a big club. Only big clubs can get 80,000 crowds. I felt there was a little bit of snobbery from some of the more regular Spurs fans I knew from going to the Lane. Some of them didn't want to admit it was quite nice going to Wembley and taking their wife and their daughter and their uncle. But as the season went on they grew into it. It was only the yearning for home that meant they didn't embrace Wembley as they might have done. It was a different atmosphere but I think I went to sixteen or seventeen games. I didn't see any fighting. I didn't see dads covering ears of boys because there were things going on behind them that there shouldn't have been.

'It was a different football atmosphere. And hopefully that new breed of Spurs fan, as well as the old stalwarts and the people who have been going for years, will take all that to the new ground as well.

'There are certain elements they've got to keep. But you're never going to replicate White Hart Lane. The same as any club that has moved grounds. The mistake Arsenal made and some of the others is that they tried to replicate the old ground in a brand new stadium. And that just doesn't work. I hope that Tottenham will learn all the lessons. Keep the same music to walk out to, so when you come to the turnstiles you can tell by just what you hear whether you have to run or not in case you miss kick-off. And at half-time and at the end, when "Glory Glory" plays, it has the right feel to it.

'But I don't think they should be concerned about trying to manufacture atmosphere. I think they've learned the lessons, with the White Wall behind the goal and the acoustics they've talked about off the roof, I'm sure that will work. And there will be such a massive buzz because it's the new stadium we'd all been waiting to see for so long. I loved White Hart Lane, absolutely adored going. But as long as the new stadium is half as good as they're promising, I don't think I'll miss the Lane. In a similar way to Wembley, I'll appreciate and treasure the memories we have but I won't pine for it. I think we're ready to move on.'

Before that, there was one last 90 minutes of that Wembley season. A game that was utterly bonkers, swung wildly but ended with Kane's second of the afternoon securing what was, incredibly, the first 5–4 win in Tottenham history, his 30th Premier League goal of the season – two short of Salah – and third place, ahead of Liverpool. Not bad for a season which saw 38 away games, with the final moments echoing to a simple, heartfelt chant, to the tune of 'Three Lions': 'Tottenham's going home, we're going home, we're going home, we're going . . .'

Nobody, not even the Spurs hierarchy, knew that in fact there would be one last Wembley game, at the very start of the next season. But Pochettino, wary of his side starting with four straight away matches, as they otherwise would have to do to ensure the new stadium passed the required safety inspections, got his way to see the match with Fulham on the second week of the season played underneath the Arch, with the grand opening agreed for 15 September, a lunchtime kick-off against Liverpool, the official beginning of the Spurs future.

Attention in the aftermath was taken by Pochettino's press conference. The Argentine spoke from the heart: 'Our fans need to know what we are doing and feel the reality of club. We need to tell the truth and we need to create an expectation you can achieve. You cannot create dreams thinking that we cannot achieve. We need to create dreams that are possible to achieve.

'We cannot think we are the cleverest people in the world winning trophies spending small money. We need to think our reality is different. We cannot invest crazy money. We need to feel we are a special club. I think Daniel is going to listen, of course. You know me, I have crazy ideas. You need to be brave. In this situation you need to be brave and take risks. It is the moment the club needs to take risks. We need to work harder than the previous season to be competitive again. Today the Premier League is a tough competition, you can see not only the big clubs but the clubs behind us, like West Ham, Leicester, Everton, are working so hard to be close to the top six clubs. I'm sure Daniel will listen to me and we will create together.'

Pochettino knows that the new stadium will bring intensified expectations. So do his players.

But for them, there is a real buzz about the future. Just before he left the stadium, heading for a pre-World Cup week in the Bahamas, Kane stopped in the Wembley mixed zone to tell me about his own feelings. The striker, who had scored 22 Wembley goals – all but one of them for Spurs – in the Wembley season, conceded: 'I'm really looking forward to going back home. I've been to the stadium and seen that going up. It's been difficult for us to play at Wembley rather than home. But if you look at the season, we've done really well, better than a lot of people thought we would, and come out the other side.

'It's been tough for us as a team to have to adapt. It was a tough year. When other teams have come here, it's been like a big final for them. It's got them going because they don't get the chance to play here very often, so for us as a team we've had to cope with that. I do think we did well. Yes, we started a bit slowly, as maybe we were always likely to, but we became more used to playing here, got better and better as the season went on, and it was good to end on a high with those three wins that ensured we finished third.

'White Hart Lane, for me, was amazing but the new ground is going to be incredible. When I went to the stadium with Hugo Lloris a few months ago and looked round, even though it was only half-built, I think you could see what it meant to us both. And when we walk out there for a game, in front of 62,000 fans, it is going to be incredible. It was pretty amazing for me to look round it even then, empty. But we can't wait for the atmosphere on big nights, for the crunch games and Champions League nights, which is what we were aiming to ensure we'd have. It's going to be absolutely amazing. I know everyone in the dressing room is so looking forward to getting out there and the feeling from all of us is that we can't wait. I think it will feel as special as White Hart Lane did for me. The great thing, for us and the fans, is that we're going back to the same place, where we are used to playing. For me it's going back home. It's not that we're going to a new stadium, we're just going back home, but to a bigger and better place. The fans are going to be excited. We're going to be excited. It's going to be a great place to be.'

It surely is, although, until I set foot inside Spurs' new home for a match, I was determined not to visit. Building sites have never really appealed to me and while I, like so many Spurs fans, keep an eye on proceedings through the club website and social media postings, I had deliberately not headed to N17 since that final day at White Hart Lane. I wanted to go back, but to a finished new ground, a place for dreams to start all over again. And, much like Alan Fisher, I will embrace that future with some trepidation. He told me: 'We will be there, taking the chance to make new relationships, and the team will be there. Hopefully there will be enough noise to feel like home. There really could be some atmosphere and I felt White Hart Lane needed that towards the end in some games. Any ground is what the fans make it. For those ninety minutes what happens behind the stands doesn't matter. It's about what the supporters make it. This will be a new ground for the fans to take over and get behind the team. Leaving Wembley was the chance to say "good riddance and goodbye – and see you a few times in the future but just for big cup ties". Wembley is for finals, that's its proper use. Let's hope there's a few of those. Now I'm looking forward to the new ground. But it will never be the Lane, for me. It will never be the same . . .'

STATISTICS

Record at White Hart Lane

Competition	Played	Won	Drawn	Lost	Goals for	Goals against	Goal difference
Southern League	147	104	25	18	334	107	227
Football League	1412	846	340	366	3167	1819	148
Premier League	481	251	119	111	812	530	282
FA Cup	188	121	44	23	463	184	279
League Cup	105	71	15	19	234	100	134
Europe	95	70	18	7	246	71	175
Total	2533	1472	565	496	5272	2798	2616

Notable matches at White Hart Lane

First game: 4 September 1899 – Tottenham 4 Notts County 1

First League game: 9 September 1899 – Tottenham 1 QPR 0
(Southern League)

First Football League game: 1 September 1908 – Tottenham 3
Wolverhampton Wanderers 0

Last Football League game: 25 April 1992 – Tottenham 3 Everton 3

First top-flight game: 11 September 1909 – Tottenham 2 Manchester United 2

First Premier League game: 19 August 1992 – Tottenham 0 Coventry City 2

Last Premier League game: 14 May 2017 – Tottenham 2 Manchester United 1

First FA Cup game: 8 February 1901 – Tottenham 1 Preston North End 1

Last FA Cup game: 12 March 2017 – Tottenham 6 Millwall 0

First League Cup game: 25 September 1968 – Tottenham 6 Exeter City 3

Last League Cup game: 21 September 2016 – Tottenham 5 Gillingham 1

First European Cup game: 20 September 1961 – Tottenham 8 Górnik Zabrze 1

Last Champions League game: 13 April 2011 – Tottenham 0 Real Madrid 1

First Cup Winners' Cup game: 31 October 1962 – Tottenham 5 Glasgow Rangers 2

Last Cup Winners' Cup game: 18 March 1992 – Tottenham 0 Feyenoord 0

First Uefa Cup game: 28 September 1971 – Tottenham 9 Keflavík 0

Last Europa League game: 17 March 2016 – Tottenham 1 Borussia Dortmund 2

Biggest win: 3 February 1960 – Tottenham 13 Crewe Alexandra 2

Heaviest defeats: 19 December 1914 – Tottenham 0 Sunderland 6; March 6 1935 – Tottenham 0 Arsenal 6

Most appearances

Steve Perryman (1969–1986): 436 games
Gary Mabbutt (1982–1998): 307 games

Pat Jennings (1964–1986): 304 games
Glenn Hoddle (1975–1987): 260 games
Cyril Knowles (1964–1976): 258 games
Ted Ditchburn (1939–1959): 256 games
Jimmy Dimmock (1919–1931): 241 games
Ron Burgess (1938–1954): 240 games
Tom Morris (1899–1913): 239 games
Alan Gilzean (1964–1974) 233 games

Leading goalscorers

Jimmy Greaves (1961–1970): 176
Bobby Smith (1955–1963): 130
Martin Chivers (1967–1976): 111
Cliff Jones (1957–1969): 106
Len Duquemin (1946–1957): 102
George Hunt (1930–1937): 91
Jermain Defoe (2003–2014): 90
Alan Gilzean (1964–1974): 86
Bert Bliss (1911–1923): 79
Les Bennett (1939–1955): 76

Notable goals

First goal scored: 4 September 1899 – Tommy McCairns (Notts
    County v. Tottenham)
First Tottenham goal scored: 4 September 1899 – Tom Pratt
    (Tottenham 4 Notts Co 1)
First Southern League goal: 9 September 1899 – Tom Smith
    (Tottenham 1 QPR 0)
Last Southern League goal: 18 April 1908 – George Payne
    (Tottenham 3 Norwich 0)

First Football League goal scored: 1 September 1908 – Vivian Woodward (Tottenham 3 Wolverhampton Wanderers 0)

Last Football League goal scored: 25 April 1992 – David Unsworth (Everton v. Tottenham)

Last Tottenham Football League goal scored: 25 April 1992 – Paul Stewart (Tottenham 3 Everton 3)

First Premier League goal scored: 19 August 1992 – John Williams (Coventry v. Tottenham)

First Tottenham Premier League goal scored: 22 August 1992 – Gordon Durie (Tottenham 2 Crystal Palace 2)

First FA Cup goal scored: 8 February 1901 – unknown (Preston v. Tottenham)

First Tottenham FA Cup goal scored: 8 February 1901 – Sandy Brown (Tottenham 1 Preston 1)

Last FA Cup goal scored: 12 March 2017 – Son Heung-min (Tottenham 6 Millwall 0)

First League Cup goal scored: 25 September 1968 – Jimmy Greaves (Tottenham 6 Exeter 3)

Last League Cup goal scored: 21 September 2016 – Erik Lamela (Tottenham 5 Gillingham 0)

First European goal scored: 20 September 1961 – Danny Blanchflower (Tottenham 8 Górnik Zabrze 1)

Last European goal scored: 17 March 2016 – Son Heung-Min (Tottenham 1 Borussia Dortmund 2)

Last Tottenham goal scored: 14 May 2017 – Harry Kane (Tottenham 2 Manchester United 1)

Last goal scored: 14 May 2017 – Wayne Rooney (Manchester United v. Tottenham)

ACKNOWLEDGEMENTS

Football, it is said, is a fickle mistress. When it comes to Tottenham Hotspur, fickle is an understatement. A club that regularly promises so much, only to deceive, to under-achieve, to be so damn Spursy.

But even as this book was being written, something bigger was taking shape in N17. Not just physically, vastly bigger as the new stadium grew at a bewildering pace, but organically, spiritually as well. A team that, genuinely, appears to have the same *esprit de corps* and desire that all those who were around at the time tell me was the essence of Bill Nicholson's side. And a sense that everybody within the club was, for once, pulling in the same direction.

We will see if that is the reality or another typically Tottenham dance of the seven veils, a misleading moment before we are all dragged back to confront harsh facts head-on.

Yet if ever there is a time to put the past in context, live in the present and look positively towards the future, it surely is when, for the first time in two decades, even rival fans have to take Spurs seriously.

Of course, this was as much about me and my relationships – with the club, my family, even myself – as it was about Tottenham Hotspur. The love affair has left my heart scarred so many times yet I keep on going back. And in my son and daughter I see, all over again, the wide-eyed innocence and powerful belief that I myself carried in those early days.

But I would not have been able to embark on this journey, into my own past and that of the club, without the encouragement and belief of so many people, and the kindness and help of others.

Thanks to my agent, David Luxton, who tempted me with the promise that he genuinely believed I could make this work, even when we both wondered if we were walking down a blind alley. And Paul Murphy at Orion, a calm voice when I needed one.

Thanks, too, hugely, to Mike Collett. A friend and inspiration for many years but there so often when I needed guidance and correction. Any errors remaining are entirely down to me, not him.

At Spurs, so many. Donna Cullen, Simon Felstein, John Fennelly, Joe Bacon and Jonny Davies, among a host of others. Without your time and patience, this would not have been possible.

Of course, all those who spared the time to talk to me, to give me their memories and thoughts. I apologise to those who feel short-changed for the hours I badgered out of you.

I was helped, too, by my colleagues at the *Sun*, among them Shaun Custis, Ian Passingham and the peerless Russell Lanning. Thanks to some I have not mentioned but played their part in my Spurs story, especially Mike Mahoney, who spent far too many journeys listening to me jabbering, on that line from Wickford to Liverpool Street.

And to my brothers, Trevor, Jerome and Gideon, and my parents, especially my father. Dad, without you I suspect none of this would have happened. But I might not have suffered so much for the past 30 years.

But most of all, thanks to Christine, Emma and Ollie, who had to put up with the angst and effort that putting together 'TDB' caused for so many months. Without your love, help and understanding, I would simply never have been able to complete this book. Thank you.

BIBLIOGRAPHY

Ron Burgess, *Football – My Life* (Souvenir Press 1952)

Martin Cloake and Adam Powley, *The Boys from White Hart Lane* (Vision Sports 2008)

Martin Cloake and Alan Fisher, *A People's History of Tottenham Hotspur* (Pitch Publishing 2016)

Hunter Davies, *The Glory Game* (Penguin 1972)

Terry Dyson with Mike Donovan, *Spurs' Unsung Hero* (Pitch Publishing 2015)

Ralph L. Finn, *Spurs Supreme* (Robert Hale & Co. 1961)

———, *Spurs Go Marching On* (Robert Hale & Co. 1963)

The History of the Tottenham Hotspur (Crusha & Son 1921)

Bernard Joy, *Soccer Tactics: A New Appraisal* (Phoenix House 1963)

Brian Scovell, *Bill Nicholson: Football's Perfectionist* (John Blake Publishing 2011)

Alan Sugar, *What You See Is What You Get* (Macmillan 2011)

INDEX

INDEX

INDEX

INDEX